**I don't know who owned this horse and fine buggy, but I do know the horse's name – "Old Dan" as it is written on the back. I love him so much, I just had to put him in the book!**

People ask why I started doing these books. The history of this part of Grayson County around Pottsboro MUST be preserved. I have lived here all my life and my ancestors came here in 1866 and I know how much rich history is here and want all these people to be remembered, so I thought, if no one else will do it, I will. I am still writing with no end in sight. All pioneers were exceptional people to be able to travel here in the first place, so the people of Texas had interesting lives and we Texans know that because we know what it took to get here and survive once they got here. We are proud of them and of our state. Because of them, we have what we have, and we are what we are, so we honor them! NCB

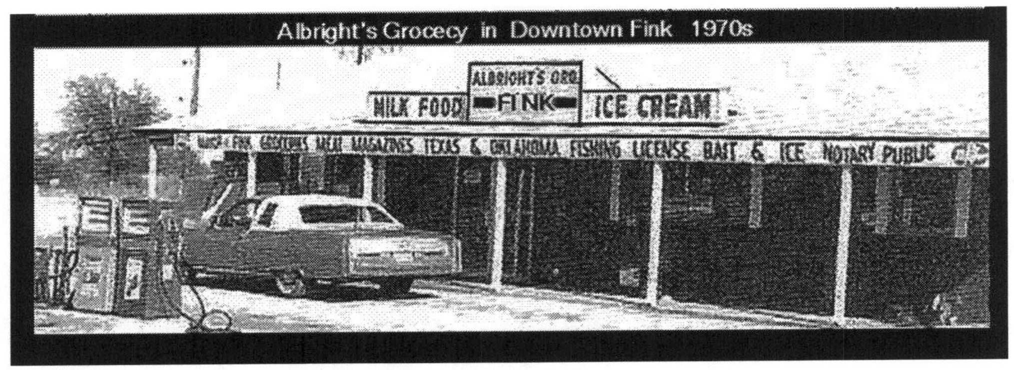

Albright's Grocecy in Downtown Fink 1970s

# GHOST TOWNS OF TEXOMA

## VOLUME FOUR

## GEORGETOWN, FINK & REEVESVILLE

# UPDATED EDITION

**By NATALIE CLOUNTZ BAUMAN**



**LOST TOWNS OF GRAYSON COUNTY TEXAS AND**

**THE POTTSBORO AREA**

# CONTENTS



# UPDATED VERSION

# GEORGETOWN, FINK & REEVESVILLE

In the 1830s and 1840s, Georgetown, Preston Bend and Old Warren were the only Forts and population centers in the county. Fort Johnston and Georgetown were major hubs of activities at that time. Georgetown was an integral part of the early expeditions of exploration and and a base of operation for the protection of the entire area. Georgetown was host to a fort, a military road, the starting point for important exploratory expeditions and was an oasis for weary travelers. The community at the site became known very early as George's Town, from which the name Georgetown came, named after George Ivey who lived in the area, perhaps as early as the mid 1830s. This supposition is stated at the time in the Clarksville Standard newspaper in 1852 in article describing the area. Much later, people wrongly attributed the name to be in honor of Georgetown land owner, George R. Reeves, who was county Sheriff from 1850 to 1854, and represented Grayson County in the Texas State legislature for many years after that, serving as speaker of the House.

Fort Johnston (or Johnson as some have called it), was located in **the Old Georgetown community**, just south of the present day Georgetown Road and west of Hwy 289 and Squirrel Lane. There is an historical marker near the site. The old fort was not a formal large fort, but a temporary shelter for soldiers as they trained and built the military road. It was built near the mouth of three natural springs to provide water for the horses and men. There is still evidence of fencing wrapped around pecans trees at the site which may have been temporary corrals for the horses. Georgetown and Fort Johnston played an important role in many significant events and episodes in the exploration of the area at that time. Early Georgetown was a rural farming community, and grew to have a post office, cotton gin, school, church and stores.

## GEORGETOWN / FINK QUICK TIMELINE

1830s and onward – Early settlers receive land grants or buy land in the area: like William Steele Reeves, George and Jefferson Ivey. Cherokees arrived from the Trail of Tears and established farms in the area, only to be forced to move north of the Red River soon afterward by white settlers.

1840 – Fort Johnston was built on the military road in Georgetown.

1843 - Snively expedition mustered and departed from Fort Johnston.

1845–46 – winter - Lyman Wight, leading a congregation of defecting Mormons into Texas, used Fort Johnston as his headquarters. At this time, his people also built Glen Eden for Holland Coffee at Preston and another similar mansion just across the River in Indian Territory.

1846 - The commissioners' journey to Comanche Peak in connection with the Comanche treaty of 1846 passed through Georgetown.

1849-1852 - Marcy's Expedition passed through Georgetown.

1852: Clarksville Standard, while mentioning George Robertson Reeves in the article, says Georgetown was first called George's Town after early resident George Ivey, NOT George R. Reeves as many believe today.

1850 – George R. Reeves donated land for a cemetery and a school/church combined. A Masonic Lodge met in the second floor of the school. The old Georgetown School was established on the corner of present day Georgetown Rd & Squirrel Lane.

1927 – The old Georgetown school was moved to land donated by the Finke family.

Then later, when the last modern brick Georgetown school was built, the old building was moved briefly to the Georgetown Baptist Church grounds, then sold and moved to SW Denison on Coffin St. according to James Clement and others.

There was also a Colored school on Reeves Rd on Dr. Alexander Morrison's land west of Katy Ln (probably established by Dr. Morrison). The house and Dr. Alexander Morrison gave or willed to his colored son still stands on Reeves Rd where he gifted him 50 acres.

Late 1860s or early '70s - W.J. Bilderback opens a general store at Georgetown. 1875 – settlement of Reevesville existed nearby, perhaps near Reeves land – ( probably established by George R. Reeves or in his honor). One proof lies in a dry Goods store receipt from R. H. Pierce owned by Robert Daniel descendant, Natalie Bauman

1882 - Fred Finke, a German immigrant, arrives in Grayson County.

1897 - The settlement becomes known as Fink after a post office is established in honor of Finke family. It could not be named Georgetown since that town name and post office already existed in southern Texas.

1906 – J.A. Porter has a grocery store in Georgetown. G.W. Bailey buys Porter's store. 1908 – Grayson County plat map shows businesses at Georgetown located at intersection of present day Hwy 289 and Georgetown Rd/Spur 406: H.C. Mercer, Marion & Bilderback, G.W. Bailey Grocery (formerly Porter's Grocery), Holley & Taylor gin, J.W. Bilderback (grocery), C.B. Williams, Allen Bros. Nursery

1936 - The population in town limits is estimated at 15.

Mid-1940s to mid-1970s - Population fluctuates from an estimated 25 down to only 3 in the confines of small "downtown" Fink, but there were many more people in the much larger Georgetown school district. Fink Day celebrations become popular events.

1979 - Texas Legislature declares every fourth Friday in June as Fink Day.

1984 - Fink is officially shown on the county highway map.

2010 - Surrounded by Pottsboro, Fink's commercial center consists mostly of a motel, cafe, convenience store - all closed – except gas station and a liquor store. Ghost town status.

2020s – Fink Day is revived, more businesses open.

SOURCES: Newspaper articles, first person recollections, The Handbook of Texas Online; Texas Historical Commission, 1908 Grayson Plat Map

## From Red River to Fannin to Grayson County to... GEORGETOWN

At first, even during the Republic of Texas, there was no such thing as Grayson County. Prior to 1837, the southern Red River Valley was known as Red River County. Because of rapid population growth, Dr. Daniel Rowlett presented a petition to the Texas Congress on October 5, 1837, requesting that a new county be formed from a section of Red River County west of Bois D'Arc Creek. The county was originally to be named Independence, but during the course of opening debates over the bill the name was changed to Fannin, in honor of James Walker Fannin, Jr., a martyred hero of the Texas Revolution. The legislation, approved on December 14, 1837. The entire shaded area of the map below shows the original Fannin County. Fannin County was again divided into Grayson, Collin, Cooke, Denton, Montague, Wise, Clay, Jack, Wichita, Archer, Young, Wilbarger, Baylor, Throckmorton, Hardeman, Foard, Knox, Haskell, Stonewall, King, Cottle, and Childress counties, as well as parts of Hunt and Collingsworth counties – the present-day boundaries were established and approved on March 14, 1846.

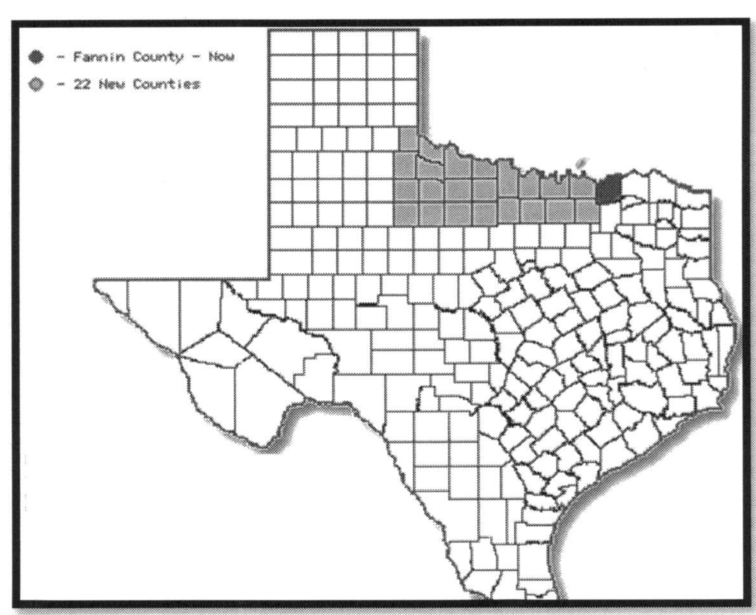

# The Cross Timbers – The Beauty of Georgetown

## GEORGETOWN – PART OF THE CROSS TIMBERS REGION

Many untouched areas of Georgetown still have the same dense impenetrable growth that was described below in 1834, though most are not the original "old growth" timbers. The trees they mention are still here, as well as the underbrush, the grapevines and the impassable, vicious briar (thorn) vines which hang from every tree. It reminds me of a line in a song by Johnnie Horton, "they ran through places where a rabbit couldn't go." Those exist here in Georgetown. You can barely see through them, if there is a cedar tree there, and there usually is, you **won't** see through it. In the 1800s, it was paradise for animal predators, Indians and outlaws who wanted to hide and use it for ambush, and it still supports a varied and vigorous animal population today for the same reason.

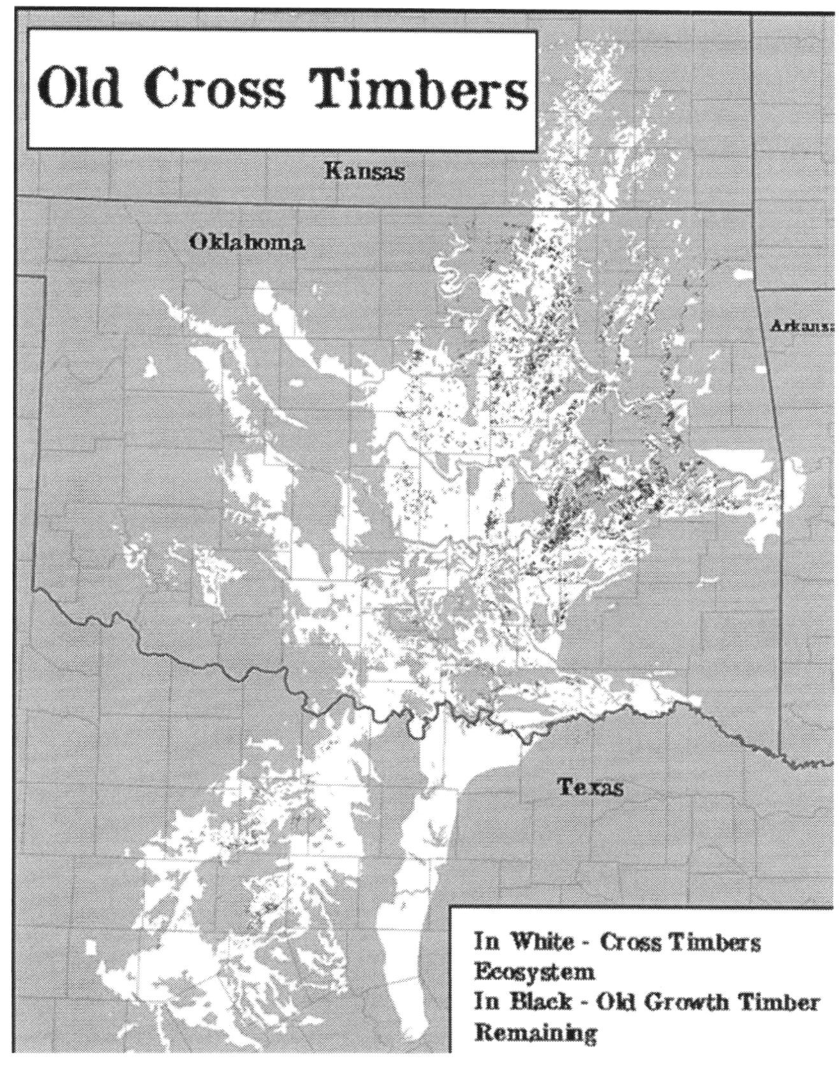

# NATIVE AMERICANS - THE FIRST SETTLERS OF GEORGETOWN WERE Caddo Indians -

# Earliest Immigrants Included Cherokees Who Lost Their Land Twice in a Few Years

June 23, 1841 Austin City Gazette Indian News From the East– "By Mr. Cordelius, who arrived in town on Sunday last, direct from the East, we learn the following particulars of a late engagement with the Indians in Fannin County. It being suspected that an Indian village was located on the waters of the Red River, some hundred miles above the settlements, a party of citizens, about sixty in number, started in search of them. They proceeded about one hundred and fifty miles up the river but without any signs. They then altered their course, intending to return to their homes by the most direct route, passing through the **Cross Timbers**. They had, on the 27th of May, returned within forty miles of the settlements, and some of their comrades had that morning left them, considering all chance of finding the enemy at an end, when about 9 am, they discovered an Indian village with several flourishing fields of corn; they immediately charged and routed the enemy, who retreated to a second village; here the conflict was renewed with like results, the Indians retreating to a third village, from whence they were likewise driven; they then fell back on a fourth village where they concentrated their whole force which now amounted to some two or three hundred warriors. The Texians, finding the enemy too strongly posted and in too large a force to enable their small party to act successfully against them, retreated to the settlements, having lost one of the most esteemed and talented citizens in that section of country, John B. Denton. Capt. Stout was wounded. The loss of the Indians is variously estimated. The volunteers being reinforced had, at last accounts, started in pursuit of the enemy, with a full determination of avenging the death of their comrade. **The Indians were principally Cherokees,** and had planted some three or four hundred acres of corn. From appearances, they had been located there eighteen or nineteen months." (These were probably people who had been uprooted from their lands back east a few years earlier, i.e. Trail of Tears. They settled here, only to be driven from their land once again by the Texians.)

## EARLY DESCRIPTION OF THE CROSS TIMBERS

From Sep 15, 1841 in the Austin City Gazette - "The Cross Timbers is a continuous series of forests, extending from the weedy region at the sources of the Trinity River in a direct line north, across the prairies of north Texas and the Ozark Territory, to the south bank of the Arkansas River. Between the Trinity and Red River, it is generally from five to nine miles wide; and is so remarkably straight and regular, that it appears to be the work of art. When viewed from the adjoining prairies on the east or west, it appears in the distance like an immense wall of woods stretching from south to north in a straight line, reaching to the horizon. There appears to be no peculiarity in the surface of the ground over which the Cross Timbers passes, to distinguish it from the surface of the adjoining country; but where the country is level, the region traversed by the Cross Timbers is level; where it is undulating, and where it is hilly, that also is uneven, conforming in every respect to the general features of the adjoining country. The trees composing these forests are not distinguishable by any peculiarity from those which are occasionally found in the adjoining prairies, or in the bottoms bordering the streams which intersect the Cross Timbers. Oak, hickory, elm, white oak, holly, and other trees are found in it. The elm is often found growing luxuriantly far from any stream, and in apparently poor and sandy soil. The black jack, a species of oak, is met with throughout its whole extent, from the Arkansas to the "Black Jack Ridges", at the sources of the Trinity. The Cross Timbers, in its general direction, does not perceptibly vary from the true meridian. Dr. Irion, (formerly Secretary of State of the Republic), a few years since, accompanied a party of surveyors, who measured a line extending forty miles due south from the bank of the Red River, near the Cross Timbers; and found, to their surprise, that the western border of the Cross Timbers continued parallel with this line through the whole distance. The Cross Timbers forms the grand landmark of the western prairies; and the Indians and hunters, when describing their routes across the country in their various expeditions, refer to the Cross Timbers as the navigators of Europe refer to the meridian of Greenwich. If they wish to furnish a sketch of the route taken in any expedition, they first draw a line, representing the Cross Timbers, and another reporting the route taken, intersecting the former. Thus, a simple, but correct, map of the portion of country traversed in the expedition is at once presented. The remarkable uniformity which characterizes the Cross Timbers and its apparently artificial arrangement, under a particular meridian, has induced some persons to believe it owes its origin to the unknown race of men who have erected the mounds and ancient fortifications of the Mississippi Valley. It is difficult to conceive, however, for what useful purpose it could have been intended, unless as a landmark to distinguish the boundary between two nations. But whether it be the work of art or of nature, will probably never be determined. The lines of civilization are rapidly extending towards it, and soon the scrutiny of science will be forever checked by the destroying axe of the pioneer." Many of these Indian mounds still exist here, one in Collinsville.

**More Early Descriptions of the Cross Timbers:** Agnew, Brad. 1975. Dodge Leavenworth Expedition of 1834. Chronicles of Oklahoma. 53 p. 385 - "The Cross Timbers vary in width from five to thirty five miles and entirely cut off the communication betwixt the interior prairies and those of the Great Plains. They may be considered as the 'fringe' of the great prairies, being a continuous brushy strip composed of various kinds of undergrowth; such as black-jacks, post-oaks, and in some places hickory, elm, etc., intermixed with a very diminutive dwarf oak, called by the hunters 'shin-oak.' Most of the timber appears to be kept small by the continual inroads of the 'burning prairies;' for, being killed almost annually, it is constantly replaced by scions of undergrowth; so that it becomes more and more dense on every reproduction. In some places, however, the oaks are of considerable size, and able to withstand the conflagrations. **The underwood is so matted in many places with grapevines, green-briars, etc., as to form almost impenetrable roughs,'** which serve as hiding-places for wild beasts, as well as wild Indians; and would, in savage warfare, prove almost as formidable as the hammocks of Florida." p. 283. Gregg, Josia. 1844. Commerce of the Prairies (The 1844 Edition.) (Author's note: it is STILL like the underlined portion in places!). "The next day the regiment entered the Cross Timbers, a natural border separating the Plains Indians from the eastern tribes which was described as a great thicket composed of nettles and briars so thickly matted together as almost to forbid passage."

Grayson, Fannin, Cooke, Montague, Clay and Wichita Counties are located on the northern border along Red River. The general surface is rolling, with wide level valleys along the numerous streams. The bottom lands along the Wichita and Red rivers and their tributaries are well wooded, with walnut, bois d'arc, elm and pecan, while in the eastern counties of this group, notably in Fannin and Grayson Counties, are large tracts of hickory and oak.

Realization.

The soil is admirably adapted to agriculture, and all standard grains and vegetables are grown profitably. In the bottom lands along the streams the soil is a deep black loam. In other localities it is of black sandy, chocolate and sandy loam. In the central and southern parts of Fannin, Grayson and Cooke Counties, the soil is principally what is known as the black waxy soil, a soil that is rich and productive and capable of the most trying cultivation.

These counties are well watered by numerous streams, by wells, at depths from 25 to 50 feet, and artesian wells from 600 to 800 feet in depth.

Fannin, Grayson and Cooke Counties are noted for their enormous crops of small grain, cotton, corn, oats and hay (alfalfa is also grown very successfully), and fine stock (the hog industry is large), while Clay and Wichita Counties are noted for their large wheat and oat crops, and the big cattle interests.

## Peter's Colony at the Cross Timbers

Peters Colony (also "Peters' Colony") was formed as a result of a contract (which was authorized by the Republic of Texas Congress on January 4, 1841) between William S. Peters and his associates, a group of English and American men, and the President of Texas, Mirabeau Lamar. It began on August 30, 1841. Three other contracts modifying the original would be signed, followed by numerous legal battles, some remedied through the Texas Legislature. In the end, the colony created little to no income for its investors. It did, however, bring 2,200 families to Texas, distributing to them 879,920 acres of land. September 24, 1842 Civilian and Galveston Gazette - The Clarksville Northern Standard said that Messrs. Johnson and Peters, contractors, with twenty two other immigrants from Kentucky, passed through Clarksville on the 25th on their way to the colony at the Cross Timbers. The immigrants were generally of the better sort; all well-armed, some of them finely mounted, and having along some three or four superior wagons. They were in good health and highly pleased with the country; fancying particularly the appearance of the corn fields upon our prairies. Another party which started before them is hourly expected. Mr. Peters informs us that two hundred families will leave Kentucky this fall, for the Colony. **(The corn fields observed by the Peter's Colonists may well have previously belonged to the Cherokees mentioned in an earlier article in 1841.)** The policy of colonizing by contracts was continued from the Mexican period into the Republic. In February of 1841, an act by Congress became effective by which colonizing could progress and under this law, President Lamar entered into a contract with W. S. Peters, D. S. Carroll, and eighteen others, for the introduction of six hundred families in Texas within three years from the date of the contract. This was called 'Peters' Colony' and the eastern boundary line began where Big Mineral Creek joins Red River in Grayson County, thence due south 164 miles. This places part of Grayson County in the northeastern corner of Peters' Colony. Colonists who were the head of a household received 640 acres if he built a house and lived in it, and remained on the land for three years and cultivated at least fifteen acres. A single man received 320 acres.

## Peter's Colony Map in Grayson/Fannin County

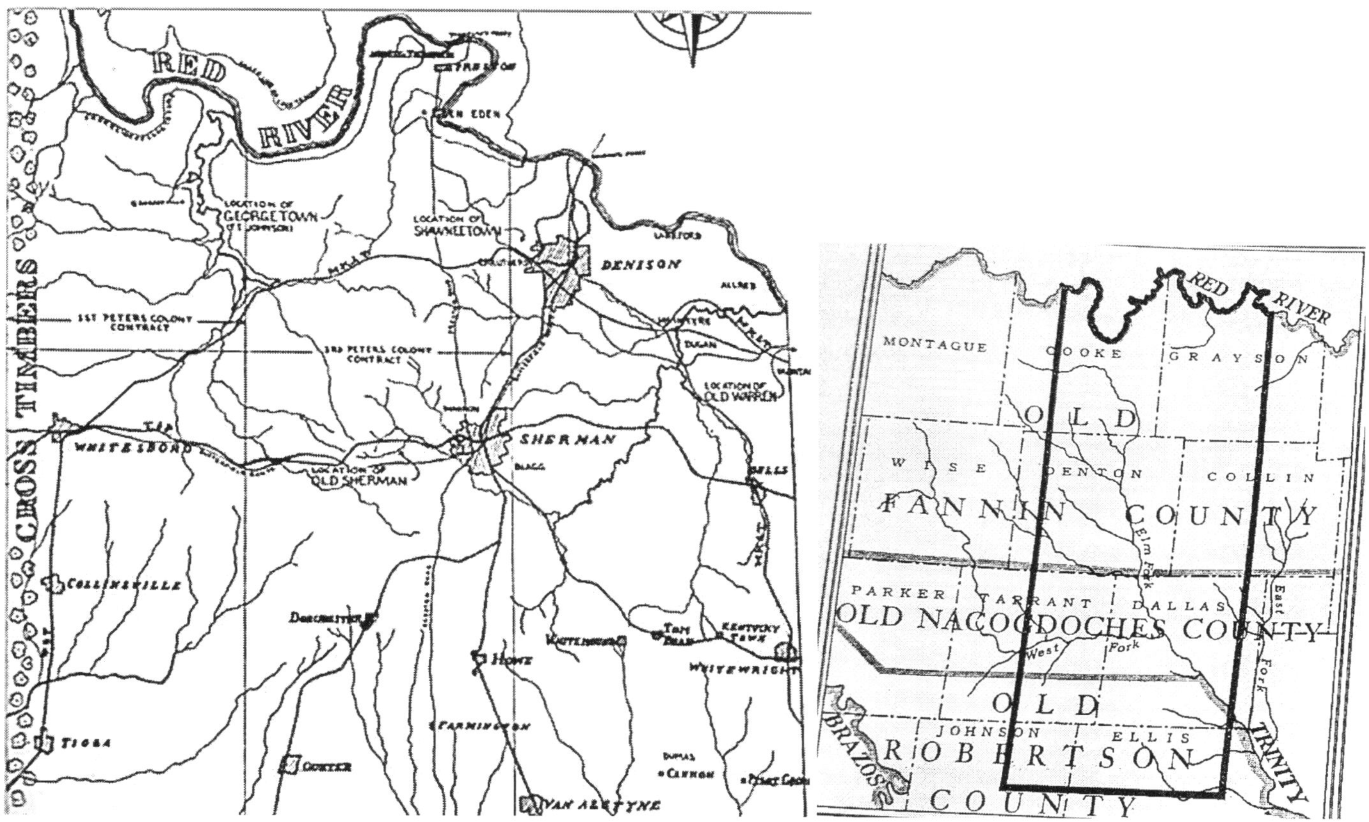


# RANGERS, A MILITARY ROAD and a FORT IN EARLY GEORGETOWN

There are several passages in a history book of this area written in 1936 that mention Fort Johnston and Georgetown, along with many of its important residents. The name of the book is "A history of Grayson County, Texas by Mattie Davis Lucas (Mrs. W. H. Lucas) and Mita Holsapple Hall (Mrs. H. E. Hall). It lists the Rangers who served this area: "Rangers served for a period of three to six months and were under the jurisdiction of the Chief Justice, who in 1840 in Fannin County, was J. R. Oneal. Fannin County Rangers were in the 2nd Regiment, 4th Brigade; Jacob Snively, paymaster; Daniel Montague, Lieutenant Colonel. Among the companies in North Texas, the following "Captains" are listed, in April 1839; Jesse Stiff, N. T. Journey, J. P. Simpson, H. B. Stout, M. R. Roberts, S. Adams, J. Emberson, J. Todd, J. E. Hamilton, John B. Denton, J. Sowell, and J. Durst. Capt. Jesse Stiff's company in 1838, shows the names of: Wm. Foster, Neely Dobson, T. J. Shannon, James Thompson, and James Blagg. Muster rolls of N. T. Journey's company showed: N. T. Journey, first Lieutenant; R. W. Sowell, second Lieutenant, Nushnell Garner, first sergeant, Solomon Chandler, Joshua Sharpless, Jefferson Ivy, Gibson May, Charles Jackson, Willis Boone, James Rulland, Franklin Davis, Wm. Morten, Wm. Taylor, Issac Camp, Santa Arga, John Yates, Wm. Wimlick, Wm. Casly, Taylor Patterson, Garrett Pangburn, John Seymour, Lorenzo Tula, John Ferguson, James Pierce, P. L. Lankford, W. W. Kennedy, James Jeffries, Jas. A. Wood, Andrew Panero, John Russell, Daniel Jackson, George Ivy (the George for whom Georgetown was named – NB), Hosea Myrear, J. M. Garner, Wm. Foster, Nicholas Carter, Garrett F. Lankford, Wm. T. Lankford, Silas Colville, Renee Allred, Wm. R. Caruthers, Jas. G. Keathley. Jefferson Ivy sold his survey of land in Preston Bend to Holland Coffee in 1837. **George Ivy lived where Georgetown and Fort Johnston was established in 1838 or 1839. George Ivy was said to have had a small store or trading post where the Fort was built.**

The young Republic of Texas made an effort to protect the settlers along the frontier, despite the handicap of insufficient finances to maintain the soldiers. Capt. Henry Stout was a famous hunter and Indian fighter, living in North Texas at that time. He came to Texas in 1836 and fought in the battle of San Jacinto. In January 1839, he received orders from Gen. Rusk to continue in constant service along the frontier for six months, so with a company of seventy-two men, he ranged from the Cross Timbers eastward to Lake Soda. He was active and vigilant, but unable to accomplish much owing to his scanty supply of supplies and other problems. Mr. McIntyre, on Choctaw Bayou, had two young sons killed during this time. Capt. Stout built a number of small stockades which gave protection to the families of the settlers, and he assisted at Coffee's Station. His force of Rangers was disbanded in June 1839. One reminder of the service of Capt. Stout is Stout's or Spout Springs, just northwest of the intersection of present day Georgetown Road and Spout Springs Road today. Clear, cold water still flows from the sheer rock face as it did during the days when Capt. Stout and his Rangers made camp there. Capt. John Emberson, who resided near Red River for twenty years, raised a company about a month before the expiration of Capt. Stout's service, and for five or six months ranged the frontier. This company disbanded in September, 1839, and from then until May, 1840, there was no organized force operating, so the Indians became very bold in their attacks. Gammel's Digest of Texas Laws records all the laws passed by the Republic of Texas. One of these was an effort to provide mail service to the settlements. In January 1839, an act was passed to establish mail lines, with an extension to Coffee's Station in Fannin (now Grayson) County, from the seat of justice in Fannin County at Warren. The contract for carrying the mail was granted to James A. Caldwell for 1839. In the fall of 1839, under an act of the Legislature passed in 1838, Albert Sidney Johnston, the secretary of war of the Republic of Texas, sent a company of men, under the command of Col. William G. Cook, to lay out a military road from the Brazos to Red River and to establish small forts for the protection of the settlers. Following is a copy of the report of Col. Cooke on his expedition:

"Camp on Bois d'Arc
November 14, 1840.

I joined the troops at Little River, according to my agreement, on the 9th of September, and remained five days waiting for the mules which were to be furnished me at that place, but which were not delivered. In the meantime, the beefs escaped through the neglect of the guard. The Quartermaster made arrangements to furnish others but as they could not be obtained immediately, I started for the Brazos without them, where I had ordered Capt. Holliday to join me, with directions to have the beefs driven on as soon as possible. I arrived at the Waco village on the 19th where I remained until the Quartermaster came up with the supplies, when I again took up the line of march for the Trinity, making but slow progress, on account of crossing the creek bottoms with our wagons. On account of the dryness of the season, we were obliged to camp in two or three instances, without water. Upon one of these occasions at Chambers creek, some of our men went back upon the trail for water, and contrary to orders, without their muskets. They were attacked by Indians, probably 10 or 15 in number, and some of them were killed. Upon the same night, a severe norther blew up, during which our cattle again broke away from the guard and escaped though every effort was made to recover them. They were probably driven away by the Indians, who were prowling about our camp from the Brazos to the Trinity. We made about 6 or 8 miles per day, owing to the difficulty of getting through the bottoms as our mules were in bad condition. After the loss of our beefs, we were entirely without provisions with the exception of sugar and coffee. No corn was taken on the expedition.

From Little River to the Brazos we found buffalo in abundance, and also for several days after we crossed Chambers creek, but as we approached the Trinity, game became scarce, and before we reached the main bottom, we were obliged to subsist for several days upon our dogs, mules, and horses. In this state of affairs, I saw it was impossible to get to the settle-

++++++++++++++++++++++++++++++++++++++++++++++++++++++++++++++++++++++++++++++

ments with the wagons and even with the sick; and being informed by the pilot that it was but two days ride to the settlements on the Sulphur Fork of Red River, I concluded to leave a part of my command, and march on for supplies, calculating to reach the settlements in four days.

Lieut. Col. Clendennin, at his own request, was left on the west side of the Trinity, with the wagons, sick, and forty men as a guard. The fifth day after leaving the Trinity, we struck a thicket, supposed by our guard to be the headwaters of the Sabine, which we were five days cutting through. On the tenth day after leaving Lieut. Col. Clendennin, we struck the trail of the Chihuahua traders, which took us to the settlement on Bois d'Arc, fork of Red River, where we were treated very hospitably by Mr. Bailey Inglish, and furnished with supplies after having been without beef for 22 days.

Arrangements were immediately made to send assistance to the command on the Trinity, and a company was sent back with beefs, and oxen to haul the wagons, etc. Four men who have returned, state they arrived there on the 5th inst. but too late to meet with Col. Clendennin's command.

Captains L. Knott and Haynton were there with forty men who had followed us from Austin. They had reached there on the 4th inst. They stated they had found a note signed by Col. Clendennin, dated the 3rd inst., stating that he had been starved out, that he had eaten the most of his mules and horses, and that he was obliged to leave for the settlements and that he expected to return in 8 or 10 days. I hear nothing of Col. Clendennin, but I expect he has gone down the Trinity. He had, when I left him, about 20 horses and mules. Upon the arrival of Capt. Smith with his command, I shall proceed to obey my orders respecting the military road.

The soldiers here are in fine health and condition. I have selected a fine situation for the post on Red River, ten miles above Coffee's Station, where supplies can be easily obtained, and where it will afford most protection against the Indians. I am told by Mr. Coffee that he, with many of the settlers, were about to leave, but that our arrival has altered their determination.

I am respectfully your obedient servant,

Wm. G. Cooke,

Col. Command, 1st Infantry."[1]

This post established by Col. Cooke was known as Fort Johnston and was midway between Coffee's Station and Basin Springs. He also established a supply post (not a stockade fort) at Coffee's Bend, and this became known as Fort Preston for Capt. William G. Preston, who was there with a company of men in 1840. It is known now as Preston or Preston Bend. In 1840, Col. Cooke received information that a party of hostile Indians, supposedly Cherokees, were leaving the Chickasaw Nation for Texas, in an invading manner and were said to be possessed of large quantities of ammunition. Col. Cooke, with forty volunteers, immediately started north for the purpose of intercepting them and cutting off their supplies. He crossed Red River at the mouth of the Washita and marched up Red River some hundred and fifty miles. During the expedition they met only friendly Indians and molested no one, returning to Fort Preston without locating the hostile Indians. Complaint was made about this expedition by the United States government and charges made against Texas. In May, a large group of men, commanded by Gen. Tarrant, with Capt. James Bourland left Fort Johnston, above Coffee's Trading Post, for a village of Indians on the headwaters of the Trinity, the inhabitants of which had been raiding the settlements. It was on this expedition that Capt. John B. Denton, who divided the command with Capt. Bourland, was killed. Capt. Henry Stout and Capt. Griffin was both wounded. William N. Porter, acting brigadier inspector, gave the report of the expedition June 5, 1841.

## Capt. Stout & Rangers Search For & Engage Indians in the Cross Timbers

They find only Cherokees who had, a few years earlier, arrived from the Trail of Tears resettlement march from the east. Between 1836 and 1843 Capt. Henry Stout and his brother Capt. William Stout served in several ranger expeditions against Native Americans throughout North Texas. Stout/Spout Springs in Georgetown bears their name. Below: Captain Henry Stout and Captain William Stout

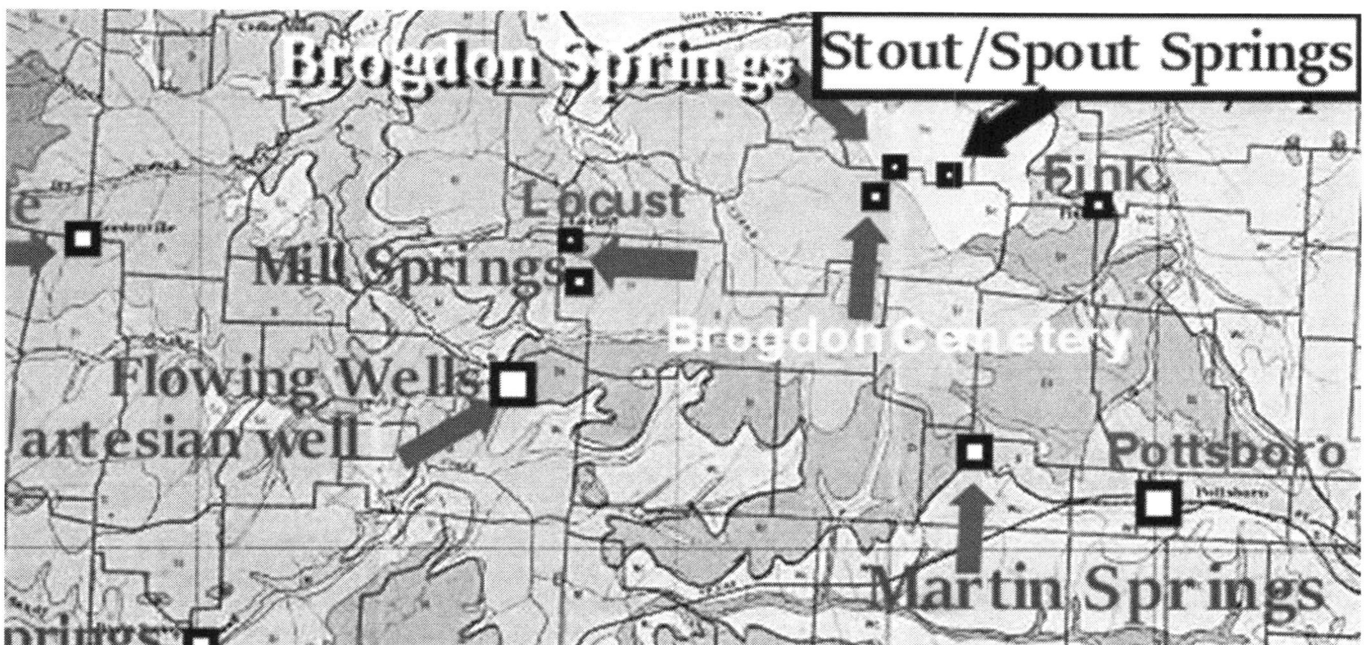

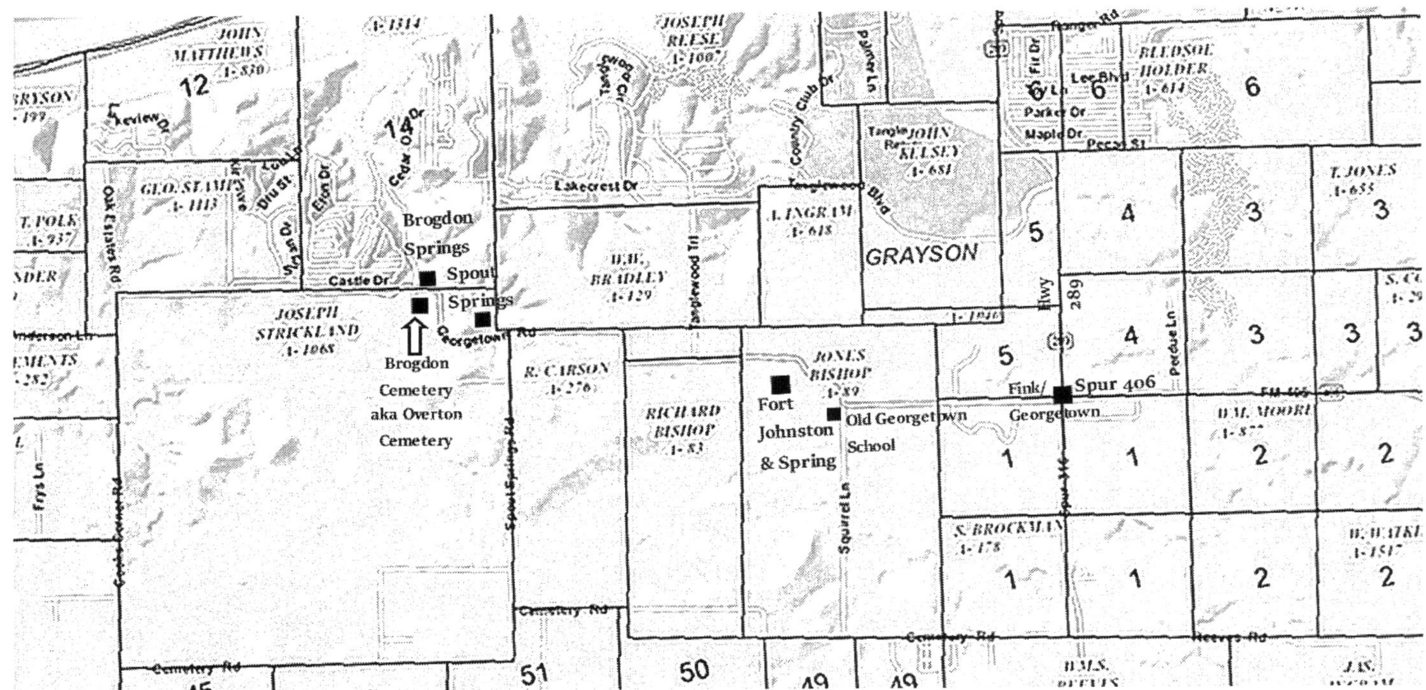


Above: Maps of Georgetown today with Georgetown in the middle going east to west; showing the location of Spout Springs, Brogdon Springs, Brogdon Cemetery, Fort Johnston and spring, location of old original Georgetown school/church.

## GEORGETOWN SPRINGS

The success or failure of any place is dependent on its water, or lack of it. In order for people to exist in Georgetown, like other areas, there had to be a ready supply of fresh, clean water. The Georgetown area is very blessed with springs. I will mention the major springs in the area. In the old times, even up until fairly modern times, people did not dig wells unless the water table was very, very shallow – they depended upon natural springs. People would haul water in barrels from the springs back home for their use. Areas with flowing springs were always populated first, and this area is filled with small flowing springs and large artesian wells. Land which had a spring on it was very valuable and was often bought for that reason, like W. S. Grant did when he purchased a 1 X 11 acre tract of land in order to acquire the **Spring on Reeves Road.** Mr. Grant also later purchased another spring – Spout Springs. His life will be discussed later.

**Brogdon Springs, Spout Springs and the Hanging Tree** Left; Mr. Richardson at Brogdon Springs 1936; right: Tom McQueen at Spout Springs, who lived across the road from the spring.

Neal Henderson lived near the site of William Quantrill's camp at "Camp Lookout at Mineral Springs" and had a trough that he found which was carved by Frank James to collect water from the hillside spring there at Brogdon and Spout Springs. (Quantrill's Raiders were Confederate Civil War guerilla fighters who camped here in the winter during the war. See my book Quantrill's Raiders in North Texas) Brogdon Springs had a large depressed basin where the water could collect and 15 men could bathe at one time. Mr. Henderson also found carved inscriptions in the stones around the springs and dug up pots which contained coins from the Civil War era. James Clement said that there is a large "hanging tree" a walnut that was still located at Brogdon Springs during his lifetime.

Henderson's Ferry was just north of Brogdon Springs on the Red River. This ferry took advantage of a very narrow portion of the river. This spot and nearby Bounds Ferry was also used by outlaws like Jesse James and many others over the years to easily cross to and from Indian Territory into Texas. They used the nearby Brogdon Springs and Stout/Spout Springs situated below the hill which is the highest point in Grayson County. This provided shelter, water, an easy getaway across the Red River and a perfect vantage point to see approaching danger. Quantrill called this place Camp Lookout for this reason. These springs are mentioned in the book Springs of Texas, Volume 1 By Gunnar M. Brune: He stated about 0.55 lps still issued in 1976 from the cliff of Woodbine sandstone where the spring is located. He also saw many carved names and dates there just as Neal Henderson stated. Downstream he described a waterfall at Brogdon Springs west of Stout Springs and 300 meter north of Brogdon springs, and he described a water seeping from cliffs of Woodbine sandstone covered with maidenhair ferns, bittercress and moss and called it Dripping Springs (not what locals call it). He also repeated that horse thieves had been hung from a walnut tree that apparently still stood there in 1976.

**Spout/Stout Springs –** is just north and west of the intersection of Georgetown Road and Spout Springs Road. There is a very sheer high cliff there. Out of the east side of that cliff, the water flows. This was named for Texas Ranger Henry Stout. The old Overton/Pinchum school used to come to this spring and to Brogdon Spring just to the west of it to have picnics.

**Brogdon Springs** - is just to the west of Spout Springs at the intersection of Georgetown Road and Cedar Oaks Dr.

**Martin Springs –** is just east of the intersection of Kyker Lane and Hwy 120 about two miles west of Pottsboro. It still flows into a pool of water that currently sits just north of the road there. To learn much more about Martin Springs, see my book: "Ghost Towns of Texoma – Vol 3 – Martin Springs and Mineral City". There are multiple springs in this immediate area, just as there are in Georgetown. There are many other small springs in the area and of course the largest spring is the artesian well called Flowing Wells near Hagerman which is now under water. Check out my books "Pottsboro Texas and Lake Texoma, Then and Now Vol 2" & "Ghost Towns of Texoma Vol 2 – Hagerman" for more information on this spring.

**Fort Johnston's three springs** - The reason the location for Fort Johnston was probably picked was because of the proximity to a set of three springs. According to long-time Georgetown resident James Clement, who lived across from the old Fort site, the springs are now at the bottom of a stock pond. He said the digging of that pond was very difficult since the springs kept filling the hole up with water and mud and causing the machinery to become stuck and swamped before the hole could be dug. Old artifacts have been found at the site by the landowner and Mr. Clement has found wires grown into VERY old trees there where there may have been fences or horses picketed.

## TRADE ROUTES AVAILABLE TO SETTLERS IN THE AREA

February 21, 1844 Weekly Houston Telegraph - **Colony in the Timbers –**

"The settlements in the Cross Timbers are rapidly extending. Numerous families are now on their way from Kentucky and other States to settle in the new Colony. Col. Coffee, who lately visited Washington (D.C.), stated that the number of Emigrants who arrived in Fannin County during the last years exceeds the whole number who have removed to that section in any former year. The roads in all directions are furrowed by the numerous wagons of the emigrants, so as to resemble the well-beaten roads in the densest settlements in the United States. It is estimated that at least 200 families will remove to the colony in the Cross Timbers this year. The contractors are required to locate in the colony at least two hundred and fifty families each year. Two single men are rated as a family. Each head of a family is entitled to 320 acres of land, provided he cultivates fifteen acres and builds a house upon it. Each single man is entitled to one hundred and sixty acres upon similar conditions. The beauty and fertility of this section are well known. Its distance from navigable waters is the main objection to it; but this difficulty will in a short time be in a great measure obviated. Good roads have been opened from the extreme settlements on the Brazos across to the colony, and there is now but little more difficulty in transporting families from Houston to Galveston to this colony than there is in transporting them to Austin or Seguin. The distance from the Falls of the Brazos to Bird's Ford in the colony is about 65 miles, and from Houston to the Falls as about one hundred and thirty miles, making the whole distance from Houston to Bird's Fort about one hundred and ninety five miles.

The road extends over an undulating country intersected by few deep ravines; and settlements are scattered at intervals of about thirty-five or forty miles along the whole route. There is a nearer route by the Trinity of steamboat navigation as far as Magnolia, which is about one hundred miles by land, and two hundred and seventy miles by the meanderings of the river to Dallas in the colony. Whenever the rafts shall be removed from the Trinity between the Bird's Fort and Magnolia, steamboats will be enabled to ascend quite to the fort, as the river is as wide and deep at Bird's Fort as at Magnolia. The main raft is situated about twelve miles below Dallas and is three quarters of a mile long, the river here divides into three branches, and canoes can easily descend by the raft in high water. The rafts below are all very small and could be removed for an expense of a few hundred dollars.

The opening of the navigation of this river, is of immense importance to Galveston. The distance by water from Dallas to the mouth of the Trinity is six hundred miles, and if the navigation were opened between these points, the trade of the whole country bordering the Trinity throughout this extent would be turned to Galveston.

The country bordering Red River and its tributaries above Coffee's old Station (at Preston Bend), would also be turned to Galveston during a large portion of the years; for the Red River is not susceptible of navigation above the great raft during the dry season.

The distance from Shreveport to Coffee's old Station on Red River by water, is about one thousand miles, and three or four hundred by land. But from that Station to the nearest navigable point on the Trinity River is only ninety miles.

Whenever the Red River therefore is closed, the planters of that section will find it to their advantage to transport their produce to Dallas, and thence to Galveston. Whenever the Trinity is closed, however, the planters of the Colony will be compelled to procure their supplies by land from Houston or some point near Shreveport on the Red River. Houston will probably be the nearest point from which they can procure supplies, and we may ere long expect to see a profitable and extensive trade opened between this city and the settlements in the Cross Timbers."

## Safety for Settlers? The answer was ……. Fort Johnston and the Military Road

The Indian troubles in the Indian Territory, Georgetown, Warren and Preston caused a need for the security of a military road and forts were to be set up in the area to ensure the safety of future settlers. In December 1839 the Congress of the Republic of Texas passed a law directing military personnel to cut a road between Austin and Fort Inglish (near Bonham). The road was intended to protect and advance the frontier by connecting a series of forts to be set up from San Patricio northward to a point near Coffee's Station on the Red River. Col. William Gordon Cooke, commanding the First Regiment of Infantry, was in charge of the expedition, which set out in the fall of 1840 with instructions to begin the road on the Texas side of the mouth of the "Kiamishia Red" river in what is now northwest Red River County and terminate at the Brazos. Drought, loss of supplies, bitter cold, and a scarcity of game delayed the effort to construct the forts and lay out the road. Cooke ultimately camped on Timber Creek north of Fort Inglish and established Fort Johnston, southwest of Coffee's trading post. He chose not to terminate the road at the mouth of the Kiamichi because of the western settlements that would be left unprotected.

## 1842 - SURVEY GROUP For MILITARY ROAD ARRIVES IN GEORGETOWN BARELY ALIVE

The Standard (Clarksville, Texas) **1842** - The line of travel of the group, from the upper Colorado to Red River as late as 1842, was by the way of Nacogdoches, Marshall and the ferry on Big Cypress by which Jefferson now stands, thence by Stephenson's Ferry on Sulphur, now in Morris County. In pursuance of an act passed Dec. 21st, Col. Wm. G. Cooke, started from Austin with a well-appointed armed body, "to define the northern extension of a road, authorized under an act to protect the northern and western frontier, and cut out a road from the Nueces to the south of Kiamichi, and establish military posts thereon."

Their route was over "a terra incognita", and involved serious privations, and somewhere south of the Trinity, perhaps on "Four mile" or Post Oak creek in the present county of Dallas, they ran out of provisions, and scattered; some dying from hunger and the remnant straggling into Fort English (Inglish) (near present day Bonham) and Old Warren, in Fannin County, and some into **Old Georgetown (Fort Johnston)** in Fannin (present day Grayson) County. **These facts are cited to show how remote was the Red River country from any settled part of the state,** and its connection with the formation of the independent existence of Texas as a separate government, discovered from its original association with the Mexican State of Coahuila. Article reprinted August 25, 1882

# EARLY ROADS AT GEORGETOWN Go Through Fort Johnston

The Denison Press Nov 21, 1951 - One of the oldest and most historic roads of Northeast Texas figures in highway modernization plans for the Dallas area. This is Preston Road, which echoes the creak of covered wagons, the crack of freighters' whips, and the tramp of Longhorn herds. Today, as in the early periods of settlement and cattle trailing, Preston Road is the quickest route between Dallas and the Red River.

The Preston route was in use long before it acquired its present century-old name. Because it followed high prairies and kept away from the Cross Timbers, Indians used it as a trade route, a trail, a road for hunting buffalo and in raiding the early white settlements in Central Texas to steal horses and capture prisoners for ransom. Many of the early emigrants, coming down through the Indian Territory in Conestoga wagons, entered Texas by this trail. They called it and the route through the eastern edge of the Indian Territory, the Texas Road.

The first survey of what is now Preston Road, along with that from Dallas to Austin, was made in the days of the Texas Republic. In the fall of 1839, under an act of the Congress of Texas, passed a year earlier, Albert Sidney Johnston, Secretary of War, sent north a company of soldiers under the command of Col. William G. Cooke. The purpose was to lay out a military road from the Brazos to the Red River and to establish small forts for the protection of the settlers.

Colonel Cooke joined the troops at Little River and proceeded to the Waco village. There he waited for the quartermaster to catch up with supplies, which included beeves on the hoof and several wagons with provisions. Five of Cooke's men, carelessly leaving their muskets when they went to get water, were killed by Indians. Soon afterward, in a norther, the cattle broke loose and ran away. This left the party with nothing edible except sugar and coffee and whatever game they could kill. When game ran out, they had to eat dogs, mules, and horses and they barely reached **Georgetown** alive. Having reached the Red River, Colonel Cooke established a stockade called **Fort Johnston**, midway between Coffee's Station and Basin Springs. He also set up a supply post that became known as Fort Preston. It took its name from that of Capt. William G. Preston, who was in charge of a company of men there in 1840. The village that grew up there was called Preston Bend and then just Preston; and the trail from Dallas to this point became known as Preston Road. The road surveyed by Colonel Cooke and his men is shown on manuscript maps prepared in 1841. They have been preserved in the General Land Office and the University of Texas archives. **<u>They show the road starting south from Fort Johnston, between the mouth of Mineral Creek on the west.</u>** A few miles to the south, the road crossed the Chihuahua Trail, which later became known as the Butterfield Trail. The Cooke military road followed a route already in occasional use. Between the Red River and the Trinity, it was roughly that of the present Preston Road. It crossed the Trinity just below Cedar Springs, now a part of Dallas. The upper Preston

Road was the first highway to be improved by Grayson County after the formation of a county government in 1846. The route was staked out in October of that year from Sherman to Preston landing and was developed as a county road in 1847. By this time the route was in frequent use by emigrants headed into Texas and was beginning to be used by cattlemen trailing herds to northern markets. For the southwestern cowmen, Preston Road became part of a much longer cattle trail that began in South Texas and extended through the eastern edge of the Indian Territory – past Fort Gibson and Boggy Depot. At Baxter Springs, in the southeastern corner of Kansas, it divided into several branches. One went north to Independence, Missouri. Another led west along the southern border of Kansas, and then turned north. The third pointed northeast toward Sedalia, St. Louis, Quincy and Chicago. At first, this route was called The Trail, the Cattle Trail, or the Kansas Trail; Kansas called it the Texas Trail. In time it became known as the Shawnee Trail. It crossed the Red River just above an Indian settlement on the Texas side called Shawneetown, passed through Shawnee country, and skirted the Shawnee Hills. It remained the principal cattle trail from Texas to Kansas until the Chisholm Trail was established farther west in 1867. After that, its use for cattle began to diminish. The northern drives became larger in 1849 and more so in 1850.

Map of three Early Forts which existed in the 1840s below:

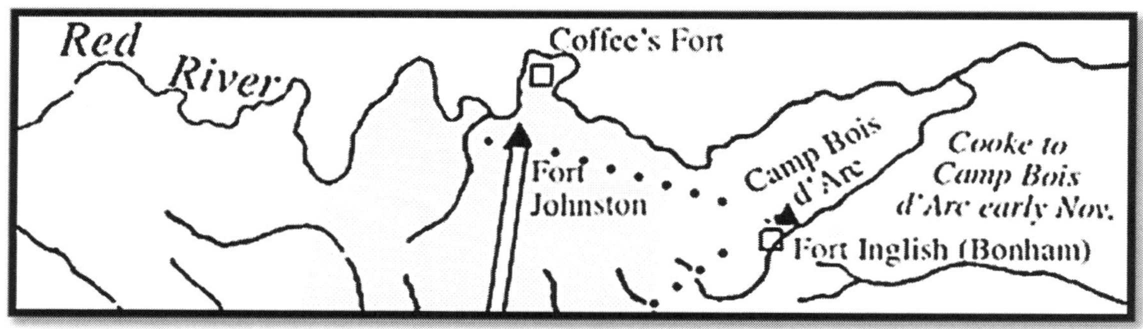


**Map of Emigrant Trail and Butterfield Trail, Grayson County**

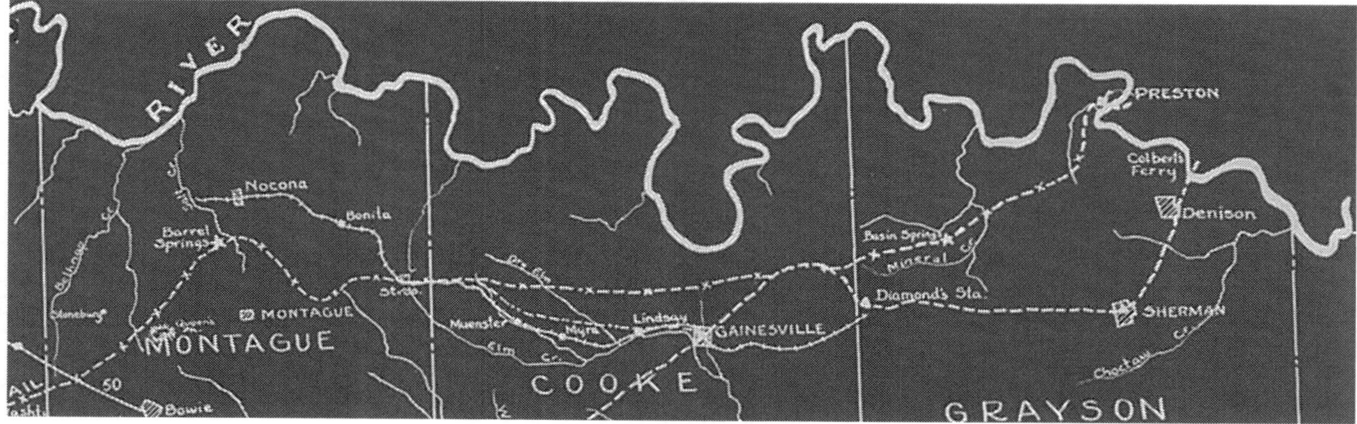

## Texas Roads/Trails

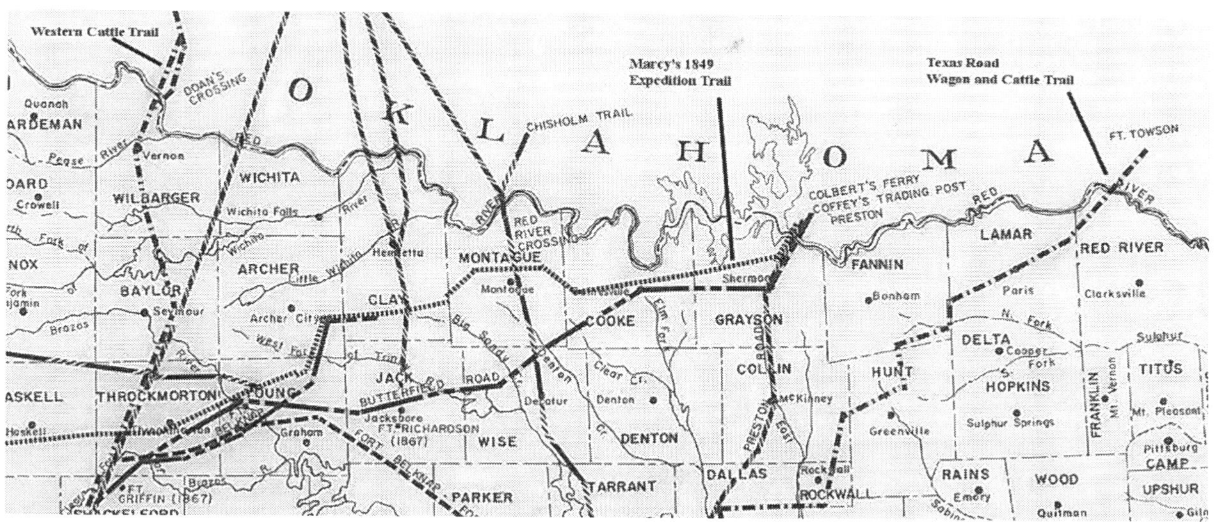


# FORT JOHNSTON / JOHNSON IN OLD GEORGETOWN

Fort Johnston (or Johnson), was located in the Old Georgetown community, just south of the present day Georgetown Road and west of Hwy 289 and Squirrel Lane. There is an historical marker near the site which is on private land.

Below: Historical Marker, James G. Bourland and William G. Cooke

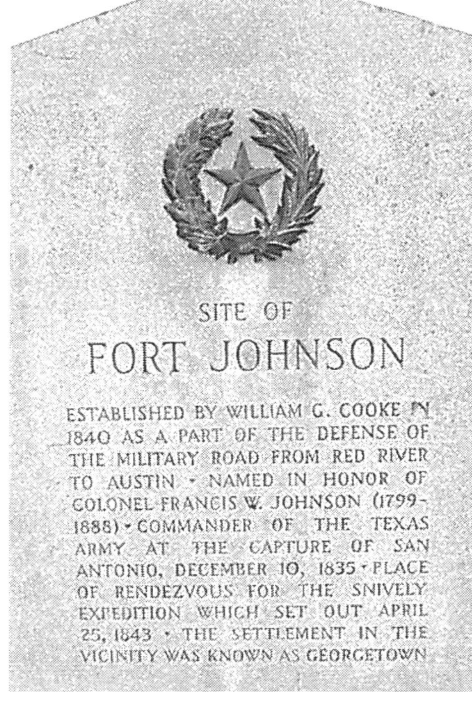

Fort Johnston was a small, temporary fort of the Republic of Texas. It was meant to be equally distant between Coffee's Station and Basin Springs in a line of forts on the military road protecting settlers from Indians in northern Grayson County. It was established in November 1840.

The site, **east of the Cross Timbers and near Little Mineral Creek,** was selected by William G. Cooke, commander of the Military Road expedition, immediately after his arrival on the Red River. The post was constructed in November - December 1840 by First Infantry companies D (commanded by John Holliday) and E (commanded by James P. Goodall) under the command of Holliday.

On Feb. 3, 1841, Capt. Goodall wrote that Corporal George Taylor and five privates deserted. On his muster roll of 1841, he wrote the company was stationed at Fort Johnston, using it as a base of operations as they worked on the military road. He said building was progressing rapidly, but there had been many more desertions and he was not able to retrieve many of them except Private Michael Riley, due to lack of funds and horses.

Fort Johnston was to be the upper post in a line of frontier forts proposed by Albert Sidney Johnston. But in March or April of 1841 the post was abandoned. After learning of the disbanding of the Army of the Republic of Texas, Holliday left Coffee's Station on April 19. He joined Capt. William D. Houghton, from Camp Jordan, and arrived in Austin on May 3.

### Indian Treaty –

President Houston appointed three commissioners, Messrs. Stroud, Durst and Williams, to make treaties with the Indians so as to stop the attacks. They met "at Georgetown, otherwise known as Fort Johnston," and made plans for meeting the tribes. Later in the summer, tribes of Caddos, Biluxies, and Ionies met the commissioners near Red River, and signed a treaty. Red Bear, chief of the Caddos was spokesman for the tribes, and the treaty was attested by Holland Coffee, James A. Caldwell, J. Bourland, and others. Col. R. M. Jones, Col. Sloan Love, and Col. Stroud were among the speakers. By this treaty, the Indians were assured of their hunting grounds as all that portion of Texas lying west of the following limits: Beginning on the Rio Roxo or Red River at the lower edger of the Cross Timbers, thence along the said Cross Timbers to the south fork of the Trinity River, thence in a direct line to the Comanche Peak, on the south side of the Brazos River, thence in a southwest course to the River (Rio) Grande, including all the prairie west of said line to the Rocky Mountains, except that inhabited by the Mexicans. This eastern boundary of the Indians as far as it affected Grayson County came through Whitesboro. Conditions with the Indians improved after the treaty, but attacks on settlers did not stop entirely.

**TREATY WITH THE INDIANS** - Telegraph and Texas Register Houston, Aug 20, 1842 - A gentleman from Fannin County informed the newspaper that Messrs. Stroud, Durst and Williams, the Commissioners appointed by the President, to treat with the various Indian tribes who had been harassing the frontier for some years past, met a few days ago at Georgetown, otherwise known as Fort Johnston, and organized for business. Communication was had with the various tribes, and time and place was appointed for arranging the treaty. These tribes, numbering about three thousand men, have assembled near the head of Cash Creek, in the mountains above the lower Cross Timbers, about ninety miles northwest of **Coffee's Station,** and on the north side of Red River. Runners have sent for the representatives of other tribes, who will all meet at that place. The Commissioners will accompany some of the principal Chiefs, who are now at the Depot in the Choctaw Nation. Our informant entertained no doubt the treaty would be effected. If so, and its provisions fairly adhered to, relief would be given to an immense extent of most desirable country, and probably none more desirable than the frontier county of our own district – the county of Fannin. There is now a considerable population in that county and we presume that a large emigration will pour into it and the balance of this district, this fall (after the threat of Indian attack is removed).

Everywhere in the district, the corn crops are great beyond recollection, and pork will be very low. The citizens of the Western States of the Union who are pushed and harassed, from the effects of excessive and fraudulent issues of worthless bank paper based upon nothing but impudence and the ill-judged confidence of their victims, can find here a country with but little money, cheap land of the richest character, which will yield great returns for the labor of cultivation; moral and most worthy neighbors and a degree of personal and mental independence, which we think is without parallel. There is here, no artificial system to cramp the energies of a man, or defraud him of his earnings, by causes beyond his control.

Telegraph and Texas Register Houston, Sep 21, 1842 - **Treaty with the Indians!** The editor of the Clarksville TX Northern Standard was informed by a gentleman from Fannin County, that the commissioners mentioned in the communication of the Creek Nation Agent, Mr. Logan, which was published a few weeks ago, met with the tribes about the 12$^{th}$ of Sept. **at Fort Johnston**, **now called Georgetown**, and organized for business. Communication was made with the various tribes, and a time and a place appointed for arranging the treaty. The tribes, numbering about 3,000 souls, had assembled near the head of Cash Creek, in the mountains above the lower Cross Timbers, about ninety miles northwest of Coffee's Station (at Preston Bend), and on the north side of Red River. Runners have been sent to the representatives of the tribes who had not come in. The commissioners intended to accompany some of the principal chiefs to the place designated for the meeting. These chiefs were waiting for the commissioners at the depot in the Choctaw Nation. The citizens of that section manifested great satisfaction that the treaty was about to be concluded. It is worthy of notice, however, that at the very time these arrangements were in progress, parties of Indians were committing depredations in the vicinity of Austin, Milam and Franklin. Possibly, however, the authors of these attacks were merely renegades or outcasts from the other tribes. The prairie Indians of Texas have so long been distinguished for treachery that even if a treaty should by concluded, some doubt the ability to place much reliance upon it. Before the (Texas) revolution, the Indians residing east of the Brazos, were accustomed to make treaties with the inhabitants of Eastern Texas, and frequent Nacogdoches and other towns in the most friendly manner to trade, while at the same time, their warriors were murdering families on the Colorado and Guadalupe. The Apaches play a similar game in Mexico. They murder and plunder the people of Chihuahua and sell the spoils in Albuquerque or Santa Fe. But the one great advantage of a treaty will be to enable our traders, for a while, to visit the Indian villages, and ascertain the precise number of the warriors, and the features of the country they occupy. Then if hostilities again ensue, we shall know the force with which we have to contend, and the direction in which we are to seek the enemy. We shall also be enbled to make distinctions between the tribes, and thus conduct a war against one or several of them, without involving them all in hostilities. The treaty was finally concluded on the 24th with only the Caddo, Biloxi and Ioni Tribes. There would be other treaties signed by more Indian tribes with the Republic of Texas and the Federal Government in the next few years in North Texas. Conditions for settlers improved after the treaties, but hostilities did not entirely stop, especially with non-participating tribes.

**Fort Johnston** was short-lived, but was host to many important events. The Snively expedition mustered and departed from Fort Johnston in 1843. In the winter of 1845–46, Lyman Wight, leading a congregation of defecting Mormons into Texas, used Fort Johnston as his headquarters. The community is mentioned in the log of the Leach family wagon train and their trip west. The commissioners' journey to Comanche Peak in connection with the Comanche treaty of 1846 passed through Georgetown, as did Randolph B. Marcy's Expedition on his return from Dona Ana in 1849. The old road became the upper part of the military road from Preston to Fort Belknap. The site of the fort is now just west of Fink, a few miles from Lake Texoma. A Texas Centennial historical marker located there says that the post was named for Francis W. Johnson. It was probably named Fort Johnston in honor of Albert Sidney Johnston who proposed the fort system in the first place. It is called by both names in historical sources. info from Gerald S. Pierce, "The Military Road Expedition of 1840–41," Texas Military History (Summer 1967). Gerald S. Pierce, Texas Under Arms: The Camps, Posts, Forts, and Military Towns of the Republic of Texas (Austin: Encino, 1969). Northern Standard, July 31, 1852.

## Map showing location of Fort Johnston superimposed over modern map

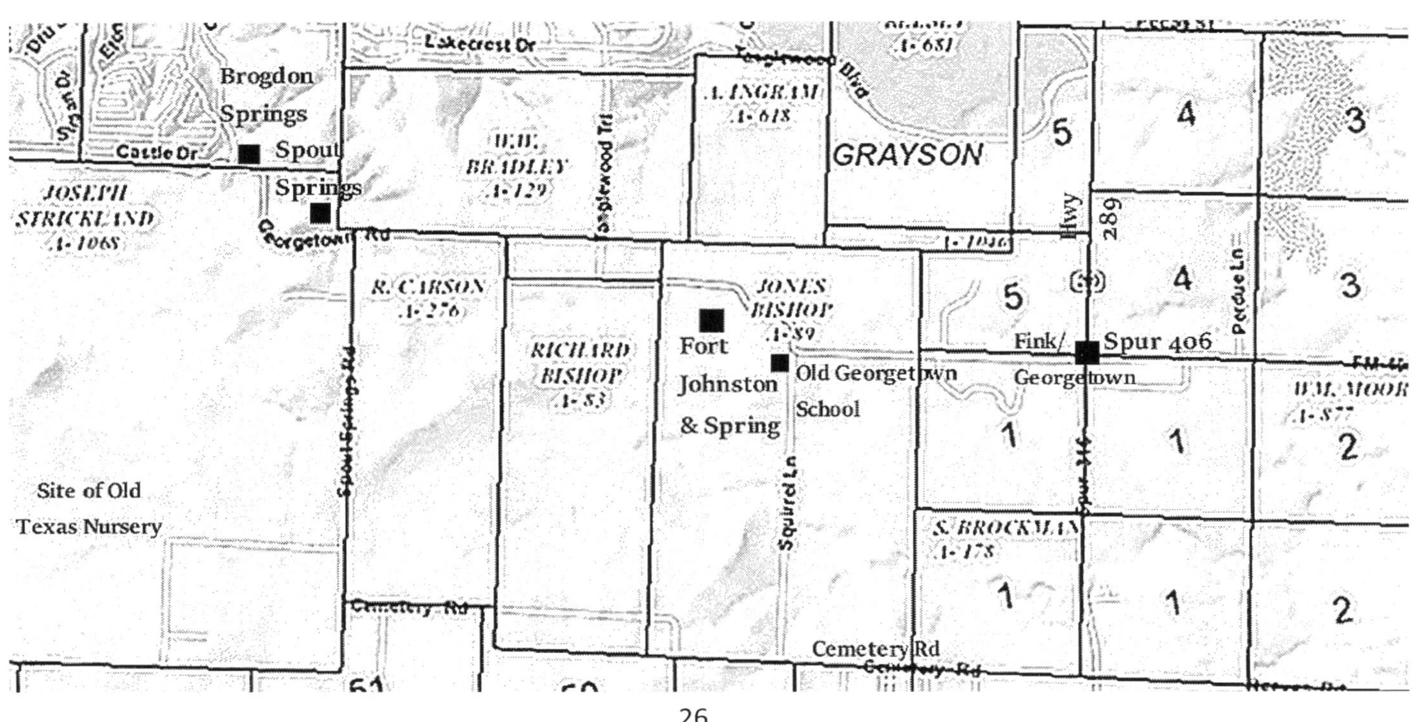

# FORT JOHNSTON & GEORGETOWN - STARTING POINT FOR THE SNIVELY EXPEDITION - Colonel Snively's Expedition is Organized at and Leaves From Fort Johnston in Georgetown Apr 25, 1843 With many Georgetown residents as members of the expedition.

By way of clarification, you must understand at this time, Grayson County had not yet been formed. All of what would become Grayson County was part of the much larger Fannin County as mentioned in this article. Also, the Santa Fe Expedition had previously been commissioned by the president of Texas, Mirabeau Lamar who had a vision for expanding the Republic of Texas into New Mexico. He sent an expedition to Santa Fe in order to convince the people of New Mexico to join Texas. Lamar selected José Antonio Navarro as a commissioner. The Texan-Santa Fe Expedition left Austin on June 19, 1841. The expedition was a disaster from the beginning. They quickly became lost, their food was short, water was scarce, and the group got lost again on the high plains. Several men deserted and some died on the way. Finally, after a three-month journey, the group arrived in New Mexico. They were met by an overwhelming force of 1,500 Mexican soldiers. The Texans had no choice and surrendered without firing a shot. The prisoners were marched 1,500 miles to Mexico City suffering mistreatment along the way. Waiting for them was Santa Anna, ready to take revenge for his defeat against the Texans. Santa Anna especially wanted to punish Navarro, who he considered a traitor. After diplomatic efforts by the United States, Mexico finally agreed to release the Texans and send them home, but not Navarro. He was convicted of treason and sentenced to death. But Santa Anna offered Navarro a deal: if he renounced Texas, he would be forgiven and allowed to take a prominent government position in Mexico. Navarro refused. He remained in prison for more than three years returning to Texas as a hero. Texans of course, were not happy to hear about the mistreatment of their fellow Texians especially since their nemesis Santa Anna had a hand in it. The Snively expedition was one of a series of forays in which Texas engaged during the early period of the Republic to retaliate for indignities heaped upon the Texans in trading expeditions like the one just mentioned above.

Telegraph and Texas Register (Houston, Tex.), August 2, 1843 "The expedition was sanctioned by the Executive, and a majority of the men were raised in the Red River District, and were commanded by Colonel Snively. They left Georgetown, in Fannin County, on the 25th of April (1843) and it was their expectation that they would meet Col. Warfield and company at or near Bent's Fort, on the Arkansas River, and then make a descent on Santa Fe, and avenge the wrongs which had been done their countrymen. They were not a banditti, as some of the papers of the United States styled them, but citizen soldiers going to battle for the rights and liberties of their adopted country, and to avenge the death of their treacherously murdered countrymen. We have heard nothing of them since they left, but wherever they may be, we wish them success and know them to be gentlemen, there is no danger of any traders belonging to the United States being molested by them; but woe betide a Mexican trader should any be caught by them, as they could not forget the treatment of the Santa Fe expedition."

Jacob Snively, on January 28, 1843, petitioned the government of the republic for permission to organize and fit out an expedition to intercept and capture the property of Mexican traders who might pass through territory claimed by Texas on the Santa Fe Trail. On February 16 the War Department authorized the organization of a force not to exceed 300 men. The spoils of the campaign, taken hopefully in honorable warfare, were to be divided equally between the government and the members of the expedition. The place of **the rendezvous was Fort Johnston at the settlement of Georgetown near Coffee's Station** on the Red River in what was then Fannin County but is now Grayson.

By April 24 about 175 men had assembled, and on that day the expedition, which was called by the members the Battalion of Invincibles, was organized into four companies with Snively chosen as the commandant. They marched along the old Chihuahua Trail, crossed Red River two miles below the mouth of the main Wichita, followed a north northwestward course across present Oklahoma, and on May 27 reached the Arkansas River and the Santa Fe Trail in the vicinity of present Edwards County, Kansas. Upon reaching the Arkansas, the first plan was to familiarize themselves with their surroundings. The spy company of ten men became active, while the main command moved along the south bank of the river. On May 30 the spies' discovered evidence of a wagon train, but learned that the train belonged to some traders from Bent's Fort. Snively then moved his force south of the Arkansas, first to Mulberry Creek and to the head of Crooked Creek, thus allowing the Texans to command the Cimarron branch of the Santa Fe Trail and hiding their own presence in the area. Charles A. Warfield and three or four of his followers joined the Snively party. When the Texans struck the Santa Fe Trail about fifteen miles below the crossing, they encountered 100 Mexican soldiers. In the fight, seventeen Mexicans were killed and eighty-two taken prisoner, while no Texans were injured. June 28, boredom and division in the group caused them to break up. The prisoners were released, the mules, saddles, and weapons taken from the Mexicans were divided among the Texans, who divided into two groups called the "mountaineers" and the "home boys." The home boys, about seventy-six men, selected Eli Chandler as their leader. Chandler led his followers back toward the Arkansas.

The mountaineers, with Snively in command, also marched to the Arkansas, where on June 30 they were discovered by United States Dragoons under Capt. Philip St. George Cooke, who, largely as a result of the murder of Antonio José Chaves attributed to the Warfield expedition, had been sent to protect a Mexican caravan. Cooke told Snively he believed the Texans were on United States territory, and that his men must be disarmed. Snively insisted that he was on Texas territory, but had to relent and disarm when Cooke surrounded him. Cooke first only allowed the Texans ten muskets for 170 men, but later he returned to the Texan camp and on July 1 offered to escort all who wished to accompany him to Independence, Missouri. About fifty men went with him. Snively and the others rejoined Chandler on July 2. Snively was still determined to chase Mexican caravan, which the scouts reported on July 8, had crossed the Arkansas; but he found the majority of his command unwilling to continue on the expedition any further; so he resigned his command on July 9. Chandler and his men then set out for home. The remaining Texans, deciding to continue in their attempt to capture the caravan, elected Warfield as commander and set out on their march. Several of them later rejoined Chandler's party; less than seventy were still holding to the original purpose of the expedition on July 13, when they discovered what they thought to was a large group of Mexicans under Governor Manuel Armijo escorting the caravan. Believing their few men incapable of capturing the caravan, they abandoned further pursuit and turned for home. Warfield resigned; Snively was reelected to command; and on August 6, the Texan force was disbanded at Fort Bird on the Trinity. The Texas government complained that Captain Cooke had invaded Texas territory in arresting Snively's forces.

**The Sante Fe and Snively Expeditions started out with high expectations which remained unfulfilled, but accomplished only confusion, conflict, misery and death.**

**More articles detailing the Snively Expedition:** The Northern Standard. (Clarksville, Tex.), September 14, 1843; Northern Standard. (Clarksville, Tex.), September 21, 1843; Telegraph and Texas Register (Houston, Tex.), Sept 27, 1843; Telegraph and Texas Register (Houston, Tex.), October 4, 1843

## More Indian Troubles on Little Mineral and Cross Timbers

The Standard (Clarksville, Texas) 1844 – 1845; from the Standard, March 27, 1844: "We were called upon on Saturday by Mr. J. Eliot, who is an agent of the Trinity Colony Company, and who was direct from the colony. He informed us that everything was progressing well, and that there was no difficulty with Indians, (but) the colonists have organized themselves into two militia companies to act in case there should be need, and a third company will soon be organized." From the Standard, March 13, 1845: "About the last of January, four persons in company with an old man named Rice and his two sons, one a boy of about 18, and another man, were out on Rowlett's Creek, a branch of the East Fork of Trinity, bear hunting. The Rice boy was killed by Indians and scalped. The Indians were wearing blue hunting shirts and sealskin caps (acquired via with northwestern tribes??). Rice and his companions pursued them for some time but had to give up. They suspected they were Cherokees or Creeks from the United States territory. On the 9th February, a man named Helms living on Wilson's Creek, a branch of the east fork of Trinity, was out hunting with a neighbor, whose name we do not know and concluded that they would drive home their horses which ranged some six miles from home. Their horses not being together, they separated, and Helms went on until he found his horses. He found one of them with a lariat around him which of course caused his suspicion. As he drove them homeward, the horses crossed the creek at an unusual place, and shortly after, about mile on his way homeward, Indians started up around him, and giving a tremendous yell, discharged several guns at him. Raising the yell in return, and starting his horses, he presented his gun at them and they gave back. Helms then started for home, turning every once in a while as the Indians got too near, and presenting his gun, which always made them give back. He noticed that his horse after running a piece, stopped, and four of the Indians went after them, and must have gotten them, as they have not been seen since. Helms rode home, the Indians firing at him occasionally, and the last shot which was made at him, when within a half mile of home, just grazed his heel. This was in the morning about eight hours after a party of 16 men started in pursuit of the Indians. They followed the trail of the horses, and so they got into the edge of the lower Cross Timbers, they discovered an Indian, on foot, which they took to be a spy, watching the rear of the returning party. They came upon him, Helms being convinced he was one of the party that attacked him, shooting him. They then came up to him, and commenced questioning him, but could learn nothing from him, except that there were five more camped on the trail, ahead. They then rode and came upon a camp where they found two Indians. They professed to be Caddoes, and one of the spoke very good English. He said there were others belonging to the camp, who were out. One being shown the gun and shot-bag taken from the Indian just shot, he claimed them as belonging to one of his hunters, and was then taken to the body, which he claimed as a cousin of his wife. The mistake was explained to him (if mistake there really was) and all the circumstances which it had grown out of; and he seemed to be satisfied, that no wrong had been intended. He said that he had seen a trail of twelve Indians going down to the settlement, and threatened vengeance upon "the damned Wichitas" who, he said, had been the cause of the mischance. Whether satisfied, or not, with the course of the Whites, he seemed to be so, but we suppose the first evidence of dissatisfaction, will be the taking of a scalp. On the same day that Rice was killed, an old man named Underwood, and his son, a small boy, living at a new settlement in the **Cross Timbers**, were upon **Little Mineral,** some six miles from the **residence of James Shannon (one of the Rangers?)**, gathering cattle to drive to their new place, and were killed by Indians, what tribe, not known, probably the same that pursued Helms. Depredation in the way of killing cattle and stealing horses take place daily as well as attacks on settlers. A line must be drawn at once to safeguard lives and property.

## INDIAN SKIRMISH IN THE CROSS TIMBERS

Weekly Houston Telegraph, April 23, 1845 – The Northern Standard reported the Indians have recommended hostilities upon the frontier settlements in the Cross Timbers. It appears that a party supposed to be Creeks or Cherokees from the United States, made an attack upon one of the settlements and in the skirmish an old gentleman named Underwood, his little son, and a boy named Price were killed. Several Indians were also killed. These Indians have probably become enraged and jealous of the settlers in that section who are rapidly encroaching upon their old hunting grounds. Every effort of our Government to restrain them by peaceable means has been found ineffectual. Whenever the American flag is unfurled, the Indian shrinks back with dismay and leaves the weakest settler to pursue his avocations unmolested.

## Marcy Expedition Began at Georgetown's Fort Johnston

Randolph Barnes Marcy, in 1849, determined the route of the Marcy Trail, from Fort Smith to Santa Fe. In March 1852, Marcy was assigned the command of a seventy-man exploring expedition across the Great Plains in search of the source of the Red River and directed to "collect and report everything that may be useful or interesting." Second in command of the Marcy expedition was Capt. George B. McClellan, who later became his son-in-law, and during the Civil War, his commander. Among Marcy's scouts was Jim Ned, a Delaware Indian whom Marcy called "the bravest warrior and the most successful horse thief in the West." Between May 2 and July 28, 1852, Marcy's party crossed a thousand miles of previously undocumented Texas and Oklahoma territory, discovering numerous valuable mineral deposits as well as twenty-five new species of mammals and ten reptiles. Marcy also recorded a prairie dog town that covered

400,000 acres. He discovered the sources of both forks of the Red River, as well as the Palo Duro and Tule canyons, and he became the first white man to explore them. The expedition encountered and documented the little-known Wichita Indians and compiled the first Wichita Indian dictionary. He returned with information on Cynthia Ann Parker. Eastern newspapers erroneously reported that Marcy died at the hands of the Comanches. Marcy's 1852 expedition has been called the most significant of his career and "the best organized, best conducted, and most successful" venture into the region to that date. It was the first to locate the headwaters of the Red River, which Zebulon M. Pike, Stephen Long and Thomas Freeman had all previously searched for and failed to find. Marcy's report on his expedition, “Exploration of the Red River of Louisiana, In the Year 1852...With Reports on the Natural History of the Country”, supplemented by a handsome collection of lithographs, was published in 1853.

**EARLY 1853 map below.**

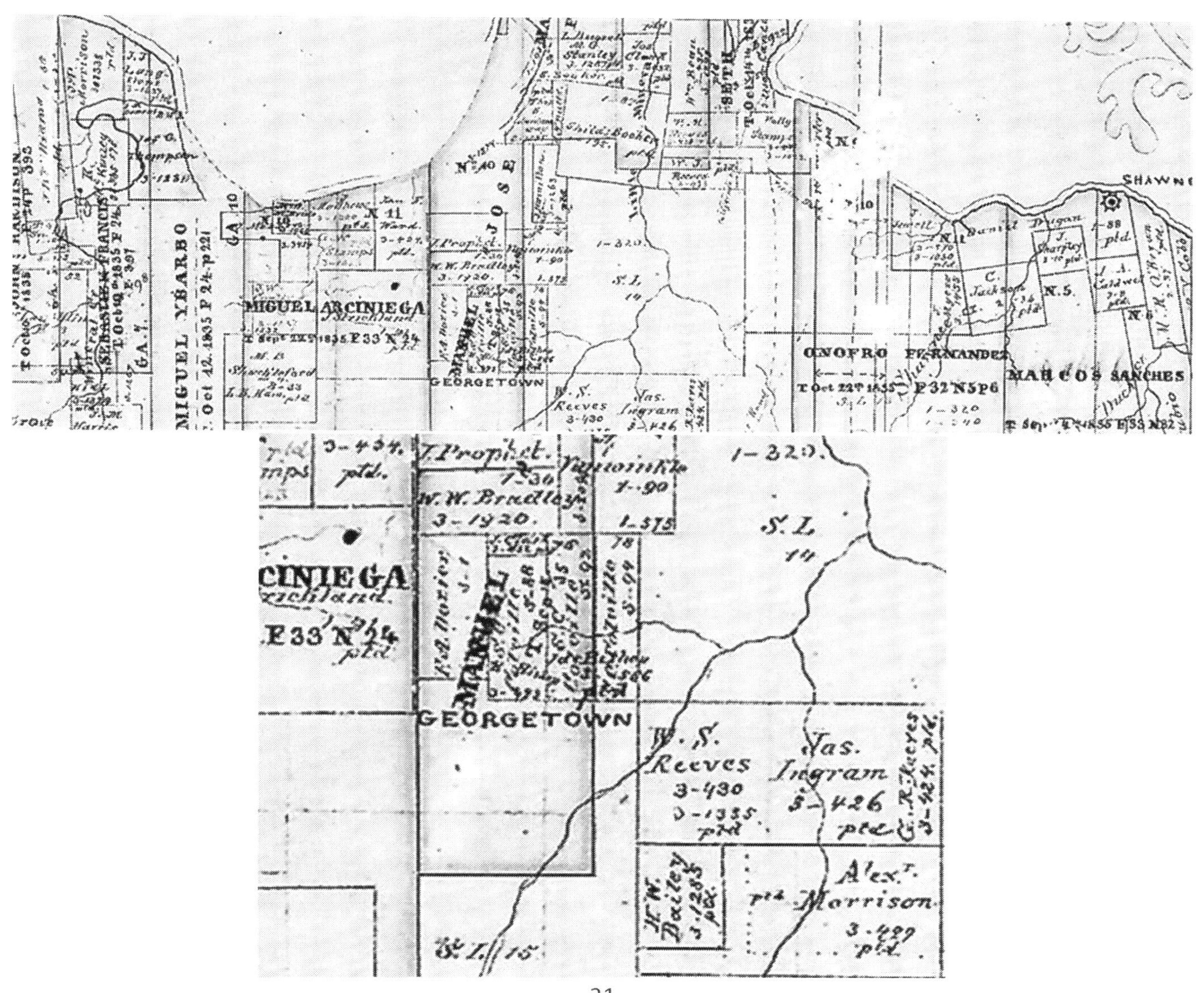

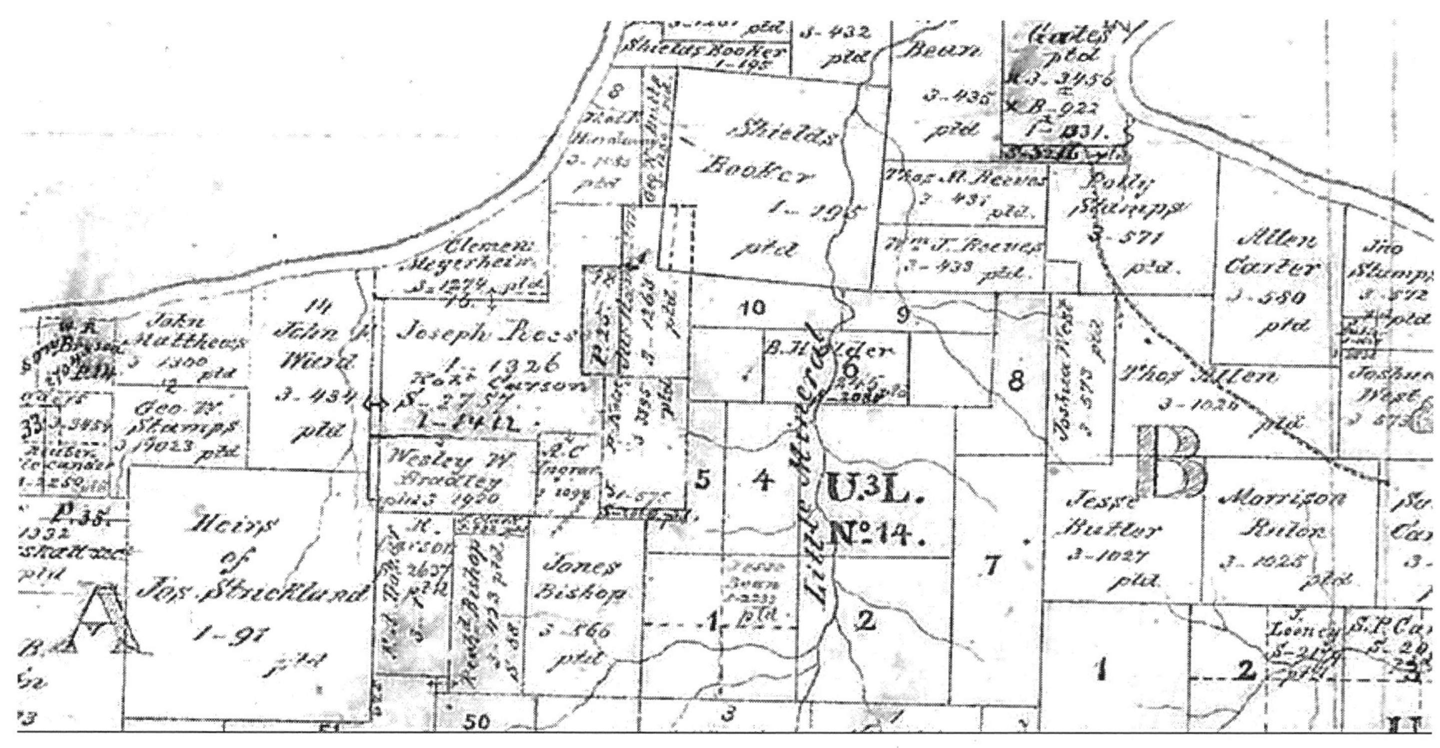


**Above: January 19, 1859 map Below: 1871**

# George's Town, Old Georgetown, Reevesville, Fink – Little Town With Many Names

**Fink, Texas, north of Pottsboro, as it stands today, started out in the late 1830s and early 1840s and has gone by many names.**

Georgetown or George's Town was named for early pioneer **George Ivey.**

The community was originally referred to as George's Town, in honor of a local resident at the time, who lived near Fort Johnston - George Ivey. This information is according to a newspaper article in The Northern Standard. (Clarksville, Tex.), Saturday, July 31, 1852 From Reeves' Monday Evening...by C. De M.

"This morning after breakfast, we left McCarty's and after travelling about the neighborhood somewhat, we got here this afternoon, **after crossing Big Mineral, a clear creek, with a muddy bottom,** cut up by the Government teams, hauling to the Northern line of Forts. **The road which we struck into a little the other side of Spring creek, and which continues to Preston, is termed the Military Road, and is broad, plain and much travelled by wagons, carrying supplies for the Posts, and express riders from the Post to the Depot at Preston.**

Just beside the residence of Mr. McCarty, the view of the surrounding country becomes distinctly visible. This place is a very pleasant one, well divided between timber and prairie, with highlands in view from the house. Around it, are three leagues of University land, two of them almost entirely prairie, but of fair quality, save the lack of timber, the third a superb league, well timbered. Of the 50 appropriated by law for two Universities, twenty eight leagues have been surveyed in this (Grayson) and in Cooke Counties."

Shawnee Town, Wednesday Evening. (Let's look at Old Georgetown!)

**"Went this morning with Col. Reeves, all over the Georgetown tract, famous ever since I have been in the district, as a magnificent tract of land, and in 1840 or thereabout, the station of a company of Rangers.**

**It's pretensions as a Town are about these, as near as I can learn – a man named George Ivey once lived there, and from that circumstance, it was called George's Town or Georgetown, its town character being perhaps increased by the residence of the Rangers. Some of the cabins erected by the troops are still standing. (Author's note: There was an old cabin on Pete Christman's land across from Fort Johnston which had 1840 carved in the mantle piece. It was said by some modern informants that this mantle was moved to an old cabin or house at Texoma Estates on Georgetown Road near modern day Russwood).**

**The tract is part prairie and part timber, lying finely either as regards cultivation or beauty. The land in some places is black sandy, and in some, red sandy. Of the thousand acres, every acre is tillable. There are several fine springs; one a Chalybeate, welling up strongly, in a little ravine.**

Came from Georgetown to Shawnee Town, which has a coexistent reputation with Georgetown, and is at present the residence and plantation of Col. William C. Young.

Shawnee Town however, was once an Indian town. Their fields and some of their cabins are still here, and the creek which runs through the tract has always been known to the whites as Shawnee creek. This tract is of red sandy land, very rich, and has a front of two miles on Red River, the tract containing 1200 acres.

On the east side of the Creek, is a high hill, the commencement of a range, which are bald, save grass and cacti, and run from the edge of the bottom, for some distance out in the prairie, and also sinuously with the course of the river. From it may be seen the surrounding country for miles. The locality is such a one as Indians always choose for villages when practicable; the conjunction, Hills, rich valleys and clear running water. The creek affords perch, trout, and suckers (catfish).

The under layer of the banks is of argillaceous limestone, with great number of Ammonites and other shells imbedded. Petrifications (fossils) are deposited upon the little bars at the bends. In places, benches of white limestone occupy one side of the bed, creating basins for the water. **The soil here, as at Georgetown**, is shown by the creek banks to be eight or nine feet deep. This is the place whose product of corn last year, with indifferent cultivation, was 70 bushels to the acre, as published last Fall. There is an apple orchard on it, which bore last years, fruit of very large size, and excellent flavor. This tract of land, was originally nearly all, heavily timbered.

There is a region of country about here, on the river, which I should like to visit, if I had time. It is in Cooke County, has now only a half dozen settlements upon it, but is said to be magnificent land, with heavy timber. Bottom prairies extend out a mile from the timbers, affording rich fields cleared by Nature, ready for tillage.

Red River at the place of John D. Black, which is the highest settlement, is fordable, nearly always. Col. James Bourland has a trading place, for Indian traffic, in that region, and his brother William H. Bourland, lives also in the vicinity. It is a portion of country which must soon command attention, for its great richness, and its convenience to the market furnished by the frontier posts, for grain. Friday Evening.

Have been today, upon the hills by the bottom and sauntering about for curiosities, have found upon the summit, scallop, oyster and muscle shells petrified. The oysters were most of them in halves and at first, I was disposed to doubt their identity, but at last I came upon one whole, whose rough coat and irregular shape could not well be mistaken, and pointing the point of a big knife to the seam, it opened some familiarly that I almost expected to see the ancient inhabitant within it. I found three kinds of cacti upon the hills." C. De M

# Where Was REEVESVILLE?

# What does it have to do with Fink?

Historic Marker at Fink: Fink, a community, also known as Georgetown and Reevesville, grew up near Fort Johnson on the Texas Military Road (also known as the Shawnee Trail) in the 1840s. The settlement became known as Fink when a post office 500 feet north of the historic marker, was established in 1897 and named for Friedrick Finke (1858-1920), a German immigrant who had come to Grayson County in 1884. The post office was discontinued in 1908. Never incorporated, Fink was eventually included within the boundaries of Pottsboro. In the 1960s local residents began annual Fink celebrations.

Fink/Finke is a German name. Fred Finke and his wife Katherine who lived in Fink, were both born in Germany. According to the 1920 census, they immigrated to the US in 1882 and became citizens of the US in 1891, as well as citizens of a town named in their honor. The least known name for the area around Georgetown / Fink is Reevesville. The name of Reevesville was mostly used in the time period of the 1870s, and was used until the early 1900s. The three names, Georgetown, Fink and Reevesville seemed to be used interchangeably for the same town. See documentation following to show this. The name Reevesville was being used before the establishment of Pottsboro as a town. Reevesville was probably named in honor of an important pioneer family there - William Steele Reeves and his son George Robertson Reeves and his grandson George E. Reeves.

I have the receipt below that my ancestor Robert Daniel obtained from the business of R. H. Pierce in Reevesville in 1875. I am not sure exactly where this store was located.

OFFICE OF R. H. PIERCE,

—DEALER IN—

DRY-GOODS, GROCERIES, PRODUCE AND DRUGS, Etc.,

R. H. PIERCE, Notary Public, REEVESVILLE, TEXAS, ............ 1874.

Received, Reevesville Tex Dec 29 - 1875 of Robt Daniels the sum of Eight and 4/100 Dollars in full payment of account —

R H Pierce

# POSTMASTERS OF OLD POST OFFICES OF Reevesville, Georgetown, Fink

There was mail distribution to the settlements from very early days, even if they had no official post office designation. This was true of Georgetown. However we know by January 1876, there must have been some sort of post office in Georgetown because of the following article in the Denison Daily News on January 22, 1876: "A petition is being circulated in the vicinity of Georgetown and receiving a long string of signatures, asking that the Denison postoffice be made the distributing office for mails going west, and tat a mail route be opened from this point to Clay County and intermediate offices. The petition will be sent to on. Mr. Throckmorton. Under the existing arrangements, mail matter to Georgetown, even from the North, is frequently a week in transit from Denison in consequence of its having to go around by Sherman for distribution. The citizens of Whitesboro, Gainesville and other pints farther west are also sufferers in a similar degree. We believe the authorities at Washington will correct the evil if the matter is presented in its true light." **We will see Georgetown was NEVER used as the name for the local postoffice, the only names used were first Reevesville, then Fink.**

**REEVESVILLE** (Grayson) which is at Old Georgetown had a post office - postmasters, Douglas, Thos. D., 7 Oct 1872 - Orme, Wm. R., 13 Mar 1876. But Washington in its usual wisdom solved the problem of Georgetown's mail distribution problem by discontinuing this post office on 17 Apr 1876. The **Georgetown/ Reevesville** postoffice closure was said in the Sunday Gazetteer in Denison on May 20, 1876 to be an inconvenience to Col. Chiles and other residents in the area who had to travel too far to send and receive mail. This was because Denison was then the nearest post office (as the town of Pottsboro had not yet been established). Since **Reevesville** was the post office that closed, therefore, it seems the names **Georgetown and Reevesville** were used interchangeably for the same town.

Georgetown received some relief when **Reevesville** post office was Re-established April 3, 1878 with -Post Master William R. Orme. "A post office has been re-established at Reevesville, in the north part of this county, **near old Georgetown**" - Denison Daily News May 21, 1878 and The Galveston Daily News. Wednesday, May 22, 1878. Then in typical government fashion, it was discontinued again after only two years on 17 May 1880.

## List of Grayson County Post Offices

Reevesville at the top, William R. Orme, postmaster Apr 3, 1878. Discontinued May 17, 1880

322 Grayson County

| | | | | | |
|---|---|---|---|---|---|
| dis | √ Reavesville | Wm R. Orme | 3 Apr '78 | discontinued | 17 May '80 |
| changed | White Wright | James A. Patzell | 8 Apr '78 | Peter McKenna | 31 Dec 85 |
| dis | Kendall | Emery W. Frost | 13 May 78 | discontinued | 12 Dec '80 |
| | Pottsborough | Wm P. Richelieu | 19 May 79 | David J. Lake | 24 Nov 79 |
| | | Geo. E. Reeves | 17 Sept 84 | Bascom N. Greenup | 17 June 89 |
| Late [illegible] | √ Bells | Edward S. Aston | 8 Sept 79 | Benj R. Sanders | 10 May 81 |

**From the Daily Bulletin of Orders Affecting the Postal Service** -

May 17, 1880 Vol 1. From the Post Office Department, Washington, D. C. -

Post offices discontinued – Reevesville, Grayson Co. Papers to Pottsborough. February 26, 1899 Dallas Morning News - **Fink,** Grayson County postmaster is David S. Allen - Texas postmasters appointed today: David S. Allen, Fink, Grayson County, Ben Arnold, Milam County

November 21, 1899 Dallas Morning News - **Fink** Grayson County postmaster is grocer - Texas postmasters appointed today: Fink, Grayson County, William J. Bilderback. William J Bilderback, the post office was located in the Bilderback grocery store. In the old days, many times the post office was located in the local store.

1902 – **Reevesville** was mentioned in Lippincott Gazetteer of the World as a post village of Grayson County at the same time that it was also known as **Fink**. It said the town had four churches and an academy (school), 9 miles W. of Denison, 2 ½ miles from Red River, and 14 miles N. of Sherman. Lippincott's Gazetteer of the World: 1902

### The Masonic Lodge and area Texas Representative District was listed as being in Reevesville

We KNOW the first Masonic Lodge was located in Old Georgetown over the school at the corner of what is now Georgetown Road and Squirrel Lane. So this is where Reevesville must have been, in Old Georgetown, and consisted of more than a school, church and lodge; it had at least one store and probably more in the 1870s. Death Noted - Reevesville Lodge No. 396, Reevesville, Grayson Co.---- C.W. Thomas. 1873. Source: http://archiver.rootsweb.ancestry.com/th/read/TXFANNIN/2001-12/1007613535

George R. Reeves' official service record lists him as representing Reevesville in 1879-1881 in the 16[tthe] Texas legislature for district 49. Source: http://www.lrl.state.tx.us/legeLeaders/members/memberDisplay.cfm?memberID=4224#3

There is still a Masonic Lodge, The George R. Reeves lodge, located in Georgetown just north of Pottsboro.

## Family History of Col John Sawyers and Simon Harris

Page 39 states John B.M. Sawyers, fourth child of James C. H. Sawyers, married Lucy Bond in **Reevesville,** Grayson County, Texas Nov. 15, 1877.

On Page 40, **Reevesville is mentioned, which is in Old Georgetown.** On page 41 it says John Sawyers was buried in the **Old Reeves Pioneer cemetery** in 1875, and **he is buried in the Georgetown cemetery**. They were connected with the Martin Springs and Georgetown families of Thoma and Stalcup on Page 44. John Henderson Sawyers was married to Martha Jane McKinney, June 26, 1874. He died and was buried in the **Reeves Cemetery, Grayson County, Texas (Georgetown Cemetery). (So the Georgetown Cemetery was called by three names interchangeably in this one family history book.)**

January 13, 1878 Denison Daily News (Denison, Texas) - "J. N. Steele of Reevesville is at the Alamo" Hotel in Denison.

# Reevesville near OLD GEORGETOWN

The present day Georgetown cemetery location (on land originally donated by George R. Reeves for that purpose) is referred to as being in "Old Georgetown". "Georgetown" as a community and later as a school district was a very large area. This location is closer to Fort Johnston and the old location of the school/church/Masonic lodge located at the corner of Georgetown Rd and Squirrel Lane.

The Sunday Gazetteer. (Denison, Tex.), July 10, 1892 - The Pierce's from a tragic murder/suicide were buried in **the graveyard at Old Georgetown, a short distance north of Pottsboro. The chil-**

The Sunday Gazetteer. (Denison, Tex.), February 19, 1893 stated "quite a number of people from the city went to **old Georgetown,** north of Pottsboro, this evening, to attend the funeral of Dr. I. N. Holder.

## Reevesville Precinct # 8

Denison Daily Cresset, June 19, 1877 - In 1877, G. W. McGlothlin must have been Justice of the Peace of Precinct number 8 of Grayson County, which was known at that time as the Reevesville Precinct.

STATE OF TEXAS—GRAYSON COUNTY.
To the Sheriff or any Constable of Grayson County, Greeting:

Whereas, oath has been made this day before me by J. A. Sadler, that J. Jimerson is absent from this State, so that the ordinary process of law cannot be served upon him. You are hereby commanded that you, by making publication of this writ within some newspaper printed in Grayson Co., for three successive weeks before the return day hereof, summon the said J. Jimerson to be and appear before me at my office at Reevesville Precinct, No. 8, on the 7th day of July, A. D. 1877, to answer the complaint of the said J. A. Sadler for the sum of fourteen dollars due upon an account, dated Oct. 1st 1876 with interest thereon from date.

Herein fail not to execute this writ as the law directs. Given under my hand this 5th day of June A. D. 1877.

G. W. McGLOTHLIN, J. P.
Precinct No. 8, Grayson County.

## 11th Cavalry Mustered at Old Georgetown/ Reevesville in Civil War

Sherman Daily Register August 1, 1900

The reunion of the Eleventh Texas Cavalry will be held at old Georgetown, near Pottsboro, tomorrow and the next day. There will be quite a number of people there from Sherman—men who on Reeves' camp ground took the oath of fealty to the Confederate States and went to the war to make a name as a regiment which will last as long as time itself

The Eleventh was organized under orders from the state of Texas, and had proved its grit in battle before it entered the Confederate service. Its firs. colonel was W. C. Young, who was assassinated in Cooke county.

It went into Confederate service as cavalry, but was soon dismounted and fought as infantry. It "went across the river," and followed Joe Wheeler through many and many a tight place. When it came back home it was merely a small part of its former self. But all these things will be talked about and retold on the old camp ground, in better language than the REGISTER can ever use and by men who "were on the ground," and are prepared to tell what they saw. There is one thing that the REGISTER must say, however, and that is that the remnant of the Eleventh Texas are among the finest looking and most active of the South's chivalrous sons. May they live to reunite time and time again.

Sherman Daily Democrat, August 25, 1920 - **Funeral of policeman John M. Blaine** at West Hill Cemetery – He was a veteran of the Civil War at the age of 21, and appointed chief of police of a city of 15,000 at the age of 24. The life span of John Blaine had been filled with active, strenuous living. He served actively in the office of chief of police until the latter part of last year when he was stricken down, and since which time he has been confined to his home. He was a native of Falls County, Texas, being born in January, 1844, one year before Texas was admitted into the Union. He grew to young manhood in Texas. When the war between the States broke out, Mr. Blaine was living in Grayson County, and was then 17 years of age. **He enlisted at old Georgetown,** near Pottsboro, in October, 1861, in Company A, 11th Texas Cavalry, He saw active service the same year in the battles of Richmond and Perrysville, Ky., and Murfreesboro and Chickamauga, Tenn. Remaining in the cavalry, he went to Greensboro, N.C., having many encounters doing so. Near Rhome, Ga., he had a horse shot from under him. Mr. Blaine never surrendered to Federal soldiers. When his command laid down their arms at Greensboro, N.C., at the close of the war, he, with fifteen of his comrades escaped, and started to Texas on foot. On his long overland journey back home he had many close experiences, calling for pluck, self-reliance and personal bravery. He made his way back successfully. **When veterans of the 11th Texas Cavalry met in Sherman**

**for their annual reunion a few weeks ago,** they went to the home of their stricken comrade in a body, when it was learned that he would be unable to meet with them. Except for a few months spent in Indian Territory, Mr. Blaine lived all of his life in Texas, engaged as a peace officer. He had been a detective in the employee of the Katy, during which time he was stationed at Denison, had been a deputy constable for a time, but the greater portion of his life as a peace officer had been spent as a member of the Police Department of Sherman. For more than twenty years he was Chief of Police of Sherman, and his recent administration in that office is the second one he had held. He was appointed Chief of Police by the City Commission about eighteen months ago, following the resignation of Bart Shipp, administering the duties of that office actively until his illness a few months ago. He was known as a fearless officer, ever mindful of his duty, and undiscriminating in the enforcement of the law.

J. M. BLAIN.

**War Death of Pottsboro Man Breaks Denison Woman's Heart** - The Sunday Gazetteer September 18, 1898 - Miss Elizabeth East, sister of Bud East, died Sunday of consumption at her home west of the city. The death of this lady is particularly sad. She was betrothed to the young soldier who died at the front and was buried at Pottsboro at the beginning of the war. Miss East was laid to rest at the old Layne burial ground. There was a large attendance of sympathizing friends at the funeral. The war this was referencing was the Spanish-American War. In my research, I believe I may have found the Pottsboro soldier who was affianced to Miss East, buried in the Georgetown Cemetery under the auspices of Georgetown's Masons – Stanley Ranger Thomas Boggs who died in camp at Austin, perhaps from injuries at the front.

Sunday Gazetteer. (Denison, Tex.),
Sunday, June 5, 1898

**........There was an immense turnout last Sunday at Pottsboro to pay the last respects to the memory of Stanley Ranger Thomas Boggs, who died in camp at Austin. Deceased was buried under the auspices of the Masonic fraternity ........The call**

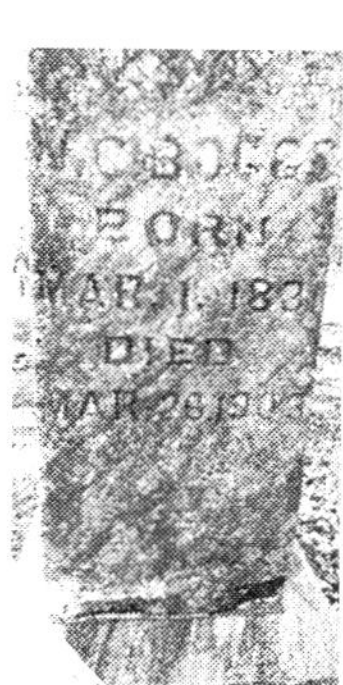


# First Texas Cavalry Decorates W.C. Boggs Grave May 31, 1903

Denison News

## AT DENISON.

**Nathaniel Lyon Post No. 5, G. A. R., and Women's Relief Corps Carry Out Memorial Services.**

SPECIAL TO THE NEWS.

Denison, Tex., May 30.—Decoration Day was observed here today. The Federal offices were all closed and a general half-holiday was observed.

Nathaniel Lyon Post No. 5, Grand Army of the Republic, and its Woman's Relief Corps No. 2, carried through an interesting series of exercises this morning. There was a parade, in which about one hundred school children took part, with the veterans and the relief corps ladies. The procession formed on the High School campus at 10 o'clock and marched down Main street to Burnett avenue and to Forest Park. The procession was headed by a fife and drum corps, and Major W. O. Kretsinger was the marshal of the day. Arriving at the park the children were given the place of honor in the pavilion. The exercises began with an invocation and the singing of "America" by the children and all present. Rev. J. A. Shoptaugh, pastor of the First Christian Church, then delivered an eloquent oration. It was a fine effort. His sentiments struck a responsive chord in the breasts of all who heard him, whether they belonged to the blue or the gray. There was no sectionalism about it. His utterances were broadly patriotic.

This was followed by the singing of "Nearer, My God to Thee," by all present. Mrs. Joanna Shelley recited "The Blue and the Gray." The fife and drum corps brought the exercises to a close by playing a medley of national tunes.

The committees took carriages for the different cemeteries, taking with them a profusion of flowers for the decoration of the graves.

At Fairview Cemetery the G. A. R. held its ritualistic ceremonies. The beautiful and impressive ceremony of decorating the graves of the unknown dead was gone through with. The grave of Rolla Whitaker, a member of the First Texas Cavalry in the Spanish-American War, was decorated by the relief corps ladies.

Father Crowley and Mrs. J. Tygard decorated the graves in Calvary Cemetery.

The decorating committee for Oakwood Cemetery was H. E. Close, Newt Ormsby, Hixson, C. E. Farnsworth and Deck Wagner. Mesdames L. W. Clark, Sallie Bray, J. F. Jordan and Durham.

Fairview Cemetery—L. H. Ruthroff, S. S. Clark and Dr. C. C. Haskell, Mesdames Rainey, Howe, Fitzgerald, Quinn, Wingrove, Morefield, Tygard, Irvin and Down-

a medley of national tunes.

The committees took carriages for the different cemeteries, taking with them a profusion of flowers for the decoration of the graves.

At Fairview Cemetery the G. A. R. held its ritualistic ceremonies. The beautiful and impressive ceremony of decorating the graves of the unknown dead was gone through with. The grave of Rolla Whitaker, a member of the First Texas Cavalry in the Spanish-American War, was decorated by the relief corps ladies.

Father Crowley and Mrs. J. Tygard decorated the graves in Calvary Cemetery.

The decorating committee for Oakwood Cemetery was H. E. Close, Newt Ormsby, Hixson, C. E. Farnsworth and Deck Wagner. Mesdames L. W. Clark, Sallie Bray, J. F. Jordan and Durham.

Fairview Cemetery—L. H. Ruthroff, S. S. Clark and Dr. C. C. Haskell, Mesdames Rainey, Howe, Fitzgerald, Quinn, Wingrove, Morefield, Tygard, Irvin and Down-ing.

Two carriages, containing members of the First Texas Cavalry, went to Pottsboro and decorated the grave of W. M. Boggs, who lies in the Georgetown Cemetery. Returning the party visited Kaufman Cemetery, where the graves of Comrades Earl Richardson and Will Simmons were decorated.

The gentlemen who made the arrangements for decorating the graves of the Spanish-American War soldiers were Quartermaster Sergt. George A. Lake, Corporal W. O. Stewart, Musician Fred Ormsby and D. Givens.

# Georgetown's 11th Regiment, Texas Cavalry

The 11th Texas Cavalry was organized by William C. Young in Grayson County during the summer of 1861. Young had been a former United States Senator.

11th Cavalry Regiment was organized with 855 men at Camp Reeves, in Georgetown Grayson County, Texas, in May, 1861. Some of its members were from Grayson, Cooke, Clarksville, Mt. Pleasant, and Bowie County. This regiment, along with the 8th Texas Cavalry, was one of the best in Confederate service. It was active in the Indian Territory and Arkansas, then was dismounted when it arrived on the eastern side of the Mississippi River. After fighting at Richmond and Murfreesboro, it was remounted and assigned to Wharton's and T. Harrison's Brigade. The unit participated in the Chickamauga, Knoxville, and Atlanta campaigns, then was active in the defense of Savannah and the campaign of the Carolinas. They fought in over one hundred and fifty engagements from Texas to Georgia, and actively opposed Sherman during his "march to the sea."

It contained 599 officers and men in the spring of 1862 and only about 50 remained when they surrendered on April 26, 1865. The field officers were Colonels Joseph M. Bounds, John C. Burks, James J. Diamond, Otis M. Messick, George R. Reeves, and William C. Young; Lieutenant Colonels Robert W. Hooks and Andrew J. Nicholson; and Majors H. F. Bone, John W. Mayrant, and John B. Puryear.

## Reunion of the 11th Texas Cavalry Held at Camp Reeves at Georgetown in 1900

**CSA GEORGETOWN PICNIC 11th CAVALRY REUNION Sherman Daily Register Wednesday, July 11, 1900**

On August 12th the Eleventh Texas, C. S. A., will hold a reunion at old Georgetown, three miles north of Pottsboro. There will be a barbecue. Wagons will convey visitors from Pottsboro to the grounds.

Sherman Daily Register July 13, 1900

LET US ALL GO.

Invitation From the Eleventh Texas to Attend Their Re-union.

I am in receipt of an invitation signed Wm. E. Baird and others, Ben F. Gafford, Secretary, requesting the Mildred Lee Camp, U. C. V., to be present and participate in the reunion of the Eleventh Texas Cavalry, which meets at Georgetown church, about two miles north of Pottsboro, on the 2nd and 3rd of August next. I am also informed by the committee that there will be ample provision to convey all ex-Confederates from Pottsboro out to the grounds, and their entertainment while there. Parties going over can go on the News train in the morning to Denison, out on the local from Denison to Pottsboro, which gets to Pottsboro about nine o'clock. I hope all ex-Confederates will attend that re-union that can conveniently. I have attended several of them and they are very enjoyable.

J. D. Woods,
Captain Commanding Mildred Lee Camp, U. C. V.

Sherman Daily Register Tuesday, July 17, 1900 George E. Reeves, Son of George R. Reeves

G. E. Reeves of Pottsboro was in the city yesterday evening. Mr. Reeves says the people in that locality are taking great interest in the Confederate picnic to be held at old Georgetown, and that all who attend may expect hospitable treatment following a hearty welcome.

**Ex-Confederates.**

The following is the revised program of the ex-Confederate association of Grayson county for the reunion to take place Aug. 10, 1900, at the Old Settler's park:

Members of the association will assemble at the north gate at 10 o'clock sharp and march in order to the speakers stand, following the band.

The marshal, J. H. Dills will form the procession and conduct the march with Mildred Lee camp in front, followed by visiting camps and all other ex-confederates present.

The sons and daughters of Confederates to follow the veterans in said march.

M. W. Bowles, color bearer.

The ceremonies of the day will be opened by a prayer by the chaplain, Dr. J. S. Moore.

Music—"Dixie" by the band.

**CLASP HANDS AND TALK -ELEVENTH CAVALRY REUNION AT OLD GEORGETOWN**

Sherman Daily Register, August 1, 1900 - In reality, that is the strength, the backbone of all reunion, especially of men who have camped and fought for and served their county – grasp hands and talk. There may be a super-abundance of good things to eat and speaker capable of making the blood run wild; but if it were not for the handshakes, the God bless you and the palavers, there would be but slim attendance at any of them. The reunion of the Eleventh Texas Cavalry will be held at **Old Georgetown** near Pottsboro, tomorrow and the next day. There will be quite a number of people there from Sherman – men who on Reeves' campground took the oath of fealty to the Confederate States and went to the war to make a name as a regiment which will last as long as time itself. The Eleventh was organized under orders from the state of Texas, and had proved its grit in battle before it entered the Confederate service. Its first Colonel was W. C. Young, who was assassinated in Cooke County. It went into Confederate service as cavalry, but was soon dismounted and fought as infantry. It "went across the river", and followed Joe Wheeler through many and many a tight place. When it came back home it was merely a small part of its former self. But all these things will be talked about and retold on the old campground, in better language than the Register can ever use and by men who "were on the ground" and are prepared to tell what they saw. There is one thing that the Register must say, however, and that is that the regiment of the Eleventh Texas are among the finest looking and most active of the South's chivalrous sons. May they live to reunite time and time again. Reunions were held yearly for many years at various locations throughout the region to make it easy for people to attend at least some of the reunions without traveling too far.

## 11th CAVALRY REUNION Sherman Daily Register July 21, 1900

PROGRAMME.

Twenty-third Annual Reunion of the Eleventh Texas Cavalry

At Camp Reeves, near Pottsboro, Texas, Aug. 2 and 3, Thursday and Friday, 1900. All Texas comrades have been provided with tents and will camp on picnic grounds. Reduced rates on all railroads. Grand barbecue and two days picnic.

Gen. Joseph Wheeler, U. S. A, in whose division the Eleventh Texas served, has been invited and has promised to be present.

Welcome address to the comrades by Jas. A. Landram, of Pottsboro, Texas.

Response by Comrade George W. Diamond of Whitesboro, Texas.

Hon. Cecil H. Smith of Sherman will deliver an address on Aug. 2nd.

Hon. J. W. Blake will speak on Aug. 3rd.

Other noted men will be present.

Baseball games: Sandusky vs. Georgetown, Aug. [illegible] Pottsboro vs Tioga, Aug. 2; Ge[illegible]. San-

ville, Aug. 3rd. [illegible]

Foot, sack and whe[illegible] races Greasy pigs to catch an[illegible] poles to climb. Band concert morning and evening by Pottsboro band. Abundant shade and free ice water. Every effort will be made to most cordially entertain the hundreds expected.

Committee: G E Reeves, W B Chiles, J A Potts, W S Grant, A W Hulett, Jas Vaden, John Blain, Ben F Gafford, Sam Vaiden, W S Reeves, W E Baird.

Just Received—The new Campaign and Rough Rider hat for both ladies and gentlemen. Douglas & Livingston, North Travis.

The Sunday Gazetteer. (Denison, Tex.), August 5, 1900

light.......... Quite a large number of our people went to the Georgetown picnic yesterday. There was a Confederate reunion among other events

Eleventh Texas Cavalry - Dallas Morning News, Aug 05, 1900

## ELEVENTH TEXAS CAVALRY.

### Veterans Dine with the Widow of Their Colonel—Officers Chosen.

Special to The News.

Sherman, Tex., Aug. 4.—When the first call to arms sounded in 1861 at old Georgetown, Grayson County, 1,260 men in gray gathered under the flag of the Confederacy and took the oath to uphold its Constitution even to death. Thirty-nine years afterward, within a quarter of a mile of where they were mustered in as the Eleventh Texas cavalry, C. S. A., thirty-eight survivors came together and for two days, surrounded by hundreds of descendants of comrades, spent two days in reunion.

Mrs. G. R. Reeves, relict of the gallant soldier, the Colonel of the Eleventh Texas cavalry, still resides at the old Georgetown homestead and the remnant of the regiment dined in a body with her yesterday. Congressman Bailey has asked as a special favor when the regiment meets in Gainesville next year that they be his guests for at least one day.

The mortuary report for the year ended Aug. 1, 1900, was the largest for any year since the civic organization was effected, eleven veterans having answered the last bugle call. Of the 116 men who went out from the town of Sherman but three reside here. Chief of Police Blain, ex-Com-

**Picture of Reunion of 11th Texas Cavalry**

35th Annual Reunion of 11th Texas Cavalry in Whitesboro Texas 1912

Front row: J.C. Burk, S. Hudgins; M.M. Deaver; S.R Etter; A.L. White, W.S. Buster. Second Row: J.M. Blaine; G.C. Stephens; J. T. Woodward; S.R. Stiles; T.A. Sinclair; H.S. Waller; S.W. Saunders; D. Douglass; G.W. Walker. Third Row: P.B. Franklin; A.J. Harris; W.J. Brewer; N. B.Ross; J.C. Witcher; T.N. Obrien; T.A. Stephens; H.H. Cook; P.T. McBride. Back Row: A.J. Mathews; J.B.Wells; G.B. Dean; A.W. Wall; Isaac, Guest; Nathan Grant; Rich Merrill; W.H. Penick; A.J. Devault; C.C. Hornbuckle; T.S. Barnett.

**Reevesville was almost certainly named in honor of the important resident Reeves family, which included the most famous of the family: the son of W. S. Reeves - George Robertson Reeves.**

Reeves Family – were Early Pioneers in Georgetown - William Steele Reeves Had A Gin in Georgetown Sunday Gazetteer, November 24, 1895

Confirming the report of Denison cotton buyers, which appeared in the News a few days ago, and refuting the late ridiculous bureau report, I submit the following additional ginners' and farmers' reports from Grayson county and the Indian Territory:

Mr. P. W McConnell, Basin Springs, Texas, put up at his gin last year 642 bales. This year up to date he has put up 196 bales, and thinks he will yet get fifteen bales more this season, or less than one-third of last year's crop. He says the top crop is ruined by frost, and the crop will average about one eighth of a bale per acre, or about sixty-two bales of lint per acre against the bureau's 151 pounds per acre.

Thompson & Henderson's gins at Brownville, I. T., put up last year 1150 bales. This year they have put up about 165 bales, and will not get over 50 bales more, or not quite one-fifth of last year's crop.

The Georgetown gin, west of Denison, put up last year 935 bales, against 200 this year.

The two gins in Denison have not put up one third of last year's business to date, and there is but little cotton coming in how.

W. T. Davis writes from Martin Springs that the cotton crop will not average more than 33½ pounds of lint per acre, and 90 per cent of crop gathered and sold.

Thirteen planters at Colbert, I. T., report they planted 245 acres and the total yield is 5000 pounds lint, or just 20 pounds per acre.

Eight farmers report a yield of 21,440 bales lint from 333 acres, or about 64 pounds per acre.

From all I can gather the crop of Grayson county and the Indian Territory, all told, will fall far below 100 pounds of lint per acre, with no top crop at all, and at least seven-eighths gathered and sold

So far as our section is concerned the absurdity of the bureau report is fully exposed. R. M King.

**William Steele REEVES GIN BURNED -** Dallas Morning News - October 4, 1897 - This morning about 9 o'clock the steam gin owned and operated by W. S. Reeves and located 3 miles north of Pottsboro, burned to the ground. About 100 bales of cotton and $800 or $1,000 worth of cotton seed were destroyed. The building and machinery were insured for $2,000, about half the value of same, with no insurance on the cotton and seed. October 5, 1897 - Walter Steele came in from Preston Bend this afternoon and brought the news of the burning of W. S. Reeves' gin, two and a half miles north of Pottsboro, (in Georgetown) this morning at an early hour. The gin and all the machinery was a total loss, valued at $3,000. The fire caught, supposedly, from a match in the cotton. The lint caught in one of the gin stands and the fire spread through it like it was gunpowder.

Below: William Steele Reeves and Nancy Totty Reeves

### William Steele Reeves' Gin Burned at Pottsboro, (Georgetown) AGAIN

October 20, 1902 Dallas Morning News - October 19 – This morning at 7:20 o'clock, William S. Reeves' ginhouse was struck by lightning and consumed by fire. Loss is $4,500, insurance $2,000. W. S. Reeves was also deputy clerk for Grayson County. Denison Daily Herald - August 2, 1906

County Judge G. P. Webb and Deputy Clerk W. S. Reeves went to Denison this morning to try a lunacy case.

J. F. Thompson of Pottsboro, county commissioner, was here today taking in the picnic.

Yesterday afternoon at 5 o'clock Willie Graham, aged 17 years, was tried as to his sanity before County Judge G. P. Webb and was adjudged insane. The lad was taken into custoday and brought into court at the instance of his father who testified that he believed the boy to be insane. The lad will be taken to the asylum as soon as a place can be provided for him.

G. E. Reeves went to Sherman Tuesday.

W. D. Mortan of Locust was here Wednesday.

Mrs. William Hull was called to Sherman on account of the serious illness of her daughter, Mrs. W. S. Reeves.

Mrs. Mollie Looney returned from Gunter Wednesday, where she had been visiting her daughter, Mrs. J. D. Rowland, for the past week.

Denison Daily Herald March 30, 1906

## Wife of W. S. Reeves, Mrs. Nora Hull Reeves Buried at Pottsboro

Denison Press November 12, 1937

Funeral services for Mrs. Nora Reeves, 63, a former resident of Pottsboro living in Austin the past eight years, who died at 5:20 p. m. Thursday at her home in Austin, were held Friday afternoon at 3 o'clock at Georgetown, with Rev. White of Sherman officiating.

Interment was held at a Pottsboro cemetery with Short-Murray directing. Pall bearers were R. M. Wilson, E. Loney and A. S. Allen of Pottsboro, Judge J. J. Loy of Sherman, Earl Myer of Houston and J. N. Dickson of Sherman.

Mrs. Reeves, nee Miss Nora Hull, was born April 27, 1874 to Mr. and Mrs. William Hull of Pottsboro at which point she was reared and received her education.

She married William S. Reeves, a banker and county clerk, during September, 1896 at Pottsboro, where they resided until 1905, moving then to Sherman but taking up residence again at Pottsboro during 1919.

Mr. Reeves died April 30, 1929. Mrs. Reeves moved to Austin where she has since resided. She became ill November 8 and was removed to a hospital Nov. 9, where she later died.

The remains, accompanied by relatives, arrived in Denison at 11:25 a. m. today and were removed to the home of her son, Tom M. Reeves, 830 West Crawford street where the body will lie until time for the funeral at Georgetown.

Surviving are four sons, Tom M., of Denison; W. S. of Tyler; R. G. of San Francisco and Jack H. of Austin; one daughter, Mrs. Mary Belle Federer of Austin; three brothers, W. E. Hull of Pottsboro; H. B. Hull of Kilgore; R. H. Hull of Pasadena, Calif. Also are four sisters, Mrs. Nina Steele, Mrs. Fred Riddel, Miss Della Hull and Mrs. Edith Allen, all of Pottsboro.

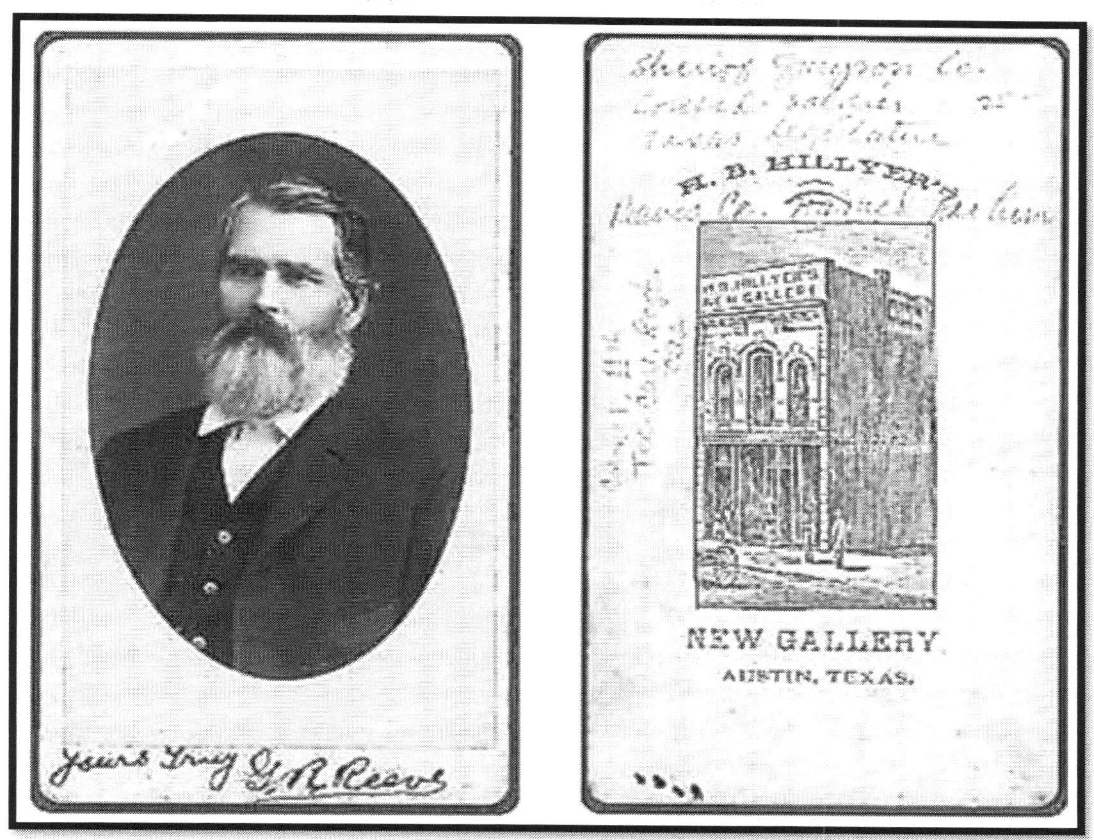


# Colonel George Robertson Reeves

The ancestors of Col. George R. Reeves emigrated from Ireland to the United States about the year 1794 and located in South Carolina, where his father, William Steele Reeves, was born in 1796. After the death of both his parents in 1798, William Steele Reeves, at the age of 3 years, was taken to Nashville, Tennessee, then a frontier village and brought up by an uncle, a pioneer settler.

He served in the wars of 1812 and in the Creek War, and after living a few years in Arkansas, where he represented his county (Crawford) in the legislature, in 1846, he moved to Texas, settling near Preston on the Red River, then the major business point in Grayson County. He then acquired land in Georgetown.

George Robertson Reeves was born in Tennessee, Jan. 3, 1826. When about eighteen years of age, Oct. 31, 1844, he was married to Miss Jane Moore, the granddaughter of Robert Bean, a noted pioneer settler of Arkansas, and afterward of Texas. In 1846, he moved to Texas and located in Grayson County where he became a prominent figure in the public affairs of the County. In 1848, George Reeves was elected tax collector and served two years. In 1850, he was elected sheriff and served until 1854. Then he was elected to the State legislature, where, by his clear headed manner, he won the friendship of men like W. B. Ogiltree, John Sayles, James W. Throckmorton, Stephen H. Darden, M.D.; Ector Ashbel Smith, Cyrus H. Randolph and other noted men who have since figured greatly in Texas history. He was again elected representative in 1857.

At the beginning of the Civil War, George R. Reeves was among the first to respond. He raised a company for Col. William C. Young's regiment at what became known as **Camp Reeves at Georgetown,** the **famous 11th Texas Cavalry**.

Colonel Reeves shared the hardships and struggles of the 11th Texas Cavalry through many of the fiercest battles of the Civil War - among which were Murfreesboro, Corinth, Chattanooga, Chickamauga, Knoxville, and Tunnel Hill.

After the death of Col. Young, George Robertson Reeves was promoted to the Colonelcy of his regiment, and remained as its commander until the war was over.

A man who was to become even more famous than himself was at that time merely his servant, a slave belonging to George's dad, named Bass Reeves, who deserted him and went on to become a deputy US Marshal in the Indian Territory and became the pattern for the fabled Lone Ranger.

When George R. Reeves came home, he found himself ruined by the war; but he was not one to give up, he went to work to retrieve his fortunes, and succeeded.

He continued his political career and in 1866, 1873, in 1878, and 1880, he was elected to the legislature from Grayson County, and at the session of 1881, was elected speaker of the house, a position which he filled with marked ability.

He was about to be brought up as a candidate for Lt. Governor, when tragedy struck. In 1882, Col. Reeves was bitten by a rabid dog and died in the agony of hydrophobia from the effects of the poison.

The four sons and three daughters of Col. Reeves continued to reside in Grayson County. His son George E. Reeves also became a prominent local politician and businessman. Edna May Bell Reeves Tyler, born 31 Aug 1877, was a granddaughter of Col. Reeves.

Some of the above information in this summary was taken from a biography which appears to be written by Edna May Bell Reeves Tyler about her grandfather, George Robertson Reeves, on note paper and placed in her Tyler Family Bible.

## George R Reeves Sheriff

Texas State Gazette. (Austin, Tex.), Saturday, September 20, 1851

**Runaway.**

WHEREAS, on the second day of this month, August, a negro boy was apprehended in this county, Grayson, by Ambrose Hilbron, and committed to jail by R. J. Bullock, a Justice of the Peace in said county. Said boy is a dark yellow complexion, about five feet ten inches high, has whiskers, has on a white silk hat considerably worn, white cotton pants, coarse shirt, and is quite slow to speak. Said boy says he belongs to one Wm. Johnson, who lives in Talladega county, Alabama, and who he says was a negro trader, and says he left him near Natchitoches in Louisiana.

GEORGE R. REEVES, Sheriff, G. C.

The Weekly State Gazette. (Austin, Tex.) August 4, 1866 George R. Reeves became Texas State Representative for Collin and Grayson County/

Denison Daily News, March 29, 1878 Brenham Daily Banner. January 13, 1881

**The Democratic County Executive Committee.**

J. D. Woods, Chairman—Hon. W. Blassergame, Cedar Springs; Geo. R. Reeves, Georgetown; Geo. L. Patrick, Denison; J. M. McMurray, Kentuckytown; Wm. H. Bean, Farmington; T. W. Hudson, Collinsville; J. H. Choice, Whitesboro.

**17th Legislature.**

Austin, Jan. 11.—The house was called to order by the secretary of state John D. Templeton. Will Lambert acting secretary. The secretary then declared the house ready to go into the election of speaker.

Baker, Reeves, Finlay, and McComb were put in nomination.

On the 4th ballot George R. Reeves, of Grayson, was elected.

Mr. Reeves was escorted to the chair and very briefly thanked the house for the honor confered.

Col. George R Reeves' Son, Thomas Reeves of Georgetown, age 31, died. - Denison Daily News, Feb 25, 1878.

George R. Reeves being put up as LT Governor - Galveston Daily News June 8, 1882

We see the name of Colonel George R. Reeves, of Grayson county, spoken of as a very proper person to be made lieutenant-governor of Texas. Colonel Reeves is an experienced and able legislator; he is the present speaker of the House of Representatives, and is a good parliamentarian; and, with all, he is a good farmer and a most excellent gentleman. Since Western Texas is to have the governor, Colonel Reeves is just the man for lieutenant-governor, and the Register hereby expresses its choice for him for this position.

## Col. George R. Reeves Quells Carousing Crowd at Masonic Lodge –

Denison Daily News, **May 8, 1875** – At a meeting of the Good Templars (Masons) in Georgetown, Saturday night, May 1st, charges were preferred against a number of young gentlemen, members of the order, of breaking the pledge. Thereupon, said young gentlemen, arming themselves with bludgeons, knives and pistols, and a plentiful supply of "the fatal enemy to civilization," marched up to the lodge room, attacked the sentinel, and attempted to force an entrance to the main lobby of the cold water drinkers in the rooms above. Mr. Winton, the sentinel, gave them such an exhibition of his valor and prowess, as soon convinced them that he was fully alive to the perils of the situation, and the sacredness of the cause he guarded. Col. Reeves coming to his assistance, they soon had three or four of them stretched on the ground, and the others beating a hasty and disorderly retreat. King Alcohol and the disciples of the fair crusaders wage war in the merry month of May, and long may victory perch upon the banners of the cold water army. - Sherman Register.

## Prominent **Reevesville** Citizen George R. Reeves Dies of Hydrophobia Weekly Democratic Statesman. (Austin, Tex.), May 25, 1882

SOME of the north Texas papers want Hon. George R. Reeves made lieutenant-governor. Colonel Reeves is certainly worthy of such and even greater distinction.

SHERMAN, September 6.—Hon. George R. Reeves, late speaker and candidate for floater from Grayson and Cooke counties, died at 12 a. m. of hydrophobia, at his home, three miles west of Pottsboro, in the northern portion of this county. He suffered with paroxysms from Monday morning until the moment of his death, with apparently lucid intervals, during which he would call for water and then reject it, saying that it was poison. It is about six weeks since he was bitten and went to McKinney to have mad stones applied. Mr. Reeves, I believe, was in his 56th year and had represented this county eight terms in the legislature, twice before the wa . He was also assessor and collector two terms and sheriff two terms. He will be buried from his farm home at 3 p. m. to-morrow by the Georgetown masonic lodge, of which he was late master. He was one of the charter members of the Travis masonic lodge, No. 117, of this city. A large masonic delegation will go from here to attend the obsequies. If Colonel Reeves had an enemy your correspondent has always failed to learn thereof, and his most lamentable and violent death casts a gloom over all the country.

**Hon. George R. Reeves Buried by Masons at Reevesville – (Georgetown Cemetery)** The Galveston Daily News. Wednesday, September 6 & 9, 1882

## Death of a Prominent Citizen—Election of Trustees.

[Special Telegram to The News.]

SHERMAN, September 5.—The Hon. Geo. Reeves, late speaker of the House of Representatives, died this morning of hydrophobia. He will be buried by the Masons from his home at Reevesville.

The election for trustees resulted in the election of W. Byers, A. L. Darnell and Mose Chapin. They are all unexceptionally good men for the position.

---

The Sherman Courier makes some touching remarks on the death of Hon. George R. Reeves, the victim of hydrophobia:

Colonel Reeves was born at Cain Hill, Ark., in 1825, and came to Grayson county in 1847. In 1853 he was elected assessor and collector of Grayson county, which place he filled with such satisfaction that he was, two years later, elected to the legislature. He then filled the office of sheriff for two terms, since which time he has been almost constantly a member of the legislature, and during the last session was chosen speaker of the house. During all his public life there has never been one, not even his bitterest political enemies—and he had no other enemies—who could say he was other than an honest and upright public servant. His name was known and revered throughout Texas, and his place can not be filled. At the commencement of the civil war he was one of the first to volunteer. He was elected colonel of the Eleventh Texas cavalry, and led that gallant regiment during all the dark days of the war. In 1845 he married a Miss Moore, of Cave Hill, who, with a family of seven children, all grown, survive him. In private, as in public life, Colonel Reeves was respected by all with whom he came in contact. He was a distinguished member of the Masonic fraternity. He was buried at Reevesville by the Masonic fraternity. The lodges of Sherman and Denison were present and assisted in the solemn ceremony.

The house met at 7:30 p. m. The special order of the evening session was the memorial services of George R. Reeves, deceased, late speaker of the house. The hall was appropriately draped in mourning, and many ladies were present to do honor to the departed speaker.

After singing by the Presbyterian choir, the resolutions expressive of the sympathy of the house for the great loss the state had sustained by his death, were taken up, and F[illegible]r, of Grayson, in a very appropriate a[illegible]ess, reviewing the life of Ho[illegible]. George R. Reeves, moved an adoption of the resolutions, which was seconded by Messrs. Cochran, Graves, Chenoweth, Frymier and others, all of whom spoke of the integrity and purity of the man.

........................

But, gentlemen of the house, as some of you had not the pleasure of an intimate acquaintance with this humantarian and philanthropist, a few little incidents in his private life will serve as a key to unlock the sacred chambers of his noble heart, that you may behold the rich troasurs it contained. When two friends would fail out and become angry at each other, as soon as the fact came to the knowledge of this good man, he would saddle up his horse, and make it his business to visit them both, bring them together, settle their difficulty and leave them friendly as before the difficulty occurred. Therefore, gentl men of this house, I feel assurred that the response of every heart will be, honor to the memory and sacred be the ashes of this friend to his race and lover of humanity, the beloved and lamented George R. Reeves.

GEORGE ROBERTSON REEVES WAS **NOT** THE ONLY FAMOUS REEVES FROM GEORGETOWN……..

Truth really IS more interesting than fiction……

# The REAL Lone Ranger Was From Georgetown and He Was BLACK

George Robertson Reeves was once Sheriff Grayson County Texas, but little did he know, his personal servant, his slave, Bass Reeves would become a much greater and more famous lawman than he.

# Deputy Marshal Bass Reeves

Bass Reeves (July 1838 – 12 January 1910), one of the first black Deputy U.S. Marshals west of the Mississippi River, arrested over 3,000 felons and shot and killed fourteen outlaws in self-defense while he himself was never wounded.

He is the REAL inspiration behind The Lone Ranger

and was similar to Rooster Cogburn the Marshal in True Grit and D'Jango Unchained.

Georgetown can be proud of Bass Reeves, their most famous native son.

(Bass Reeves is also immortalized in the Cowboy Hall of Fame)

Lawman Bass Reeves

# From Slave to Deputy Marshall to The Lone Ranger – Georgetown's Bass Reeves

Bass Reeves was born into slavery in 1838 in Crawford County, Arkansas, or possibly Paris, Texas, it is not known for sure. Bass was named after his grandfather, Basse Washington. Slaves often took the last name of their master, in Bass' case, it was Reeves. Bass Reeves and his family were slaves of Arkansas state legislator William Steele Reeves. When Bass Reeves was eight (about 1846), William Steele Reeves moved to Grayson County, Texas, near Sherman in the Peters' Colony. They subsequently acquired land near Preston and then in Georgetown. Bass Reeves may have been offered by William S. Reeves to his son, Colonel George Robertson Reeves, as a personal assistant and servant, perhaps he was even freed.

George R. Reeves of Georgetown, northwest of Pottsboro Texas, was a sheriff and legislator in Texas, serving as the Speaker of the House until the time of his death from rabies in 1882.

George R. Reeves joined the Confederacy in the Civil War as a leader in the 11th Texas Cavalry organized at Camp Reeves in Georgetown.

At some time before or around the beginning of the Civil War, Bass parted company with George Reeves, perhaps "because Bass and George got in a dispute in a card game." Bass Reeves fled into the Indian Territory (now Oklahoma) and lived with the Cherokee, Seminole, and Creek Indians until he was officially freed by the Thirteenth Amendment. (Future Oklahoma) Indian Territory was a popular location for freed people of color, run-away slaves and outlaws to hide at that time. Here, Bass became very familiar with the Indian Territory itself as well as Native culture. He learned how to ride, shoot and track, and he also became fluent in five Native American languages.

After the war, Bass became the first African American settler in Van Buren, Arkansas. There he married a lady named Nellie Jennie, built an eight-room house, raised ten children and worked the land. When his first wife died, he married a second wife in Muskogee in 1900 and fathered more children. Bass Reeves and his family farmed until 1875, when Isaac

Parker was appointed federal judge for the Indian Territory. He was known as "Hanging Judge" Parker since his sentences were swift and harsh. He appointed James F. Fagan as U.S. Marshal, directing him to hire 200 deputy U.S. Marshals to police the Territory. Fagan had heard about Reeves, who knew the Indian Territory and could speak several Indian languages. He recruited him as one of his deputies and Reeves was one of, if not, THE first African-American deputy west of the Mississippi River. Reeves was initially assigned as a Deputy U.S. Marshal for the Western District of Arkansas, which also had responsibility for the Indian Territory.

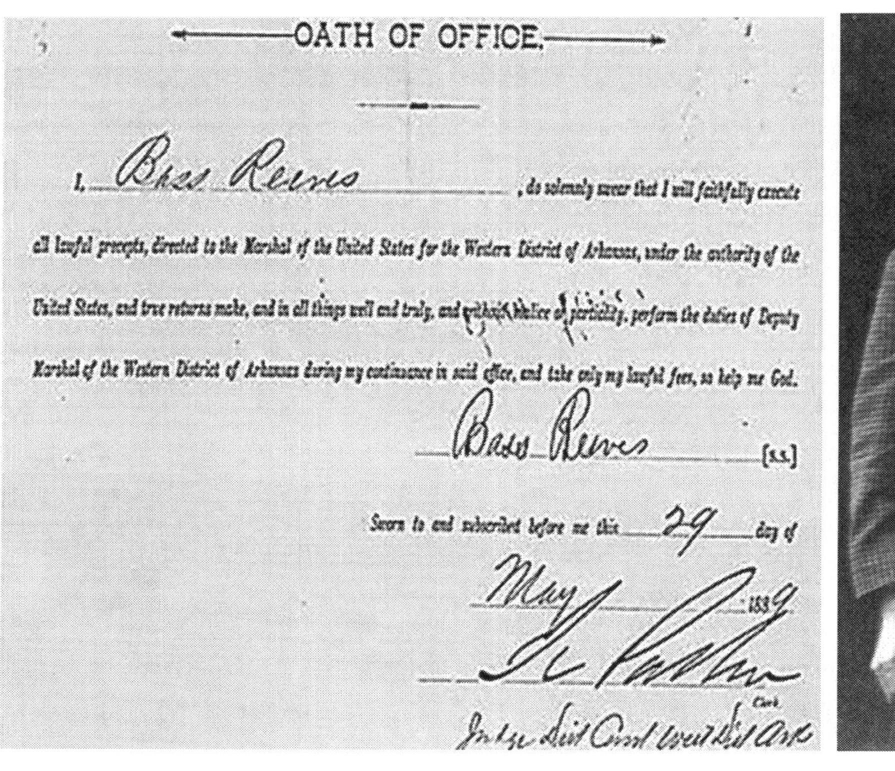

OATH OF OFFICE.

I, Bass Reeves, do solemnly swear that I will faithfully execute all lawful precepts, directed to the Marshal of the United States for the Western District of Arkansas, under the authority of the United States, and true returns make, and in all things well and truly, and without malice or partiality, perform the duties of Deputy Marshal of the Western District of Arkansas during my continuance in said office, and take only my lawful fees, so help me God.

Bass Reeves [L.S.]

Sworn to and subscribed before me this 29 day of May 1889.

Clerk

Judge Dist Court West Dist Ark

**1907**

Reeves also had a well-earned reputation for law enforcement south of the Red River. He killed fourteen men in the performance of his duty while assigned to the federal district courts at Paris and Sherman, Texas, during his thirty-two-year career as deputy. Among them were Bob Dozier, a criminal whose illegal activities included cattle and horse theft, land swindles, and murder, and who eluded Reeves for several years before being killed after refusing to surrender in the rain and mud in the Indian Territory.

While working for the Paris, Texas court, Reeves broke up the Tom Story gang of horse thieves that operated in the Red River valley. Story was a murderer who had sold stolen horses south of the Red River from 1884 to 1889, and who lost his life at the Delaware

Bend crossing on the county line between Grayson and Cooke Counties, in an attempt to beat Reeves to the draw. In 1890, Reeves arrested the notorious Seminole outlaw Greenleaf, who had been on the run for eighteen years without capture and had murdered seven people. The same year, Reeves went after the famous Cherokee outlaw Ned Christie. Reeves and his posse burned Christie's cabin, but he eluded capture.

Jim Webb, a cowboy and horse thief with eleven notches on his pistol handle, was outshot in a fierce running gunfight after a manhunt that lasted from 1893 to 1895. The dying Webb acknowledged Reeves as the better man by giving the deputy his pistol and holster. The fact that Webb died and Reeves didn't in the shootout should have been acknowledgment enough. Reeves was dependable and devoted to duty in his service to the government. Many of the district courts asked for Reeves because of his reliability in serving warrants. His devotion to duty was especially seen in this example: Once Bass Reeves had to arrest his own son for murder. One of his sons, Bennie Reeves, was charged with the murder of his wife. Marshall Reeves was disturbed by the incident, but demanded to accept the responsibility of bringing Bennie to justice. Bennie was eventually tracked and captured, tried and convicted. He served his time in Ft. Leavenworth in Kansas before being released and living the rest of his life as a responsible and model citizen.

Daily chieftain, Vinita OK., July 03, 1902 & The Muskogee Cimeter., August 30, 1907

Okla. City, Aug. 28—During the brief reign of Grover the great, there were several United States Marshalls appointed because of their ability. Robert Fortune of Wilburton holds three commissions as deputy marshall received from Democratic superiors, one from J. J. McAleseter and two from George J. Crump. Marshall Crump gave commissions to the following Negro deputies while he was Marshall under Cleveland, Grant Johnson, Bynum Colbert, Ike Rogers, Rufus Colbert, Lee Thompson, and Bass Reeves.

**DEPUTIES NAMED**

**By Marshal Bennett for Service in the New Western District.**

Marshal Bennett has announced the appointment of the following deputy marshals in the western district.

Dave Adams, Muskogee.
Bass Reeves, Muskogee.
John L. Brown, Webbers Falls.
R. D. Fought, Sapulpa.
Ed Fink, Wetumka.
Grant Johnson, Eufaula.
Frank Jones, Checotah.
Henry Kaase, Holdenville.
J. W. Matthews, Choska.
John S. O'Brian, Wagoner.
H. A. Thompson, Tulsa.
Paden Tolbert, unassigned.

Office deputies same as before in Muskogee, Wewoka and Wagoner. Office deputies will probably be appointed later at Okmulgee, Sapulpa and Eufaula.

In 1893, Reeves was transferred to the Eastern District of Texas in Paris, Texas. In 1897, he was transferred to the Muskogee Federal Court. Reeves remarried in Muskogee in 1900 to Winnie Sumter since his first wife had died in Fort Smith in 1896.

Though Reeves could not read or write, it did not curb his effectiveness in bringing back the criminals. Before he headed out, he would have someone read him the warrants and memorize which was which. When asked to produce the warrant, he never failed to pick out the correct one.

An imposing figure, always riding on a large stallion, Reeves began to earn a reputation for his courage and success at bringing in or killing many desperadoes of the territory. Always wearing a large hat, Reeves was usually a sharp dresser, with his boots polished to a shine. He was known for his politeness and courteous manner. However, when the purpose served him, he was a master of disguises and often used aliases. Sometimes appearing as a cowboy, farmer, gunslinger, or outlaw, himself. He always wore two Colt pistols, butt forward for a fast draw. Ambidextrous, he rarely missed his mark.

Leaving Fort Smith Arkansas, often with a pocketful of warrants, Reeves would return months later herding a number of outlaws charged with crimes ranging from bootlegging to murder. Paid in fees and rewards, he would make a handsome profit, before spending a little time with his family and returning to the range once again with more warrants for more criminals.

The tales of his captures are legendary. On one such occasion, Reeves was pursuing two outlaws in the Red River Valley near the Texas border. Gathering a posse, Reeves and the other men set up camp some 28 miles from where the two were thought to be hiding at their mother's home. After studying the terrain and making a plan, he disguised himself as a tramp, hiding his handcuffs, pistol and badge under his clothes. Setting out on foot, he arrived at the house wearing an old pair of shoes, dirty clothes, carrying a cane, and wearing a floppy hat complete with three bullet holes.

Upon arriving at the home, he told a tale to the woman who answered the door that his feet were aching after having been pursued by a posse who had put the three bullet holes in his hat. After asking for a bite to eat, she invited him in and while he was eating she began to tell him of her two young outlaw sons, suggesting that the three of them should join forces. Feigning weariness, she consented to let him stay a while longer. As the sun was setting, Reeves heard a sharp whistle coming from beyond the house. Shortly after the woman went outside and responded with an answering whistle, two riders rode up to the house, talking at length with her outside. The three of them came inside and she introduced her sons to Reeves. After discussing their various crimes, the trio agreed that it would be a good idea to join up. Bunking down in the same room, Reeves watched the pair carefully as they drifted off to sleep and when they were snoring, handcuffed the pair without waking them. When early morning approached, he kicked the boys awake and marched them out the door. Followed for the first three miles by their mother, who cursed Reeves the entire time, he marched the pair the full 28 miles to the camp where the posse waited. Within days, the outlaws were delivered to the authorities and a $5,000 reward was collected.

One of the high points of Reeves' career was apprehending a notorious outlaw named Bob Dozier. Dozier was known as a jack-of-all-trades when it came to committing crimes, as they covered a wide range from cattle and horse rustling, to holding up banks, stores, and stagecoaches; to murder, and land swindles. Because Dozier was unpredictable, he was also hard to catch and though many lawmen had tried to apprehend the outlaw, none were successful until it came to Reeves. Dozier eluded Reeves for several months until the lawman tracked him down in the Cherokee Hills. After refusing to surrender, Reeves killed Dozier in an accompanying gunfight on December 20, 1878.

At a time when the average man was about 5'6", Reeves was 6'2, about 190 lbs. He was broad at the shoulders, narrow at the hips, and said to possess superhuman strength. Reeves cut a striking figure on his large horse, while wearing his usual black hat and twin .45 Colt Peacemakers cross-draw style. He could shoot equally well with each hand. Some say he had a gray, almost white horse, some that he had a large red horse with a white blaze on its face. During his long career, he may have had both these horses. He gave out silver dollars as a calling card.

Bass Reeves became famous among criminals for his skills and tireless pursuit. Although shot at many times, he remained untouched by a single bullet, and because of this he was called "The Indomitable Marshal," so tough he could "spit on a brick and bust it."

A newspaper of his times reported, "Place a warrant for arrest in his hands and no circumstance can cause him to deviate." The Oklahoma City Weekly Times-Journal reported, "Reeves was never known to show the slightest excitement, under any circumstance. He does not know what fear is." This was never truer than the case where three men he was pursuing managed to get the drop on him and ordered him off his horse. The leader approached, gloating that the "Indomitable Marshal" was about to die.

Showing no fear, Reeves calmly took out his warrants and asked the three men, "What is the date today?" The puzzled leader asked, "What difference does that make?" Reeves explained that he'd need to put the date of the arrest on the paperwork when he took the three of them in — dead or alive -- their choice. The three men laughed at the ridiculous question, and Marshal Reeves used the distraction to grab the barrel of the leader's gun. One of the men opened fire, but Reeves drew and shot him dead. He then killed the leader by bashing his skull with his pistol. The third man wisely submitted to the arrest.

By the end of his career, a newspaper reported Reeves had brought in 3,000 living felons and 20 dead. He corrected the record, saying that during his amazing career he had killed 14 men in self-defense. He once caught 19 horse thieves at one time near Fort Sill. The noted female outlaw Belle Starr turned herself in at Fort Smith when she found out Reeves had the warrant for her arrest. Reeves worked for thirty-two years as a Federal peace officer in the Indian Territory. He was one of Judge Parker's most valued deputies. Reeves killed or brought in some of the most dangerous criminals of the time, but was never wounded, despite having his hat and belt shot off on separate occasions. Reeves and Parker were the REAL possessors of "True Grit". In addition to being a marksman with a rifle and pistol, Reeves, during his long career, developed superior detective skills. When Oklahoma became a state in 1907, Reeves, then 68, became an officer of the Muskogee, Oklahoma police department. He served for two years before he became ill and retired.

**Left: Bass Reeves (front row left, with cane) Muskogee, Indian Territory, White and Black policemen about 1900. Courtesy of University of Oklahoma Library; Right: Judge Parker**

Daily Ardmoreite., January 02, 1908 BASS REEVES A POLICEMAN

**Well Known Deputy Marshal Has Beat at Muskogee.**

Muskogee, Okla., Jan. 2.—Bass Reeves, for nearly twenty years a deputy United States marshal in old Indian Territory, is now a member of the Muskogee police force. Reeves is a neg.. six feet tall, and is over seventy years old. He was in many battles in the old days and a terror to the negro outlaws and bootleggers. It is said of him that he never failed to bring in a man he went after. He would get them either dead or alive. In recent years, however, the change did away with the man with the gun to some extent and Reeves was kept in Muskogee to serve subpoenas in civil matters.

Negroes in the north end who had been imposing on the negro police in the negro districts, have been compelled to walk the straight and narrow path since Bass Reeves has been on the force.

Depending on the outlaws for whom he was searching, a deputy would generally take with him from Fort Smith, a wagon, a cook and a Native American posse man (his "Tonto"). Often they rode to Fort Reno, Fort Sill and Anadarko, a round trip of more than 800 miles.

But Bass Reeves was himself once charged with murdering a posse cook.

Indian Chieftain. (Vinita, Indian Terr.), Thursday, February 4, 1886

Bass Reeves, a notorious and unprincipled ex-deputy marshal is now in jail at Fort Smith charged with murder. Reeves, who is a negro, killed his camp cook, of the same race, in the Chickasaw nation, in April 1884. He reported the killing at the time to have been done in self defense.

At his trial before Judge Issac Parker, Reeves was represented by a former United States Attorney W.H.H. Clayton, who had been his colleague and friend. Reeves was acquitted.

Reeves' health began to fail, and he died of Bright's disease (nephritis) in 1910. He was an uncle of Paul L. Brady, the first African-American appointed a Federal Administrative Law Judge (in 1972). It is widely believed that Bass Reeves was the inspiration for The Lone Ranger radio and television series by the fact that he was basically in hiding in his first years in Indian Territory, hence, his “mask”, and he was a master of disguise which he employed when necessary, his extreme skill in law enforcement, his Indian companion, his honesty and devotion to duty, riding a white horse and using a silver coin as his signature: “Hi, yo, Silver! Away!”

There are very stark parallels between him and the character Rooster Cogburn in True Grit. He was probably the inspiration for Quentin Tarantino’s film, Django Unchained. Bass was also elected into the Cowboy Hall of Fame. On May 26, 2012, a bronze statue depicting Reeves on a horse riding west was dedicated in Fort Smith Arkansas’ Pendergraft Park. The statue, which was designed by sculptor Harold T. Holden and cost more than $300,000, was paid for by donations to the Bass Reeves Legacy Initiative. Once asked why he spent so much effort enforcing the "white man's laws," Bass reportedly replied, "Maybe the law ain't perfect, but it's the only one we got, and without it we got nothing." He was a true self-made man, an inspiration to all Americans and an American success story.

The Daily Cairo Bulletin., August 31, 1884 and Galveston Daily News. August 26, 1892

**Good Work by a Bravo Officer.**

FORT SMITH, ARK., **August 30.—Buck Bruner, the Creek desporado, was killed** by Deputy Marshal Bass Reeves a few days ago on the Canadian River in the Creek Nation. Reeves had warrants for Buck and John Bruner for horse stealing, but not knowing the parties or country, and wanting guides, employed these men. At noon they camped, and while getting dinner Reeves noticed John Bruner stealthily drawing a pistol, whereupon he grabbed Bruner's pistol with one hand and with the other drew his own. Buck Bruner then drew his pistol, but without releasing John's pistol Reeves shot Buck dead, then ironed John, with whom he arrived to-day.

**Old Man Horribly Abused.**

SOUTH MCALESTER, I. T., Aug. 25.—Parties in from the vicinity of Leader, I. T., report a deplorable outrage upon an old man residing there which may result fatally. J. Lyons, who is some 60 years of age, was generally supposed to be possessed of some money on account of his thrifty and frugal habits. On Friday of last week Lyons was accosted by a young person named Billy the Kid and his money demanded, failing to produce which he was horribly maltreated, dragged some distance from home and finally struck upon the head and left for dead. He lay out in the broiling sun from Friday until Sunday, when he was found and cared for, and it is thought that there is a bare chance for his recovery. Deputies from Fort Smith were placed in possession of the facts and Deputy Bass Reeves has succeeded in capturing the Kid.

## SURRENDERS ON A DREAM OUT OF FEAR OF BASS REEVES

Black Freedmen Held for Grand Jury In Assault Case,

Daily Ardmoreite., July 16, 1903 - Muskogee, I. T., July l6. Jerry McIntosh, the black freedman, who is charged with saturating his wife's clothing with kerosene and then setting fire to them, came to this city today and surrendered to **Bass Reeves**, deputy United States marshal. McIntosh says he dreamed last night that Deputy Marshal Reeves came upon him in the brush and when he jumped up to run the deputy shot and killed him. When he awoke and realized that it was only a dream he decided to come to town and give up immediately. He was arraigned before the United States commissioner today on the charge of assaulting his wife with intent to kill. After pleading guilty, he was bound over to the grand Jury and was sent to jail in default of $10,000 bond." It seemed he would rather surrender to the court than face Bass Reeves. What a coward, not only for being afraid to face Reeves, but for assaulting his wife.

**Marshal Bennett's Deputies - Bass Reeves** July 5, 1902 Dallas Morning News

**Appointments for the Western District Announced.**

SPECIAL TO THE NEWS.

Vinita, I. T., July 3.—In taking control of the Western District of the Indian Territory Marshal Leo E. Bennett has appointed the following deputies: David Adams, Bass Reeves,. Muskogee; John L. Brown,

The Cordell Ok Weekly Beacon. July 30, 1903 **Not all Bass' calls were dramatic.**

**FOUND DEAD ON TRACK**

**Body of Conductor H. A. Shotwell Discovered on Katy Track**

MUSKOGEE: The body of H. A. Shotwell, a member of the Order of Railway Conductors, and a member of the American Federation of Labor at Wilburton, was found dead on the Missouri, Kansas & Texas tracks near Wybark, about five miles distant from this city.

Mel Bowman, Theo Stidham, Deputy Fleming and Bass Reeves took a hand car and went out to where the body was. They found it under guard of some section men. Close examination was made and the officers could find no evidence that would lead them to believe the man had been murdered. There was a cut and a bruise on the back of his head and two of his teeth were knocked out. These wounds evidently caused death, and the officers were of the opinion that the man was killed by a train, as the body was on the right of way.

The officers refused to take charge. It will be taken in charge by the railroad company.

April 1, 1904 Plaindealer (Topeka, Kansas)

# An Attempt on Bass Reeves' Life

The Norman Transcript. (Norman, Okla.), November 22, 1906

Bass Reeves' mother, Mrs. Stewart, of Van Buren, Ark., who has been in the city several days visiting relatives and friends left for home last Friday.

An attempt was made to kill Bass Reeves, a negro, who has served for thirty years as a government officer in Indian Territory. Reeves was driving in a buggy north of Wybark when an unknown man fired from a railroad trestle under which he was passing, the bullet splintering one of the ties.

Bisbee Daily Review., February 22, 1906 Denison Daily Herald. Wednesday, November 14, 1906

## FIXICO AND WILD CAT JAILED.

**Two Seminole Indians Held for Murder in Territory.**

Muskogee, I. T., Feb. 21.—Deputy Marshal Cordell brought in two prisoners, Barney Fixico and Wild Cat, yesterday, charged with the murder of Billy Cully, a Seminole Light Horseman, on the third of this month. A light horseman is a mounted Indian police officer.

When Wild Cat was put in jail here, one of the deputy marshals, Bass Reeves, recognized him as a man he had arrested once twenty years ago. Reeves arrested him on a murder charge and was taking him to Fort Smith for trial. When they reached the Arkansas river, Wild Cat made his escape. He had not been seen or heard of since, and the officer supposed he was dead until he turned up at the jail here today. Wild Cat and Fixico are both Seminole Indians.

## ATTEMPT AT ASSASSINATION.

**Bas Reeves, Well Known Colored Deputy, Shot at Near Wybark.**

Muskogee, I. T., Nov. 14.—Last night an assassin made an attehpt to kill Bas Reeves, a negro deputy marshal who has been in the service in Indian Territory for twenty-five years. Reeves was in the country near Wybark and driving under a trestle of a railroad bridge when some one on top of the trestle commenced shooting at him with a sixshooter. Reeves ducked at the first shot and returned the fire. The would-be assassin escaped. Reeves thinks he knows his man. Reeves occupies an unique position here. Marshal Leo E. Bennett has kept him on the force for nine years. He works exclusively among the negroes and never arrests a white man. He knows every negro in the Arkansas Valley and is very successful in arresting bad "niggers." He has never been known to show any sign of fear. He arrested his own son on a murder charge and he is now serving a life sentence at Fort Leavenworth for killing his wife.

April 4, 1907 San Diego Union

# A Terror to Desperadoes In Indian Territory

## The Career of Negro Deputy Marshal Who Has Slain Fourteen Outlaws

St. Louis, March 28.—In Muskogee, Indian Territory, lives Bass Reeves, a negro. He has been a United States deputy marshal for thirty-two years and has killed fourteen men in that time.

"For thirty-one years, going on thirty-two, I have ridden as a deputy marshal, sir, and when Marse Bennett goes out of office I am going to farming for a living," is the simple way that Reeves tells the story of his life as an officer in a country at a time when every day's service was a hazardous one. Reeves has served under seven different United States marshals, Democrats and Republicans, with the expiration of the present federal regime upon the advent of statehood, he will, as he says, go to farming for a living, laying down for the plow the six-shooter, which in his hand has been a potent element in bringing two territories out of the reign of the outlaw, the horsethief and the bootlegger, to a great commonwealth.

Reeves is an Arkansas negro. He is six feet tall, sixty-eight years old, and looks not more than forty. He was never known to show the slightest excitement under any circumstances. He does not know what fear is, and to him the one supreme document and law of the country is a "writ." Place a warrant for arrest in his hands and no circumstance can cause him to deviate. I saw him once arrest his own son, charged with murder, take him to jail and place him behind the bars. It was for a most diabolical crime. The negro had brutally murdered his young wife. This was probably the most trying moment in the whole life of the old deputy. He walked into the office of Marshal Bennett and was told that there was a warrant for his son for murder, and asked if he did not want someone else to serve it. "Give me the 'writ,'" was all he said.

### In the Days of Daring Outlaws

When Reeves commenced riding as a deputy marshal all of Oklahoma and Indian Territory were under the jurisdiction of the Fort Smith court, and deputies from Fort Smith rode to Fort Reno, Fort Sill and Anadarko for prisoners, a distance of 400 miles. In those days the Missouri, Kansas & Texas railroad, running south across the territory marked the western fringe of civilization. Eighty miles west of Fort Smith it was known as "the dead line," and whenever a deputy marshal from Fort Smith or Paris, Tex., crossed the Missouri, Kansas & Texas track he took his life in his own hands, and he knew it. On nearly every trail would be found, posted by outlaws, a small card warning certain deputies that if they ever crossed the dead line they would be killed. Reeves has a dozen of these cards which were posted for his special benefit. And in those days such a notice was no idle boast, and many an outlaw has bitten the dust trying to ambush a deputy on these trails.

In the early 80's there were two principal trails that led up from Denison, Tex., into the Indian country thre were frequented by horsethieves, bootleggers and others. They were known as the Seminole trail and the Pottawottamie trail. The former led up via old Sasakwa and on toward the Sacred Heart mission. The Seminoles hated the Pottawottamies and the two trails, though they practically paralleled each other, were never used by the same Indians. It was along these two trails, which also led to Fort Sill, Anadarko and Fort Reno, that most of the scenes of encounters with outlaws were laid.

There were three principal classes of outlaws—murderers, horsethieves and bootleggers. Added to the Indians and mixed negro and Indian, were the white outlaws that had fled from Texas, Kansas and other states.

### Man Hunting Was Profitable

Whenever a deputy marshal left Fort Smith to capture outlaws in the territory he took with him a wagon, a cook and usually a posseman, depending on what particular outlaws he was after. The government allowed 75 cents a day to feed the prisoners captured, and mileage for the distance they traveled at 10 cents a mile. A deputy going west was not allowed to arrest a man east of the M., K. & T. railroad, but he had to wait until on the return trip. If he caught a man a mile west of the M., K. & T. railroad, however, he was entitled to pay both for feeding and mileage both ways, if he carried him 300 miles west to Fort Sill and back again to Fort Smith. A deputy was allowed thirty days' time to make a trip as far west as Fort Sill and return. If he had to stop for high water he was paid for the delay. Every deputy was then on fees and took chances on making a living. It was a hazardous business, and the deputies made big money. Reeves says that he never made a thirty-day trip and got back with less than $400 worth of fees and expense money. He went to Mud creek and brought in sixteen prisoners at one time, and the fees amounted to $700, while the total actual expense to him was less than $100. The biggest killing he ever made was one time when he captured seventeen prisoners in the Comanche country and took them into Fort Smith. His fees for that trip amounted to $900. A deputy was allowed to take a posseman, a guard and a cook. The posseman drew $3 per day, the guard $2 and the cook $20 per month. The deputy paid his own expenses and got all the fees. The deputy, of course, rode horseback and ranged wide from the wagon, which was simply his base of supplies and his prison.

## He Had Many Close Calls

Each wagon was equipped with a long, heavy chain. When a prisoner was captured he was shackled with old-fashioned brads. At night all of the prisoners were shackled in pairs and the shackle passed through a ring in the long chain. One end of the chain was locked around the rear axle of the wagon. In this manner one man could handle thirty prisoners if he wished to. His only precaution was to prevent the prisoners from ever getting within reach of the six-shooters. This danger was ever present. No guard or cook was ever allowed to gamble with the prisoners for fear that they would lose their six-shooters. The first thing a prisoner wants after he is captured and shackled to a chain is to gamble.

During his lifetime Reeves has had some mighty close calls. His belt was shot in two twice, his hat brim shot away, a button on his coat was shot off, the bridle reins in his hands were shot in two, yet he has never had the blood drawn in a fight, though fourteen men in all have had their lives snuffed out by his deadly gun, and in not a single instance did he ever shoot at a man until the other fellow started the fight.

## Killed Two Men at Once

Reeves says that about the tightest place he ever got into was in 1884, when he was riding the Seminole whisky trail, looking for two white men and two negroes. He was ambushed by three Bruner brothers, who knew he was looking for them. They had their guns on him and made him dismount. He got down and showed them the warrants for their arrests and asked them to tell him the day of the month so he could make a record to turn in to the government.

"You are just ready to turn in now" remarked one of the outlaws, but they relaxed their vigilance for the merest instant, and that was enough.

Reeves whipped out his six-shooter and killed one of the Bruners quick as lightning and grabbed the gun of the other in time to save himself. He also killed the other Bruner while he was still holding the gun of the third one, who shot three times with Reeves gripping the barrel of the gun. Reeves finally struck him over the head with his six-shooter and killed him.

### The Bravest He Ever Saw

"The bravest man I ever saw," said Reeves, "was Jim Webb, a Mexican that I killed in 1884 near Sacred Heart mission. He was a murderer. I got in between him and his horse. He stepped out into the open, 500 yards away, and commenced shooting his Wincchester. cBfore I could drop off my horse, his first bullet cut a button off my coat and the second cut my bridle rein in two. I shifted my six-shooter and grabbed my Winchester and shot twice. He dropped and when I picked him up I foundthat my two bullets had struck him within half an inch of each other. He shot four times, and every time he shot he kept running up closer to me. He was 500 yards away from me when I killed him."

Reeves has been tried for murder but has never been convicted, always proving that he was discharging his official duty. One time he was out with a posseman, so the story goes, when the latter became enraged and threw some hot grease on a favorite dog belonging to Reeves. Reeves whipped out his six-shooter and shot the negro posseman dead. He pitched forward into the campfire and the deputy was so enraged that the let the body lie in the fire until it was charred. Reeves denies part of this story, but he stood trial for murder on account of it, and it cost him practically all he had ever made as a deputy marshal to keep out of jail for the offense.

### Knows Negro Criminals at Sight

The old deputy says the worst criminals and the hardest to catch are the Seminoles and negroes. They stick together better, fight quicker and fight to kill. A Seminole on the scout is always on horseback, never sleeps until after midnight and gets up with the sun; every minute he is not asleep he is on his horse. He does not get off to eat. Riding up to a house he says "hombux," which means he wants something to eat. He is given a piece of meat and bread,and sits in his saddle and eats it, watching all the time for an expected oc.

**<u>Muskogee Phoenix, Thursday, January 13, 1910</u>**

**BASS REEVES DEAD;**
**UNIQUE CHARACTER**
**Man of the "Old Days" Gone**
**Deputy Marshal Thirty-Two Years.**

Bass passed away on January 12, 1910. He is buried in what is a now an unattended cemetery. His grave was marked with a simple wooden cross.

Daily Ardmoreite January 18, 1910

**BLOODY RECORD OF "BLACK BASS" REEVES - FEDERAL OFFICERS MOURN THE DEATH OF BLACK DEPUTY MARSHAL, WHO KILLED 14 MEN.**

Muskogee, Okla. Jan. 17 - He killed fourteen men, but nothing more true could be said of him than that he did his duty, and today the federal officers and ex federal officers in eastern Oklahoma mourn the death of old Bass Reeves, "Black Bass," as he was known, for he was a black man. No history of frontier days in Indian Territory would be complete with no mention of Bass Reeves, and no tale of the old days or "Hell on the Border" could be told without the old deputy marshal as a prominent character.

He died Wednesday, after several months of illness at the age of 71 after a career of thirty-two years, beginning way back in the eighteen seventies and ending in 1907. Bass Reeves was a deputy. During that time he was sent to arrest many of the most notorious characters that in those days were located in the Indian country, and because he was gifted with a mind that knew how to find his quarry, and an intensity of purpose that led him to follow criminals day and night, dogging the fugitive's trail- because of this, he rarely failed to land his man in the Muskogee federal Jail. As his record shows, it often happened that he was to get him alive, but the old deputy often said that he had never shot a man except in self-defense. He was once tried for murder but was acquitted on the ground that he had killed the man in the discharge of duty, and to save his own life.

Bass was a slave, and a few years after the close of the civil war a court was set up with jurisdiction over Indian Territory in Fort Smith Arkansas. Bass was appointed a deputy marshal there. <u>An incident which shows his devotion to duty was the arrest of Bass Reeves'</u>

own son for the murder of his wife. It was suggested that someone else should serve the warrant on him, but Bass insisted that he be the one to bring him to justice, and he did.

Reeves had many narrow escapes, but was never wounded. At different times, buttons were shot from his coat, his hat punctured, his belt shot, his horse reins shot from his hand, but no bullet ever touched his body. All this, too, in spite of the fact that he had never fired a shot until after someone fired at him.

Shawnee Daily Herald. (Shawnee, Okla.), January 14, 1910

**BASS REEVES, 32 YEARS DEPUTY U. S. MARSHAL AT MUSKOGEE PASSES AWAY.**

Muskogee, Okla., Jan. 13.—Bass Reeves, famous old negro deputy marshal, who served thirty-two years up to the coming of statehood and later was a member of the Muskogee police force, is dead. As a former expert with a six-shooter and any other implement of warfare for that matter, Bass was a winner and many are the strange tales told of his early days in the service against outlaws and desperadoes. No story of the conflict of the government's officers with those outlaws which ended only a few years ago with the rapid filling up of the territory with people, can be complete without mention of the old negro who died yesterday.

For thirty-two years, beginning 'way back in the seventies and ending in 1907, Bass Reeves was a deputy United States marshal. During that time he was sent to arrest some of the most desperate characters that ever infested Indian Territory and endangered life and peace in its borders. And he got his man as often as any of the deputies. At times he was unable to get them alive and so in the course of his long service he killed fourteen men. But Bass Reeves always said that he had never shot a man when it was not necessary for him to do so in the discharge of his duty to save his own life. He was tried for murder on one occasion but was acquitted upon proving that he had killed the man in the discharge of his duty and was forced to do it.

Reeves was an Arkansan and in his early days was a slave. He entered the federal service as a deputy marshal long before a court was established in Indian Territory and served under the marshal at Fort Smith. Then when people started to come into Indian Territory and a marshal was appointed with headquarters in Muskogee, he was sent over here.

Reeves served under seven United States marshals and all of them were more than satisfied with his services. Everybody who came in contact with the negro deputy in an official capacity had a great deal of respect for him and at the court house in Muskogee one can hear stories of his devotion to duty, his unflinching courage and his many thrilling experiences, and although he could not write or read he always took receipts and had his accounts in good shape.

Undoubtedly the act which best typifies the man and which at least best shows his devotion to duty, was the arrest of his own son. A warrant for the arrest of the younger Reeves, who was charged with the murder of his wife, had been issued. Marshal Bennett said that perhaps another deputy had better be sent to arrest him. The old negro was in the room at the time and with a devotion to duty equalling that of the old Roman, Brutus, whose greatest claim on fame has been that the love for his son could not sway him from justice, he said, "Give me the writ," and went out and arrested his son, brought him into court and upon trial and conviction he was sentenced to imprisonment and is still serving the sentence.

Reeves had many narrow escapes. At different times his belt was shot in two, a button shot off his coat, his hatbrim shot off and the bridle reins which he held in his hand cut by a bullet. However, in spite of all these narrow escapes and the many conflicts in which he was engaged, Reeves was never wounded. And this, notwithstanding the fact that he said he never fired a shot until the desperado he was trying to arrest had started the shooting.

Bright's disease and a complication of ailments together with old age, were the cause of his death.

The deceased is survived by his wife and several children.

## Georgetown Baptist Church

George R. Reeves, a prominent landowner and law enforcement officer in Grayson County, donated land for the combination school, church and Masonic Lodge. It is believed the school classes and church services were held in the same building downstairs, while the upstairs was dedicated to the Masonic Lodge. A Masonic Lodge at Georgetown still exists and has been named in Reeves' honor. A marker honoring George R. Reeves has been installed at Fink by the Texas State Historical Society. The Georgetown Baptist Church was organized in the 1870's, using the local school building for worship service.

**Tragedy at Church** - Denison Daily News, March 13, 1879 - Shocking news reached town regarding the death of Reverend J. L. Davis. It appears he shot himself fatally at 5 a.m. and was found in the hall by his son-in-law, C. A. Clamp. He was dead when found with the pistol grasped firmly in his hand and within an inch or two of his head. The deceased was a Baptist minister, and the cause of the rash act was troubles in his family. He left in his room a slip of paper with the following directions in pencil marks: "Please bury me just as I am. J. L. Davis."

The church was disbanded in 1939 as many people were leaving the area. In 1947 people gathered together and reorganized the church. Land for the church facilities was donated by **Mr. & Mrs. Carl Finke**. Land was donated for the minister's home by **Mr. & Mrs. A. H. Sharpe.** The parsonage was a Sears Roebuck kit home delivered unassembled on a truck, and the members of the church put the house together. The new church building was completed in 1948. Through time, the sanctuary and educational facilities have been expanded, and a new building built. Now there are three buildings making up the large church complex with plans to soon expand further with a brand new church building. The Georgetown Baptist Church is one of the most well attended churches in the area. Below: Georgetown Baptist 1948 & 1980s

## 1908 Grayson County Plat Map Georgetown School district

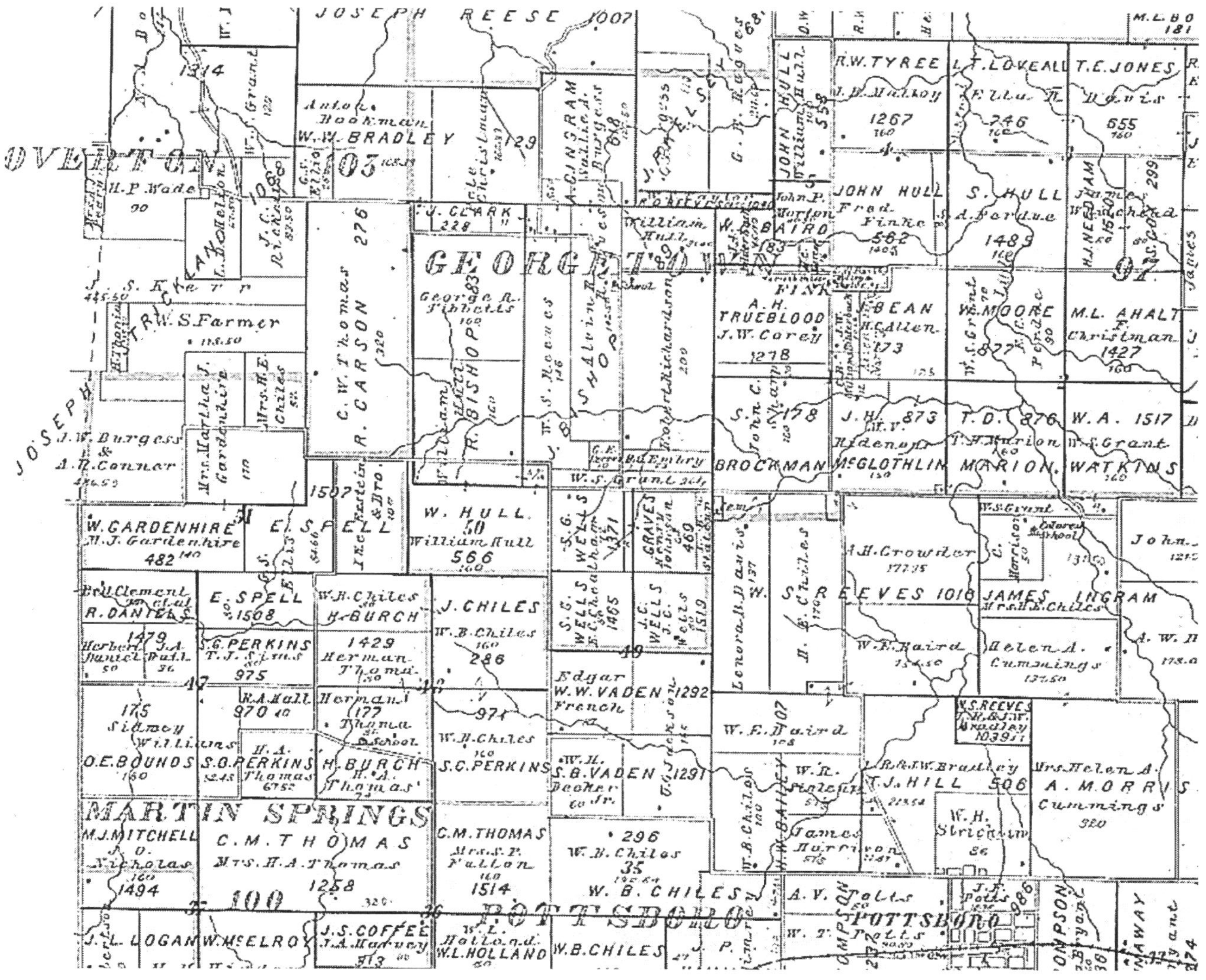

# SCHOOLS AT GEORGETOWN AND FINK

COMMUNITY BENEFACTORS OF THE GEORGETOWN AREA – SCHOOLS – CHURCH were the Reeves and Finke families

The Reeves family was very instrumental in seeing to the needs of their community, including schools, churches and cemetery facilities provided for the people in Georgetown. George R. Reeves came to Texas from Tennessee via Arkansas. About 1844, he donated land for a cemetery and a school and church. Later the Finke family also contributed land to build a school at Georgetown. The 1908 map of Georgetown below shows the school was located at the corner of Georgetown Road and present day Squirrel Lane, west of the town of Fink. Mr. Edgel Clement, a long-time resident, said his father attended classes there at the original school in 1875 and Edgel himself attended in 1921.

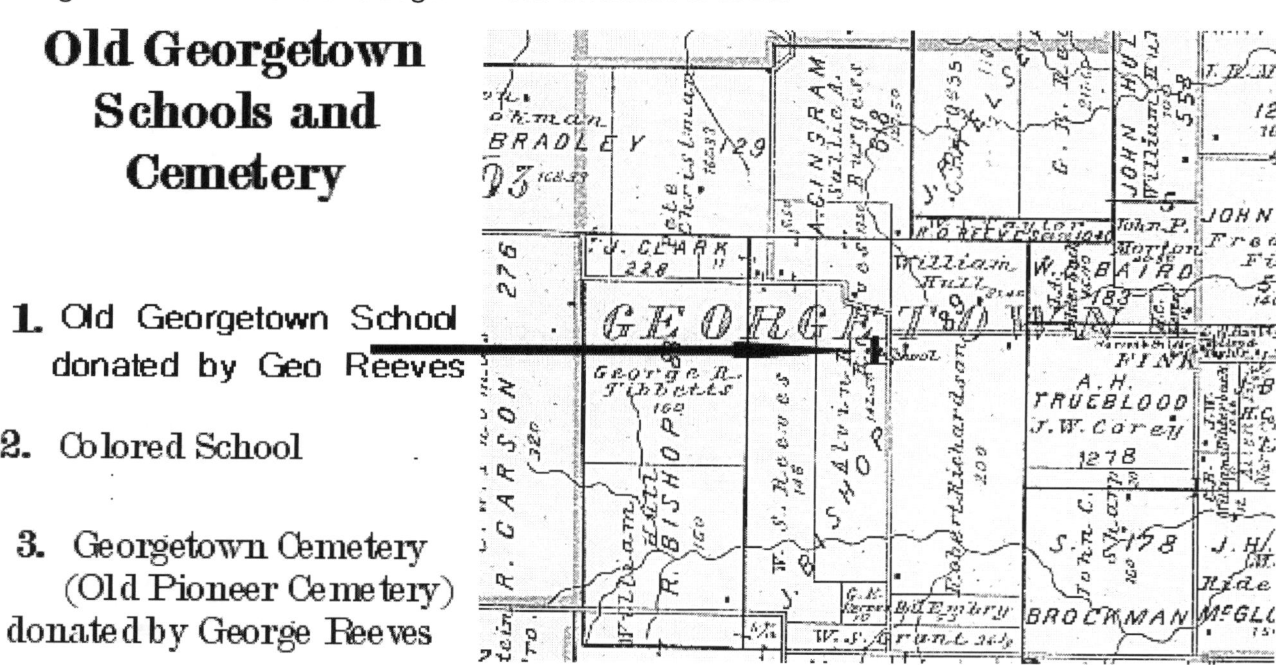


The teachers in the 1920s were Miss Margaret McEwin, Miss Nina Carr, Mary Carroll, Misses Maggie and Rommie Summerville and Miss Ruth Beane. Later teachers were Mrs. Moreland, Troy Martin, L. Bolin, Mrs. Timberman and Mrs. Hodges. Some of the trustees were Horace Hale, William R. Perdue, Bill Cantrell, Fred Finke and A. Sharp

In 1927 the Georgetown School was moved to the Preston Road location north of Fink on land donated by the Finke family. The land where the school had previously been was donated back to the Reeves heirs. The school still operated under the name of Georgetown and became a part of the Pottsboro consolidated district. It contained all the elementary grades until the 1970s when it had only 4th and 5th grade classes. In the early 80s, it only had 1st and 2nd grade classes. Some of the families whose children attended the school were the Mosers, Daniel, Finke, Arthur, Burgess, Perdue, Clountz, Clement, Henderson, Christman, Bilderback, Allen, Hall, Hull, Montgomery, Reeves, Sharpe, Griffith, Thomas, Travis, Mollenhour, Roy, and many more.

Georgetown school above in 1905 or 06 with Etta Sharpe, Bunt Reeves, Lottie Sharpe, Beulah Riddle, Bob Richardson, Wallace Burgess, Raymond Hull, Earl Burgess, and Carl Burgess. Below: Georgetown Sunday School picture from Jim Allen

Georgetown School in 1917-1918 from Jim Allen, names of students on next picture, the sons of all the leading citizens and pioneers of Georgetown.

Jackson, Sison, Swan
Marion, Emil Chrisman, Charlie
Campbell Lloyd Bilderback, Ed Swan
Fred Perdue, Fritz Christman
Luther Vale, Burgess Buchanan
Dick Christman, Lester Geis
Taken
When I was in 4th Grade
in 1917-1918

**Very Early picture above of Georgetown School from Jim Allen**

Photo below from Jim Allen, he said this may be the Georgetown School after it was moved from Old Georgetown in 1927. Many people have said this building was finally moved to a location on Coffin Street in Denison west of where the Sonic is and it is still there. The new school was built on the north intersection of where Hwy 289 and 406 are now, next to the old Allen residence.

**Georgetown school 1935?, pic by Jim Allen**

**More early pictures of Georgetown school about 1935 from Jim Allen**

**More early pictures of Georgetown school from Jim Allen**

Above: Georgetown School in the mid 1940s owned by Natalie Clountz Bauman. Teacher Mrs. Moreland, student George W. Clountz in front row, center with long shadow across face and body.
Below: Mrs. Moreland teacher at Georgetown in the 1940s and Mrs. Timberman in the early 1970s

When I (Natalie Clountz) was a student of Georgetown School in 1968-1971, the school had only fourth and fifth grade and it was right next to the Fink store. Eddie Vessels was the principal and Mrs. Timberman was the fourth grade teacher (my favorite!) and Mrs. Hodges was the fifth grade teacher. We even studied Spanish in those grades, and I think Mrs. Hodges taught that. Our gymnasium was, as I recall, an old curved top Quonset hut-like structure which I was told was salvaged from Perrin Field Air Force Base when it was closed. We had a storm cellar, but I don't think it was big enough for everyone to fit in it. Thankfully, we never had to go into it when I was there. Our favorite class was recess of course! We had one of those tall metal slides that bakes your skin when it's hot especially the girls who frequently wore dresses in those days. Our favorite play equipment was the merry-go-round. The outer seats were always full. Periodically, we would all take turns getting in the middle and being the "horses" to turn it. We would run as fast as we could and push it as hard as we could until it threw people off the seats, or they got so dizzy they fell off or threw up. The teeter totters were fun because it was like a game of "chicken" to figure exactly when the other person was going to jump off the board while you were up in the air, letting you come crashing down with a jolt, but do it to him first before he knew what you were planning! It was a wonderful lesson in gravity and strategy! Boy, was it all fun! Schools probably wouldn't allow such equipment on their playgrounds now, no one was hurt, and we all toughened up and learned some lessons from them too. I'm sure the teachers appreciated all the energy we burned off out there playing so we would be ready to pay attention in class. Georgetown School below in 1970s with the red hot slide, centrifugal force merry go round and the "who can jump off first" teeter totter. Principal Eddie Vessels is near the slide approving the daredevil high jinks with a grin.

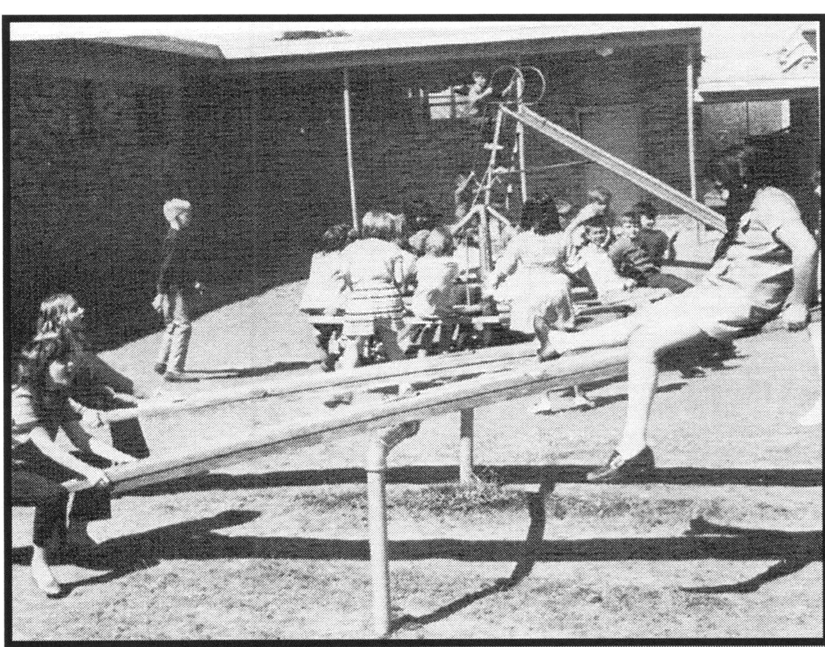

1970 Georgetown 5th graders in Mrs. Hodges class – 1st picture: Steve Atkins left, Natalie Clountz bottom right. 2nd picture: same class, Natalie Clountz left, Cindy Vessels right.

Fifth grade students on their assignments.

# Georgetown Had a Black School – here's how it happened......

through one of Georgetown's Greatest Doctors -

## Dr. Alexander Morrison

BIRTH 31 OCT 1813 • Scotland
DEATH 28 MAR 1891 • Denison, Grayson Co., TX.

### Facts

Name
Dr. Alexander Morrison

Name *(Alternate)*
Alexander Morrison

Gender
Male

Birth
31 Oct 1813 • Scotland

Birth *(Alternate)*
31 October 1816 • Scotland

Marriage
1839 • New York
Harriet Newell Deveaux/Devoe
(1817–1882)

Birth of Daughter
6 May 1841 • Napoli, Cattaraugus Co., NY.
Helen Alexandria Morrison
(1841–1936)

Birth of Daughter
20 Nov 1843 • Sparta, Ontario, Canada
Harriet Eugenia Morrison
(1843–1926)

Birth of Son
15 Sep 1855 • Texas
Charles Morrison (1855–1935)

### Family

Parents

Spouse & Children

Harriet Newell Deveaux/Devoe
1817–1882

Helen Alexandria Morrison
1841–1936

Harriet Eugenia Morrison
1843–1926

Spouse & Children

Janie Smith
1830–

Charles Morrison 1855–1935

## Pioneering Doctor From Scotland in Georgetown – Dr. Alexander Morrison

Alexander Morrison is the Doctor in this story and he was born in Scotland about 1813. He married Harriet Newell Deveaux/Devoe in 1839 in New York. His daughter Helena Alexandria was born on May 6, 1841, in Napoli, New York. His daughter Harriet Eugenia was born on November 20, 1843, in Sparta, Ontario, Canada.

During the time of the Texas Republic (1836–1846), the Morrison family traveled on a steamer on the Mississippi River, going to Shreveport, Louisiana. They traveled with a man named Dr. Stewart. Then the group traveled on by ox cart to Old McKinney in Collin County, Texas. One source says Dr. Morrison went from McKinney to Weston, in Collin County. He bargained for a headright and a little cabin from a man who wished to dispose of his right. They stayed there for several years, but the Reservation Indians came to steal cattle and horses and sometimes even to kill people. This convinced them to move away from there to Grayson County in 1852. The Morrisons lived for a while at **Preston Bend,** on the Red River, where the doctor set up his practice. He was one of, if not the earliest physician in the area. The closest doctor other than himself may have been in the new town of Sherman. On April 14, 1855, he sold his lots in Preston to James G. Thompson, early settler and the first county judge of Grayson County.

Since he was a pioneer, Dr. Morrison was able to claim a headright of 640 acres of land which is the Morrison Survey adjoining the old James G. Thompson Survey on one side, and the James Ingram Survey on the other. Later he bought 100 or so acres of the James Ingram Survey. Around 1854, the family and their slaves moved there, staying throughout the Civil War. The farm was just north of where Pottsboro was founded twenty four years later, with early census records listing Sherman as the post office for his farm. In the 1908 plat map, this area was defined as being part of "Georgetown."

Dr. Morrison came to Georgetown in 1854 where he farmed and practiced medicine there for eighteen years before he moved to Denison. He is best known for being a Denison physician, but he did not move to Denison until soon after the town was mapped out in 1872. Here he continued medical practice throughout his life. He still kept the land in Georgetown in his family even after his move to Denison, because in 1908 on the plat map, it all still belonged to his two daughters and his lesser known son Charley Morrison. He had two female children, Mrs. William Chiles, and Mrs. James Cummins, both of whom were at his bedside at the hour of his death. Dr. Morrison's residence at the time of his death was 815 West Main in Denison which would have been across the street from the present Waples Methodist Church. Dr. Alexander Morrison died on March 28, 1891, in Denison and his wife, Harriett, died on Valentine's Day in 1882. Harriet became the first person buried in Fairview Cemetery. [Source: Sunday Gazetteer, Denison TX, March 29, 1891]. The cabin/house that Dr. Morrison built was the first built in Denison. After his death, Mr. Esler in Denison (who had the Esler Paint store on Main Street, which still stands with his sign intact) kept Morrison's cabin in his yard for years preserving it, trying to convince city leaders to preserve it for posterity but was unsuccessful. Sadly, he ended up using the logs of the house for firewood. Just one more important historic home lost due to disinterest. Below: Dr. Morrison's cabin in Denison.

**Compassion of a Doctor and The Cruelty of Another Man, Brings Two People Together To Begin A Family**

## Dr. Morrison – a Georgetown & Preston Resident - A Man Ahead of His Time – The Father of Charley Morrison (Mulatto)

By 1850, census records show Doctor Alexander Morrison had land in Grayson County, Texas as a physician and farmer. Dr. Morrison was a well-respected physician all over Grayson County, and at the time, the only one in the Preston area. In the early days of Preston Bend, slavery was legal, and there were hundreds of black slaves living in the Preston and Georgetown area. **But Dr. Morrison treated white and black patients alike.** Perhaps his Scottish origins helped. He came from regions removed from the specter of slavery. Being a Doctor, he no doubt believed people were people, no matter their complexion. By 1850 Grayson County had a population of 2,008, most of whom had come from Southern states; they had been raised in different circumstances. The census enumerated 186 slaves, used mainly by farmers and stockmen along the Red River and its tributaries to raise grains and livestock, cotton being a minor crop in the area until much later. There were probably some white men who had "romantic" relations with black slaves which resulted in children, some were with mutual consent between both parties, some may not have been. Dr. Morrison had come to Texas from Scotland, which was a very different culture. Dr. Morrison did have black servants, and a Morrison descendant, Jack Chiles, stated that they stayed with Dr. Morrison after they were freed by the government. It could be they were not considered by him to be slaves. He must have been good to them, and I also believe that he provided them a school on his land, believing they deserved the same chance in America everyone had (per 1908 plat map). It was the only black school in this area and it was on his land. On Sep 15, 1855, a mixed-race baby boy was born named Charley Morrison. In the 1910 census, Charley was listed as a Mulatto, part white, Indian and black, according to his present family. He served as a houseboy since he was part white, according to his descendant Finus Roy Potts.

| | | | | | | | | | |
|---|---|---|---|---|---|---|---|---|---|
| 148 | 148 | Morrison, Charles | Head | M | Mu | 54 | M | | |
| | | — Lucy | Wife | F | Bl | 51 | M | 11 | 4 |
| | | Lornt, Jesse | Boarder | M | Bl | 14 | S | | |
| | | Pegue, George | Grandson | M | Mu | [illegible] | [illegible] | | |
| | | Morrison, Anthony | Nephew | M | Bl | 21 | S | | |
| 149 | 149 | Marion, Charles H | Head | M | W | 38 | M | 12 | |

According to military records, on August 6, 1863, Dr. Morrison, at age forty-seven, enlisted for six months in the Confederate army at Camp Stonewall in Collin County. He was a private in Company B, Cavalry, 15th Battalion, Texas State Troops, under Capt. John Goode; the company's ranks were drawn from Collin and Grayson counties. The doctor worked as a military surgeon during this time. Information from descendants Ray Potts and Newell Cummins stated that one of Dr. Morrison's servants, Charley Morrison, who was a houseboy in the doctor's house, went through the Civil War with Dr. Morrison as a personal servant. After the slaves were freed and the Civil War came to an end, the African Americans who had been his slaves stayed with him, probably working as sharecroppers.

Dr. Alexander Morrison's wife and daughters managed the farm while he was away serving the Confederacy. Soon after the war ended, both the Morrison daughters married Confederate veterans from Missouri. Helen Morrison, on August 24, 1865, married James Hunter ("Jim") Cummins (1842–1890), from Harrisonville, Cass County, Missouri. Harriet Eugenia Morrison, in 1866 married William Ballinger ("Bill") Chiles Sr. (1844–1900).

Alex Morrison was an extremely intelligent man, who loved reading and learning; and valued education for all people. He spent his life furthering education and it is believed he was instrumental in installing a colored school on his land at Georgetown. He was ahead of his time in seeing that "colored" people at the time had equal opportunities.

He also saw to it that his own daughters were well educated, something else that was not common at the time. Females were not encouraged to be scholars at the time. He even had hopes that one of his daughters would follow him in becoming a doctor. He often took his daughters with him on house calls as would-be apprentices.

His daughters were also well versed in the social graces. They were well known in society, both were good dancers and went to many parties at 'Aunt' Sophia Porter's house Glen Eden in Preston Bend" (The History of Grayson County, Texas, vol. 1, published by Grayson County Frontier Village).

1908 Plat Map for Georgetown below shows the only local colored school located on the land belonging to half black Charles Morrison, son of Doctor Alexander Morrison. Land just to the east and south belonged to the other heirs of Dr. Alexander Morrison – his daughters Helen Morrison Cummings, and Harriet Eugenia Morrison Chiles, his white half-sisters.

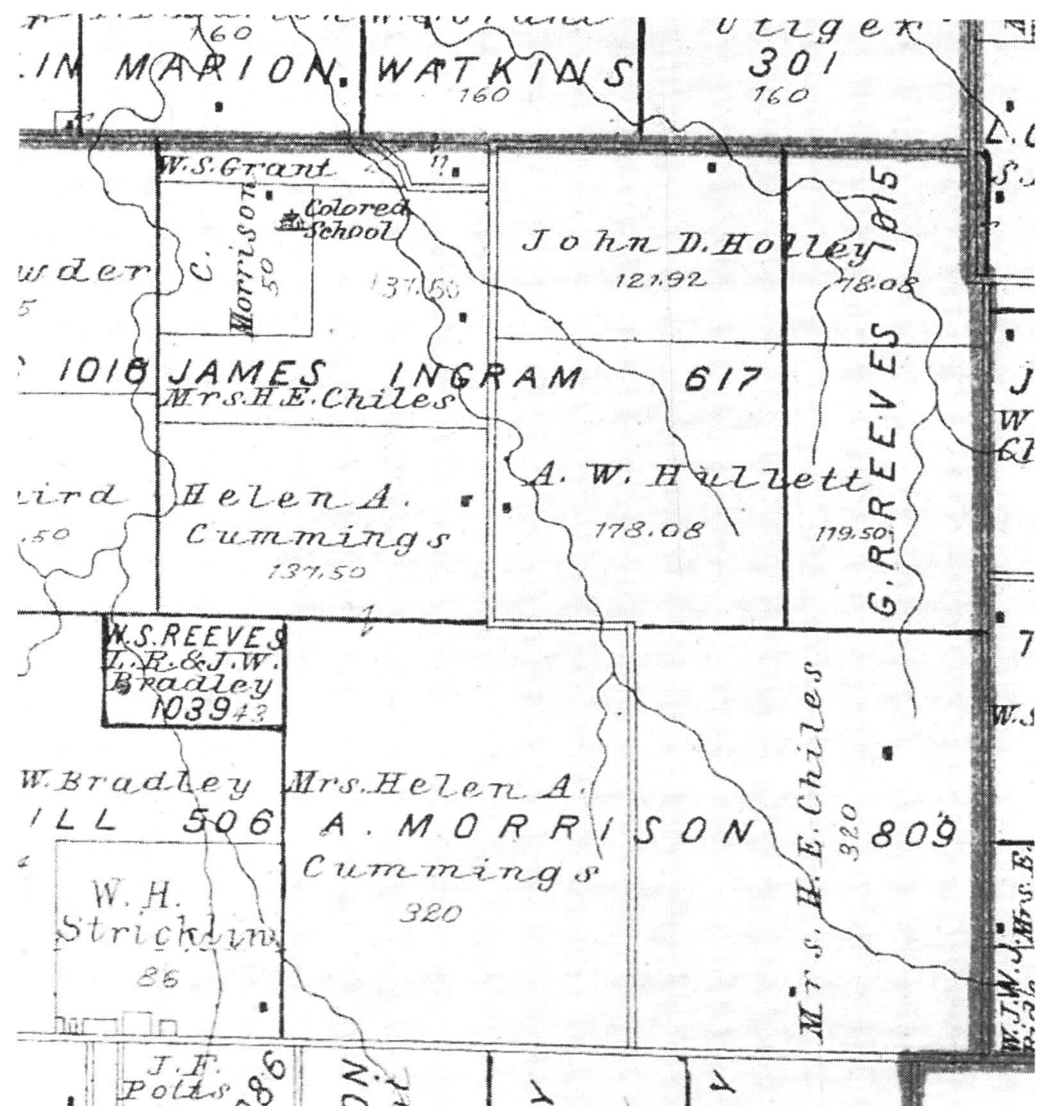


According to Jack Chiles' family information and Charles Morrison's death certificate, and his inheritance from Dr. Morrison, Alex Morrison had some sort of an affair with a black lady named Janie Smith with Charles Morrison being the son, because he made him an heir with his own two white legitimate daughters to receive land. Plus, it was Charley Morrison's own daughter Myrtle Johnson who listed Dr. Morrison as her father's father. Also, I spoke to James Clement, lifetime Georgetown resident, and he recalled that at the time, local people were surprised to learn that this black family had received an inheritance of 50 acres from a white doctor who had other children, and thought he must be Charley's father for this to have occurred. In 1935, when Charley died, and his daughter Myrtle inherited the 50 acres of land that Charley had gotten from Dr. Morrison, James Clement recalls that people were still shocked they had received this, but realized it confirmed their suspicions that Charley had a white father (Dr. Morrison as Myrtle said) who had given him land. But, Mr. Clement recalled that some thought T. D. Marion could have been the father since he also lived nearby. But there is no doubt Charley got part of Morrison land, not Marion land. Also, Charley's last name was Morrison.

The most definitive information came from Finus Ray Potts of Sherman, a descendant of Dr. Morrison and Charley Morrison. He has some great stories about his ancestors which have been passed down through his family. He said he had multiple Native American ancestors who came west on the Trail of Tears. Janie Smith, who was said to be the mistress of Dr. Alexander Morrison, and the mother of Charley Morrison, was reported to be mixed race Native American and African from the island of Madagascar. He also stated that Dr. Morrison's white wife was aware of the Doctor's relationship with Janie and that Charley was his son. Ray Potts told the interesting and tragic story of how Charley Morrison and his wife met each other. Lucy was a young servant at **Preston Bend** for one of the wealthy farmers there, whose name Mr. Potts cannot recall. But records indicate her last name may have been Young, which means she or her parents once "belonged" to a farmer named Young since it was the custom for slaves to take the last name of their masters. Lucy made the man angry with her for some inconsequential reason, and he hit her on the head with an axe and threw her out into a field to bleed to death. He ordered that no one was to help her. After dark though, some of the other servants sneaked out to get her and summoned Dr. Morrison to come to tend her to save her life. Charley came with him, and their acquaintance began and grew into marriage with children. Charles "Charley" Morrison married Lucy Young (according to a Grayson County marriage license) in 1872 and one of their daughters was named Lillie Myrtle Morrison. She married Jack Johnson and they lived in Georgetown there on the site of the old colored school on her father and grandfather's land just south of present-day Reeves Road. The house where Myrtle lived was built in 1890 and as of today is still standing and is in surprisingly good shape inside and out, considering its age and its vacancy. It is located in the spot where the 1908 map says the colored school was located. There is an old foundation there on the property which may be that of the original school or Charley's old home. One of Charley Morrison's daughters, Myrtle, continued to live in the home Dr. Morrison left Charley near Pottsboro up until the 1980s. Below is the house on Reeves Road in Georgetown where Myrtle Johnson lived, which still stands.

In 1880, there were a couple hundred free blacks in the Preston, Pottsboro and Georgetown area. By the last days that Jack and Lillie Myrtle were living in Georgetown, they were the last black people still left in the area. Myrtle's grandfather, Dr. Morrison had probably had a hand in building the house she lived in, which may have also served as the colored school around the turn of the 20th century.

Charley Morrison (1855–1935) died of pellagra in Denison in 1935. His death certificate, signed by Dr. William M. Freeman, stated that Charley's father was "Dr. Morrison."

TEXAS STATE DEPARTMENT OF HEALTH
BUREAU OF VITAL STATISTICS
STANDARD CERTIFICATE OF DEATH

Dr. Freeman.

County of Grayson — Registrar's No. 603

City or Precinct No. Denison — No. 1330 Street W. Crawford St. (If in an Institution, give name of Institution instead of Street and No.)

Length of residence in city where death occurred: yrs. 2 mos. 13 days. How long in U. S. if foreign born? yrs. — 28397

2. Full name of deceased: Charley Morrison. Pottsboro Texas

Residence: No. — Street — (If non-residence give city, or town and state)

PERSONAL AND STATISTICAL PARTICULARS

3. Sex: male
4. Color or race: col.
5. Single, Married, Widowed, Divorced (Write the word): Widowed
5a. If married, widowed, or divorced HUSBAND of (or) WIFE of: —
6. Date of birth (month, day, and year): Sept 15 1855
7. Age: 79 Years 8 Months 2 Days. If LESS than 1 day, hrs. or min.

OCCUPATION
8. Trade, profession, or particular kind of work done, as spinner, sawyer, bookkeeper, etc.: farming
9. Industry or business in which work was done, as silk mill, saw mill, bank, etc.
10. Date deceased last worked at this occupation (month and year): Nov. 1929
11. Total time (years) spent in this occupation: life

12. Birthplace (city or town) (State or country): Grayson Co. Texas

FATHER
13. Name: Dr. Morrison
14. Birthplace (city or town) (State or country): Mo.

MOTHER
15. Maiden name: Janie Smith
16. Birthplace (city or town) (State or country): Texas

17. Informant: Myrtle Johnson
(Address): Pottsboro Texas

18. Burial, cremation, or removal: Place Georgetown Cemetery Date 6/15 1935

19. Undertaker: T. E. Grant
(Address): Denison, Texas

20. File date and signature of registrar: 6-15 1935 W. A. Lee

MEDICAL CERTIFICATE OF DEATH

21. Date of death (month, day, and year): June 13 1935

22. I HEREBY CERTIFY, That I attended deceased from June 1 1935, to June 13 1935; I last saw him alive on June 13 1935; death is said to have occurred on the date stated above, at 6 p.m. The principal cause of death and related causes of importance were as follows: Pellagra — Date of onset: 1934

Other contributory causes of importance:

Name of operation — date of —

What test confirmed diagnosis? Symptoms — Was there an autopsy? No

23. If death was due to external causes (violence) fill in also the following:
Accident, suicide, or homicide?
Date of injury — 19
Where did injury occur? (Specify city or town, county, and State)
Specify whether injury occurred in industry, in home, or in public place.
Manner of injury
Nature of injury

24. Was disease or injury in any way related to occupation of deceased? No
If so, specify

(Signed) Wm. Freeman M. D.
(Address) Denison Tex

His mother was Janie Smith (born in 1830). Charley's youngest daughter, Clara George Morrison Bell (1893–1960), was the mother of Charles Samuel Bell (1909–2008), a landscaper who worked for prominent white families in Denison for many years. His obituary said, "Charles would always look his best, even wearing a shirt and tie while working in the yard. He was proud of his profession and handed his knowledge and work ethic on to his grandchildren. . . . He was a faithful deacon for over 65 years at Hopewell Baptist Church. Charles was also a member of the H.A. Coleman Masonic Lodge, where he served as Senior Warden and Senior Deacon until his health failed." It has often been said that the African

American founders of Hopewell Church came from Preston Bend. This makes sense because, in the earlier days in Preston Bend, there were many people of color, and the "colored" church there was very strong and active. When these spiritual people moved to Denison, they took their faith with them. Charlie Bell and Clara Morrison Bell are both buried in Jeremiah Cemetery southeast of Denison. They were among Dr. Morrison's descendants – **a family brought together by both cruelty and kindness.**

Myrtle and Jack Johnson were long-time neighbors of the Marion family across the road.

THOMAS D. MARION 1910 Census

| | | | | | | | | | | | | | |
|---|---|---|---|---|---|---|---|---|---|---|---|---|---|
| 146 | 146 | Halley, John D. | Head | M | W | 43 | Wd | | | | Alabama | Alabama | |
| | | ——— Myrtle | Daughter | F | W | 17 | S | | | | Texas | Alabama | |
| | | ——— Ramah | Daughter | F | W | 13 | S | | | | Texas | Alabama | |
| | | ——— Newman | Son | M | W | 9 | S | | | | Texas | Alabama | |
| | | ——— Ben | Son | M | W | 6 | S | | | | Texas | Alabama | |
| | | ——— Buddie | Son | M | W | 2 | S | | | | Texas | Alabama | |
| | | Elliott, Rufus E | Son in law | M | W | | M1 | 0 | | | Georgia | Georgia | |
| | | ——— Ava | Daughter | F | W | 21 | M1 | 0 | 0 | 0 | Texas | Alabama | |
| 147 | 147 | Steele, Leon E | Head | M | W | 35 | M1 | 13 | | | Missouri | Missouri | |
| | | ——— Margaret | Mother | F | W | 67 | Wd | | 6 | 5 | Missouri | Virginia | |
| | | ——— Annie | Sister | F | W | 26 | S | | | | Arkansas | Missouri | |
| | | ——— Lee | Son | M | W | 12 | S | | | | Texas | Missouri | |
| | | ——— Roy | Son | M | W | 8 | S | | | | Texas | Missouri | |
| | | ——— Maud | Daughter | F | W | 8 | S | | | | Texas | Missouri | |
| | | Jones, Rebecca | Sister | F | W | 37 | Wd | | 2 | 2 | Missouri | Missouri | |
| | | ——— Earl A | Son | M | W | 18 | S | | | | Arkansas | Arkansas | |
| | | ——— Willie | Daughter | F | W | 16 | S | | | | Arkansas | Arkansas | |
| 148 | 148 | Morrison, Charles | Head | M | Mu | 54 | M1 | | | | Texas | United States | |
| | | ——— Lucy | Wife | F | Bl | 51 | M1 | | 11 | 4 | [illegible] | Unknown | |
| | | Lorent, Jesse | Boarder | M | Bl | 14 | S | | | | Texas | Texas | |
| | | Pogue, George | Grandson | Mu | Mu | [illegible] | S | | | | Texas | Texas | |
| | | Morrison, Anthony | Nephew | M | Bl | 21 | S | | | | Texas | Texas | |
| 149 | 149 | Marion, Charles H | Head | M | W | 38 | M1 | 12 | | | Texas | Ger German | |
| | | ——— Janie | Wife | F | W | 31 | M1 | 12 | 1 | 0 | Texas | Tennessee | |
| | | Elkins, Bettie | Aunt | F | W | 61 | S | | | | Tennessee | Tennessee | |
| | | Stratton, Nellie | Cousin | F | W | 4 | S | | | | Texas | Kentucky | |
| 150 | 150 | Marion, Thomas D | Head | M | W | 7[illegible] | M1 | 44 | | | Ger German | Ger German | Ger German |
| | | ——— [illegible] | Wife | F | W | 65 | M1 | 44 | 4 | 1 | Missouri | Kentucky | North Carolina |

**Jack Johnson is mentioned in an obituary for helping his neighbor Charles Marion:**

**DEATH ROLL Charles Marion** - The Denison Press Monday, February 3, 1941 - Enroute from his home near Georgetown from Pottsboro Sunday to secure medicine for his ill wife, Charles Henry Marion, 69, a farmer, died in his automobile approximately half a mile from his home, according to Justice of the Peace E.A. Wright who conducted an inquest. Marion's car became stuck in the mud, caused by the heavy rains before noon, and hailed a passer-by, **Jack Johnson, colored**, to secure help and pull his car out. When Johnson returned with neighbors they found the farmer dead behind the wheel of his car. He suffered a stroke of paralysis a year ago. A Pottsboro physician was summoned who notified Judge Wright.

Mr. Marion was born February 21, 1872, son of Mr. and Mrs. T. D. Marion of Pottsboro and was reared and educated here. He was married to Miss Jennie Bilderback at Sherman Dec. 10, 1898 and was a member of the Presbyterian church. Surviving are his widow; a daughter, Mrs. Millie Taylor of Foster, Texas; two nephews, Tom Marion of Kermit, Texas and Glen Marion of California, and two grandchildren.

---

Below: Jack Johnson's World War I registration form in 1918.

42-2-14-C

REGISTRAR'S REPORT

DESCRIPTION OF REGISTRANT

| HEIGHT | | | BUILD | | | COLOR OF EYES | COLOR OF HAIR |
|---|---|---|---|---|---|---|---|
| Tall | Medium | Short | Slender | Medium | Stout | | |
| 21 | 22 X | 23 | 24 | 25 X | 26 | 27 Brown | 28 Black |

29 Has person lost arm, leg, hand, eye, or is he obviously physically disqualified? (Specify.)

30 I certify that my answers are true; that the person registered has read or has had read to him his own answers; that I have witnessed his signature or mark, and that all of his answers of which I have knowledge are true, except as follows:

E. A. Wright

Date of Registration Sept-12-1918

Local Board
Grayson County No. 2
Denison, Texas

(STAMP OF LOCAL BOARD)

REGISTRATION CARD

SERIAL NUMBER 3545 ORDER NUMBER 1954

1 Jack Johnson

2 PERMANENT HOME ADDRESS: Route 2 Pottsboro Grayson Texas

Age in Years 3 33 Date of Birth 4 Oct 11th 1884

RACE

| White | Negro | Oriental | Indian Citizen | Indian Noncitizen |
|---|---|---|---|---|
| 5 | 6 X | 7 | 8 | 9 |

U. S. CITIZEN / ALIEN

| Native Born | Naturalized | Citizen by Father's Naturalization Before Registrant's Majority | Declarant | Non-declarant |
|---|---|---|---|---|
| 10 X | 11 | 12 | 13 | 14 |

15 If not a citizen of the U. S., of what nation are you a citizen or subject?

PRESENT OCCUPATION 16 Farmer

EMPLOYER'S NAME 17 Self.

18 PLACE OF EMPLOYMENT OR BUSINESS: Route 2 Pottsboro Grayson Texas

NEAREST RELATIVE 19 Name Lillie M. Johnson 20 Address Route 2, Pottsboro Grayson Cnty

I AFFIRM THAT I HAVE VERIFIED ABOVE ANSWERS AND THAT THEY ARE TRUE

P. M. G. O. Form No. 1 (Red) Jack his mark Johnson

Myrtle Morrison Johnson, daughter of Charley Morrison, used to make a living by doing people's ironing, taking in sewing, and was a Nanny for the Guilloud family. When Myrtle's husband Jack Johnson died in 1958, it was only Myrtle there until she died at age 86 in 1973. Lots of people here today still remember Myrtle. By the time Myrtle was old, some in the Guilloud family (Laverne) looked after her and she gave her land to them. She and Jack are buried in the black section across the road at Georgetown Cemetery.

1. PLACE OF DEATH a. COUNTY GRAYSON; b. CITY OR TOWN DENISON; c. LENGTH OF STAY 1 month; d. NAME OF HOSPITAL OR INSTITUTION MADONNA HOSPITAL

2. USUAL RESIDENCE a. STATE TEXAS b. COUNTY GRAYSON; c. CITY OR TOWN POTTSBORO; d. STREET ADDRESS ROUTE 1 Pottsboro, Texas

3. NAME OF DECEASED MYRTLE NMI JOHNSON; 4. DATE OF DEATH JULY 3, 1973

5. SEX FEMALE; 6. COLOR OR RACE NEGRO; Widowed X; 8. DATE OF BIRTH APRIL 29, 1887; 9. AGE 86

10a. USUAL OCCUPATION HOUSE WIFE; 10b. KIND OF BUSINESS OR INDUSTRY DOMESTIC; 11. BIRTHPLACE TEXAS; 12. CITIZEN OF WHAT COUNTRY U.S.A.

13. FATHER'S NAME CHARLIE MORRISON; 14. MOTHER'S MAIDEN NAME LUCY ( UNKNOWN )

15. WAS DECEASED EVER IN U.S. ARMED FORCES? NO; 16. SOCIAL SECURITY NO. 405-64-7435; 17. INFORMANT LAVERNE L. GUILLOUD, FRIEND

TEXAS DEPARTMENT OF HEALTH REC'D AUG 8 1973 BUREAU OF VITAL STATISTICS

IMMEDIATE CAUSE Cardiac arrest; DUE TO Bed Rest; Parentia Leiomorrne

# THE OLD BLACK CEMETERY AT GEORGETOWN

This cemetery is located directly across the road from the large, main Georgetown cemetery on present day Cemetery Road. GPS N 33.78850 W 096.8766 There are many funeral home markers that are faded and unreadable and there may be many unmarked graves.

### Old-Time Man Dead - His Remains Properly Interred

Dallas Morning News 30 Aug 1904 - Pottsboro, Tex., Aug. 28 -- Andy Rice, born about 1849, an old-time colored man, who has lived here for twelve years, died Friday night. Andy Rice was formerly from McKinney and was but 55 years old. He was good friends of all people here, and they had the body embalmed, bought him a nice casket and will bury him using a hearse. **His white friends were going to bury him in the Georgetown Cemetery, but local landowner Captain William Sidney Grant gave the colored folks some of his land to start a separate cemetery. This was the beginning of the black cemetery at Georgetown.**

## Known burials at Georgetown's black cemetery:

Rice, Andy 1849 26 Aug 1904

Bennett, S P 23 July 1876 15 August 1938

Johnson and Morrison family plot:

According to Georgetown resident James Clement, Jack Johnson used to walk from his and Myrtle's house on Reeves Road to help dig most of the graves at the Georgetown cemetery whenever there was to be a funeral.

In 1912-1916 I found a Jack Johnson that matches his description in prison at Huntsville TX for 2nd degree murder and he served his 5 yr sentence, not sure if it was him.

Johnson, Jack 15 October 1884 15 April 1958

Johnson, Myrtle 29 April 1886 03 July 1975

Morrison, Charley 15 September 1855 13 June 1935

Ring, Della 11 October 1874 31 December 1917

Ring, Della Texas Death Certificate Name : Dellar Ring

Birth : 11 October 1874, Texas female, Black, married

Father : Charlie Morrison, born Grayson Co. Mother : Lucy, born Tennessee

Death : 31 Dec 1917, Pottsboro, Texas Age : 42 years, 2 months, 20 days

Cause of death : tuberculosis Burial : 1 January 1918, Georgetown Cemetery

Brown family plot:

Brown, Aaron 17 September 1896 13 March 1962

Brown, Charlie 10 October 1905 14 August 1948

Brown, Infant 27 April 1940 05 May 1940

Brown, Josephine 24 July 1874 23 December 1941

Brown, Luther born 1900 12 Nov 1918 Died of Spanish Flu

Brown, William 15 June 1866 20 June 1964

**Right across the road from the Black Cemetery is the very old very large**

# GEORGETOWN CEMETERY

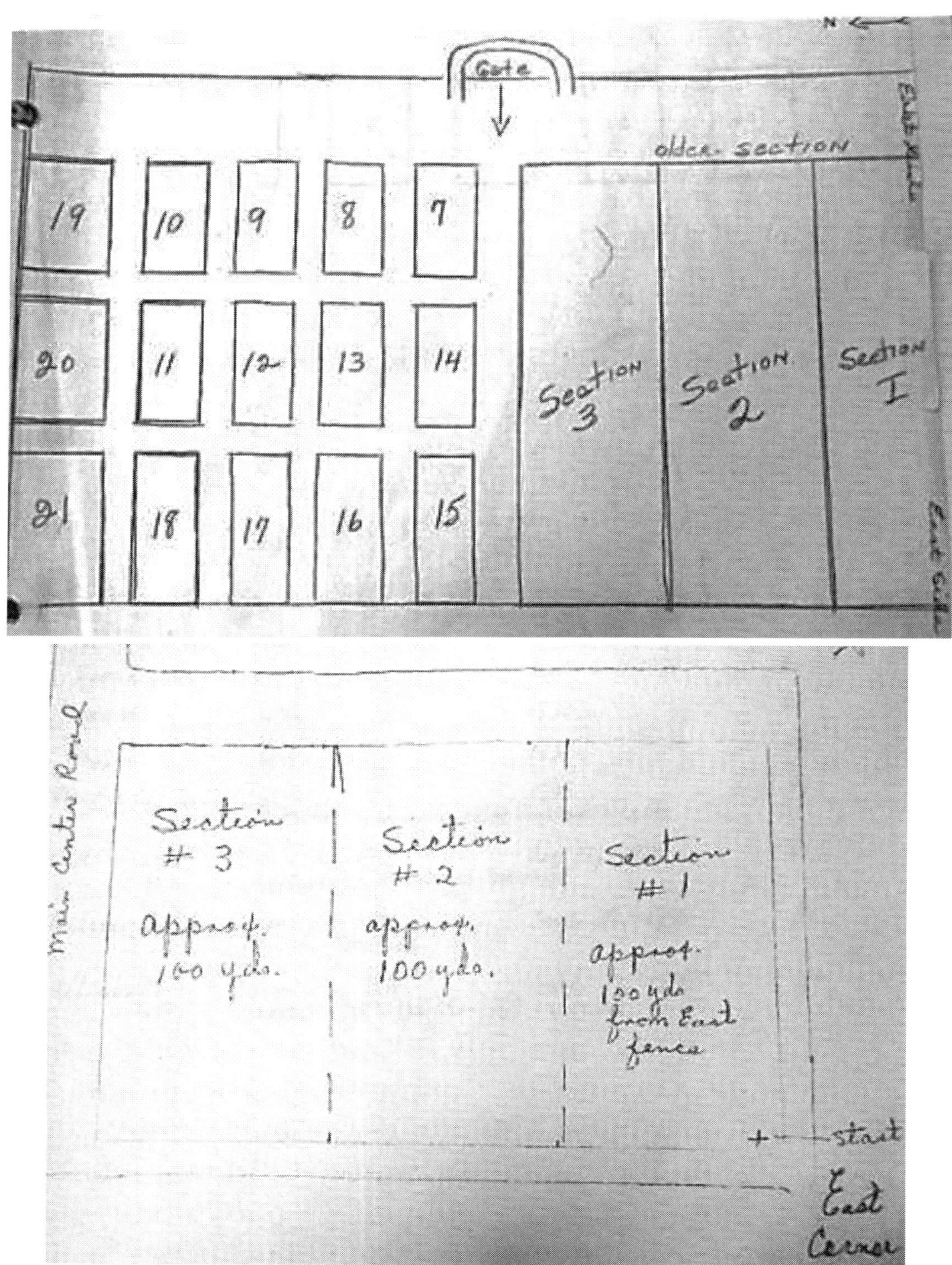

# GEORGETOWN CEMETERY – more than a cemetery

The Old Pioneer Cemetery (as it was referred to many years ago) on Cemetery Road north of Pottsboro is more than just a place to go when there is a funeral, although it is still used by most people in the area and still expanding.

First, it is living history. Land for the cemetery was contributed in about 1850 by early pioneer George R. Reeves. The oldest grave in Georgetown Cemetery is Mary T. Reeves, the daughter of J. R. and Jane Reeves, the granddaughter of George R. Reeves. She was buried on Reeves family land. She died January 8, 1850. George R. Reeves then donated four acres surrounding her grave for public use as a cemetery probably to make sure her burial ground would always be preserved and not ever forgotten in a pasture somewhere as many lone graves have been. She only lived about 2 ½ months, but she is still remembered today. The inscription reads: Mary T. Reeves 28 October 1849 - 8 January 1850 d/o J.R. & Jane Reeves "Erected by Georgetown Cemetery Assn in Memory of Mary T. Reeves, the First Person Buried in Georgetown Cemetery".

G. P. (Pat) Baker stands in 1973 with the tombstone and historical marker of George R. Reeves' grave.

There are many burials in this cemetery from the Reeves family from the 1860s, 1870s, 1880s including George R. Reeves himself.

There are probably MANY early burials here from the 1850s and subsequent decades before access to local tombstone providers was available which will remain unknown to us unless we find outside references to them. There are many burials in the old section of the cemetery where simple stones have been erected as headstones and markers, some with crude markings, some unmarked, but obviously placed. Some stones may have been moved, and we KNOW over the years some marked tombstones have been stolen (including some from my own relatives, so I know this to be true, NB).

One such stone which existed in 1973 which is still there and deeply embedded in the soil now is the one referred to in the Denison Herald article on August 19, 1973 pictured below. This appears to be a typo of the name and should be "Lucy A. Crabtree" who died in 1856 and was buried here with an ironstone rock as a marker with a carved inscription.

A native ironstone rock stone has the inscription carved in with a knife. It reads: "Lucy A. Crabee, age 24 years, 7 months, 14 days, A.D. 1856."

There are many interesting old burials here, and is even more interesting if you allow yourself to delve into their history. It is an interesting, peaceful park-like place to walk with large oak shade trees and plenty of old tombstones to view. Across the road is the historic old black cemetery on land donated by W. S. Grant, who is buried at Georgetown and whose tombstone is said to be the infamous "glowing tombstone". Second, it is a place to discover one's family history and a place to come to feel close to departed loved ones and friends and express our esteem. A full list of burials can be found now online at the Grayson County GenWeb by Elaine Bay. I have provided a list of burials to the local Pottsboro public library also, complete to the time of the printing of that book.

This cemetery is the showplace of Georgetown, a beautiful park. What more peaceful place could one want for a quiet walk in the woods, for exercise or calming reflection? There are many roads through it and the grounds are excellently maintained by those in charge of the cemetery.

**Simcox graves**

**Mrs. Mary Reeves**

The flat round top rock above is massive and looks to me to be a hard yellowish limestone rock that is so plentiful here. I personally took this picture a few years ago. I can see what is still visible above the ground says "Mrs. Mary Reeves. Mrs. Fritz Finke in 1973 was the secretary of the Georgetown Cemetery Association, and here she examines the two brick-covered Simcox graves dating back to 1886 in the old section of the cemetery. They are the only burials of this kind above ground in the cemetery.

# GEORGETOWN CEMETERY – THE HISTORICAL PARK

In the "Old Section" of the Georgetown Cemetery

There is an ancient and weather beaten old oak. (ca. 2014)

It has something to say if we will listen closely.........

## **"A Living Monument"** by Natalie Bauman

"Underneath my Tangled Branches;

Beside my Gnarled and Twisted Bark

Stand many Sentinels of the Past

Who bear Witness of Those long Gone.

Our Aged and Weathered faces, Scarred by Hardship,

Yet rendered Strangely Beautiful,

Much like the Beautiful Weathered Faces of those We Honor Here."

# THE OLD MAN OF THE CEMETERY By Natalie Bauman

I have always been fascinated by the old gnarled tree pictured below in the Georgetown Cemetery. It is a stand-out in a large cemetery absolutely full of large, old beautiful oak trees; the Grandfather of them all, carrying the scars of time. It didn't take too much imagination for me to see the majestic burl-y shoulders, the vigilant eyes, the prominent nose, the pensive lips and the strong chin, elongated by old age (or perhaps he grew a manly beard?. I wondered, how many years has this venerable guardian of the cemetery overseen the cycle of life played out at this place each day? This tree has weathered many storms, many invading insects, perhaps obstacles standing in the way of its growth (hence the burl-y shoulders – burl is a name for the rough growth on this tree). However, these trials, instead of making this tree ugly - its survival has made it unique, interesting and much more beautiful aesthetically than its more "normal" companions, or any young, straight, perfect sapling - at least in my opinion. Any wood worker will tell you, burled wood like that found on this tree, is beautiful and highly prized. In 2014, I was inspired to write the poem on the previous page about the tree because I was afraid it was approaching the end of even its long life.

Sadly, The Old Man of the Cemetery, ever reminded of the brevity of life, and the certainty of death by the silent monuments around him, quietly succumbed to old age and went the way of all the living. R. I. P. January 14, 2016 He is now gone, but not forgotten, and not without a monument among this land of monuments. His burly shoulders remain to remind us to overcome obstacles, persevere to the end and let those scars of adversity and wrinkles of old age make us unique, interesting and more beautiful than those not yet tried and tested by time.

# Glowing Tombstone of Georgetown Cemetery

A Ghost Towns book about Georgetown would not be complete without a story about the infamous Glowing Tombstone of Georgetown Cemetery and it is purported to be connected with the grave of Julia Grant, the wife of William S. Grant, whose life is discussed at length in the book.

The big black jack oak that was once next to the "glowing" stone has now been cut down. The picture below is taken from Cemetery road looking west in 2016, zoomed in.

I made a personal reconnaissance of the area. It looks like the glow may also have possibly come from similarly shaped nearby tombstones of Nancy Utter and J.W. & Mary Bradley, noted below. There is even an inscription on Mary Bradley's tombstone – "Passed through the golden gate into the beautiful shining land". However, it is more likely that the Grant stone is the luminous culprit because it has the smoothest, most polished surface of the three and would be more likely to reflect light (i.e. moonlight).

Photo above is taken from a different angle, and after a large tree near the glowing tombstone was cut down, but still looking west.

The inscription on Julia Ann Campbell Grant's obelisk shaped tombstone that she shares with three other family members, in itself, incites some fearful feelings, even without the light show at night. Julia, wife of W. S. Grant, was born in Anderson County, S.C., on March 27, 1843. She died on July 7, 1906, and was buried there next to her loved ones. Her tombstone reads, "Take warning by me young people as you pass by. Cast a glance at this and think as you are now, so once was I. But now I am lying in the cold, cold grave."

When the moon is bright, a glow can sometimes be seen from the road, radiating from the tombstone. This phenomenon has been scaring teenagers for decades and has become quite well known in the area. But **don't go into the cemetery at night** to investigate. It closes after dark and the glow is best seen from Cemetery Road anyway. Due to people vandalizing the cemetery, **trespassers** in the Cemetery at night **will be prosecuted**. Ghostly apparitions may not be the only ones watching!

It is up to you whether you believe that the smooth, polished finish of the tombstone is merely reflecting the moon light at the right time; or that a ghostly presence is shining a light, so that her message from the grave can be illuminated in order to be read at night, as well as in the day.

Grant tombstone from the road inside the cemetery on the south east side looking north. See the stump of the big black jack oak on the left.

## WILLIAM SIDNEY GRANT

In an earlier article about the Black Georgetown Cemetery, we learned that William S. Grant gave land for the people of color to have a proper burial place of their own across from the larger Georgetown Cemetery. W. S. Grant became a very prominent landowner in the community of Georgetown.

The father of W. S. Grant, William B. Grant, was born in 1809 in Union District, Spartanburg, South Carolina to Rev. Humphrey Grant and Elizabeth Bryant Grant. A few months before his marriage, on February 16, 1837, William Benton Grant purchased land from Amos Robinson. This land is in Northwestern Hall County Georgia near the Chestatee River in what is now the Cool Springs Community. It was there that William B. Grant and his wife Elizabeth raised their nine children. The land on which they lived, which was not flooded when Lake Sidney Lanier was built in the 1950's, is still in the Grant family.

William Sidney Grant was born on April 11, 1839. He was educated in what at that time was called a subscription school. The parents would get together in an area, select a teacher or teachers, then "subscribe" or pay the teacher the agreed upon amount for each pupil.

His family was engaged in farming, stock raising and merchandising. He followed this type work and met a pretty young girl named Julia Ann Campbell, daughter of Zilron and Jane McKinney Campbell. She had moved with her parents to North Georgia from Anderson, South Carolina where she was born on March 27, 1843. They were engaged to be married when he enlisted in 1861 in Company B, Fifth Arkansas Infantry Regiment where he advanced to the rank of Captain.

He fought in the Civil War battles of Chickamauga, Stone River, and Kennesaw Mountain near Marietta, Georgia where he was taken prisoner by a regiment of Illinois troops largely composed of miners who undermined the Confederate's position and blasted away their defenses. He was taken to a prison camp on the shores of Lake Michigan where he was almost starved and was nearly frozen during the bitter winter that followed.

During the time he was away Julia Campbell spun and wove her wedding dress. It was made of cotton and woven in a small plaid pattern in shades of blue and white with a tiny bit of red. The dress was lined with fabric woven in a stripe in shades of blue and gray.

William Grant returned to Georgia following the War Between the States. He and Julia Ann Campbell were married in Hall County, Georgia in 1865. She wore her pretty blue dress. It was her wish that the dress stay in the family a hundred years. She kept it as a dress for many years, then decided it could be more easily kept as a quilt; so one was made from the fabric. After her death in 1905, William Grant kept the quilt until 1914, when shortly before his death, he gave it to his great niece, Ruth Taylor. She kept the quilt until her death in 1977. It is now owned by her children: so Julia Grant's wish for the fabric to last a hundred years came true.

The South suffered greatly during and after the war and the economy was bad. Many families were large and there was not enough acreage to support so many children, especially many sons. Some people chose to leave and head West and Texas was thought of as the "Promised Land" where there were many free land grants available. Many people left during the post war era and marked the letters "GTT" on their doors. Everyone around knew that meant "Gone To Texas".

William and Julia Grant farmed in Lumpkin County, Georgia and their son, Egbert E. Grant was born there on August 8, 1866. When this child was six weeks old William and Julia Grant, her mother Jane Campbell and William's sister Amanda "Mandy" and her husband Lewis Keith left Georgia for Texas. This would have been about the middle of September 1866.

Photograph is of Julia and William S. Grant – courtesy of Barbara Kerby. 9/21/1865: Marriage to Julia Ann Campbell in Hall Co., GA.

They came by wagons, many times in areas where the roads were very poor and many of the bridges had been destroyed because of the war. They crossed the Mississippi River on a ferry. Julia Grant was an accomplished horsewoman and she brought her horse with her. When they had to ford a river, he would get the mules and wagons across, and she and the baby would ride her horse across. She trusted her horse more than she did his mules.

It is assumed Julia Grant's father Zilron Campbell died in Georgia prior to their leaving as there is no record of his being in Texas. He is not buried beside Jane Campbell in Georgetown Cemetery in Grayson County, Texas.

On reaching Texas, they came to the northern part of Grayson County of which Sherman is the county seat. They found land they liked in **Georgetown,** two miles north of where the town of Pottsboro now stands, though it did not exist at that time. The land they wanted had been filed on by a W. A. Watkins. William Grant contacted this man and he had found a place he liked better, but you could only file on one place. William Grant filed on a place which was north of Denison in the Rock Bluff area and the two men then traded claims.

There was a one room house on this land which had been built by the drovers who would camp there and hold their cattle near a spring which was nearby. This house had a fireplace, dirt floor, wooden bunks, and wooden shutters on the open windows. But it afforded comfort and shelter after being in the wagons and camping by the trail for so many days.

The Lewis Keith family settled on land west of Sherman and lived there a number of years but then moved back to Georgia.

By 1871, William B. "Buck" Grant, at age sixty-five, decided to go to Texas himself. He traveled by wagon to Gainesville, Georgia, then by train to Savannah. From Savannah he took a boat around Florida into the Gulf of Mexico. After entering Texas around Galveston, he traveled up through East Texas to Grayson County to visit his son and daughter and their families.

The trip was long and tiring. Somewhere along the way he contracted yellow fever. By the time he reached Texas he was very ill. He hoped he would recover once he arrived at his daughter's home. But he only weakened. Finally he was taken to the home of his son, **William Sidney Grant, at Georgetown, north of the new settlement of Martin Springs, a few years before the establishment of Pottsboro.** They had a spring there at his home, and hopefully the cool spring water would be just what he needed, plus they wanted him to be near Dr. Alexander Morrison who lived in the area. But he continued to decline, and on April 24, 1871 he died. It would have been virtually impossible to bring his body back to Georgia for burial, **so he is buried in the Georgetown Cemetery**. William Sidney Grant later died on December 01, 1914 and he and his wife Julia are also buried there at Georgetown.

William Grant wished to buy the acre of land on which the spring near their house was located. It was owned by James Ingram and he did not want a jog in his land line, so William bought a strip of land one acre wide and eleven acres long in order to obtain the spring. This land joined the one hundred and sixty acres he had gotten from W. A. Watkins on the south.

On the map see T. D. Marion's land at the top middle and W.S. Grant's land to the right of his and see the narrow strip of Grant's land that was 1 by 11 acres under Marion's land.

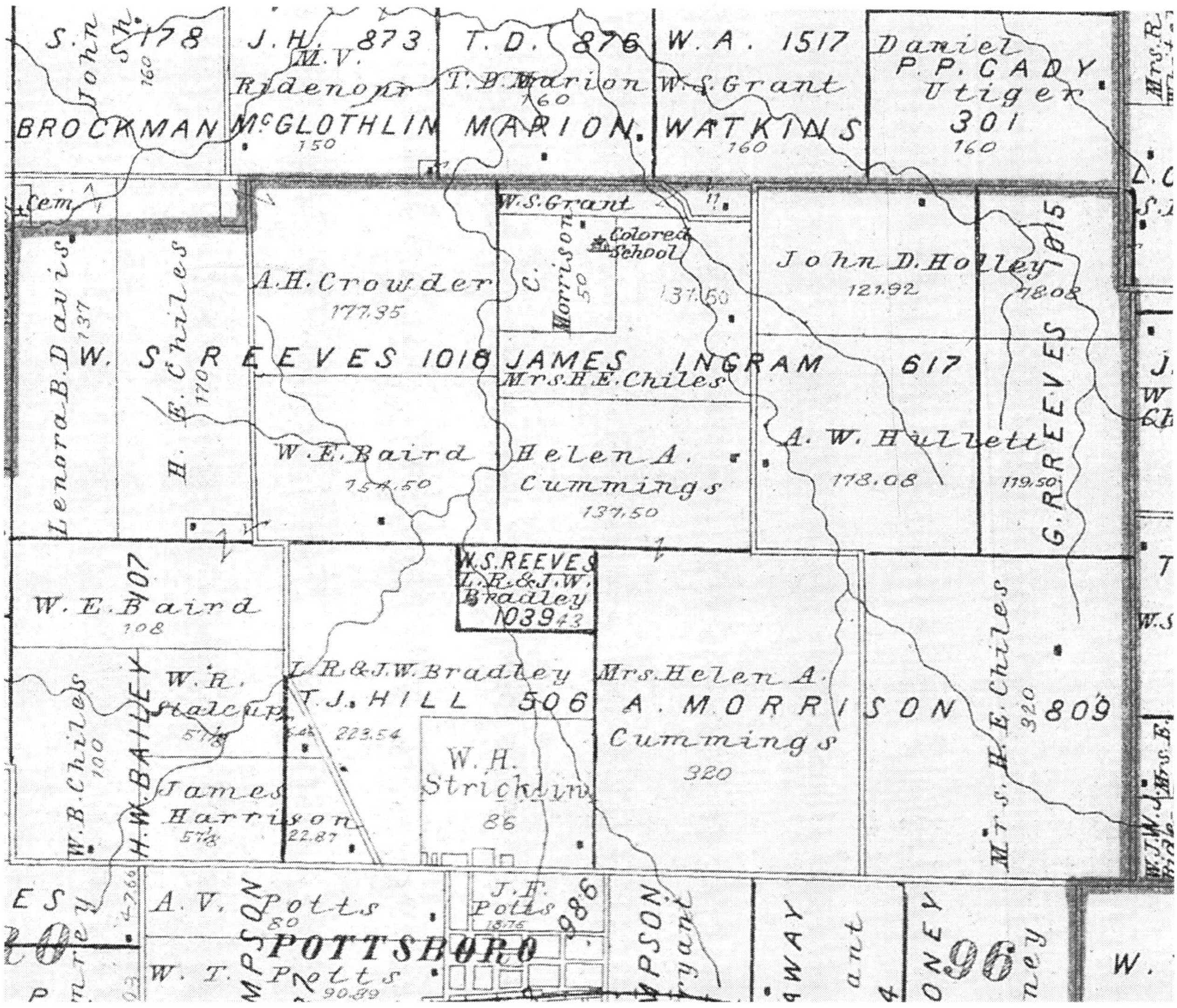


They broke the sod with oxen borrowed from a neighbor, T. D. Marion, because the plow to break the sod was too heavy for the mules to pull.

There were no suitable trees in this area, so all lumber had to be hauled from Jefferson, Texas which was in East Texas one hundred and fifty miles away near the Louisiana line. The trees in east Texas are straight pines, the trees here were knobby and crooked. If you try to build a cabin out of logs that aren't straight, there will be very large gaps in between them, too large to be practically filled with mud to keep out moisture and wind. The smooth, straight pine logs made for thinner gaps in between and less air leakage and required less filler. As soon as possible, they hauled the lumber and built a house just north of where the present house now stood. This house had one large room, a side room, a fireplace and glass windows.

About this time, William Grant started a freighting business hauling merchandise to Sherman from Jefferson where boats could come up the river and land. He did this in order to pay for his land, which was seven dollars per acre to be paid to the state.

Shortly after this, he built another house identical to theirs just east of his house for J. D. Holley and his wife Sarah, "Sally". They were not related, but John Holley was a carpenter and stone mason, and he had claimed land next to the Grant land which later was known as the Wall farm. He could also be near so Julia Grant and her mother would not be alone while William Grant was away on the freighting trips which took about six weeks.

Residence of J. D. Holley.

In March of 1889 while William Grant was away on one of these trips, a relative of theirs whose name was Smith had stopped there en route to the land rush in Oklahoma. He had cleaned his gun, went outside and shot it to see if it was all right. It was very windy and shortly afterward, it was discovered that the top of the house was burning. They never knew if it was set from wadding from the gun or if a spark from the fireplace set it. They were unable to save much, but Julia got out with the quilt made from her wedding dress.

When William Grant returned and saw his home in ashes, the first words he said were, "Did you save my old gray Confederate cap?" Unfortunately, they had not been able to do so. That cap was highly treasured and he never forgot what it stood for.

They stayed in the house with the Holleys until lumber could be hauled from Jefferson to build another house. This house was built in the latter part of 1889 so they could be in it by winter. A well was dug which was on the back porch and was much more convenient than carrying water from the spring. These two rooms are now the south two rooms of the present house.

He acquired cattle and land and horses, and sometime around 1890 a flood in Preston Bend on the Red River caused it to change its course, and left some buildings damaged and abandoned. One of these was a saloon made of oak logs. He bought the logs and moved it to his farm and made it into a barn. An unusual feature of the saloon was a fireplace in the side of the wall rather that the end.

As he acquired more cattle, William Grant, along with two neighbors, Will and Ben Holder, started taking their herds up through Indian Territory which was later Oklahoma. They would drive them through good grass letting them fatten along the way. They would then take them to Fort Sill where the cattle would be sold to the government for food for the soldiers and Indians there.

Many years later the great nephew of Will and Ben Holder married the great niece of William S. Grant. They were Ernest Guilloud, Jr. and Julia Ann Taylor (who related some of this story). The mother of Julia Grant lived with William and Julia until her death. She was Jane C. Campbell nee McKinney. She was born in Anderson County, South Carolina August 9, 1816 and died February 17, 1880 in Grayson County, Texas. She is buried in the Georgetown Cemetery.

Toward the early part of the eighteen eighties, a severe drought hit Grayson County leaving no grass and little water for the cattle, so the family moved to Wise County and bought land near Decatur, Texas. Egbert Grant finished school there and fell in love with a beautiful classmate whose name was Eva Hart. By 1886, the rains had come back to Grayson County so the family sold the land in Wise County and moved back to their Home in Grayson County. In the meantime, Eva Hart's family and a group of people from Decatur had moved to Ellensburg, Washington Territory to homestead. Most of these people were former neighbors and friends of the Grant family, including Will Wallace who had been a foreman on William Grant's Decatur ranch.

In July 1887, Egbert Grant left Grayson County by train to go to Ellensburg, Washington to claim Eva Hart as his bride; on August 1st after three days and nights he reached his destination on the morning of his wedding day. The Harts had invited all the people who had come up from Wise County and they were to have the wedding dinner at noon, the wedding at 3:00 P.M. Will Wallace was to be the best man. When everyone was seated at the table, and with Eva at his side, Egbert Grant fell back in his chair and died with a heart attack. That was August 1, 1887, seven days before his twenty-first birthday. He was buried in Ellensburg, Washington Territory. Will Wallace handled all the funeral arrangements.

William Grant bought another farm northwest of his original one hundred and sixty acres at Spout Springs and some town lots in Pottsboro, Texas. He raised horses, cattle and hogs and was interested fruit trees, berries, and grapes. His wife Julia had many flowers. W.S. Grant bought a small place west of Georgetown which included a spring called Stout or Spout Springs because of a spring that ran out of a stone wall. In his older years he especially enjoyed his gardening and grape vines on this place. There are still many wild grape vines growing in this area to the modern day, perhaps descendants of the root stocks he planted.

Denison Daily Herald April 13, 1908 & Sunday Gazetteer March 8, 1891

W. S. Grant, a well-known farmer of near Pottsboro, spent several hours in the city yesterday on a visit to friends. Mr. Grant is a candidate for the legislature from Grayson County and in speaking of his race yesterday said: "I am for fewer laws and more common sense ones. I would work for the interest of Grayson County and the State in general by urging a bill exempting all new enterprises such as cotton factories from paying taxes for a period of ten years."

Monday night the home of Mr. and Mrs. W. S. Grant was the center of attraction for a score or more of happy young people. The gathering was in the nature of a reception extended Miss Mamie Grant, who had just returned home from an extended visit among friends and relatives in Illinois. Elegant refreshments were served; parlor games, music and recitations filled to repletion the evening hours. Those present were: Misses Anna Mixson, Maude Overaker, Rachael Dickerson, Etta Dickerson, Pearl Nicewarner, Lillian Eskew, Lena and Maggie Whiteacre and Miss Levey. Messrs. Ed Burget, Chas. Mayfield, Harry Phillips, Chas. Muggard, Frank Galvin, Dick Jarvis, John and Allen Whiteacre.

W.S. Grant was a delegate to the county Democratic Convention more than once. Grant Was Candidate for Legislature Denison Daily Herald April 8, 1908

## CAPT. W. S. GRANT.

In response to a largely signed petition of his neighbors and friends in north Grayson County, Capt. W. S. Grant has consented to become a candidate for the Legislature from Grayson County in Class Two, and it is with genuine pleasure that we present his name to the Democracy of Grayson County for this important position.

Capt. Grant is a farmer, having come to Texas from Georgia, the State of his birth, in 1867, and since which time he has lived in the northern part of Grayson County near Pottsboro, and has pursued the vocation of farmer and stockman. He is in no sense a politician, but is a sterling, old-fashioned Democrat. He has always fought in the ranks of Democracy, and has voted the ticket and fought the battles without wavering and without hope of reward, or desire for any reward.

Capt. Grant was a gallant Confederate soldier, having served the full four years in Patrick Cleburne's Division of the Tennessee army. His bravery, courage and devotion to the cause of the South is testified to by those who wore the Gray and fought with him during those trying times.

Capt. Grant was a gallant Confederate soldier, having served the full four years in Patrick Cleburne's Division of the Tennessee army. His bravery, courage and devotion to the cause of the South is testified to by those who wore the Gray and fought with him during those trying times.

Capt. Grant is a broad-guaged, level-headed, liberal-minded citizen. He is a reader and thinker, without polish, but big-hearted and big-brained, and is just the kind of man that North Grayson, or all of Texas, needs in Austin. He is without prejudice, represents no class or special interests. He is in full possession of his faculties and physical energy, with an honest, loyal Democratic heart, and we feel that Grayson County is to be congratulated on the opportunity of sending such a man to represent her and Texas in Austin. Honest, intelligent, patriotic and sure-footed on all Democratic questions, he represents the ideal type of a Texas Representative and old-time Democracy, and we commend him to the consideration of the Democratic voters of Grayson County.

W.S. GRANT Speaks At GOOD ROADS CONVENTION Sunday Gazetteer. (Denison, Tex.), February 5, 1905 - (Note: We are fortunate today in that we have excellent paved roads almost everywhere we want to travel. Even less than a hundred years ago here, this was not the case. My own mother, Florence Clountz, who lived in Georgetown, recalled the roads here in the 1920s and 30s were so deep in mud and red clay after a rain, travel in a car or even a wagon was impossible. Everyone out here in the country were very far away from any town and even school. Farmers in particular suffered because they couldn't get their goods to town to sell it before it spoiled.)

The opening number on the program was a piano duet by Mrs. T. J. Odell and Miss Lillian Royce, but they gave way to hear the views of a real farmer, a pioneer of Grason county, Capt. W. S. Grant, who, in spite of bad weather and worse roads, had come from his home 15 miles away to attend the convention. Capt. Grant has given the subject of good roads much thoughtful study and like the practical man he is, goes at once to the root of the whole matter, to the source from which the money neccessary to make good roads is to come. It is his belief that good roads can be secured only by cooperation among and the direct financial support of the people, and that no man is too poor to contribute something toward making them and be made the richer by the contribution. His idea is that the people of Grayson county can make macadamized roads across the county,

Capt. W. S. Grant, an old Texan and farmer living north of Pottsboro, came fifteen miles to attend the Good Roads convention. He is an enthusiast for good roads in Grayson county. He also attended the Sherman convention Thursday.

Capt. W. S. Grant, of Pottsboro, an old confederate veteran, a sterling democrat, and one of the GAZETTEER's oldest friends and patrons, left last Monday for several months' tour in the Southwest, for improved health and recreation. He will be absent several months and will visit California, the State of Washington, Idaho, and points in Canada before his return. The GAZETTEER wishes its old friend bon voyage.

1905, 1906

**Below: William S. and Julia Grant - Right: Julia ALICE McKinney Helvey Grant**

Below: **Henry and Marie Guilloud and Family**

– Henry came from Azenge Switzerland in the 1880s. Marie came from Lyss, Switzerland. Interestingly, they were married on Apr 21, 1890 in Georgetown, Williamson County Texas, and moved to Grayson County Texas in 1897 and ended up in, where else – Georgetown. Children: Henry Jr, Lee, Ernest, Marie, Fred, Sam H, Todd

Georgetown 1910 Census showing Henry Guilloud family from Switzerland and speaking French in house 145 living close to Holley and Taylor in house 146 & 131 on Pearce Dr. According to information from Linda Taylor Guilloud Thurston and Lila Guilloud Schnitker provided to the Grayson County history book compiled by the Frontier Village, the Guillouds first lived north of Denison and Henry worked for the railroad. Then the Guillouds moved to the Georgetown area on Pearce Drive and raised cotton, corn, hogs and chickens. They milked cows and made their own cheese. They would haul these products into town on a two wheel hack drawn by mules until 1916. Life was not easy. People used to come by their house with rabbits they would trade so Mrs. Guilloud would fix them a home cooked meal. Many times at Christmas, the children didn't get such things as toys, they received practical gifts like a shirt or some ducklings. She said that at cotton picking time, the Guilloud men would spend the night in their covered wagon out in the cotton field with their BB guns to keep people from stealing the cotton they had picked that day, since each bale was worth $50. (I guess times haven't changed that much after all!) Another source of income for the Guillouds, and many others, was hunting and trapping for hides. They would skin the hides and hang them on the wall to dry and sell them. They got $1.50 each for skunks (the blacker the fur, the more it was worth), possums and rabbits only brought 15 cents. They sold live horned toads to help catch insects in people's gardens for 15 cents a pair.

(Too bad we don't have any of them left around here anymore, there are still plenty of bugs in my garden to feed an army of horned toads!). In 1946, the Guillouds moved west of Pottsboro to the old site of Martin Springs about where Guilloud Circle is today.

**Georgetown' s Taylor, Guilloud and Farrell Families closely linked to W. S. Grant family.**

Frances "Frank" Marion Farrell born April 13, 1857 married Martha Isabelle Waddle and had eight daughters:

Spouse and children

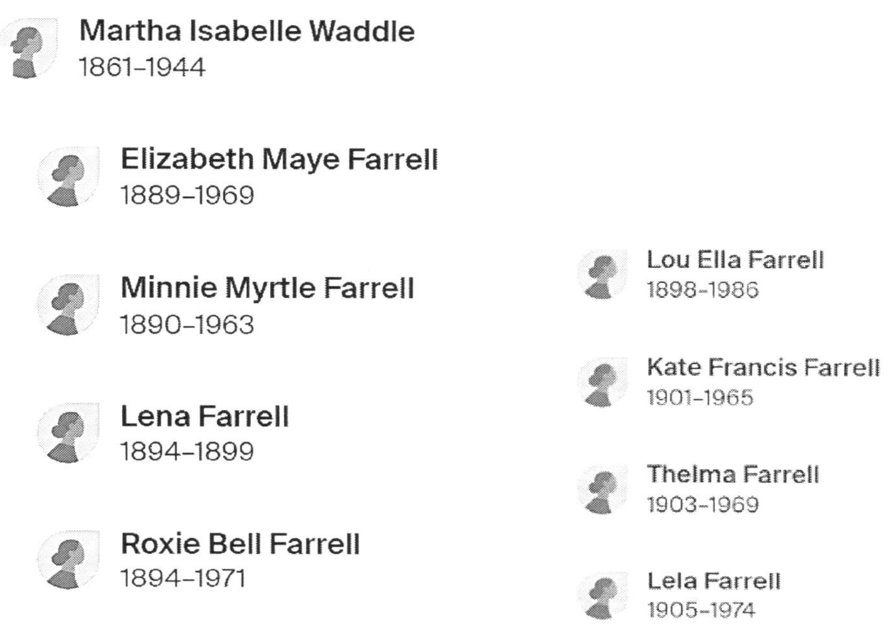


They moved to the Indian Territory and were often sick with fevers and malaria and had to take quinine every day to stay alive. Their daughter Lena died of strep throat in about 1898, so they decided to move to a better place like Texas before they all died, and they decided to stay in Georgetown. There they first rented the Grubbs farm in eastern Georgetown and that is where Luella was born. When Maye was 11 in about 1900, they moved to the Utiger farm in the adjoining Cashion community so the girls would be close enough to the Cashion school to attend. The Denison Daily Herald, on December 3rd, 1904 in the Cashion news section said Mr. Farrell moved from the Utiger farm to a farm west of Georgetown. Maye Farrell married James Homer Taylor in 1907. Minnie married Abner Allen, Roxie married Alex Christman with Justice McAden officiating. In 1917 the Farrells moved to farm the Christman place on the old Preston Road near Cashion School and stayed there a year. Then they moved to Sam Hull's farm just north and east of the Georgetown store where Ralph Finke later lived. At this time Kate Farrell married Lloyd Allgood and Kate worked for Ab and Minnie Allen in their grocery store at Fink. After this the Farrells moved to the Skaggs place north of Georgetown, then to a little square house on the west side of the road on the Coonrod place south of Georgetown. Lela/Lelia married Oliver Montgomery. At that time, the Farrells were older and went to live with Lelia and Oliver at the old George Hull place south of the Georgetown cemetery and then to the Lambert place south of Georgetown. Then to Maye Taylor's daughter's house – Julia Taylor Guilloud.

Obituary of Frank Farrell gives the married names of all his surviving daughters in Georgetown. Denison Press July 15, 1941

**F. M. FARRELL**

A resident of route 1, Pottsboro for 43 years, F. M. Farrell, 84-year-old farmer, died Monday afternoon at 1:35 at his home, following an illness of three months.

Funeral services were held this afternoon at 2:30 from Georgetown cemetery, Rev. G. W. Wall officiating. Interment was at Georgetown, Short-Murray directing.

Mr. Farrell was born in 1857, son of Mr. and Mrs. James Farrell of Cincinnatti, where he was born and reared. He went to Tennessee a young man, later to Fort Gibson, Indian Territory, where he resided until coming to the Pottsboro community in 1898. He was married to Miss Martha Waddle at Butlers Landing, Tenn., Jan. 29, 1888.

Surviving are his widow; seven daughters, Mrs. J. H. Taylor, Mrs. A. S. Allen, Mrs. Alex Christman, all of Pottsboro, Mrs. J. L. Allgood of Dorchester, Mrs. J. M. Stephens of Sherman, Mrs. Clifford Stephens of Tom Bean, Mrs. O. S. Montgomery of Denison, fourteen grand children and six great grand children.

# FINK, TEXAS.

Fink Texas, located near the old Preston Trail, was a "watering place" for cowboys traveling between Pottsboro and the Red River. Finke is a German name for bird we call a finch. The town of Fink, in the old days, was known as a German settlement. Fink was bypassed by the railroads, resulting in an early demise. The area was known as Georgetown and Reevesville since the 1840s. At the end of the 19th century, when the residents of Georgetown were petitioning to get a post office re-instated, Fred Finke was one of the petitioners. The post office was to be named Georgetown, but the post office department checked and discovered there was already a Georgetown, Texas - near Austin in Williamson County, which would cause too much confusion. German immigrant, Fred Finke owned a large amount of land in the town, so it was suggested that the post office be called “Finke” in his honor. He did not want to have the town named for him, so a compromise was made to drop the “e” and name the town and post office “Fink”, while the school and church kept the name Georgetown.

Denison Sunday Gazetteer April 10, 1904 - MAX BECK Store in Denison carried creamery butter from the German settlement at Fink Texas.

The original Georgetown school was located about a mile west of the present site of Fink. The old school was moved in 1927. The new school building was built just north of the Fink general store, and the old school building was moved to sit next to the Georgetown Baptist Church around 1950 where it stayed until it was sold and moved to Denison.

The fourth Thursday each June was National Fink Day. On this day a huge bonfire was lit in the shade of the Fink Horse Apple tree (bois d'arc). Fink Thursday is an attempt to restore honor and dignity to the name Fink. The town died out but was revived in the 1950s. The celebration included a gala golf tournament at Tanglewood Country Club.

Fink, Texas does not show up on every map. But it is marked on the official Texas Highways map. It is located on Hwy 289, three miles north of Pottsboro and ten miles northwest of Denison. Source : The Fantastic World of Fink by John Cliff, April 1972

Georgetown and Fink Stores: The first store was built in the mid 1800s by Mr Bilderback. Mr. James A. Porter also operated a grocery store there in Georgetown. Later it was operated by Mr. G. W. Bailey.

**SPECIAL SALE OF** Fruit and Shade Trees, Roses, Grape Vines, Shrubbery, Evergreens, etc., orchard size, trees, 25c. Roses 35c, Shrubbery 25c, Grape Vines 15c. Allen Brothers Nursery, Pottsboro, Texas. j31-12tp

The Allen Brothers Nursery had a store front in Georgetown, with the actual nursery being about a mile west on Allen's land north of the intersection of present day Squirrel Lane and Georgetown Road. A.S. "Abb" Allen bought the land with the original store building on it. Allen never liked the name "Fink." He had the name "Georgetown" written across the store front in foot-high, block letters. The Allen Brothers had a nursery, but at the same time that Allen Bro. shows up on the 1908 plat map at Fink, Ab Allen was also an agent for the nearby Texas Nursery Company.

Denison Daily Herald March 1, 1906 GEORGETOWN NEWS

Mrs. W. J. Bilderback spent Saturday and Sunday with her son, Sam Bilderback, at Preston.

Miss Minnie Lostic has accepted a position with Sidney R. Elkin of Denison.

Mr. and Mrs. Mack Jones went to Denison Saturday.

Ab Allen has resumed his duties as agent for the Texas Nursery Company.

# Stores at Fink

.....W. S. Grant, James Homer Taylor and John D. Holley

W. S. Grant later sold this small place to James Homer Taylor.

At some time about 1889 or 1890, W.J. Taylor and George Cantrell, son and son-in-law of Millie Grant Taylor, sister of William Grant, came to Grayson County to visit and to see if they wanted to move to Texas. They visited with the William Grants and since they were from Gainesville, Georgia they went to Gainesville, Texas but did not like to country, so they returned to Georgia. W. J. Taylor lived in Georgia the rest of his life, but George and Mandy Taylor went on to Montana and made their home and raised their family there. In the fall of 1896, William and his wife Julia returned to Georgia with a twofold purpose: they wanted to visit their families and to find a young man who would be related to them, would come to live with them and on whom they could depend to help care for livestock, farm and be a part of their family. After visiting several days, they went to the home of Henry and Millie Grant Taylor. Millie Taylor was William Grant's sister. There were five Taylor children: Mary Amanda, William Jefferson "Jeff", James Homer, Mattie Jane and Louella "Cooney".

At this time **James Homer Taylor was twenty years old and working at a cotton gin for Dr. Charles Thompson.** When he returned from work that afternoon, William Grant and Henry Taylor were standing on the front porch. He met his uncle and went inside to meet his aunt. She stood up, took one look at him and ran from the room crying. She later said it was just as if her son and walked back into the room and her son had been dead for almost ten years. She loved him as a son from that day until the day she died. After consulting with his parents, they asked him to come to Texas to work for them and he did in December 1896. He lived with them working at breaking horses, hauling grain and helping with the cattle until 1904 and although he continued to make his home with them **he bought a cotton gin at Fink, Texas and a grocery store. John D. Holley was co-owner of the gin for a number of years, then sold his part to James Homer Taylor who ran it for years.** The store was co-owned by Wallace Cannon, a cousin from Georgia, Homer then bought his part and Wallace Cannon went to Montana.

**In May 1906, the Denison Herald said J. W. Bilderback purchased the grocery stock of James Homer Taylor.**

A Look at 1908 town of Fink on the Grayson County Plat Map with J. W. Bilderback grocery store, Allen Bros. Nursery, Bailey's Grocery, Holley & Taylor cotton Gin, Marion & Bilderback store, C. B. Williams and H. C. Mercer: This intersection can be seen today located at intersection Hwy 289 and Georgetown Rd/Spur 406.

**1908 map of Georgetown/Fink showing location of Holley & Taylor & 1904 picture of gin**

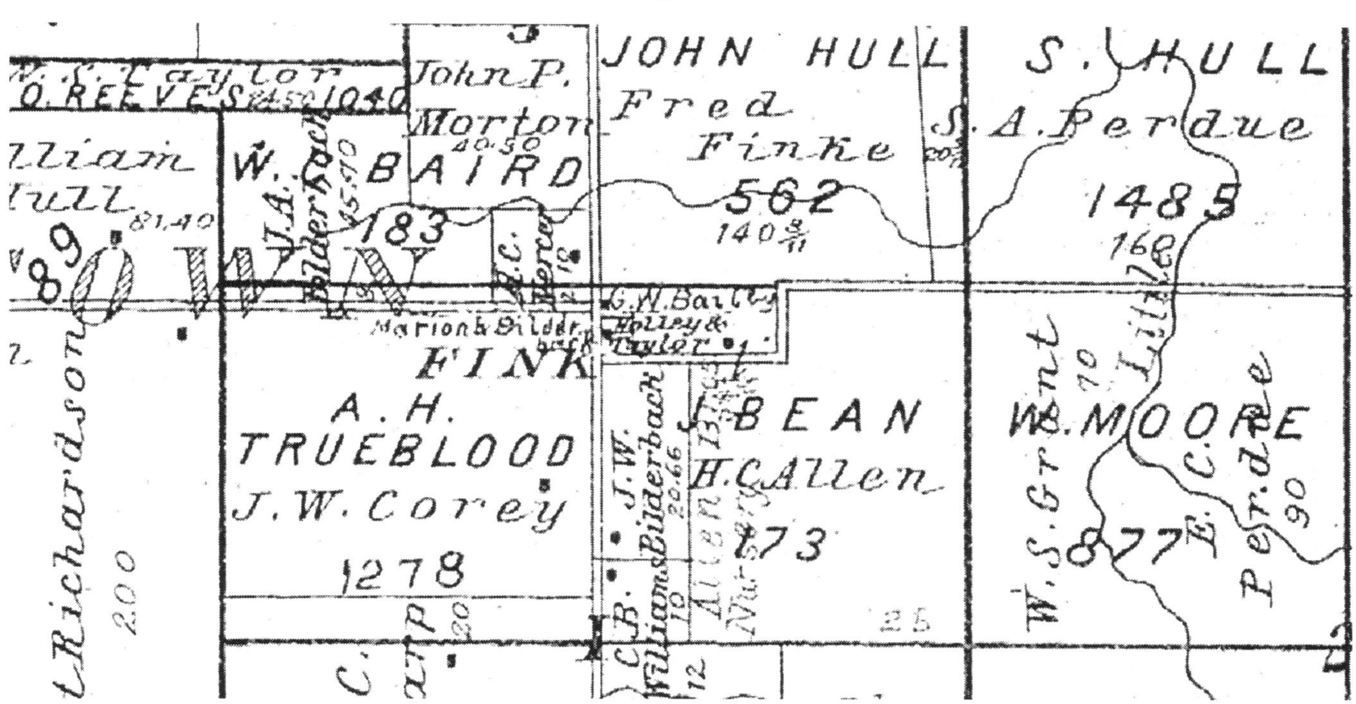

**Cotton Gin of Holley and Taylor at Georgetown in 1904**

Julia Grant became very ill in 1905. She died July 7, 1905. For a story about the "glowing tombstone" at the Georgetown Cemetery possibly being Julia Grant's stone, see stories about the Cemetery. W. S. Grant's land in the town of Fink/Georgetown was immediately to the right/east of the section shown above. After Julia Grant's death, William Grant and James Homer Taylor continued to make their home together and in 1906 in order to keep a promise made to Julia Grant, the two of them made a trip to Ellensburg, Washington. A small marker had been placed at Egbert Grant's grave, but she wanted a better one and had made them promise to go do it, so they did. En route to Washington, they went to San Francisco and arrived just a few hours before the devastating earthquake which leveled most of the city. They were uninjured, but had to remain there for days before transportation was available for them to leave. They then went to Ellensburg WA to have the tombstone made and visited in the home of Eva Hart, Will Wallace and other friends from Decatur. Next they went to Seattle and on to British Columbia, then came back to Missoula, Montana where they visited relatives. They next went to Yellowstone Park where they camped out for a week, then to Kansas City to a cotton ginner's convention and came home.

J. A. Porter has been repairing his store building the past week.

Capt. J. C. Sharpe, who has been very low, is some better at this writing.

Captain W. S. Grant and Homer Taylor returned last week from a two months' visit in the Northwest.

Vance Sharp of Wynnewood, I. T., who has been at the bedside of his father, has returned home.

Ernest and Ab Allen will leave this week for a six weeks' trip through Oklahoma, New Mexico and Western Texas.

Denison Daily Herald March 2, 1906

James Homer Taylor was born in Georgia Sep. 25, 1875, and came to Georgetown at age 21 to work for his uncle and aunt W. S. and Julia Grant who were here since 1866. In 1907 James Homer Taylor married Elizabeth "Lizzy" Maye Farrell, daughter of Frank and Martha Waddle Farrell of Georgetown. They were married by W. H. McAden, Justice of the Peace in Pottsboro on December 3, 1907. Their attendants were Bill Cantrell and Ava Holley. James and Maye Taylor made their home with William Grant after they married. **Taylor and John Holley became partners in a business together at Georgetown, the Taylor and Holley cotton gin.** Taylor also owned a grocery store in Georgetown at the turn of the century. There were two at that time and his was on the west side of the road. William's wife Julia died in 1906 of cancer. He then married Julia **Alice** McKinney Helvey for whom he named the **Alice Hotel.** William Grant owned some town lots in Pottsboro and built a hotel there which was called the Alice Hotel and they made their home there. The two-story Alice Hotel was located north of the depot on the east side of the street. He had two other town lots there. One was a grocery store, and a blacksmith shop in the other. This marriage did not work out and when William Grant's health began to fail, he returned to the farm and lived with James Homer and Lizzy Maye Taylor until his death in December 1914. Prior to his death, William Grant had sold the northwest farm to Bill Cantrell. He deeded eighty acres of the W. A. Watkins survey, eleven acres of the James Ingram survey, and the two lots in Pottsboro to James Homer Taylor. He gave the north eighty acres of the W, A, Watkins survey and the Alice Hotel to his wife, Alice Helvey Grant. She kept the property until her death, and it became the property of her son, Loy Helvey of Howe, Texas. He sold the hotel to Bill Wilson about 1933, and it was torn down and the lumber was used to build a house on the Wilson farm, southwest of Pottsboro. He kept the eighty acres of land until his death, and was then owned by his only child, Wanda Helvey. **In 1922 a fire destroyed the grocery store and blacksmith shop along with most of the buildings on the west side of the street in Pottsboro. Several years later James Homer Taylor sold these lots to Issac Clements and E. P. Crowder (who lived in Georgetown). Part of the trade to E. P. Crowder included a Model T Ford.**

James Homer and Maye Taylor continued to live at the William Grant home place until his death on April 23, 1949. Maye Taylor lived there until September 1967 when a stroke caused her to go the Dalhart, Texas where a daughter, Julia Guilloud, lived. She died there on July 22, 1969. After her death the farm was owned by her daughters, Ruth Taylor Waldrop and Julia Taylor Guilloud. Julia Taylor married Ernest Guilloud. Ruth Waldrop died September 10, 1977, and the land was owned by her five children James D. Waldrop, George A Waldrop, John T. Waldrop, Janell Martin, and JoAnn Stanberry. In May 1980 Julia Guilloud sold her surface interest in the farm to JoAnn and Lonnie Stanberry. This farm has been in the family since 1866, and the home of William and Julia Grant was then occupied by their great, great niece, JoAnn Stanberry and her husband, Lonnie. James Taylor was a happy out-going person who loved people. Maye Farrell Taylor was a conservative dresser, favoring starched aprons and bonnets with no jewelry except little pins. Most of her life she weighed all of 89 pounds until later in life when she rose to 120. She had borne a heavy burden of losing several children at birth or soon after.

The information for this article had been compiled from recollection of events as told by James Homer Taylor, records from Grayson County Census 1836-1969, Biographical Souvenir of the State of Texas, Illustrated History of Grayson County, Texas and the family Bible of William and Julia Grant and stories from Julia Taylor Guilloud.

# The Porter Family

James A. Porter had a grocery store in Fink for a few years in the early 1900s which George W. Bailey bought from him. In the 1930s, Abb Allen had the same store location as Porter and Bailey and was only grocery store left at Georgetown at the time.

Denison Daily News, July 20, 1906 - Georgetown News - The recent rains will ensure a good corn crop in this neighborhood. June corn is doing nicely. Threshing has commenced in this community and the grain crop will be fair. **James A. Porter has been repairing his store building** this past week **at Georgetown** after the storm.

James Porter settled at Fink and opened a grocery store before the turn of the twentieth century for a few years, which he sold to George Washington Bailey. After this, Porter moved to Oklahoma, continuing in the grocery business. Albert Sidney "Abb" Allen took over this grocery store from Bailey in about 1919.

Below, Porter family information from Porter descendants: Dr. Frank W. Porter of Ohio and Arthur F. "Fred" Porter currently from Indiana. - James Porter [1781-1830] and Susannah Elizabeth Keith [1772-1853] lived in Grayson County, VA. The death certificate of their son James Porter [1803-1874] identified his parents as James and Susannah. James and his parents lived along Elk Creek. James' father died in 1830. In the inventory of his father's estate are the names of his children: Alexander (1800), James (1803), Elizabeth (1805), George (1803) and William (1809). Elizabeth married Thomas Carr. She died on March 25, 1886 and is buried at the Cross Roads Primitive Baptist Church Cemetery in Grayson County, Va. Alexander married Sarah Roberts. Their children were: Elizabeth Porter 1829; William Creed Porter 1830–1907; Lydia Porter 1835; Andrew Jackson "Jack" Porter 1838–1921. Alexander eventually moved to Granby, MO. Sarah had passed away in 1852 in Grayson County, Virginia. In 1860, Alexander was living with his son, William Creed, in Granby. He died in 1860. William married Margaret Bedwell. Both William and Margaret are also buried in Grayson County, in the Old Bethel Church Cemetery. After Alexander passed away in Granby, MO, one of his sons, William Creed Porter, moved his wife and family to Grayson County, TX, where he served as a constable for 30 years and owned a hotel, The Pacific House, also known as The Creed Porter hotel. Creed is also believed to have built the first dwelling to exist in Pottsboro, TX. Creed and his wife, Thursie, are buried in the Georgetown Cemetery in Grayson County, TX. Creed had a long and colorful history and life in Grayson County, TX. According to his obituary, Creed, served three years in the Civil War. Another of Alexander Porter's children, William Creed Porter's brother - Andrew Jackson "Jack" Porter married Lucinda Catherine. Their children were Harvey Lewis Porter 1858–1913; James Leeson Porter 1866–1955; James Alexander Porter 1868–1950; S.S.B. "Sallie" Porter 1873–1892 and Floyd Arthur Bud Porter 1878–1952. **James Alexander Porter** was the son of Andrew Jackson "Jack" and Kate Porter, born in Grayson County Virginia on May 25, 1868. He married Ettie E. Billings, born March 24, 1871 and had four daughters: Lillian, Ollie Mae, Sarah and Mineola. They moved from Elk Creek, Grayson County, Virginia, to the Pottsboro, Grayson County area in 1903 where James' uncle Creed Porter was already living. Creed owned a hotel in Pottsboro and was the area constable for many years. A relative, J.N. Porter, also had a very prosperous grocery store in Denison. Denison Sunday Gazetteer ad from 1883:

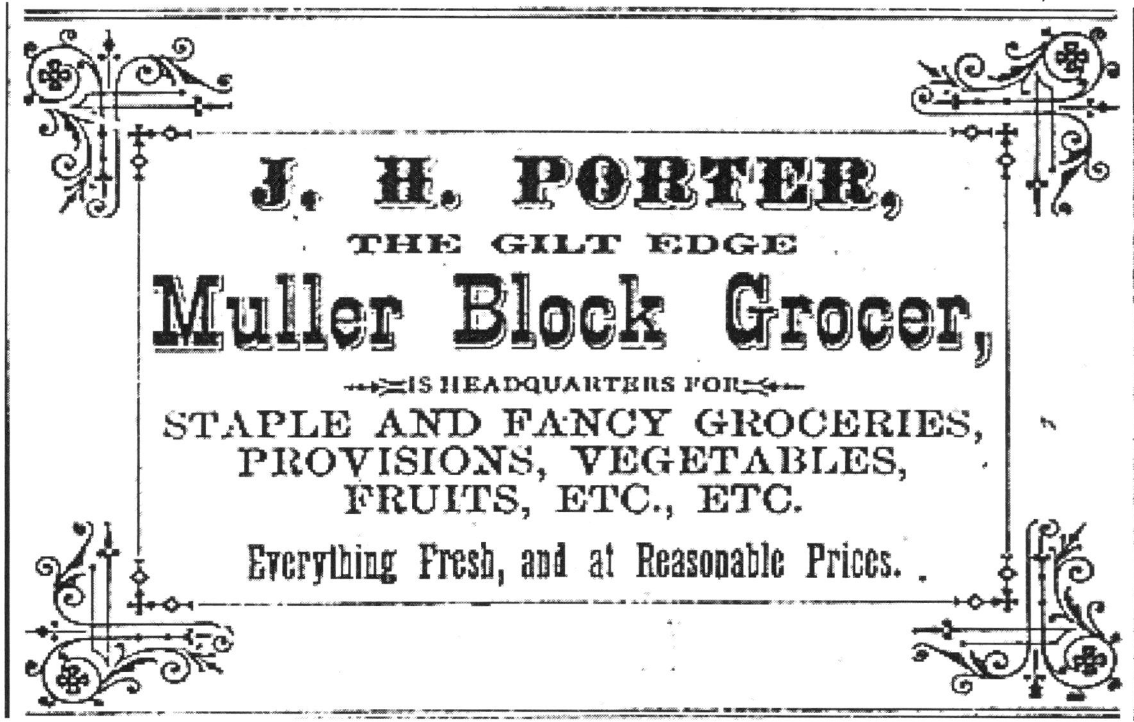


In the late 1860s or early 1870s - **W. J. Bilderback** opened a general store in Georgetown and the post office was in this store. Below: 1908 Grayson County Plat Map Bio page

Bilderback, S. F., Pottsboro, R. F. D. No. 3, Farmer, established 1907. Located in Grayson County 1879. Born on July 16, 1879, in Monroe County, Tennessee. Married on November 17, 1896, to Emma Beatty. Wife born December 12, 1879, in Alabama. Two children: one boy, Lloyd; and one girl, Ethel H. Pottsboro Pottsboro Precinct.

Bilderback, W. J., Pottsboro, R. F. D. No. 3. Grocery and Ex-Postmaster, established 1893. Located in Grayson County 1879. Born on October 11, 1840, in Monroe County, Tennessee. Married on August 9, 1859, to Louisa Elkins. Wife born June 12, 1839, in Roane County, Tennessee. Seven children: six boys, W. M., T. C., G. S., J. W., J. A. and S. F., and one girl, Jennie Ann. Pottsboro Precinct.

Bilderback, J. A., Pottsboro, R. F. D. No. 3, Farmer, established 1907. Located in Grayson County 1878. Born August 18, 1873, in Louden County, Tennessee. Married on November 30, 1898, to Miss Nannie Henderson. Wife born August 16, 1873, in Grayson County, Texas. Two children, Otis and Loyce. Pottsboro Precinct.

Bilderback, J. W., Pottsboro, R. F. D. No. 3, Farmer, established 1900. Located in Grayson County 1882. Born on June 6, 1870, in Louden County, Tennessee. Married on December 13, 1900, to Miss Carrie D. Sharp. Wife born on April 8, 1870, in Alexander County, North Carolina. Pottsboro Precinct.

Mr. and Mrs. J.W. Bilderback

## John Bilderback Follows Wife in Death at Georgetown

Friday, April 6, 1923 Dallas Morning News - April 5 – John Bilderback, 83 years old, died at his home near Georgetown community, west of Denison, this afternoon a short time after the death of his wife, who was 85 years old. A double funeral will be held for the couple at the home of their son, Sam Bilderback at the Georgetown community Friday afternoon. The couple had been residents of Grayson County for many years. They are survived by four sons and a daughter. Pneumonia was the cause of both deaths.

## ALLEN FAMILY of Georgetown

The Allen family had land at Fink, where their storefront for Allen Brothers Nursery and their grocery store was located. The article seems to place "Old Georgetown" at present day Fink. A March 2, 1906 article states "Pottsboro and the vicinity were visited Friday by one of the heaviest hailstorms that has fallen here in years. It was specifically severe about Georgetown and Fink." **It seems that at that time, the names Georgetown and Fink were being used separately in the same way that the Grayson County Plat Map two years later referred to the "business district" as Fink and the over-all area, or school district, as Georgetown.** Below: William Earnest Allen Dies May 28, 1930 Dallas Morning News

## Pottsboro Nurseryman Dies at Sister's Home

Special to The News.

SHERMAN, Texas, May 27.—W. E. Allen, 52, a Pottsboro nurseryman, died Monday of bronchial pneumonia while on a business trip to Tulsa, Ok., where he had nursery interests. The body was taken to the family home near Pottsboro, Grayson County, where funeral services were held Tuesday afternoon.

Mr. Allen was born Feb. 20, 1878. He is survived by his wife, Mrs. Edith Allen, and the following children: Mary, Lorene, Ruth, Hull, Dick and W. E. Allen Jr.; by three sisters, Mrs. Sam J. Hull and Miss Thelma Allen of Pottsboro and Mrs. Albert Burgess of Tulsa, in whose home he died, and three brothers, A. S. Allen, Pottsboro; Jack Allen, Wichita Falls, and James G. Allen of Henrietta. He was a nephew of Mrs. J. P. Wheat of Sherman and a cousin of George Stewart, Mrs. Clay Fitch and Miss Annie Stewart and Miss Bess Stewart of Sherman.

Sherman Daily Register July 21, 1900

**Miss Vella Stewart has gone on a visit to her aunt, Mrs. Clay Allen, at old Georgetown.**

Below: Abner Sidney Allen and his brothers below, picture from Jim Allen.

Henry Clay 1852
William Earnest 1879
Abner Sidney 1882
Jack Stetson 1889
James Grover 1892

The Allen Brothers

**William Earnest Allen was the brother of Abner Sidney Allen, known as "Abb", who owned the grocery store at Fink since 1919.**

## Abner Sidney Allen

BIRTH 17 JUL 1882 • Tuscaloosa, Tuscaloosa, Alabama, USA
DEATH 26 APR 1956 • Sherman, Grayson, Texas, USA

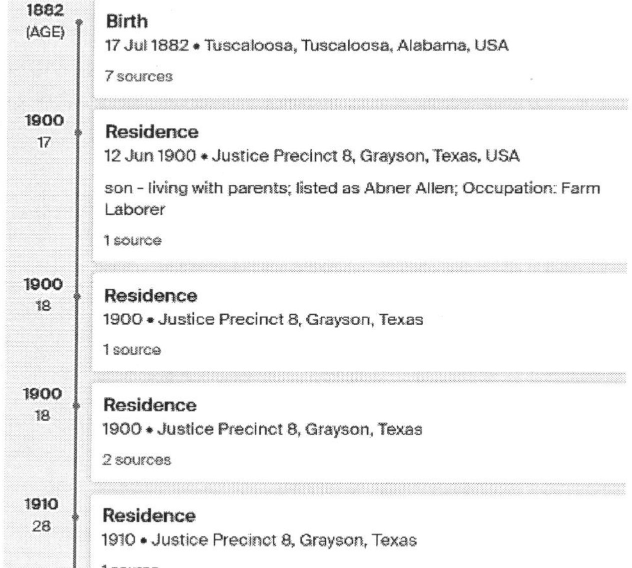

1882 (AGE) — **Birth**
17 Jul 1882 • Tuscaloosa, Tuscaloosa, Alabama, USA
7 sources

1900 17 — **Residence**
12 Jun 1900 • Justice Precinct 8, Grayson, Texas, USA
son - living with parents; listed as Abner Allen; Occupation: Farm Laborer
1 source

1900 18 — **Residence**
1900 • Justice Precinct 8, Grayson, Texas
1 source

1900 18 — **Residence**
1900 • Justice Precinct 8, Grayson, Texas
2 sources

1910 28 — **Residence**
1910 • Justice Precinct 8, Grayson, Texas

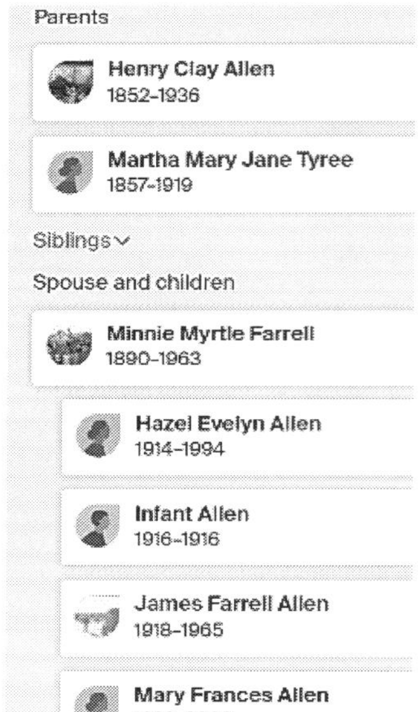

Parents

**Henry Clay Allen** 1852–1936

**Martha Mary Jane Tyree** 1857–1919

Siblings

Spouse and children

**Minnie Myrtle Farrell** 1890–1963

**Hazel Evelyn Allen** 1914–1994

**Infant Allen** 1916–1916

**James Farrell Allen** 1918–1965

**Mary Frances Allen** 1923–2020

### FAMOUS FINK HEADQUARTERS STARTED IN ALLEN'S GROCERY STORE

As stated earlier, Abb Allen's Grocery Store in Fink opened in 1919 and was in the same location as former owners J. A. Porter, and G. W. Bailey. Mr. Allen moved the old grocery building to the back of the lot, using it as a garage. Abb and Minnie Allen's house was just north of the store and the last Georgetown school was just north of their house.

When the new Spur 406 was built, the county sold the old Allen residence which was in between the Georgetown school and Allgood's Store to the Allen family for $10 and they moved the house to the intersection of Georgetown Rd and Spout Springs Rd where it remains today.

**Above: Allen residence moved to Spout Springs, pictures from Jim Allen.**

**Grandma Allen below, who lived in the house in the two previous pictures. Minnie Myrtle Farrell Allen, wife of Abner Allen with her grandchildren James R. Allen, Judith Ann Allen & William Jack King Jr.**

Mr. Allen never agreed to the using the name of Fink for the town, so when he built his store, he installed the name "Georgetown" in foot tall block letters on the store so everyone visiting would know where they REALLY were! This was according to Mrs. Luella Allgood, a sister of late Mrs. Minnie Allen who was Abb Allen's wife. Minnie and Luella Farrell also grew up in Georgetown. Luella Farrell married J. L. Allgood who took over the running of the Allen Grocery store in 1956. Allgood liked the name Fink just fine and was the first to exploit the name to attract more visitors to the little town and create events to give them a good reason to come.

Fink became very famous and very quickly attracted much media attention, especially from the popular Dallas Morning News columnist, Frank X. Tolbert who promoted Fink and its events for many years. It all started in 1963 when Allgood complained about Fink being overrun with stray dogs and cats being dropped off by "city folks." (This nefarious irresponsible action is a common occurrence in rural communities.)

Tolbert was the one who dubbed Allgood as the "mayor" of Fink and a tradition was born. Once when a reporter asked Mr. Allgood why he had Georgetown in big letters written on one side of the building and Fink on the other, he explained that Mr. Allen still owned the building and wouldn't allow its removal. The original Fink grocery store was at the northeast corner of the intersection of what was at that time Hwy 120 and Georgetown Road. The construction of Spur 406 destroyed the location of the old store which used to sit it the intersection of what is now Spur 406 and Hwy 289.

Sunday Gazetteer April 9, 1893 & Sherman Daily Register August 3, 1900 - This article below should read Mr. William Allgood, on the Farrell farm.

Mr. Wm. Allred, residing on the Farley farm, three miles northwest of old Georgetown, about twelve miles west of Denison, has a very fine Kentucky Jack, and last week Mr. Allred was in Denison getting up posters and other advertising matter for the season. Mr. W. A. Ayers, a prosperous farmer residing on the Denison and Savoy wagon road, eight miles east of the city, was here the same day on the same mission. The gentlemen had their work done at the Murray Power Printing House.

Mr. Ed Moore, Mrs. T. J. Murphy, Clarence and Victor Moore attended the picnic at old Georgetown yesterday.

The picture below is taken at Allgood's Store at Fink where the corner of Hwy 289 and 406 are now. Probably taken in 1963. It was used in a Dallas Morning News article in 1963 and belongs to and is printed courtesy of Emma Stratton Cayton. Upper left - Walter "Son" Moon; left to right, Ray Stratton; Lloyd Allgood; unknown man on right (may be William Driggers). The photo is courtesy of Emma Stratton Cayton.

Next: Jim Allen's aunt wrote stories about her life in Fink and Georgetown, including one about her Dad "Abb" Allen's Grocery Store. It gives a good snapshot about life in a small rural town in the past. Her name was Mary Frances "Mickey" Allen King, the daughter of Abner and Minnie Allen. Jim Allen's father was James Farrell Allen, Ab's son.

## LET'S GO TO THE STORE

When you got to my daddy's store the first thing you saw was the front porch and on it were two benches. Often, in good weather, it was hard to find a seat. My brother, James, was mechanically inclined and I will never forget when he drove big nails into one of the benches at various intervals and wired the nails to a battery located in the store. When the bench would get full it was his greatest delight to slip into the store and touch the wire to the battery and cause some real excitement.

The two gas pumps at the front had handles on the sides for pumping gas up into the big glass containers that held ten gallons. It was marked at gallon intervals for easy dispensing. Regular gas was ten cents a gallon and ethyl was fifteen cents. No "self service" here unless you just had a "hankerin'" to put it in yourself.

On one corner of the porch was a water faucet to use for filling radiators. It was used mostly, however, to fill ten gallon milk cans with good soft water to take home. Sometimes it was because their well had gone dry but more often it was because they preferred the taste of the store water. It was bad when hot summer arrived and the wind was reluctant to blow long enough to make the windmill pump enough to fill the big tin storage tank. Then water really became scarce. There were also other times when the windmill would break down and daddy would have to call for volunteers to help pull the "sucker rod".

For kids, especially the girls, one of the best things about the front porch was reading the "plusses" written on the wall. I don't recall the store ever being painted so there was an accumulated mixture of initials dating back for years. If you wanted to be real mean you would put someones initials plus someone they did not like or plus someone claimed by another. Occasionally there would be an ugly word, but it didn't stay up long. Daddy would remove it promptly and if he ever found out who wrote it that kid was in for it.

Starting about 8:30 in the morning the men would begin to arrive to wait for the mail. There were about ten to fifteen mail boxes located at the store. The paper was published in the afternoon in Denison and as soon as Mike arrived with it the men took off for home where the women were waiting to read the "continued story" and everyone wanted to see what "Boots and Freckles" were up to.

The front porch was the favorite place to pick up news. It was called news since it was men doing the talking. If it had been women it would have been called gossip. Kids that hung around and listened could acquire quite and education that was not available from books. In election years the politicians liked to arrive when a big crowd was gathered to promote themselves and their causes. They handed out their cards, books of matches, packets of needles, with their names and the office they were running for printed thereon.

The milk truck driven by Russell Lane, and later by Ray Stratton stopped at the store every morning to get gas. It was the favorite waiting place for people to gather if they wanted to ride the milk truck to Denison. Lots of people didn't have cars.

The big double front doors were locked with a key from daddy's key ring that had an assortment of about 25 keys. It was interesting about that front door lock. Any skeleton key would unlock the door, or, if you just leaned real hard against the door and gave it a little shove it would come right open. To my memory there was never a break-in or robbery at the store.

The floors of the store had to be swept every night. Daddy had a unique way of keeping the dust down and flies to a minimum. Before he used the broom he went to the coal oil barrel and ran coal oil over the broom straw and sprinkled the whole floor lightly, then swept with the oil drenched broom. Do you know we never had a fire in that store and daddy didn't have a penny of insurance.

What were the store hours? It was opened as soon as daddy finished breakfast and closed when mother called him for supper. However, if anyone needed anything at any other hour he only had to call out to the house and say: "Mr. Allen, I need to get in the store." There would go daddy in that lively step of his.

Self-Service was a long time in coming to the Georgetown Store. Until then there were long counters on each side and all the merchandise was placed on shelves behind the counters. Customers came to the counter and told Daddy what they wanted. He went to the shelves, got the merchandise and gathered it all together on the counter. At that counter there was string that was guided from a high shelf, a big roll of wrapping paper, a hoop of cheese with a knife attached for slicing, an adding machine and a cash register. The adding machine seldom had paper and it was a favorite plaything of all kids. To my knowledge, however, it never had to be repaired and still registered correct addition.

The cash register had compartments for different sizes of money but it was always mixed together and in the wrong place. In one of the back compartments there was an opening that no one knew about. Much to Daddy's surprise during the depression he moved the cash register and found it very heavy. When he tipped it back he heard rattling in the bottom. He removed the bottom and found over $100 in old coins. Money was hard to come by in those days and our whole family was treated to a new motorola radio with a magic eye.

What did you buy at the store? There were beans, rice,

sugar and many other things that came in barrels, boxes, or kegs and could be bought by the pound or more often, by ten or fifteen cents worth. Daddy would just get a sack and measure out the amount you wanted. You could go to the store with a dollar and get something of everything you needed by just dividing that dollar up in equal amounts for the number of things on your list, and there were no sales taxes added.

Remembering the beans, I shall never forget the time grandsons, Jack and Jimmy, were in the store with their granddad being very busy and not bothering anyone.
It was soon discovered, however, that their business was mixing pinto and navy beans, with rice and black-eyed peas in their respective bins. What a job it was to dump all those dried beans on the counter and separate them....

There was cheese in a big round hoop with a knife attached for cutting. Chewing tobacco came in wooden boxes and there was a tobacco knife to cut it. Patent medicine was on the shelves near the door and if you were sick you could read the labels for what the medicine was meant to cure and then diagnose yourself. The brooms were held up by the handles from a contraption of wire hung to the ceiling. If you were skilled you knew just how to lift one broom and get it released. The vineger was in a big wooden barrel with a wooden pump and you brought your own jug. You also brought your own can for coal oil which was in a 100 gallon metal barrel with a crank that you turned to dispense one gallon at a time at five cents a gallon. Everyone used coal oil to burn in their lamps as well as to pour on wood for a quick fire.

The flour was in the screened-in compartment in the back room. You could get Smith's Best or Gladiola in 10, 25 or 50 lb. bags as well as corn meal. Cow, chicken, and hog feed was also kept in the back room. The men were told by their wives what kind of a sack to get their feed in because the women would be collecting a certain pattern to make a dress, curtains, quilts or other things they were sewing. It was an exciting day when a new load of feed arrived to see what kind of sacks it was packed in.

The candy case was a delight. When a family would do a week's or month's grocery shopping and, if there were children in the family, daddy would always have a big sack of penny candy to send home with the groceries. There were all kinds of candy such as banana caramels, chocolate soldiers, taffy strips of pink and white, baby Butterfingers and Baby Ruths, peppermint and peanut butter sticks, all day suckers, taffy caramel suckers, O'Boy chewing gum in grape flavor, and jelly beans with a small wooden barrel to measure a penny's worth.

Elmer brought the bread every day. Early years it was not sliced but later you had a choice. Folks liked to wait around for fresh bread that was so soft it would squash.

Credit was available and there were times when the bill would only be paid when a bale of cotton was sold. Daddy could never refuse credit for food if he had it on the shelf and he knew someone was hungry. There were times when the bills would get too big and he would have to tell the man that he would have to pay on his bill or he would have to cut off his credit. A family could be real desparate and the next time send one of the children to the store to charge the order since they knew that daddy would never refuse a child who needed food.

When eggs were brought to the store to be sold they would often be packed in cotton seed to keep them from breaking and it was real fun to hunt the eggs deep down in those soft seeds.

In the summer 300 lb blocks of ice were kept in the ice box and you could send to the store for a nickles worth of ice, wrap it in a toe sack or old quilt and take it home for iced tea. Daddy kept bottled drinks but kept them on ice only when it was really hot. People would come to the store and ask: "Mr. Allen, are the drinks cold?" His reply would be: "They drink about like well water" an you knew he didn't have them on ice. In the summer the side doors were opened for extra ventilation and that was also the favorite place to cut a big red watermelon in the late afternoon.

In the winter it was different. The wood stove was kept going at "full blast" and it was not unusual to see red hot spots on the metal stove. Nail kegs and much used chairs were available for all. Daddy's chair, however, had a pillow on it and no one but a stranger would take that chair even when daddy had to get up to wait on a customer.

Winter was a favorite time for men to spend an afternoon or morning playing checkers or dominoes. In the summer the favorite passtime was croquet. It was played in the area just to the back and side of the store. Croquet was not played as a game but as a "business and skilled sport". Even though only four players could play at one time, I have known of 50 or more standing around watching a croquet match.

There were no restaurants in the area but you could get a gourmet meal at the store. Daddy would tear off a piece of wrapping paper,put it on the counter and you could make your selection from vienna sausage, potted meat, sardines with pepper sauce, cheese, crackers, big sweet onion and a coke. Who could ask for anything better?

The only time we had fresh fruit was in the fall and then you would find a stalk of bananas hanging from the ceiling and a wooden box of oranges and apples opened and leaning against the counter.

For years the only telephone for many in the community was at the store. Calls would come through to send word to someone that a relative or loved one was seriously ill or had died. The first person who passed going in the right direction was given the message to deliver. And shortly the message had been received.

Two incidents stand out as very unique in daddy's experience. One night he was called out to the store after dark. A car was parked at the gas pump to be filled. At the front door stood a woman holding a big rock as if she intended to throw it. Daddy filled the gas tank, sold the couple some food that required no cooking and left without harm not knowing who the strangers were. The next day the newspaper reported that Bonnie and Clyde Barrows had been seen in Grayson County the day before.

The other incident pertained to a customer who had stopped at the store and in his conversation with daddy had brought up the fact that the Baupmans probably had a lot of money. After the Baupman girl was murdered the sheriff was in the community investigating and asked daddy if he had seen any strangers recently. Daddy remembered the stranger that had stopped a few days before the murder and was able to describe him to the sheriff. The description was good enough to identify a convict from McAlester, Oklahoma. He was caught and convicted as the murderer. A few months later when True Detective ran a story about the murder, daddy's picture was printed with him standing on the front porch of the store.

In my memory the store had only two employees: Daddy's sister-in-law, Kate Farrell and later Louella Clements. You could not get a person to work for one hour now for what Louella was paid for a week.

The store has been gone many years, but I am glad that in my memory bank there are stored those happy days to recall, aren't you.

Mary (Mickey Allen) King

Note: the family she recalled as Baupman or Bauptman, used the possibly Anglicized version of their name – Brockman. More about the Brockman murder and the Bonnie and Clyde visit are mentioned in this book.

Congratulations you Millionaires

by Mary (Mickey) Allen King

The date is between the years 1930-40. It is sunday night and cars are beginning to arrive at the Georgetown School house for the Sunday night singing. On sunday morning G.W. Walls or Emmett Dinwiddie had preached, and the sunday school classes had met in different corners of the one large school room. Mrs Edythe Allen had the card class and Alice Waldrop Christman taught the couples who met up on the stage with the curtain lowered for privacy. That curtain was colorful with ads from stores such as Longs Drugs, Earn Looney Grocery, Potts General Merchandise, Dr. Slaughter M.D., Clement Auto, and Youngs Telephone Exchange. Miss Della Hulls young peoples class was very active as they were participating in a contest to see which of the two teams of members could read the most Bible Chapters. Fritz Christman served as Suprientendent and Snooky Allen was secretary. Faithful attenders were Eula Hull, Alex and Roxie Christman, Gladys and Lloyd Hrrison, Yvonne and Martha Eldredge; Johnny, Evelyn and Yvonne Bothe; Mr and Mrs Odell; Bill and Della Cantrell; Bob and Lou Perdue; Horace and Eva Hale, and occasionally Op and Johnny Clontz brought Dorothy. Hattie did not attend very often when she came home. But back to Sunday night....

The time for singing to start was when everyone arrived, and Mr. Brooks was usually one of the last. There was always a good crowd because parents had to come bring kids or get kids who had spent the day together. How early singing got started was determined by how early the cows came in to get milked. Abb Allen would go to the stage and with the end of his pocket knife knock on wood and say, "Lets come to order". "Edith Odell will you come to the piano and our first song will be led by William Montgomery, followed by Carl Fink, Vivian Brooks, Chester White and Lorene Donohoe."

The songs we all liked best were those Stamps-Baxter numbers with lots of parts that would end with us all singing together. Lots of folks enjoyed singing such as Sally and Alvin Henderson, (Bess when she was home); Wilmer and Bessie Nichols, Melvin Lee, Pauline and Bill Crook; Billie Jean and Lavada Lou; Ma Christman and Howard; Homer, May, Julie and Ruth Taylor; Arthur Sharpe, and Ed and Ruby Hale. Then there were the Densmores, Emily and Rufus and children Vernis, Nowassa Eva Mae, Melva, R. G. (Speedy), Wanda and Tommy. Also Mr. and Mrs. C. A. White and Lela and Charles; Doll and Alex Moser.

Doll and Alec Moser. After about 45 minutes of different ones leading a song, recess was called so kids could run around, go to the little out houses in the ditch (one for boys and one for girls and dont you ever try to slip in the wrong one) and if you were thirsty you could go to the store for a drink of water. After recess, "William Lee will you go to the piano", and it was time for some quartets. Lots of times there would be a visitor like Jack Horner from Denison and that would really thrill us.

On this sunday night in November Mr. Allen announced it was time for the pie supper if we were going to have a Christmas tree. Everyone agreed, yes yes, we wanted a Christmas Tree. So next saturday night we would have a pie supper to make money for the Georgetown Christmas Tree.

For the Pie Supper four benches were moved together facing each other to form a place to put the pies. Each lady had her name slipped under the edge of her pie so that whoever bought it could hunt her down to help eat it. Speaking of pies....there were chocolate, lemon, chocolate, bananna, egg custard,chocolate, coconut, chocolate, apple, cherry and did I mention chocolate? Some of the big girls like Hazel Allen,Jessie Lee and Lottie Brooks; the Moser girls- Ada Lee,Esther, Ethyl, Lena and Annie Mae; Loreda Hale, Beulah May and Mabel Hunter; Evelyn Sharpe, Lorene and Ruth Allen; Jessie Lee and Lottie Brooks fixed decorated boxes. Mr. Allen was the auctioneer and he would tease the big boys about what a pretty girl fixed this box and what good things he could see inside. Those big boys would bid on their girls box, and sometimes William Hull, Harold and Edwin Jones; Nun or Don Steel; Joe or Gene Cantrell; Fred or Willie Perdue; Raymond, Waymond, Luther, Mutt or Willie Hale;Paul Montgomery or John Bill Hull would get the right box. It was always the desire of several of the girls to have a ball player from Tom Bean like Cotton Franklin or Pie Smith be the one to get theirs.

We never found it necessary to provide drink, just pie and if you were desperate there was still water at the store. Around $100. could be raised at one of these events then the next thing was to appoint a chairman for the Christmas Tree. "Willie Sharpe and Etta Finke will you be co chairmem?", Yes they would be glad to and everyone was glad they would because they were experienced. By being chairman that meant you got some men to cut the tree, drag it in, and put it up. That cedar tree had to be big enough to climb in to hang presents, high enough off the floor to walk under, limbs strong enough to hang dolls on, and have the top branches stripped so the small end of the trunk could be forced thro the hole in the ceiling where someone could go to the attic and secure it.

The ladies would also buy the crates of apples and oranges, mixed nuts (in shell), hard candies and some nigger toes.

They would supervise kids who had graduated from the 7th grade in filling the sacks and decorating the tree. How you looked forward to the day you would be old enough to help decorate that Christmas Tree! It was an all day job. Finally Christmas eve day arrived as did kids such as James Allen,J.B. Lowe, Mervin and Choice Christman; Edgel Clement, Durward Payne, Louella Hale,as well as Lois and Allene; Hull Allen. Laverne and Richard Sharpe; Chig Arthur, Minnie Ola Brooks, Hattie and Dewey Montgomery; Leona McKee, A.L. MOSER and Turner Stuckey. You could just count of Mickey Allen trying to slip down and peep in the window only to have someone go tell Minnie (who was home boiling a ham) what Mickey was up to. She would be called back home, scolded, and told Santa Claus just might not bring her a doll (which she had alread found under James' bed)if she wasent nice.

Back to filling those sacks. It was done like a mass production line, all items were opened and placed on a long row of benches and starting at one end with someone opening the sack (sometimes red net but later brown paper) and each person had their one thing to put in, be it an apple, orange, hand full of nuts, or pieces of candy. Of course you poped a candy in your mouth every so often. Those sacks were so full it was difficult to tie name tags on them. It was an unbroken rule that every man, woman, and child in Georgetown community was to receive a sack, whether they were present or not, and, every visitor at the Christmas tree was to get one.

Those sacks went to Mrs Cathrine Finke, Earl and Minnie Montgomery; Charles and Robert; Joe Adams (remember his tent on the creek), Jack Allen and Earl Jones; The Biggs on the Grubbs Farm-Turpey and Leon and sister; Fred and Carrie Jones, Jim and Minnie Clement, John and Jessie Clement, Mace ~~and~~ Nina Steel, Mr and Mrs Camel, H.C. Allen, Myrtle Foshee, Sam Guilloud family, Negro Myrtle and Jack, Ebb and Lottie Hull; Slim Allen (August Finks hired man); Miss Minnie and Mr Bostic; the Brochman sisters, Tom McQueen; Katie and Gus Ruland, Mary Lou and Delbert; Mrs Davis and Francis. Mrs. Davis would probably have lots of callers at her smoke house after dark so would not want to be away from home. Also sacks for Woody and Edna Faulkner, ~~also with~~ Tommy , Eugene, Gladys Faye and Cathrine; and, the three families who lived in the W.P.A. box car houses, the Joe Cooks, Odie Stuarts and Virgil Taylors.

When the tree was decorated, cedar, red berries and mistletoe hung on the walls, the curtains hung for the program (why did kids like to get behind them and peep out?) the days work was finished. When dark started to set in, Mr. Allen would start the Delco and turn on the lights and by that time people were arriving and bringing boxs full of gifts to put on the tree. If Earl Gill had been leasing some land there would be an extra large amount of gifts but even of the years of the depression that tree was well filled. By the time everyone arrived that tree was hanging full of big dolls, bright wrapped boxes, pretty handkerchiefs, beads, pocket knives, ties, etc. Underneath was boxes for breakables. There were some of the prettiest glass serving bowls exchanged by the ladies as well as embroaderied cup towels made from bleached feed sacks.

Anyone that had ever lived in Georgetown or associated with the folks there would find their way to the Christmas tree. Visitors would include Mrs Summerville, Maggie and Romey, Eunice Weist, Cecil, Bryan, C.T., Lovell and Euleen McKinney; Ray Stratton, Peachy Mozelle and Arnold Waldrop; J.N. and Nell Taylor; Randolph Parham; Ray Gibson and Earn Looney, if they were running for Commissioner next summer; Mike Wilson knew everyone since he delivered the mail - as did Henry Guilloud his substitute. Then there was Russell Lane in his milk truck, Ella Mae Steel, Ella & Eddie B. Jennings and Juanita and Earlene; Paul Owens, Beulah and Fred Riddle; Dock Nichols and family; Thad, Paul, and Madge Steel; and Dub Brown. Then there would be babies like Doris and Carl Fred Finke on pillows.

Many people did not put up a tree at home and they would bring all the family gifts and put them under this tree. These could include Jenny and Charley Marion, Mr and Mrs Frank Farrell, Lela and Oliver Montgomery, Jack Arthur, August and Ruth Finke along with Henry, ~~and~~ Ralph, Carl Fred; Luther and Zellie Kennon with Lawrence and Vernon; Mr and Mrs H.C. Lawrence and C. A. Sparks.

Before the tree and Santas arrival there was the school program. One thing for sure every kid in school was in the program. It included songs, skits, drills, readings and plays. Those kids were so excited it was hard for them to remember their parts. There was James and Clarene Clement, Mickey Allen, Helen Finke, Laverne Dawson, Frosty Jones, Aldene and Lavern Donohoe, the Quassa girls, Lucy Mae and Elizabeth; Dick and Junior Allen, Ruby Lee Hunter, L.C. Payne, Pauline Finke; Dorothy, Pat, Bill and Jack Moser; Grace; Francis, Curtis and Margie White; Olen and Roy Brooks,

Jacqueline Payne, Leona McKee, Turner Stuckey,E.C. and Lillian Hardenberg; and the twins, Jacqueline Payne, Edith Cook, and teachers like Mrs. Johnson and T. B. . We were so glad when they brought Pee Wee and Wanda Myrle.

When the program was over, Santa arrived, the presents were hand delivered, sacks of goodies were sent by friends to those absent, old friends were greeted and another wonderful christmas had become a memory.

Hal Boyle once wrote, "Memory is the money of the Mind, A Possession that can never be taken from you."

Arnt we a rich bunch of folks that have roots in the Georgetown Community?

Mary A. King
(Mickey)
June 30, 1984
Georgetown School
Reunion

# THE BIG LITTLE TOWN OF FINK KNOWN AROUND THE WORLD for "FINK DAY" & "FINK WEEK"

Below: Fink in the 1950s looking north

## Fink Folk Dislike The Town's Title

June 11, 1963 Dallas Morning News by Frank X. Tolbert - Fink folks have long been displeased with the name of their town. They want it to be called **Georgetown**, and "something always happens" to the "Fink Texas" signs put up by the highway department. Joseph Lloyd Allgood, Mayor of Fink, and operator of Fink's Georgetown general store, said at that time, at least 15 sets of those signs had disappeared in recent years. He said the highway department was stubborn and kept replacing the signs and refused to let them call the town "Georgetown" because there was another town with the same name in Williamson County Texas. He was happy to note however that the school children did not have to attend a Fink school, the local school was known as Georgetown School. Fink was settled by planters from Mississippi in the 1850's and was informally called Georgetown. The town's post office was called Georgetown, then changed because of the one in Williamson County causing confusion. Someone had the idea of titling the post office Finke in honor of Fred Finke, a popular early German settler. But Fred Finke did not agree, he felt it was Georgetown and he didn't want them pinning his name on it. As a compromise, the "e" was dropped from the name producing the name Fink. In 1963, The town was in the news because Mayor Allgood was complaining to the Dallas Morning News that Fink was being overrun by dogs and cats. People from nearby Sherman and Denison had been coming to Fink to abandon their unwanted animals. "We will have to hire a dog catcher if this keeps up", said the Mayor, which would be too expensive for a small town of only 24 people with two of them currently away in the Navy. (He was inflating the census!) Gordon McLendon of Dallas Radio Station KLIF in one of his regular "Fink It Over" editorials, asked Dallas folks to come to the rescue and adopt a Fink dog. He said, "The question seems to be whether Fink is going to the dogs, or the dogs are going to Fink. What do you Fink?" Two of the station's disc jockeys, Irving Harrigan and Charley Brown, will broadcast from the whittler's bench on the front gallery of Mayor Allgood's store Tuesday morning. While the author of this article was in Fink interviewing Mayor Allgood, a 6-year-old Nicki Hamrick, came running up to the store, calling to a parent, "Someone just gave me another dog!"

# City of Fink Plans 'Fink Celebration'

June 9, 1965 Dallas Morning News (Dallas, Texas) by Frank X. Tolbert - Mayor J. L. Allgood is planning a big celebration in Fink on the week of June 20-26, which is "National Be Kind To Finks Week". He stated that Fink needed all the kindness it could get. The mayor invited Judge James Bates Fink to be the principal speaker. He was formerly the Justice of the Peace of Bug Tussle (the court is now in Ladonia) in Fannin county. The celebration of "National Be Kind To Finks Week" marks a new attitude in Fink, perhaps one of resignation. The Fink highway signs are still disappearing, and locals are suspected of being the culprits. Mayor Allgood's son Joe, has been appointed dog catcher of Fink and he has been kept busy, as the unwanted canines are still being dropped off. A line of "Fink Furniture" is soon to be sold at the general store in Fink. The first sample was a small end table with the words "Fink Town" inscribed on it. Joe Allgood said the other furniture will have "Fink Texas" written on it instead, because "we don't think Fink Town sounds too good".

June 23, 1965 Dallas Morning News - Fink Texas was the Fink Capital of the world this week. Mayor J. L. Allgood of Fink was swamped with messages of encouragement and goodwill on National Be Kind To Finks Week, and Monday was "the big day" of a gala week. At noon there was a big fish fry at Mayor Allgood's general store. Hundreds of Finks, Finkes, Fincks were in attendance. Others mailed greetings to the Texas Finkites. One message came from Dr. Frederick C. Fink of Port Washington, Long Island, New York. Dr. Fink said he longed to be at the Fink Reunion in Texas and "I am finking of you on this memorable week. Frankly, the abuse of the name of Fink does not phase me nor does it bother my four sons." This column about Fink Day was picked up by the wire services and printed all over the globe. Mike Fink of Seymour, IN, a US Navy man serving in submarines and stationed on the island of Guam, wrote to Mayor Allgood that he'd seen the story in Stars and Stripes. A prominent Finkite, J. T. Stephens, caught a boat load of catish on Lake Texoma and did an artistic job of frying them, along with hush puppies for the Be Kind To Finks Luncheon. Oscar Fink, a double cousin of Judge Fink, was there displaying his hand-made "Fink Town Furniture", and he displayed a new item which he'd made, a "Fink Fiddle". Fink has a "brave" new sign in front of the general store: "Welcome to Fink, Texas. Population 12 (One Fink)." Still, some Fink residents are bitterly disappointed with the community's name. Kent Biffle of the Dallas News staff has a suggestion if the town abandons the name of Fink, change it to "**The REAL Georgetown Texas".**

Photo of Fink store in 1966 from Jim Allen

JUL • 66

Photos of Fink in 1966 from Jim Allen

**Below: Late 1960s advertisement**

2/28/1967 – Fink, Texas – Pat Albright confessed the 1967 observance of Fink Day in Fink, Texas will have to get along without her if an invitation works out to celebrate at Hans Fink's restaurant in Bressahone, Italy, with some other Finks. Hans Fink invited her to a celebration in his restaurant June 26. With the tourist season at hand, Mayor Albright put up her sign to welcome all to Fink.

**Above: Fink Day hayride and wagon rides**

## ALBRIGHT'S GROCERY

Sporting Goods
Tires Gas Ice

Highway 120
Located on the Road to Lake Texoma

Phone ST 6-9943 Fink, Texas

JUDGE FINK OF BUG TUSSLE

**Poem About Judge Fink For National Fink Day**

June 9, 1969 Dallas Morning News by Frank X. Tolbert - All day a band will be playing to people from all over the nation named Fink, Finke, Finkenstein, etc on National Fink Day, Tuesday June 17. Oscar Fink of Denison will recite a memorial poem in honor of the late James Bailey Fink, for many years the beloved magistrate of Bug Tussle Texas in Fannin County. He was the first principal speaker for the National Fink Reunion and was in the forefront of the anti-defamation of the Fink name, especially against comedians like Steve Allen. The Fink celebration, conceived by John Clift of Denison, started out as "National Be Kind to Finks Week", urging people to "fink it over" before saying cruel things about people named Fink. The Fink Festival will start with a three day golf tournament at Tanglewood Hills Country Club. You don't have to be a Fink to play in the Fink tournament. Fink's Mayor Patricia Albright (her husband Willard refused the office), nor John Clift could remember who had won the 1968 golf tournament. It seems stray dogs and cats are still a problem according to Pat Albright, "Fink needs a dog catcher, but Willard won't volunteer". A project has been discussed to raise a statue of famous frontiersman Mike Fink in Fink's town square.

# Texas Town Celebrates Fink Day

June 21, 1970 Dallas Morning News - The Smiths, Joneses, Browns and others, including at least 17 Finks, poured into this North Texas hamlet Saturday to celebrate National Fink Day. Fink, hardly more than a wide spot in the road near the Oklahoma border west of Denison, trembled with hundreds of tourists seeking conversation with other Fink lovers at Albright's general store. Mrs. Pat Albright, mayor of Fink, handed out free soft drinks to visitors at the store, the sole business in Fink. Even those 17 Finks who signed Mrs. Albright's guest register were not spared from the 95 degree weather. "We were going to have a bonfire, but it's too hot outside to burn," the mayor said. Mrs. Albright said the bonfire was planned Sunday to commemorate the final day of National Fink Week and the first day of summer. National Fink Week, some say, began in honor of the surname Fink. Others claim it began about the time "fink" came into usage as slang for stool pidgeon or informer. Mrs. Albright said Fink's poet laureate Oscar L. Fink, 87, of Denison, would recite some of his works in front of the store later in the day. The mayor will play in the traditional "celebrity foursome" of golf Funday at nearby Tanglewood Country Club, site of the 3rd Fink International Golf Tournament Saturday. Mrs. Albright said earlier she expected possibly 12 Finks would appear from the Saturday celebration. She was delighted when 17 signed the register. About 500 non-Finks signed too.

**Fink's Mayor Pat Albright named Admiral of Fink Navy**

# National Fink Day

June 5, 1972 Dallas Morning News Fink Day on June 22 will be an international event. The distinguished founder of National Fink Day, John Clift of Denison, recently received a letter from Co. E. J. DeQuincey Fink of Crabtree House, Arrathorne, Bedale, Yorkshire, England: "Having read in the British newspapers that the freedom of your town, which includes its citizenship, would be granted to all those bearing my illustrious name, I write to inquire whether this is a fact. I am particularly interested as I shall be tooling around in the United States soon. In the meantime, believe me, sir, your obedient servant...." Col. E. J. DeQuincey Fink has been given an invitation to share the freedom of the town on Fink Day. His letter was one of the "Fink Letters" in a paperback book which John Clift has written called "The Fantastic World of Fink". Mayor Pat Albright has corresponded with Finks all over the world. There is to be a fund to place a statue of Mike Fink in the Fink town square. Mike Fink (1770-1823) was a frontier hero in real life who was made out as something of a comedian-villian in his role as an adversary of Davy Crockett in the old Disney movies. The Finks have finked out on this statue project. So far only about 50 bucks has been contributed. Over 1000 Finks from all over the world ended up attending Fink Day in 1972.

## Few Finks Left On National Fink Day

Anniston Star June 10, 1971 - FINK. Tex. IAP - Poor Fink. It has just lost 80 per cent of its population. And with the big National Fink Day celebration only two weeks away: "It's liable to be a rather sad celebration," commented the mayor. Pat Albright. The population shrinkage came when 12 persons in two families vacated two houses with the closing of nearby Perrin Air Force Base. That left Fink with a population of three: Mr. and Mrs. Willard Albright and an employee of their store, the only business in the crossroads village. The celebration of Fink Day was officially set for June 24, although people started dropping by the Albright General Store and Service Station a month ahead of time to get the affair rolling. Already Mrs. Albright's telephone is jammed with calls from Finks saying they will attend. When National Fink Day was announced in 1965 by the store's previous owner, Finks throughout the world leaped to applaud this new status affair--something to polish the term of "fink" which means stool pigeon in slang. Also joining in the affair have been Fincks. Finkes. Finques. Phinques, Funks, and last year, a Zink. Mrs. Albright estimated that "several hundred" persons celebrated last year. Previously, National Fink Day was celebrated with free cake and soda pop. This year it's free barbecue and pop. Unfortunately, the poet laureate of Fink, Judge Oscar Fink, 85, is indisposed and can't return to read his verses nor play his homemade fiddles. He is a former justice of the peace and resides in Denison, 10 miles away. Mrs. Pat Albright is importing a substitute from Pottsboro, four miles away. He is Dick Barrett, a retired western band fiddler. "I think the red hot hoedown fiddling might be just what we need to cheer us up." Mrs. Albright said.

The residents applied for a post office many years ago and picked the name of "Georgetown." There already was a Texas town of that name. The petition was signed by a gentleman named Finke. Butt he U.S. post office named it Fink, dropping the "e". There is no post office now.

An honorary title of mayor goes to the owner of the store. Albright didn't want the honor and appointed his wife. The store makes its money from fishermen on Lake Texoma, a mile and a half away on the Oklahoma border. Three years ago. Mayor Albright began selling printed Fink honorary citizenships for a dime. So the true population of Fink, honorary and actual, is somewhere around 5.000, she estimates. When football is mentioned in Fink, Texas (population 8), the name of J. Kingsley Fink comes to mind. He was a student at the U.S. Military Academy and made everybody's All-American list. Fink hailed from Eau Gallie, Florida. He came from a prolific family who liked to start the male children off with a first name beginning the letter "J". By the time J. Kingsley Fink arrived, the family had run out of first names beginning with "J". So they named him "J. Kingsley Fink." When the U.S. Army football team from West Point played Texas A&M at College Station in 1972, the entire town residents of Fink were guests of the Military Academy in hon or of Cadet Fink. At half-time, Cadet Fink and Mayor Pat Albright met in center field where West Point Fink was made an honorary citizen of Fink, Texas.

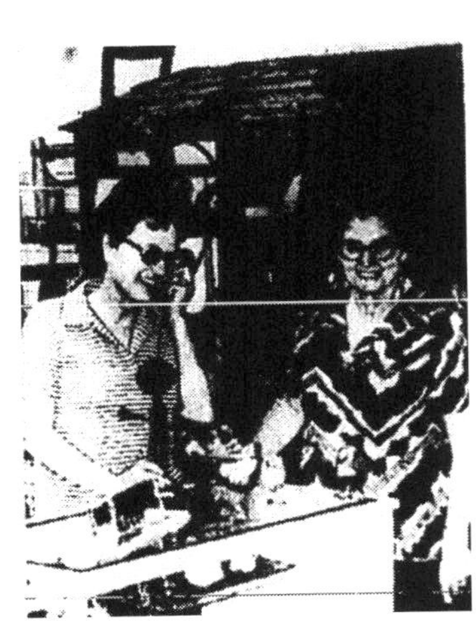

In the picture above left, are Mayor Patricia Albright and Vice Mayor Lucy Clement in the new general store/Fink museum and city hall of Fink, population 6. The picture on the right shows the mayor and Fink's official poet laureate and fiddle maker, Oscar Fink. Mayor Albright's husband Willard said there were two new houses going up in Fink, so they may just double the population any day now.

## Fink Day Fete Invites Finks and Non-Finks

- June 15, 1973 Dallas Morning News - The Mayor is the chief moving force behind Fink Day, which is dedicated to all Finks of the world who suffer jokes about their name, which is the same work as gangland slang for informers. On 1972's Fink Day, Mrs. Albright said they fed more than 1,000 and expected to feed more in 1973. For the rest of the year, Fink helps supply fishermen on Lake Texoma. For the first time in fifty years, Fink has two business houses. The Albrights moved their store into a new building which will also house the museum and city hall. Another business moved into their old place. A professional building is going up, to be occupied by Dr. Gordon Lillie, a dermatologist who lives on Lake Texoma. It will have room for another doctor, two dentists and a lawyer. The Albrights are really going to whoop it up on Fink Day, there will be free barbecue. Despite the soaring price of beef, Mayor Albright said "It's on the house as long as it lasts. I'm not finking out on that".

## Pop. 6 - Town Swells to 2,500 for Fink Day

June 22, 1973 Dallas Morning News - Out beside the road the every third weekend flea market was going strong and old Ellis Parker was selling old bottles: A Dr. Kilmer's swamp root kidney cure bottle, and a liver and bladder remedy bottle were some of his prizes. Back in the pasture under the Bratcher Funeral Home tent, the mayor's aides dished out free bar-b-que and cold drinks. Near the corner of the tent sat Oscar L. Fink wearing blue denim overalls and a straw hat. He was surrounded by fiddles and canes constructed from match sticks and every 10 minutes he recited a poem. "You know why I do it?", he asked. "If I'm not busy, me and the old lady get to fussing and she always wins". A poet AND a philosopher.

## Fink Museum

1973 – Eureka – She found it! The picture below shows Fink Mayor Pat Albright holding a historic old postcard carrying a postmark from the old Fink Post Office. This artifact is just one item in her growing Fink Museum, housed in a corner of her store. Former Grayson County Commissioner Ray Stratton found the post card, dated 1898 in an old family Bible and sent it to Mrs. Albright who had been hunting for a genuine cancellation for over a decade. Below: 1975- Pat Albright at her Fink Museum in her store showing an old postcard stamped "Fink Texas". I do not know what happened to all the items she had in her museum when the store closed.

## National Fink Week, One Day isn't Enough to Celebrate this Huge Little Town!

Oscar Fink, poet laureate of Fink and fiddle and toy wagon maker in the overalls.

**FINK FOLK FESTIVAL ON FINK DAY** May 19, 1974 Dallas Morning News

The Fink Folk Festival will feature everything from an old-fashioned quilting bee to exhibits of buttons and barbed wire. There will again be free barbeque. "If the crow gets much bigger than last year" said the mayor's husband Willard Albright, "I may have to go steal a cow to feed all the folks." Fink Poet Laureate Oscar L Fink, 87, reportedly has been ill in recent weeks, but his wife says he has still been polishing up his verbiage for his annual Fink poem. "Oscar's getting pretty deaf," said Mrs. Fink, "but that won't keep him away from Fink on National Fink Day. He's been busy making **Fink fiddles, Fink wagons and Fink walking canes**." Mayor Albright said, "Fink really is growing. We have two stores and service stations, a doctor's office, city hall, Fink museum and we have rodeo arena under construction that is due to open with its inaugural rodeo on **National Fink Week.**" She said the population probably has almost doubled over a year ago and should be baker's dozen now. However, the mayor said she doesn't like this "mushrooming growth" that has gripped Fink the past year. "It brings too many problems," she said.

## Fink Day Draws 1,000 – Finks Say Name is Really for the Birds

Wilbur Finks or Columbus OH, Louis Fink of San Antonio, TX & Oscar L. Fink of Denison (oldest Fink Day attendee)

June 21, 1974 Dallas Morning News - Once a Fink, always a Fink is what the badge proclaimed, and Louis Fink of Beatrice, Neh. Accompanied by his wife, drove 600 miles to prove it. He was sporting proof he was a graduate of Fink University and no one asked for further credentials as Louis Fink mingled in a crowd of spectators, newsmen and Finks gathered Thursday in the tiny Grayson County community bearing his name to celebrate National Fink Day, the highlight of National Fink Week. The tradition swelled the town's population from 12 to 2,500 at one time last year and promises to attract even more this year. A golf tournament is scheduled June 27-29. The biggest attraction of the celebration held next to Mayor Patricia Albright's store, was a flea market with such knick knacks as used golf balls for a nickle each, pottery, old bottles and barbed wire displays. About 50 Indians, friendly invaders from Oklahoma, set up headquarters at one end of the lot and began selling beads and trinkets, but a woman in full costume said the group was reluctant to dance because the braves and singers didn't come along. Oscar Fink, the oldest Fink present, recited a specially written sonnet about the girls and about his younger days. He displayed a walking cane and two fiddles constructed mostly from used matches – he's an ecologist. A cowboy, armed with a guitar and harmonica, chanted "I'm an Okie from Muskogee" from beneath a nearby canvas sunshade. "I didn't have no business comin' out here, but I had to come to see the crowd and to hear the Fink name." said Oscar, a nearby Denison resident. "I even got to meet my niece, and I haven't seen her in 53 years". Mayor Albright said her phone had been ringing constantly since 4 am from callers asking directions to the almost invisible crossroads Lake Texoma town. Her register showed Finks from Wichita Falls, Bryan, San Antonio, plus Oklahoma, Ohio and Nebraska. For many years in America, the name Fink is associated with the phrase "rat fink", not complimentary. Fink is a German name which means "finch" (bird) and has a pleasant association over in Germany.

## Fink near famous Preston Road; It's Mystery Namesake

January 25, 1975 Dallas Morning News By Frank X. Tolbert - Fink, Texas is near the Preston Road. A mysterious character named Lt. William Preston is intriging. He was a Republic of Texas Army second lieutenant who was the first commanding officer of an 1840 fort on the Red River. It was called Fort Preston. Preston Bend on the Red River was named for him. Indirectly, so were myriads of things in Grayson County and Dallas today, including Preston Road, and yet I can't find his name in any Republic of Texas records. I have worked the archives in Austin many times, and the other day in the Barker History Center in Austin I looked through the files of the Texas Indian papers (of the Republic of Texas) and couldn't find on reference to this frontier fellow. Fort Preston, which consisted of two stout brick buildings, was in Grayson County. Graham Landrum PhD, who wrote the best history of Grayson County, said he spent days trying to research Lt. Preston. He came up with nothing much and he says he almost came to believe that the fellow never existed. After his fruitless search for details on Lt. Preston, Dr. Graham Landrum could only report in his Pictorial History of Grayson County that in 1839 many of the settlers were thinking of leaving the country along the shores of the Red River until complaints to the Republic of Texas military department in 1840 caused "the construction near present day Pottsboro of temporary **Fort Johnston** by Col. William G. Cooke, and Fort Preston by Lt. William Preston, from whom Preston Bend received its name."

'Fort Preston' was no more than just a storehouse for supplies for militia men and Rangers at Holland Coffee's trading post, not a manned stockade.

## A Blue Funk at Fink; No Finks and No Poetry

Friday, June 27, 1975 , Dallas Morning News - The world famous Fink family reunion (in conjunction with national Fink Day) hit a few snags her Thursday. By 2 pm, they'd run out of barbecue and they'd run out of Finks. Hundreds of people had gathered, with full coverage by radio and television , to help families named Fink, Finke and Finque from throughout the US acknowledge their common bond. There was a couple from Sherman who had come to watch the Shawnee Indian dances; some tourists from Nebraska who stopped to find a bathroom and some teenagers from Dallas who heard they were giving away free barbeque. But, alas, there was no one named Fink.

**Oscar Fink...the only Fink in Town**

"There was a Fink here this morning", said Fink's mayor Patricia Albright. "he came all the way from Ohio". Another fink, this one from Brenham, also came left early. "But he explained he got here on a technicality", it was noted. "His family was Polish and the original name was Funk. But when they came to this country from Poland, they couldn't write so good, and the immigration people mistakenly put the name down as Fink. But National Fink Day is always a celebration in Fink, Texas – with or without Finks. Mayor Albright explained the official population of the town is determined by the number of people she can see from here grocery store. Now that totals nine people. Earlier in the years, she bought a prize winning steer from a young boy whose surname is Fink and had it barbecued for the annual celebration. But so many people showed up this year, the food was gone while some of the food lines were still forming. But no one seemed to mind. They camped on the lawn, visited and listened to music and tried to find people named Fink. Then someone remembered there was a man named Oscar Fink from Denison sitting in the grocery store. "He's in his 80s", it was explained, "and he's called the poet laureate of Fink". "Could you give us one of your Fink poems?" he was asked. "I don't write about Fink anymore," he chuckled. "These days I write poems about Watergate. Lots more material there, don't you think?"

**Fink Bash Includes World Domino Meet** - Thursday, June 26, 1975 Dallas Morning News - Introducing the world's first intergalactic domino tournament featuring domino players from all over the universe and San Francisco. The event is open to just about anybody. All you need is a simple knowledge of the game, a tuxedo and $100. The feature event at this year's National Fink Day, (which any true Christian calendar will tell you is Thursday,) is dominoes, the sport the New York Times claims is extinct and which Fink organizers claim people from all over the world are coming to watch. The rest of the year, Fink Mayor Patricia Albright reverts to the comparative obscurity of running her grocery, the only business establishment in the north Texas town. Judge David H. Brown, chairman of the tournament, is the recognized world's champion (recognized at least as far as Lake Texoma, which is a good domino's throw from Fink) and he came up with the idea after James Reston, the New York Times columnist, said the domino theory was as extinct as the game of dominos. Fink Day attracts several thousand persons, many with with related surnames. Finks, Finkes and Finques from throughout the US use the occasion to acknowledge their common bond. All celebrants feast free on Texas BBQ and soft drinks, watch Shawnee Indian dances and mill around.

## Fink Mayor after World Mark at Unique 'Olympics' Meet

Standing on One Foot Friday, January 9, 1976 Dallas Morning News - For the last few weeks, Mayor Patricia Abright has been practicing standing on one foot. She says it's the least she can do for her country's Bicentennial celebration. This tiny North Texas community – population 9, each summer presents the world with National Fink Week. This year, however, all of Finkdom is invited to a bicentennial Olympics. The affair will be during the usual Fink Week, June 20-26, and will be based on events recorded in the Guinness Book of World Records. "Anyone who wants to take a crack at breaking a Guinness world record is welcome to compete" says Mayor Albright, proprietor of the town's only gas station and general store. "I see no reason why we couldn't have competitors in such events as baby carriage pushing, brick carrying, clapping, frisbee throwing, hoop rolling, house of cards building, rocking, see-sawing, shoe shining, skipping and many others" she says.

Since the Fink Olympics is scheduled for National Fink Week, any Olympics contestants with the legal name of Fink will get extra awards for their records. "But we're in a financial bind" Mayor Albright said. "We'd like to get some becentennial funds to help us build a permanent type covered platform area where our Fink Jinks could be held. Not just for this year, but from now on" she said. She said a series of planning session is planned the next two months to complete all of the details with several clothing manufacturers in the area. Mayor Albright would like to have Fink Olympic T-shirts, caps, decals and other souvenirs made available. In the past years, National Fink Day has been the key attraction, bringing in 300 to 400 times the total Fink population. Now, with a week-long Fink Olympics under way, Mayor Albright said she expects the visitor total to run into the thousands. "Fink should qualify for at least one new Guinness world record", she said. "It will be the site of the most assaults on the Guinness world records, and who knows, we might even break one or two". The record for standing on one foot is five hours. Mayor Albright said she expected to be ready.

**Superstar in Fink?** March 30, 1976 Dallas Morning News - Kyle Rote Jr. who recently won his second Superstars competition, is wanted in Fink, Texas on June 20-26. That's when the Grayson County port on Lake Texoma will have its annual Fink Summer Olympics. Kyle Jr. has won more than $140,000 in three years of competition with the nation's best athletes in the Superstars thing. He won't win much money in Fink (pop. 25), but Mayor Patricia Albright, declared; "Perhaps Mr. Rote will add the Fink Olympics to his other laurels". One Fink Olympics event seems right for Mr. and Mrs. Rote's togetherness; skillet throwing with husbands as the moving targets.

# Frozen Dung Flung at Fink Olympics, Banned

Friday, June 25, 1976 Dallas Morning News - The Fink Week Olympic games rules committee, saying they wished to maintain the purity of the sport, Thursday banned Texan Bill Skinner's frost hardened cow chips from use in future prairie frisbee competition. Undaunted, Skinner picked up a warmer, more flexible chip and tossed it 139 feet for a gold medal and an unofficial Fink record. He had put the cow chip in his wife's freezer overnight so it would be hard. He "wanted it to hold together better", said Nancy

Ridgeway, one of the first members of the committee to spot the irregularity. When we went to measure the throw, we found frost along the edges. We got together and decided we couldn't allow that so we made him throw it again." Along with the gold medal, Skinner also was made an honorary Fink, a title of some importance in the Northeast Texas town. The Fink Olympics are held annually in honor of everyone in the world named Fink, and Thursday was National Fink Day. Periodic rains and high winds, however, held down this year's Fink Day crowd, which in the past has numbered up to 3,000 people from all over the US. Mayor Pat Albright said although only one Fink family lived within the loosely defined city limits, the number of Finks who gathered during the week may range from 50 to 100. The Fink Olympics have been held for 14 years in the vacant lot next to Mrs. Albright's general store, with events ranging from outhouse stuffing, to brick carrying. Theoretically, at least, contestants attempt to set new marks for the Guinness Book of World Records, but as a practical matter, just about anyone who thinks he can do something better than anyone else is allowed to compete. "We gave a guy a gold medal the other day for sitting on a Brahma bull" Mrs. Ridgeway said. "He climbed up on top of it, pulled back the reins and the bull sat up on its back legs. The bull stood that way for three minutes, 58 seconds, in front of 1,000 people. We awarded him a good medal on the spot" she said.

## House Fink Thursday, May 10, 1979 Dallas Morning News

**Rep. Bob Bush, D-Sherman, sports a hat and T-shirt promoting the "Fink Week" celebration in the small North Texas community of Fink. The Texas House approved a resolution Wednesday designating "every fourth Friday in June as Fink Day" and inviting all Texans to visit the town during Fink Week to "meet a real Fink."**

# Mayor of Fink Sells Out City's Top Office

December 2, 1976 Dallas Morning News - The administration here at Fink didn't fink out, it sold out. Patricia Albright, who has been the mayor of this hamlet for 14 years, turned over the title and that of the Fink general store and Museum to new owners Wednesday. The arrival of the new mayor, Robert Lattimore, his wife, who will be vice mayor, and their three children will swell the population of Fink to 16. The transition of power went smoothly, Mrs. Albright said. "We did it in the usual Fink fashion" she said. "Willard (her husband) and vice mayor Lucy Clement and myself just voted them in after me and Lucy resigned".

Fink, set in rolling wooded countryside dotted with herds of cattle, has been the site of the National Fink Day each summer the past decade. This year the Albrights sponsored the Bicentennial Fink Olympics in connection with Fink Day. The Albrights plan to stay in Fink, where town name signs are stolen as fast as they are put up. Lattimore, a former vice president and general manager of a concrete company in nearby Denison, said his family will live in a trailer until their new house is constructed near the general store. Lattimore said he had wanted a family business and the establishment here seemed perfect. "We had been intrigued by the goings on in Fink" he said. Albright said he thought the transition would be simple. The ex-mayor said Wednesday she plans to do a lot of resting although she promised to help out in future Fink festivities. She said she thought the selling out was the right thing to do. "The time to retire is when you're on top" Mrs. Albright said. "I don't know how we could top the Bicentennial Fink Olympics we had this year."

### **TAXES AT FINK WON'T "INCH" UP** Feb 28, 1977 Dallas Morning News

Fink landowners, take heart. A tax break is on the way. The dilemma confronting the Grayson County commissioners is not with the regular Fink residents, but with those several hundred "landowners" who each bought a square inch of the town as a novelty and promotional gimmick. "We figured it up and they (the Fink inch landowners) each owe a tax bill of about one cent" County Judge Les Tribble said. "But it would cost about $2.00 (in manpower, paper and postage) to collect it." With that in mind, the commissioners next week are expected to set aside all the one square inch tracts as an historical district, making them tax exempt. Even with the several hundred landowners, Tribble said he's not terribly worried about the historical district taking a very big chunk out of tiny Fink. "It only amounts to about 10 square feet" he said.

## The Name's Still the Fame of Rinky-Fink Texas Town

June 21, 1979 Dallas Morning News - Like it or not, June 22 is National Fink Day in Fink, Texas – athough technically, it should be National Finke Day in Finke, Texas. But then again, there are some who claim the Northeast Texas hamlet, population 13, should be called Georgetown, Texas, which could mean "Where is Fink, Texas?" T-shirts will be a hot item during National Fink Week this week, and on National Fink Day Friday. "I say we're putting Fink on the map this year – and in more ways than one" said Robert Fink of Converse, Texas, president of the Texas Finks organization. For the past 14 years there have been some sort of "think Fink" goings-on in Fink, Texas, to glorify those with the surname Fink and purge the nasty connotations that go with the name. But history reveals the Finks of the world wouldn't have had their personal mecca if the U.S. Postal Department hadn't fouled up about a century ago. Settlers originally applied for a post office under the name of Georgetown, but a community near Austin already had claimed that title. Per postal custom, the town was named after the man who submitted the application, a Mr. Fred Finke, but the postal department which sometimes loses mail, lost the "E" on Fred's last name, plus Fred didn't want the town named after him. Hence, Fink, Texas and the annual Finkfest. So pervasive is Finkomania that Robert Fink convince a state representative to introdue a resolution designating the fourth Friday of June as "National Fink Day in Texas". In addition, Fink enticed the state highway department to put new signs on Highway 120 (now designated Hwy 289) announcing the municipal domain of Fink. The signs require welded bolts and extra deep posts to prevent Fink fans from stealing them. This year's Fink festivities open with the singing of the Fink National Anthem, *Fly the Flag,* and will have singing groups, puppeteers, square dancing and the Scarlett Strutters, a dance group from nearby Pottsboro High School. Robert Fink will introduce all out of town Finks – some from the US have been known to travel 2,000 miles for the fun, as well as a few visitors from overseas – and the 1979 Fink of the Year will be announced. Visitors can enjoy special Fink sandwiches, made of bread from the Fink Baking Corp. of Long Island, N.Y. "Just imagine" Fink said, "of being in Fink on National Fink Day and sinking your teeth into a ham on Fink rye or a cheese on Fink pumpernickel. That'll be heaven!"

## Proud Finks no longer say rats. Texas celebration restores honor to funny "Rat Fink" name.

June 28, 1981 Dallas Morning News by Nikki Finke Greenburg - It was a celebration to make a Fink, Finke, proud. After years of turning red because of my maiden name, of enduring the occasional chuckle, of tolerating the inevitable question "Is that really your last name?" I was finally with a family of sorts.... Finks. The occasion was National Fink Day held to "restore a little honor and dignity to the grand old name of Fink" in the words of Texas Finks President Robert Lee Fink of Converse. It was a day when Finks, could raise their heads with pride.

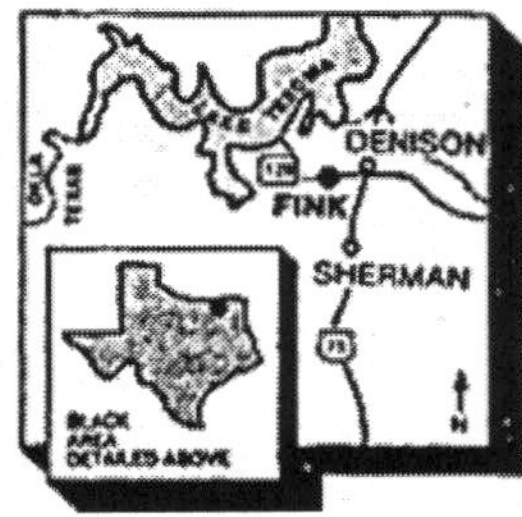


Left: Bob Fink in the Fink Museum, Middle: Brother and Sister Francis Finke Waynick and Paul Finke came from Baltimore for the Fink Week celebrations

It happens right here in Fink, a hamlet with a population of 3 and a bustling downtown comprising of 3 houses, 2 stores and an office building. Fink is even too small to be on the map. But once a year, the incoming lanes and highways overflow with Finks and well-wishers to give us poor folks with that funny surname some long overdue recognition.

1979 - Texas Legislature declares every fourth Friday in June as Fink Day. 1984 - Fink is shown on the county highway map. Mayor of Fink Ron Ivey with vice Mayor Linda Ivey in front of the Fink Motor Lodge, city hall and Fink Museum.

**Drydocks Motel and gas station at Fink where Dovie Halliburton was serving as Mayor. Check out those gas prices!**

**March 1987 Drydocks – entrance to Fink Museum**

Below: Fink in the 2000s – The old Albright Grocery is closed and Fink is a Ghost Town except for one convenience store on the corner of Spur 406 & Hwy 289

# MORE PEOPLE OF GEORGETOWN, FINK & REEVESVILLE

## Finke Family

Fink/Finke is a German name. Fred Finke and his wife Katherine who lived in Fink, were both born in Germany. According to the 1910 census, He arrived in the US in 1882. He married Katherine Wagner Jan. 3, 1889 in Sherman, TX. They moved to Georgetown about that time. Fred Finke was very involved in his community. He filed a petition for a post office, was a school trustee for Georgetown and donated land for a new school in Fink.

We would like to see the road overseer on the road from the gin past the school house use the split log or some other device on it, as there are several places that are almost impassable.

Fred Finke was re-elected school trustee in last Saturday's election.

H. C. Allen is putting in a telephone.

Crops are looking promising now, most all the corn is planted, and some few have plowed it.

Cotton planting is on; the crop will be increased a little over last year's acreage.

April 18, 1906

# Fiedrick George "Fred" "Fritz" Finke

**BIRTH** 11 JUL 1858 • Gellersen, Hameln-Pyrmont, Niedersachsen, Germany
**DEATH** 05 DEC 1920 • Grayson County, Texas, USA

## Facts

**Birth**
11 Jul 1858 • Gellersen, Hameln-Pyrmont, Niedersachsen, Germany

**Arrival**
1882

**Marriage**
3 Jan 1889

## Family

Parents

Spouse & Children

Katherine Wagner
1870–1940

Margarete Caroline Auguste Finke
1889–1954

Caroline Friedericke "Lina" Finke
1891–1902

August Henry Finke 1893–1957

Fritz George Finke 1896–1969

William Carl Finke 1898–1982

Carl Finke 1901–1961

Minnie Dorothy Finke 1905–1976

Mrs. Fred Finke Remembered - The Denison Press, Mar 22, 1940 - Mrs. Fred Finke, 69, resident of Grayson County for 47 years, died at her home in the Georgetown community March 21 following an extended illness, burial to be at Georgetown cemetery. Mrs Finke was the daughter of Mr. and Mrs. Abraham Wagner and was born May 28, 1870 at Baden, Germany. Mrs. Finke came to this country from Germany with her parents to Grayson County at the age of fifteen years and has resided in the county since that time. She was married to Fred Finke, now deceased, on Jan. 3, 1889 at Sherman. She was a member of the Lutheran church. Surviving are four sons, August and Fritz of Pottsboro, Willie of Calera and Case of Pottsboro. Daughters are Mrs. Margaret Clement, Pottsboro and Mrs. M. Montgomery of Pottsboro. A brother Abe Wagner, lives in Denison and a sister, Mrs. Anne Gresham lives at Omaha, Neb. Below: Margaret Finke Clement and family

Margaret Finke Clement; Dorothy Finke, Future Farmers' Sweetheart Denison High (Georgetown high school students went to Denison)

Land of the Hull and Allen Families highlighted in the squares

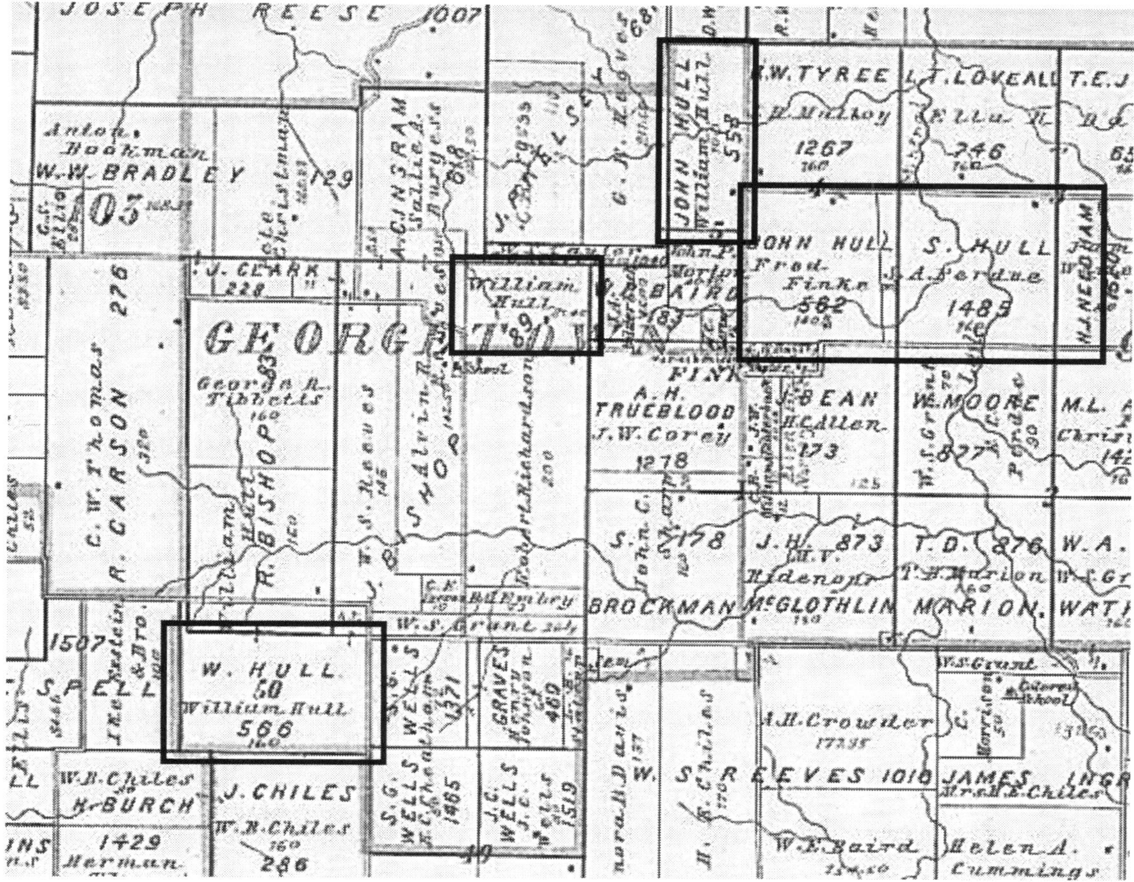


## HULL FAMILY THE JOHN HULL FAMILY

The following information on the Hull family is courtesy of descendant C. A. Parsons in 2020. The promise of free land brought settlers to the new Republic of Texas in the early 1840s. So it was that John and Sarah (Sinclair) Hull of Macoupin County, Illinois (originally natives of Pennsylvania and Tennessee respectively) packed up their three sons - Isaac, 5; William, 2; and infant John, who was just a babe in arms, and made the trip to the Red River in i844 as members of the "Peter's Colony" group. John made his claim for 640 acres on the banks of the river in the Washita Bend area about due west of the original Preston settlement. (Grayson County had yet to be formed and Texas was yet to become a state.)

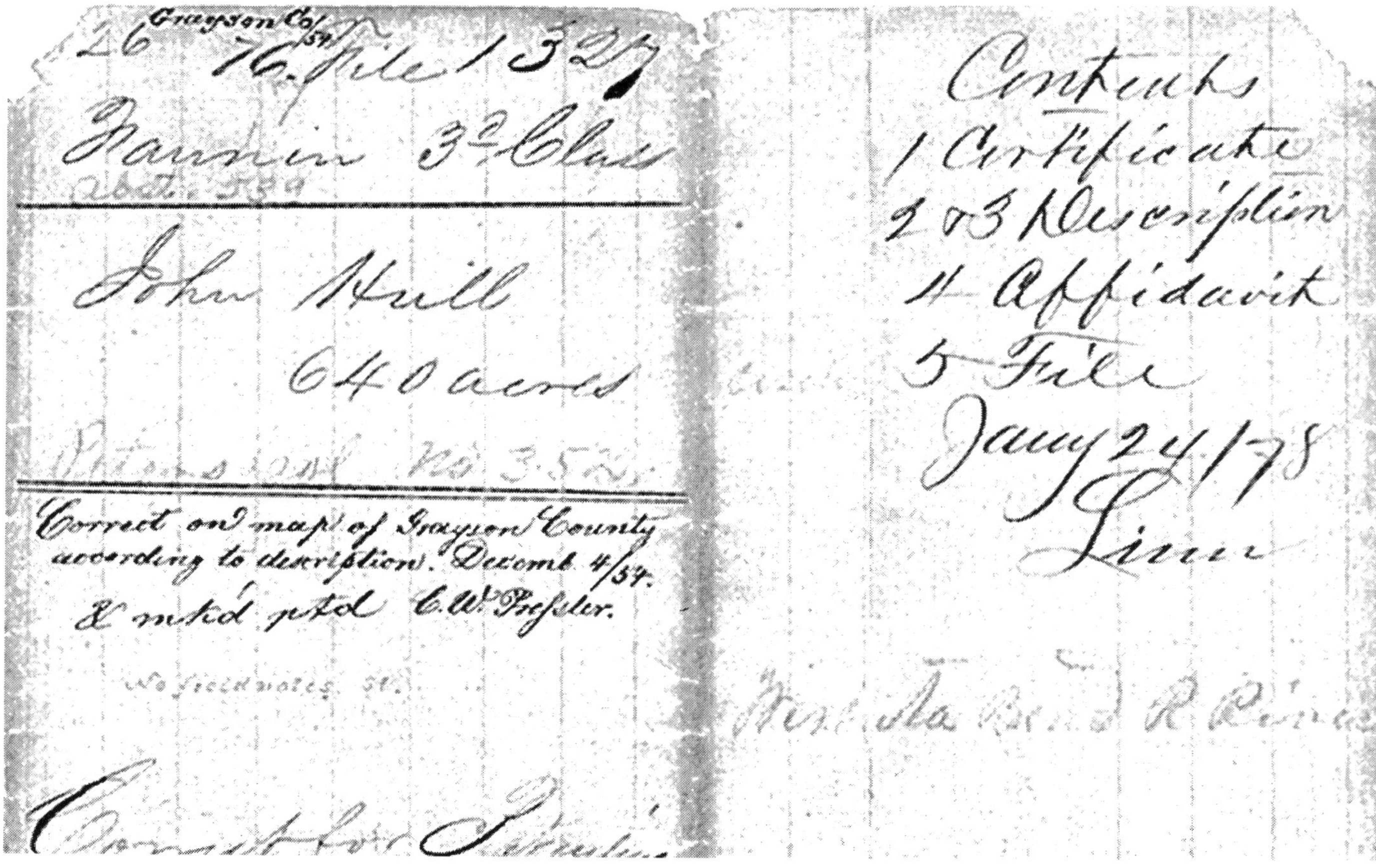

26 Grayson Co/54
16 File 1327
Fannin 3rd Class
Abst. 389

John Hull
640 acres

Patent No 352

Correct on map of Grayson County according to description. Decemb. 4/54.
& mkd ptd C. W. Pressler.

Correct for Patent

Contents
1 Certificate
2 & 3 Description
4 Affidavit
5 File
Jany 24/78
Linn

The farm prospered and a fourth son, George, was born into the family in 1851. John Hull died in 1854 but Sarah and their sons persevered and earned a comfortable living there for many, many years. Sarah married a second time to John Early of Ray County, Missouri in August of 1874. For reasons unknown this marriage wasn't of long duration and they divorced before 1880. Sarah then resided with William and his family until her death in 1882.

## THE HULL SONS

Isaac Hull joined the Confederacy in February 1862, enlisting with Fitzhugh's 16th Texas Regiment, Co. C. Isaac was killed in action June 7, 1863 during the engagement at Milliken's Bend, Louisiana. William Hull also joined Fitzhugh's 16th Texas Regiment, Co. C. He was taken prisoner by the Union forces at the Battle of Pleasant Hill, Louisiana on April 9,1864 but returned to Grayson County after the war. In January 1866 William Hull married Elizabeth Reeves. Three children were born to this marriage but all died in infancy. Elizabeth died in 1870.

April of 1873 found William marrying for a second time to Miss Mary Jane "Mollie" Baird, a native of Tennessee. In 1883 they acquired 160 acres in the rural Georgetown/Pottsboro area where William would build a large (for the time) 2-story home for his growing family. Known simply as "Hull House" by many, William and Mollie raised their 14 children there: Nora, Samuel, Carrie, Nina, Belle, Della, Bessie, Elbert, twins Beulah and Edith, John - died 1902 (age 14), Herbert, Mary - died I895 (age 3) Raymond.

William had begun to acquire a reputation for his farming and ranching skills by his management of the original family farm. By the late 1880's he was a prominent farmer/rancher in the area with over 1100 acres at his disposal and was considered to be one of the "well-to-do" of the community. William died in 1910. Mollie lived with daughter Beulah until her own death in 1929.

Sallie & John Hull, Jr. below left: Daughter of John and Sarah Hull - Millicent Hull Stalcup in this photo below right:

John Hull, Jr. took on the management of the family farm upon his brothers' departure in 1862. John married Miss Sarah "Sallie" Spence in Sherman, Texas in December 1865. Sallie was a native of Jasper County, Missouri. The couple built a home and settled down to farming and raising their family on 160 acres on the west side of Little Mineral Creek. Nine children were born to the couple: Mary, Sophia, Millicent, Elizabeth, Belle, Mabel, Connie, Jorrie (daughter), Isaac. The Hull's only son, Isaac, died at age 4 in 1889. John then bought land northwest of Doan's Crossing in Wilbarger County and moved to that area. After the daughters were grown and married, John and Sallie retired to a home in the town of Vernon. John died there in 1908; Sallie in 1912. George Hull lived with his mother until 1874. Four months after Sarah Hull married John Early in August of that year; son George married John's daughter Julia A. Early in December. The couple didn't immediately settle down in Grayson County. They opted, instead, to try their hands at farming in Wise County, Texas where they stayed for several years. In the 1880's they returned to Georgetown in the Pottsboro area and George tried his hand in the business sector owning and operating a small mercantile shop in the "downtown" area. However, financial difficulties arose which necessitated the liquidation of his property and the family then moved to Matagorda County for several years before once again returning to Pottsboro. Seven children were born to George and Julia but only six are known: Elina Rosa, Minnie, Edna, Johnny (died 1893 - 1 year), Irene, Annie from C. A. Parsons, October 9, 2020. The Allen family mentioned before was closely aligned with the Hull family of Georgetown through marriage as many families in small communities married close to home. The Hull and Allen families also married into the local Reeves, Steele and Terry families. The Hulls had land in several places in Georgetown, but they used a piece of land just north of the OLD Georgetown school at the present day corner of Georgetown Rd and Squirrel Lane, to grow many of their nursery plants. The Hull family land extended all the way south to Cemetery Road where the Hull family house shown below was located.

Above: Hull family house on Georgetown Road in the 60s and 70s. My (Natalie Bauman's) Great-uncle Joseph Cook once lived in this house above on Cemetery Rd while he worked on the Texas Nursery.

**Pottsboro Texas History Facebook comments:** Donald McElrath: "I walked through the house a few times with my grandmother, Marge Terry. We used to go over there and pick berries. The house belonged to a great-great-aunt of mine, Beulah Hull (1886-1992). The house was burned down by a bunch of drunk teenagers who were partying."

Left; Grandma Hull's house 1916; Right: John Bill Hull and Francis Hull

## Local Hero - George Hull of Pottsboro

# AGED MAN'S SACRIFICE FUTILE AS TRAIN TAKES TWO LIVES

Galveston Daily News 3 Sep 1929 Page 1, 6 An aged man sacrificed his life in a vain effort to save a child from death beneath the wheels of a southbound Santa Fe holiday passenger train, which crushed them and imperiled the lives of nine other members of a fishing party trapped on a narrow trestle bridge over Highland Bayou yesterday morning. The futile heroic effort was made by George B. Hull, 78, of Pottsboro Texas. The dead child is Lois May McCullough 7, daughter of H. C. McCullough of Brazoria, Texas. Mrs. W. T. Davis of Texas City, Mr. Hull's daughter, received a deep gash on the arm when a rod on the train scraped her arm as she hung by her hands from the trestle to escape the locomotive. The death of the child grew out of general confusion that arose among the dozen members of the fishing party when they sighted the train speeding toward them. They were peacefully fishing from railroad ties of the single track on the bridge when they discovered their peril. The bridge is near Texas City Junction, about nine miles from Galveston on the mainland. R. McCullough of Texas City, the girl's uncle, witnessed her death. Being a railroad employee, McCullough said he alone of the party members apparently realized the speed with which the train bore down on the bridge, which he estimated at fifty or fifty-five miles an hour, and shouted warnings. Summoning his wife and their child and Lois May, they started toward the south end of the bridge, which is a structure of 100 feet in length and 9 feet wide. His wife's hand was clasped around Lois May's and she held her own child in the other arm. As they began crossing the ties, Lois May's foot slipped between two ties, causing her hand to be released from Mrs. McCullough's grasp. The child regained her footing, and as she started anew across the track, the train struck her back. Mr. Hull, who was a few feet from the girl, rushed toward her as he sensed her danger, and was rushed by the train as it passed over the body of the child. Both bodies were dragged 300 feet. The aged man's body was mangled and he died almost instantly. Suffering a fractured skull and severe cuts on the body, the girl was placed aboard the train, and died en route to a Galveston hospital. McCullough shouted warnings as he saw the train approach, and ordered members of the party to seek safety on the wooden supports beneath the rails. Mrs. Davis was cut on the arm when a rod on the train scraped her as she hung from a cap. She was not injured otherwise. Five stitches were required to close the wound. In the party, in addition to Mr. McCullough and his family, were his brother and daughter, Lois May; his mother, Mrs. McCullough; W. T. Davis and wife and daughter of Texas City, and his son. McCullough said the train's whistle was blown at a distance of about a quarter of a mile from the bridge. Mrs. H. A. Palmer of Texas City, who was fishing with another party at the highway bridge over the bayou, said that they had started to fish from the railway trestle, but decided it too dangerous. While on the automobile structure, nearly a half mile away, she heard the train whistle and, looking around, saw the other group running for safety. "They were trying to get off the bridge, she said, but the train was coming fast and plowed into them before they could get out of the way." Mrs. Palmer stated that her son, Dr. F. Palmer of Houston, hurried to the scene, but Mr. Hull was dead before he arrived. She was told by those in Hull's party the he had tried to save the McCullough girl and that both were struck by the engine. Mrs. Ellsworth Benedict, whose husband and daughter and Mr. and Mrs. E. G. Benedict and Ellsworth Benedict left last night to accompany Mr. Hull's body to Pottsboro.

# MORE OF GEORGETOWN'S PEOPLE

BAIRD—Pottsboro, Tex., Sept. 6.—Mrs. Matilda Baird of this place died at Hereford, the home of her son, Sept. 3. The remains reached here this morning and were interred at Georgetown cemetery this evening. Mrs. Baird was one of Grayson County's pioneers, coming here in 1845 and living here ever since.

Dallas Morning News, Sep 08, 1902

**Above: a common sight in Georgetown, a lady proud of her chickens. From Jim Allen**

**Unknown Georgetown**

**Above: McKee Birthday Party, picture from Jim Allen. Below: Kids at Imogene Coonrod's birthday party in Georgetown, Fritz Christman, ? Bilderback, ? Arthur, Fred? Perdue, Bill Hull, Alton Gies, Lester Gies, Willie Bob Perdue, ? Arthur. Picture from Jim Allen**

# Henderson

W. M. Henderson Family in 1956 in front of Henderson family homestead at "Mrs. Tuckers" (Cedar Oaks Lane) in Georgetown just south of Red River and now Lake Texoma (east of Cambridge Shores)

Back Row. Joe, Frank, Melton, Lee, Tom, Oscar

Middle Row, Paul, Maryon, Claude, Clyde, Hurbert, Jim

Bottom Row Mollie Burges, Ella Brown, Zelma Hunt (Lida Stevens) No picture

Family of W M Henderson 1956

Taken in front of family home (WH)

Nannie Henderson Bilderback, Jennie Henderson Harrison, Mattie Henderson Shelton

# CHILES FAMILY

**Colonel James C. Chiles** - The Chiles family came to America very early. Lt Col. Walter Chiles and Elizabeth and their sons Walter II and William sailed from England in Walter's ship "The Fame of Virginia", landing at Jamestown around 1638. He was in the House of Burgesses and became speaker of the house in 1652. The Chiles family moved westward, and James C. Chiles was born in Kentucky in 1802 of John Henry and Sarah Ballinger Chiles. He married Ruth, daughter of William Hamilton, and they moved to Jackson County, Missouri via riverboat in 1834. James C. Chiles fought in the Florida War with the Seminole Indians in 1835-1837 and through his bravery became a Colonel. He also later fought in an engagement against the Mormons in Missouri. After the wars, he served in the state House of Representatives where he was Speaker for one term, he became a freighter and farmer-stockman, and outfitted and led wagon trains along the Santa Fe Trail. In 1861, Col. James C. Chiles and his wife and his minor children, gathered what possessions had not been destroyed by war, left the turmoil of Jackson County, Missouri to escape the revenge of the Kansas Jayhawkers and traveled to Sherman, Texas. After the war he moved back to Missouri for a short time, but his son moved him back to Grayson County, Texas when Ruth his wife died. James remarried in 1873.

## Cowardly Attack from the Back on Col. James Chiles Over a Dollar

Denison Daily News, September 9, 1877 – ", says a warrant was sworn out before Esquire Kirk for the arrest for the arrest of John Bowyer charged with assault to commit murder on the person of Col. James Chiles, who resides near Georgetown. The warrant was immediately issued, and John Bowyer arrested and placed in jail in Denison.

It appears the wife of John Bowyer was hired some time ago by Col. Chiles for attending to the duties of housekeeping. The Colonel at the same time told Bowyer that he could stay at the farm free of charge, and if he worked for him, his wages should be at the rate of twenty dollars per month. Bowyer, who is a carpenter by trade, says he did do considerable work for the Colonel on the premises, and on Thursday demanded a settlement. Some dispute arose in regard to the same, and Bowyer struck the Colonel twice with a fence rail – once over the head and once on the shoulder. Bowyer claims the Col. used the most abusive language towards him, and at last he could not control himself any longer and struck at the Col, but is satisfied the blows were not such as could result in serious injury, while the Colonel claims he did not use any abusive language, and the blows were delivered while he was getting into his buggy, with his back turned toward his assailant.

Grave fears are entertained that Col. Chile's skull is fractured, also, that his shoulder blade is broken. As the Colonel is nearly 75 years old, fears are entertained that the injuries will result in a fatality.

The trial for this case is set for Tuesday, Sept. 11th. We refrain from comments until we can get all the particulars as developed in the examination, but we cannot refrain from denouncing such a wanton attack on a gentleman of the age of Col. Chiles." From this author – They restrained themselves well, I think it was time for some of that abusive language and maybe a little retaliatory abusive action on the dastardly coward! P.S. He did NOT die, he lived until 1883 and died at age 81.

Denison Daily Herald, September 9, 1877 – Col. James Chiles, who lives eight miles south of Georgetown, was assaulted and beaten in brutal manner last night. The difficulty originated in regard to a settlement the Colonel had with a hired man, who had been employed on his place. The man claimed the Colonel was owing him a dollar more, and on the Colonel's refusal to pay it, the man attacked him with a fence rail, knocking him down and beating him over the head and body in a shocking manner. Col. Chiles is an elderly gentleman. The attacker Bowyer came to Denison and followed by William Chiles of Georgetown, the son of Col. Chiles, who went before Esquire Kirk to swear out the warrant for his arrest. Bowyer was found in a dwelling house in the southwest part of the city. Denison Daily News, September 12, 1877 -

The trial of John Bowyer, charged with assault with intent to kill Col. Chiles of Georgetown, was postponed until September 14th, on account of the inability of Col. Chiles to be present, he being yet confined to his bed recovering from the attack. Justice delayed is often justice denied and so it was in this case. The Dallas Weekly Herald, September 22, 1877 – The trial of J. W. Bowyer, charged with assault with intent to kill Colonel Chiles, was set for Friday. When the case was called, however, it was found that Bowyer had left for parts unknown. He was under a bond of only $100.

I bet Bowyer wouldn't have escaped justice had he been in custody in Georgetown! (Git a rope!)

James Chiles & William B. Chiles

## Col. William Ballinger Chiles

Two of Colonel James H. Chiles sons, William Ballinger and Samuel H., had already enlisted in the Confederate cause in the Civil War. William Ballinger Chiles was born on 23 June 1844 in Jackson County, Missouri. 'Bill' Chiles at age 17, on Jun 1861 at the beginning of the Civil War, was one of the first 16 to volunteer for the '8th Division' Missouri State Guard' Military Duty with the Confederate Army as a Pvt.. in Lexington, Lafayette Co., MO. in Bledsoe 1st Missouri Light Artillery Company. He was mustered into the Infantry on 11 May 1862 in Memphis, TN. William was made a Cpl. in 1863, and was in the battle until the Confederate Army surrendered on 1 May 1865 in Hamburg, South Carolina. William fought in the Following Battles: Dug Springs, Carthage, Drywood, Oakhill, Lexington and Sugar Creek all in Missouri. Pea Ridge, Elk Horn, Wilson Creek, Pine Mountain, Cronth, Luke, Ft. Gibson, Chickamauga, Missionary Hill, Raymond, Lookout Mountain, Chattanooga, Vicksburg, Altoona, Jackson, Atlanta and Nashville. William was presented a Citation of Merit by the United Confederate Veterans for serving with Patriotism, Honor and Fidelity.

William Ballinger Chiles and Harriet Eugenia Morrison were married in 1866 in Grayson County, Texas. Harriet Eugenia Morrison, Dr. Alexander Morrison's daughter, was born in 1843 in Sparta, Ontario, Canada. She died in 1926 at the age of 83 in Pottsboro, Grayson County, Texas. She was buried in 1926 in Fairview Cemetery, Denison, Texas where her husband William B. Chiles had been buried by her in 1900.

William went to his father's home 'Col. James Chiles' in Pottsboro, Grayson Co., TX. after his discharge. He was 21 years old and a veteran of 4 years of fighting. He married, and became a rancher with land in Georgetown, Martin Springs and just east of Pottsboro, TX. Bill devoted his energies chiefly to the cattle business and his wife Harriet established a land and cattle empire which embraces hundreds of acres of land in the Pottsboro area. Hard working and with a good business head, he became well known and respected all throughout Texas. Bill as he was called, worked hard under scorching summer sun and through winter blizzards. He also set up Feed Lots across the Red River in Indian Territory where he would fatten steers up for the northern market. He employed many men.

**Dipping Vat at Pottsboro.**

**POTTSBORO, Texas, April 15.—W. B. Childs, a farmer and stockman, has installed a dipping vat on his farm one mile east of town and is dipping his cattle to get rid of the ticks. This is the first dipping vat to be put in through this section and stockmen will watch with interest the results.**

## You Never Know What Will Cause Your Demise

We have already seen in this book that esteemed pioneer George R. Reeves who was on his way to be Lieutenant Governor of Texas, was taken out of this life in a most inauspicious manner – he died from rabies – from a bite from his OWN dog. Similarly, this tough man, William B. Chiles, had survived the brutal Civil War, but he was not match for a dried corn stalk. On an October day in 1900 at age 55 William Chiles died just as he had lived - in the saddle while riding his favorite horse 'Stonewall' (in honor Gen Stonewall Jackson his civil war idol). He was chasing stubborn yearlings across a frozen field of corn stubble on his ranch. His life ended suddenly when his horse stumbled and fell and Bill was thrown off with such force he was impaled on the corn stalk. His death was a great loss to family and friends.

## Just One Last Promise to Keep

October 12, 1900 - William Ballinger "Bill" Chiles' sudden death shocked all of the Georgetown and Pottsboro area and spread sorrow among his many friends and family. The sudden shocking death of Georgetown's George R. Reeves in 1882 was of a similar vein. On that day, two men stood at the death bed of their mutual friend Col. George Robertson Reeves, for whom they had just performed the last attention mortal hands could bestow, and pledged to each other that the one who survived the other should prepare the body of the dead for burial and dig his grave. It was no idle word, but a solemn promise made that day between W. B. (Bill) Chiles, who wore the gray as an artillery man under Gen. Shelby, and

George W. Green, who wore the blue as a volunteer in the Fourth Indiana. Men who faced each other unflinchingly in battle, but who met when it was over and clasped hands in friendship that never wavered. Yesterday, there was only one of those three friends who remained to fulfill the promise made. In this sorrow shrouded home in Pottsboro, a silent, gray, weatherbeaten, solitary man prepared a cold silent form for his last resting place. Scores of hands volunteered to assisted, but a chocking voice bade them stand aside. A pledge was to be kept to his dead friend, Bill Chiles. When the final work was done and they came to stand by the body, George Green broke down and wept like a child. The fact that the burial was to take place in Denison, and laws regulating the preparations of graves by that time prevented the fulfillment of George Green's announcement he was ready to go on with the completion of his pledge by digging the grave. It was at the urgent request of Mrs. Chiles that he be buried in Denison instead of the Chiles burial plot at Georgetown. The deceased resided in Grayson County for many years. The family had been staying with Mr. Chiles at his Pottsboro farm for some time due to his illness. Sherman Daily Register, October 13, 1900.

**George Green was a tough man like Col. James Chiles was.** The Sunday Gazetteer, on August 12th, 1894 reported that Green was the blacksmith in Pottsboro and he was badly injured by a wild mule he was shoeing. It pawed him down and kicked him in the head. For lesser men, this is often fatal, not George Green.

**George Green was well acquainted with sorrow long before he lost his best friends to death. Of course he had seen multiple horrors and sorrows in the Civil War, BUT George Green and his wife lost SEVERAL of their young children.**

1. Charles H. Green born September 16, 1873 - died January 11, 1884. Age 10

2. William E. Green born December 8, 1875 – died September 8, 1877 Under 2 yrs

3. Lorenzo P. Green born August 1, 1878 – died June 16, 1879. The Denison Daily News, June 17, 1879 - Lorenzo Percy Green, son of George and Sarah Green, grandchild of George Howe of Denison, aged ten months, died Monday morning at Pottsville. The remains will be brought in this morning for interment.

4. **Twins:** Norman Green born January 15, 1880 - died January 16, 1880. 1 day

5. Annie Green born January 15, 1880 - died January 15, 1880. Stillborn

6. Burnice Green born November 1, 1888 - died November 1, 1889. **Died on her first birthday.** The Sunday Gazetteer, November 3, 1889 - M.J. Fitzgerald and Charley Howe went over to Pottsboro Friday to attend the funeral of the one year old daughter of Mr. and Mrs. George W. Green. Mrs. Green is a sister of Mrs. Fitzgerald, also of Lorenzo and Charley Howe.

**More sorrow was soon to come for George Green because of an older child.**

Sunday Gazetteer, December 13th, 1903 - After a four week battle for life, on December 6th, John F. Green, aged 21 years, son of George and Sarah Green, died of pneumonia Saturday evening at 6 o'clock at the home of his parents, who reside at Pottsboro. He had been in the employment of the Denison City Water company, as water clerk, for the past 18 months and gained many friends while in Denison. He was buried at Georgetown on Monday, December 7th. His remains were followed by the largest concourse of friends ever witnessed at this place. The public school and all of the business houses of Pottsboro were closed in order that his many friends might attend the funeral. The deceased was a member of the South Methodist church, the W.O.W., the Woodmen Circle, and the C.M.A. The societies of which he was a member were represented from Denison, Pottsboro and Georgetown. The casket was covered with beautiful flowers which were the gifts of his loving friends. Pottsboro has lost, by the death of John F. Green, one of her best and noblest young men.

**George W. Green himself, the one-time Union soldier, husband, loving and embattled Father, tough indestructible local blacksmith and loyal friend, finally surrendered to death on June 11, 1923. His family are all buried at the Georgetown Cemetery.**

## Helen A. Morrison Married James Hunter Cummins

Below: James & Helen Alexandria Morrison Cummins House and Helen

James Hunter Cummins was a pioneer settler of Georgetown and Martin Springs who came from Missouri. James H. Cummins, of Scotch-Irish descent, came to the Lone Star State in 1861, and almost immediately thereafter volunteered for service in the Confederate army. He became a member of General Price's army, operating in Missouri, and toward the close of the Civil War was made quartermaster of his regiment. Upon his return to peaceful pursuits he adopted the vocation of agriculturist, and continued to be engaged in tilling the soil in Grayson County during the remainder of his life. He died July 23, 1890, with the respect and esteem of all who knew him. He married the daughter of respected Doctor Alexander Morrison, Miss Helen A. Morrison. His daughter Miss Mary Maude Cummins was a notable debutante in Martin Springs and Grayson County society at large.

# Holder, Young and Strait Family

## Nancy Clementine Young Strait Crabtree

BIRTH 1830 • Franklin, Tennessee, USA
DEATH SEP 1905 • Grayson, Texas, USA

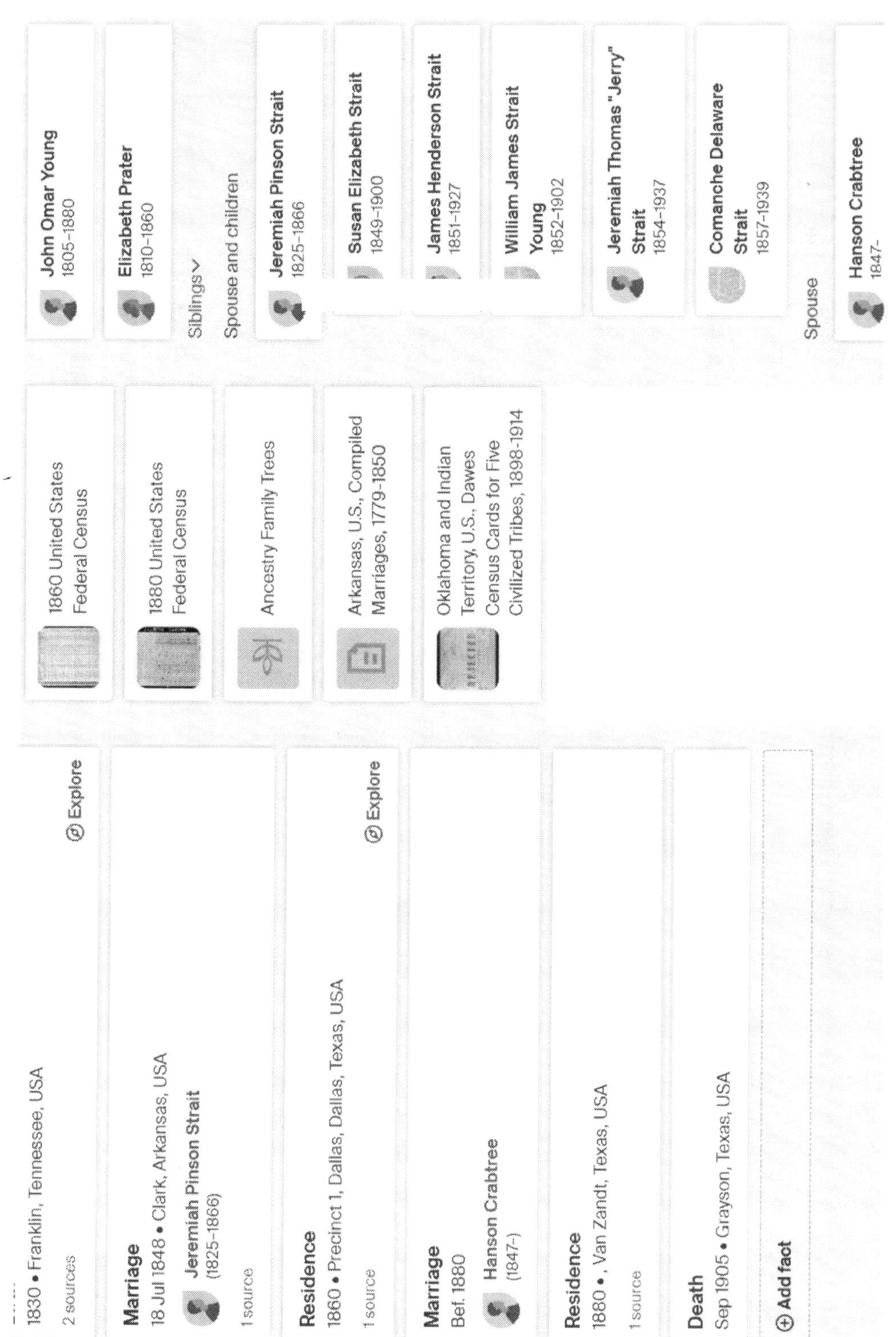

# Clinton Lafayette Holder

**BIRTH** 18 NOV 1845 • Polk, Missouri, USA
**DEATH** 18 JAN 1897 • Denison, Grayson, Texas, USA

Spouse and children

**Comanche Delaware Strait**
1857–1939

**Rufus Irving Holder**
1872–1959

**Ebby Hazel Holder**
1874–1874

**Thomas Minter Holder**
1875–1940

**Charles Fredrick Holder**
1878–1939

**Emma Eulah Holder**
1880–1929

**Susan Bulah Holder**
1882–1959

**Nancy Lilus Holder**
1887–1962

**Jerry Bledsoe Holder**
1889–1969

**Lawson La Fayette Holder**
1890–1990

**Gladys Holder**
1892–1982

# Charles Fredrick Holder

**BIRTH** 15 SEP 1878 • Pottsboro, Grayson, Texas, United States
**DEATH** 4 JAN 1939 • Denison, Grayson, TX

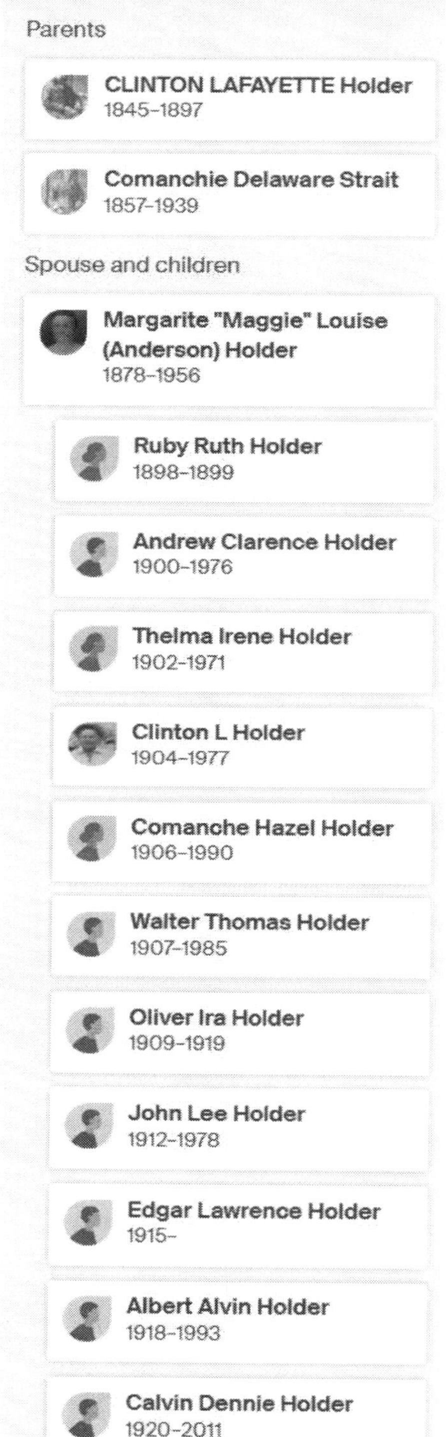

Parents

**CLINTON LAFAYETTE Holder**
1845–1897

**Comanchie Delaware Strait**
1857–1939

Spouse and children

**Margarite "Maggie" Louise (Anderson) Holder**
1878–1956

**Ruby Ruth Holder**
1898–1899

**Andrew Clarence Holder**
1900–1976

**Thelma Irene Holder**
1902–1971

**Clinton L Holder**
1904–1977

**Comanche Hazel Holder**
1906–1990

**Walter Thomas Holder**
1907–1985

**Oliver Ira Holder**
1909–1919

**John Lee Holder**
1912–1978

**Edgar Lawrence Holder**
1915–

**Albert Alvin Holder**
1918–1993

**Calvin Dennie Holder**
1920–2011

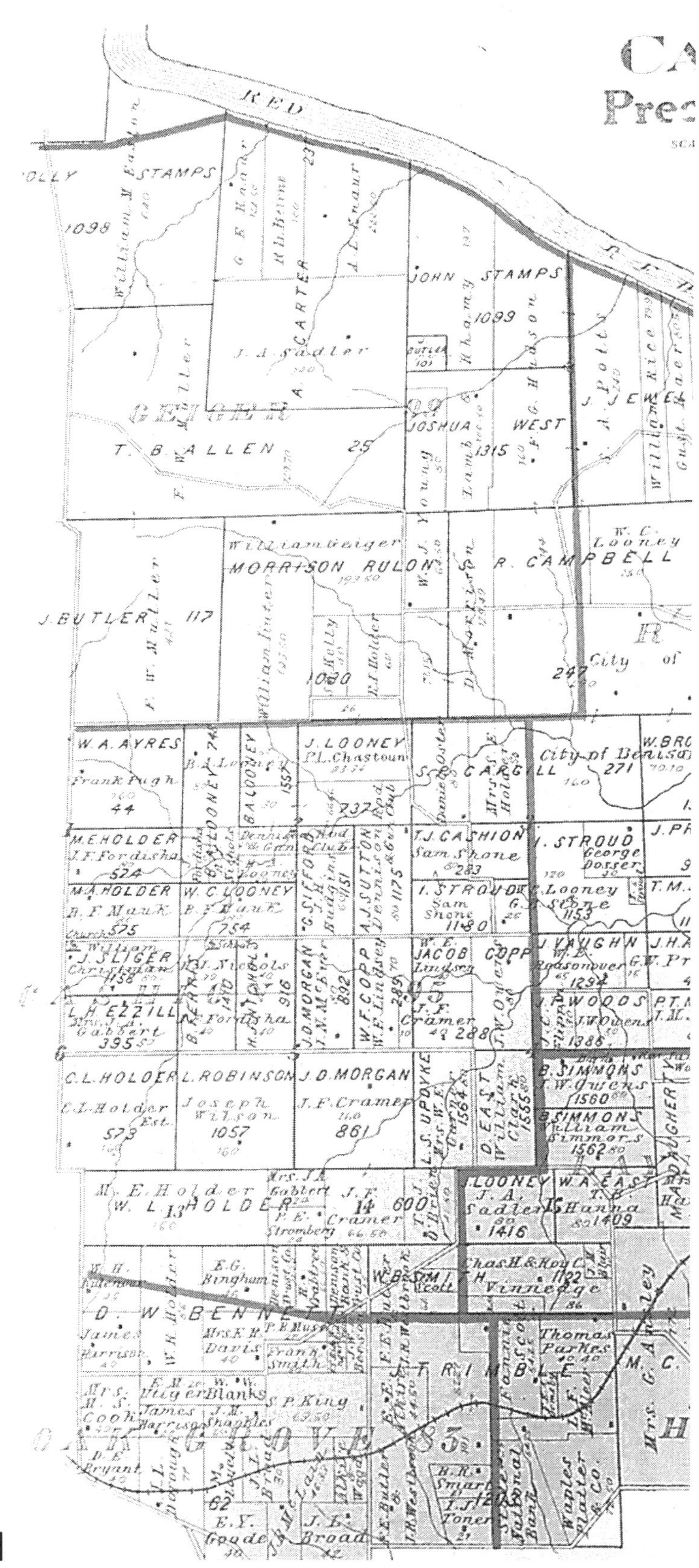


1908 Holder and Looney lands

**Most of the Holder pictures in the extensive article about the family below are courtesy of Nannette and Duane A. Martin (son of Ruby Holder Martin and grandson of Andrew Clarence Holder), and other members of the Holder family.**

## Cold Springs School and the Holders

William Lawson Holder was one of the earliest settlers in Grayson County; the family came from Alabama in ox wagons. He arrived in the very early 1840s. They lived in tents and a log cabin for two years waiting for their land grants to be approved by the Republic of Texas. The log cabin was originally built by William L Holder in the very early 1840's on William S. Reeves' land, close to the intersection of Crawford Street and Harvey Lane as a temporary residence waiting for their land grants. The little community at Cold Springs needed a school for their children and after the Holders moved they used this cabin as a school. It was believed to be the first in the county. The children paid tuition and furnished their own books. Clifton Lafayette Holder, the third of eleven children born to W.L. Holder and Mary Ann Looney, was raised in the eastern Georgetown area.

The patriarch of the Holder clan, W. L. Holder, built several other houses in the Cold Springs area, hauling the lumber by ox teams from Jefferson. They went to Shreveport, Louisiana once each year to buy sugar, coffee, salt and flour, lead & powder to mold their bullets. They killed wild game to eat - deer, turkey, prairie chickens and quails, which were plentiful in the area at the time. The family's clothing was made from cotton and deer skins. William Lawson Holder owned 900 acres; he later fenced off 80 acres with split rails in order to raise corn and cotton. Mr. Clinton L. Holder (the son) and his wife both attended school in the log structure. C. L. Holder bought the school in 1876 and moved it to Preston Road to use as a residence; located just north of what is now Highway 120 on old Preston Road (in between current Hwys 120 and 406) about five miles west of Denison. The original log structure was veneered with milled lumber, expanded and converted into a dwelling.

**Picture above shows the Cold Springs School after it was moved and had rooms added by the Holders.**

The first teacher, Miss Maudie Mangrum, slept in the loft and ate with the families of her students. A fireplace was the only way the building could be heated. The building had, and still has split-log benches for the children to sit on. There are holes in some of the logs and the story handed down by the Holder descendants is that pegs were inserted in the holes with planks laid across them to serve as desks or shelves. Carved inscriptions from Georgetown and Preston Bend families like the Steeles and the Reeves are still visible on the stepping stones around the door and foundation stones.

Historical Marker on Cold Springs School: "Pioneers, who were camped near a spring on property of William S. Reeves (1794-1879) while waiting for their land grants, built this one-room schoolhouse about 1855. The leader of the group was William L. Holder (1820-1876), who migrated to Grayson County from Missouri. His son Clinton L. (1845-1897) later used the cabin as a residence. In 1974 the structure was moved to the Old Settlers Village and restored." James Robert Clement said: The school was located on Preston Road on the property just south of the railroad tracks. The Holders lived just east of the school. There used to be a road that was just south of the school that went east to the Holder property. The road also took you to the Holder Cemetery. The cemetery is still there but all grown up with trees. The cows have knocked over many of the headstones.

**Where was the Cold Springs or Cold Spring Community and the Cold Springs school?** The following newspaper articles will help shed some light: Denison Daily News, October 2, 1875 - "The undersigned has a farm of fifty or seventy-five acres, forty in cultivation, situated four miles west of Denison in the Cold Springs neighborhood, which he will dispose of, together with the growing crops, cheap for cash. Apply on the premises, or address through the Denison post office. T. N. Bradley."

Denison Daily Cresset, August 6, 1877 – "A camp meeting, conducted by Rev. Mr. Cottingham is being held at Cold Springs, three miles and one half west of Denison. A large number went from Denison Sunday. Twelve individuals confessed religion; several had "the powers" and made the welkin (heavens) ring with their shouts."

The Sunday Gazetteer. (Denison, Tex.), February 10, 1895 – "A man by the name of Weaver, hauling wood from the Cold Springs community west of Denison into the city, fell from his wagon yesterday and broke his left forearm." The Denison Daily Herald, April 18, 1908 – "40 acres of good timber land, ½ mile west of Cold Springs on Denison and Pottsboro road. Price $1,000.

The Sunday Gazetteer. (Denison, Tex.), February 5, 1893 – A new wagon road west from Denison will pass along the north side of the new rail yards. At present the main road leading out into the Pottsboro country crosses the main line of the M. K. & T., west of the city limit about one half mile. When the new yards are completed, the road will either have to be thrown south to Sheppard street or a multitude of tracks will be encountered. Should the new road, mentioned above, be opened it would require by a little exertion to have the old Sherman and Fort Washita road that used to pass north by Cold Springs and across the railway track at Alkire station, reopened by the county commissioner's court. The old road is not passable for wagons or teams at present, but with a small amount of labor, it could be made a most acceptable thoroughfare. From the point of beginning at the southwest corner of the old Alkire homestead now the property of Dr. J. G. Ellis and others of Denison, north and east to the west terminus of Bond or Walker street, would not be over 700 to 800 yards. Then the entire route into Denison would be from deep sand and not a foot of black waxy land would be encountered. At present the old south road is one of the most abominable wagon roads in Texas. In the summer season, the sand between the one and three mile posts are from six inches to a foot deep; in the winter the sticky black land clay just before entering the city gets almost impassable.

In 1974 the original Cold Springs log cabin was the second building donated to the village, by Mr. and Mrs. Henry Sory of Sherman, was restored and awarded a Texas Historical Medallion. It was in the process of being restored in 2024 because of deterioration, with the use of antique wood donatied to the Village by Natalie Clountz Bauman.

House belonging to member of Holder family at unknown time below:

# Young – Holder House at Georgetown – VERY OLD

The house below at Georgetown/Fink began in the VERY early days as a log cabin. I understand the lumber structure of the house was built AROUND the log cabin about 1880. The cabin may date to the early days of Georgetown, i.e., late 1830s to 1840s. The house was occupied by the Strait, Young, Crabtree, Holder families (who were interrelated by marriage).

The older picture of the Young house **below** was taken in 1905, showing resident Albert "Buck" Young, wife Eunice (Reed) Young, their daughter Mary Eunice Young married a Holder. Albert's mother was also a Holder - Rachel Amanda "Mandy" Holder Young, daughter of William Lawson "Squire" Holder and Mary Ann Looney. Rachel was the wife of William Jefferson Young. A very interesting note about William Jefferson "Billy" Young and his wife Rachel Amanda "Mandy" Holder Young is that, according to her obit, she was born in Grayson County in 1852 where her parents homesteaded. Rachel and her husband "Billy Young once owned the land where Denison now stands. They moved from Denison to Marshall County, Indian Territory in 1892, living there until Rachel Mandy Young's death July 16, 1930.

Holder family in front of the Young family house at Georgetown. Back row: Clinton Lafeyette Holder, Father, was born 1845, Comanche Delaware (Strait) Holder, Mother, born 1857, Eulah Holder Morrison, Beulah Holder Nicholas, Charles F. Holder, Rufus I. Holder, Front Row: Lawson L. Holder, Gladys Holder Kibler, Nancy Holder Evans, Jerry Bledsoe Holder. Dorothy Holder was born later so is not in this picture. Nancy Clementine Young Strait Crabtree (1830-1905) was the mother-in-law of Clinton Lafayette Holder, the mother of Comanche Delaware Strait Holder.

This house still stands today (as of 2024) on 289 north of Pottsboro just past Preston Emergency Services, Graves Circle is just north and south around it, address is 85737 Preston Road Pottsboro, TX, pictured below:.

**House today**

Below: Comanche Delaware Strait Holder & Clinton Lafayette Holder

Below: Mary Ann Looney Holder in 1855, and group photo: William Lawson Holder, wife Mary Ann Looney and son George Washington Holder.

## Frontier Justice – He Stole the WRONG Horse!

Sunday Gazetteer. (Denison, Tex.), Nov 1873 - Jarrett Hastings had been a terror to the owners of fine horses in North Texas since he deserted from the Confederate Army during the war and for years since then, had been leading a life of crime. After deserting the army, he was charged with several murders and horse theft, but had evaded capture. He didn't enjoy his freedom very long though. He was surrounded by a posse of men near the residence of Dr. Issac N. Holder, five miles west of Denison on October 29, where he was shot and killed. Grayson County got too hot for him in 1872 and he went down to Dallas. He was seen on the day before the killing by two men on a public road and they reported the sighting.

Galveston News, Nov. 5, 1873 – The party who went after Jarrett Hastings had passed through Denison the day previous. They came up with him about noon the next day and ordered him to surrender. A fight ensued, and Hastings emptied the contents of two revolvers on his assailants and was only stopped after his horse had been shot and himself mortally wounded. He had stolen **Dr. Issac Holder's** horse, and before he died, told him where it was. The party crossed into the Indian Nation after other horse thieves and were determined to bring no prisoners back.

### Sheriff Investigates Holder's Posse -

A Denison newspaper on Feb 28, 1874 and the Austin Weekly Statesman, March 5, 1874 – Sheriff Vaden, with a posse, arrested W. L. Holder, and three of his sons, Evan, Jack and George W., and his son-in-law, Mr. Young. They live between Denison and the Georgetown settlement. The circumstances connected with this difficulty, said the Sherman Courier, go back to the days of the Civil War, when Lew Holder, brother of W. L. Holder, and Jarret Hastings were hiding in the brush from the conscripting officer, who was trying to force them into the war as soldiers. At that time, Lew Holder made an agreement with the officers that he would catch Hastings for them if they would let him go free. The officer agreed, for the purpose of getting them both into his hands, and Lew arrested Hastings and was bringing him to Sherman, Holder riding and Hastings walking, when, about eight miles north of the city, Hastings knocked Holder off his horse with a rock and stabbed him with a knife, killing him on the spot, mounted his horse and left the country. He returned last year, however, and was killed soon thereafter, under circumstances pointing strongly to the Holders as the guilty parties. Local resident Early Looney, who knew the Holders well and was related by marriage, confirmed that Jarret Hastings did indeed kill Lewis Holder during the War.

## Holder and Posse Pursue Another Horse Thief

Denison Daily News, November 29, 1873 – A notorious horse thief, William Strait, was captured at the house of his brother-in-law, near Pilot Knob, by Buckskin Bill and John Holter (Holder), on a warrant issued by Esquire Shackelford. He was in the act of saddling a fine iron-gray mare which was stolen, branded T E on the left shoulder. Strait and two or three other stole a horse from Buckskin Bill last August as well as several other animals from others in the neighborhood. Esq. Shackleford released Strait on a $750 bond.

He got away to steal again but ran into the Holder posse! Presumably, the Sheriff found the killing of Hastings by Holder's posse as justified, because Holder's neighborhood watch rides again that year. It often required this homegrown justice to maintain the peace because actual lawmen were so few and far between in those days. Denison Daily News December 30, 1874 - Some horses were stolen from parties residing in Dr. Holder's and T. J. Cashion's neighborhood, and Wm. Holder Jr., Jacob Copp, Thomas, and Jeptha Barbee started in pursuit of the thief, supposed to be Bill Strait, who had the reputation already of being a horse thief. While hunting Strait, they came up with his step-father, Crabtree, with whom Strait had been living, and told him they didn't want his kind in the country and that he had better pack up his traps and leave. This coming to the ears of Constable Cummins, he had warrants issued and arrested the above parties, on the charge of unlawful assemblage (called a Ku-Kluk or Ku Klux). They were held to bail in the sum of $500 each for their appearance before Esquire Kirk on January 6th. So it seems that in this free country, law-abiding citizens cannot tell a man they believe to be a horse thief, to leave the neighborhood without being arrested as desperadoes. (However, the TRUTH may be that they did more than ASK him to leave, but threatened him and TOLD him to leave, OR ELSE. The arrest may have been a protective measure for not only Strait, but to help keep the "law-abiding" citizens from committing a vigilante act.) Strait is now in jail in Sherman for stealing the above horses and has been bound over by Esquire Kirk several times, on different charges. He is considered a bad man. The Strait, Crabtree and Holder families were very familiar with each other and even related because Nancy Clementine Young Strait Crabtree 1830- 1905 was the mother of Comanche Delaware Strait - the mother-in-law of Clinton Lafayette Holder.

Denison Daily Herald, May 26, 1878 – A party of twenty-five men on horseback rode through Denison on the afternoon of the 25th and caused an uproar. A Herald reporter interviewed the leader, Deputy Sheriff Cashon, and was informed by him they were an **organized vigilance committee** to protect themselves from depredations of horse and cattle thieves that infest the country in great numbers. The committee dined at the White House with Col. Budd. Nearly all are farmers living near the **Cold Springs community**, west of Denison.

Denison Daily News, January 28, 1879 – The Grayson County Protection Association No. 1 had a meeting at Cold Springs. The association has proven of great benefit to the county in suppressing crime, and has now existed for two years. Denison Daily News, July 29, 1879 – The Grayson County Protective Society was formed for mutual protection against the incursion of horse theft. The society is composed of a number of farmers living in the country surrounding Denison and Pottsboro. They are a determined set of men and have become a terror to horse thieves. Robert Boren was arrested by the Protective Society at Cold Springs on Sunday morning. He was brought to Denison and put in jail for horse theft. The society members were on his trail for about ten days. Boren was confined in the upper cell together with a Mexican who was arrested for stealing a pair of saddle bags.

Boren is a native Texan who will look you square in the eye when speaking to you. Most people would believe him to be an entirely honest man to look at him. F. C. J. Leberman, a member of the Society and a reporter for the Daily News interviewed Boren in the jail. Boren stated he traded horses with a man named Thomas on the road near Carriage Point, Chickasaw Nation. He sold the animal in Caddo and started on foot for Texas. The members of the Protective Society recovered the horse and started in pursuit of Boren, coming up with him near Cold Springs. When Boren saw his pursuers, he tried to run, was chased, while shots were being fired at him. This convinced him to stop and give up. The horse Boren stole and soldin Caddo belonged a man named Coop, who lives on the prairie about three miles west of Denison.

As stated earlier, Will and Ben Holder, took their herds up through Indian Territory. They would drive them through good grass letting them fatten along the way. They would then take them to Fort Sill where the cattle would be sold to the government for food for the soldiers and Indians.

**Don't you dare steal these horses, they belong to the Holders!**

## Death of Issac Newton Holder and Fire at the Holder Residence

The Sunday Gazetteer. (Denison, Tex.), February 19, 1893 stated "a number of people from the city went to old Georgetown, north of Pottsboro, to attend the funeral of Dr. I. N. Holder. Sunday Gazetteer, Apr 5, 1896 – Early Preston Bend doctor, Dr. Issac Newton Holder, died in February 1893. More tragedy darkened the door of this family when the residence of Mrs. I.N. Holder, on the Preston Bend road, NW of Denison, burned on Friday night. The contents were destroyed, and Mrs. Holder had no insurance.

## Comanche Delaware Strait Holder Schifflett Obituary

The Denison Press, November 3, 1939 - Resident of Denison area for 60 years passes away. Mrs. Comanche Holder Schifflett, 82, died today at her home on Route 2 Denison. She was born Feb. 11, 1857. She received her education in a private school (Cold Springs school) which was later moved (in 1880?) and made it her home up to the time of death. She first married C. L. Holder and later became the bride of J. C. Shifflet. She was a member of the Methodist church. Surviving are her husband, four sons, R. I. Holders of Denison, T. M. Holder of Washington, J. B. Holder of Apache, TX; L. L. Holder of Denison; four daughters, Dorothy Holder Guilloud of Dalhart, Beulah Nichols of Channing, TX, Nancy Lilus Evans of Grand Junction CO, and Gladys Kibler of Long Beach, CA.

SERVICE

We have taken information and prepared this MEMO as a token of SERVICE, so that in the years to come you may refer to this little keep sake with accurate information of one to whom we have paid our last TRIBUTE.

*If we continue to love the one we lose—*
*We never lose the one we love.*

COURTESY OF THE
Denison Funeral Home
PAL NOE PETE OLIVER
FUNERAL DIRECTORS

A TREASURED MEMOIR

In Memory of

Mrs. Comanche Holder Shiflett

BORN
February 11, 1857

PASSED AWAY
November 3, 1939

SERVICES AT
Denison Funeral Home

OFFICIATING
Rev. Hargrove Grounds

FINAL RESTING PLACE
Layne Cemetery

Comanche Delaware Strait Holder Schifflett pictures below:

Comanche Delaware Strait Holder below.

**Below: Holder family pressing sugar cane at Georgetown. Right: Charles Fredrick Holder next to the press.**

## Unique Holder family stone house at Georgetown/Pottsboro

Below: Photos from Nannette Martin Holder - Circa 1915 photos of stone house at Georgetown/Pottsboro where the Holder family lived. Andrew Clarence Holder, Clinton Holder

Below: Left; Adrien Fine, in the derby hat; Charles Fredrick Holder in the overalls. Clinton Lafayette Holder is standing in the door. Right; Judson Cloer

**Holders, Looneys, Cooks and other Georgetown Residents Went to Riverside School Near Baer's Ferry**

**Below: Riverside school – 1916-17 school year. Back row: 1st on the left - Andrew Holder, 6th from the left – Clint Holder; on the left standing by the teacher - Irene Holder; Middle Row: 3rd from the left; Lottie Cook (Mosier); 5th from the left; Florence Cook (Clountz); 7th from the left; Hazel Holder; man on the end; James Jackson Cook, father of Lottie and Florence; Bottom Row: 4th from the right; Walt Holder.**

The schoolhouse was also a meeting place for celebrations like on Independence Day for riverside picnics. Below: Early 1920s photos of Riverside School, Andrew Clarence Holder,

**Above: Workers constructing old Hwy 75, including Holder family.**

**Below Left: Charles F. Holder, Maggie Louise Anderson Holder**

**Above Right: Hattie Roney Cloer Holder, middle row center in white dress; Grandma Cloer is in back row , second from left.**

**Above: a baby taking a bath in the dish pan!**

**Above: Lee, Lawrence, Albert, Red, Holder sons with their "Bull Dog". Below: the Holder Farm**

**Holders who were living in the Cartwright area north of the Red River in the early 1900s were inspecting the damage done to the riverbank after the devastating 1908 flood of the River. Andrew Clarence Holder below:**

# Bradley Family in Georgetown

## Seymour B. Bradley and Holder Family in

Seymour Bradley, 1798-1844 was born in Litchfield Co. CT. He moved to Alabama and married Rebecca Du Berry Dec. 1822. Their children are:

1. **Thomas Norman Bradley,** b. 1824 AL; d. 1906, N. M.
2. **Harriet Almeda Bradley,** b. 1826 AL; d. Aug.1910, TX.
3. **Joseph Warren Bradley,** b. 1828 TN; d. 1896 TX.
4. **Wesley Walke Bradley,** b.1830 TN; d. 1867 TX.
5. **Sarah Elizabeth Bradley,** 1832 TN; d. 1911 TX. She

Sarah Bradley married Robert Whitted in 1861, he had 2 sons from a previous marriage and he died in 1862. She married S. G. Perkins in 1866, he became a merchant in Pottsboro who had three children. He died in 1877 and she married Dr. Issac N. Holder who had children from a previous marriage. Sarah never had her own children but raised many stepchildren and she outlived all of them.

## Seymour Bradley's son Wesley Walke Bradley married a member of the Georgetown Reeves Family:

Wesley Walke Bradley, the son of Seymour Bradley was born in September 1830 in TN, and died in March 1867 in Texas. He married Nancy Tennessee Reeves on August 1854. She was born in February 1839 in Arkansas, the daughter of William Reeves and Nancy Totty Reeves. They all moved to Georgetown, Grayson County Texas. The children of W. W. Bradley and Nancy Reeves Bradley are:

1. **Nancy (Becca) Bradley,** b. 1857, Grayson, TX; d. 1871, Grayson,. TX.; she died at 14 years of age.
2. **William C. Bradley,** b. May 1859, Grayson TX; d. Sept 1868, Grayson, TX.; he died at 9 years of age.
3. **Lewis R. Bradley,** b. 1863, Grayson, TX; d. 1911, Deaf Co. TX; m. Ollie Dora Womble, 1896; b. 1873, Bear Creek, NC; d. 1956, Herford, TX.
4. **Sarah C. Bradley,** b. 1865, Grayson TX; d. 1867, Grayson; She died at 2 yrs of age; buried at Georgetown, Cem.
5. **Joseph Walke Bradley,** b. 1867, Grayson TX; d. 1952, Herford, TX; m. Willie Elizabeth Bynum, 1895; b. 1867, AR; d. 1950, Herford, TX.

Wesley Walke Bradley
1830-1867

Nancy Tennessee
(Reeves) Bradley

Info from Grayson County Frontier Village Museum

The Bradley family received multiple Texas Land Grants in Georgetown and in between Georgetown and the future site of Pottsboro on 20 May 1854 for 320 Acres and on 11 Oct 1875 for 640 acres. Below: W.W. Bradley, L. R. & J.W. Bradley land in Georgetown

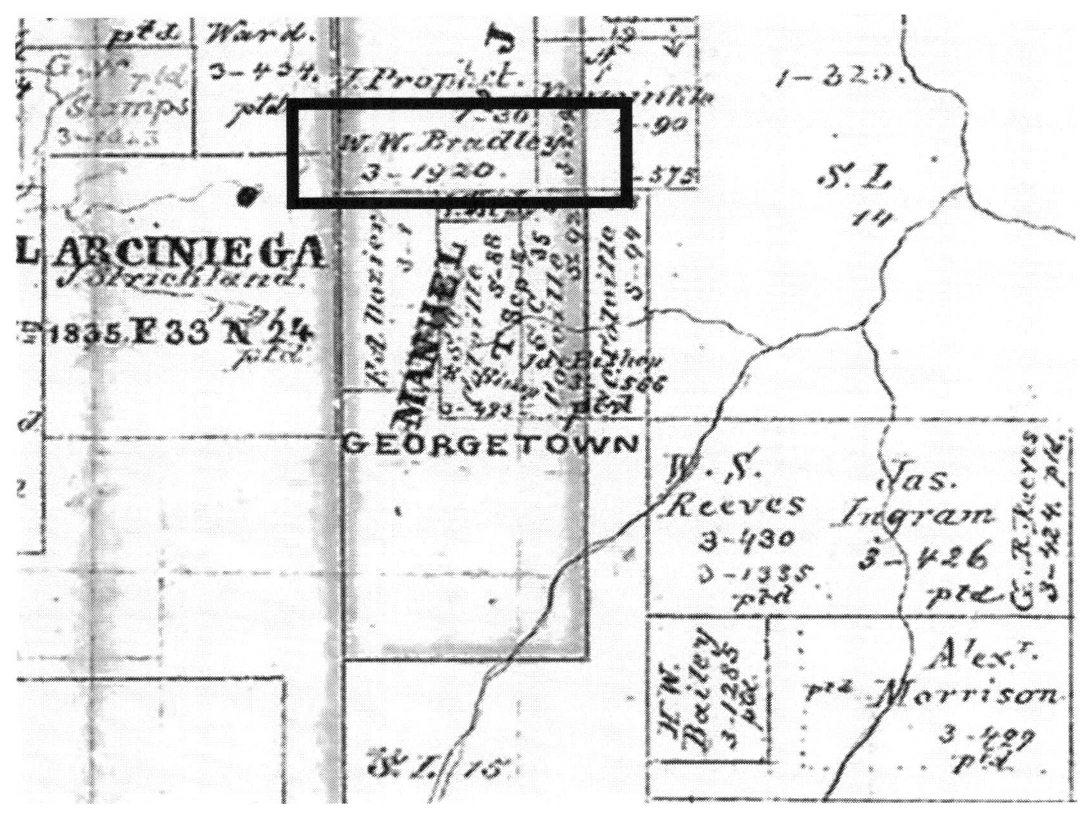

## Seymour B Bradley's son Joseph Warren Bradley – Early Texas, Grayson County and Georgetown Pioneer

He was a citizen of the Republic of Texas as is noted on his tombstone in Georgetown cemetery. PVT Bradley served with Co 8 Texas Cav, during the Mexican War with the Confederate States Army. Joseph Warren Bradley was born in July 1828. Joseph Warren Bradley and his brother Thomas Norman Bradley on the first of June 1847, enlisted in Captain Daniel Montague's Cavalry Company, 3rd Regiment Texas Mounted Volunteers for the Mexican War. Afterward, he returned to Grayson County where he drew lots with his brothers and sisters for their father's land since he had died without a will. His lot was 320 acres of the original land grant. In 1850 he was living with Micajah C. Davis and a laborer. In July 1862, Joseph and his brother Wesley Walke joined Martin's Reg., Cooper's SCA, Co., B. Randolph's Texas Cavalry. They fought in Texas, the Indian Territory and Arkansas. He married Mary Elizabeth Bostic in 1870 who was the daughter of Solomon and Elizabeth Bostic, the well-known County Clerk of Grayson County, TX. It was believed Elizabeth Bostic was a full blood Cherokee. Their children:

1. **Eliza Rebecca Bradley**, b. 1872; d. 1955.
2. **Elizabeth Seymour Bradley**, b.1874; d..1906.
3. **William Soloman Bradley**, b.1875; d..1970; m. Lita Moser, 1900; b. 1884; d. 1911. William moved to OK.
4. **Joseph Norman Bradley**, b. 1877; d. 1961.
5. **John Wesley Bradley**, b. Sept. 1879.
6. **Sarah Talitha Bradley**, b. Sept. 1883; d. March 1967.

He was an excellent horseman and had a license from the Federal Government providing breeding stallions. His death however, is attributed to his falling from a horse on December 27, 1896. Joseph Warren Bradley had written home to his sister in law during the Civil War that he wished to be buried to rest in peace with his friends and loved ones and not be buried in some mass grave with strangers, which he had no doubt often seen. He was granted his final wish.

Joseph Warren Bradley

Joseph Warren Bradley, left; Right; Elizabeth Seymour Bradley and Eliza Rebecca Bradley, daughters of Joseph Warren Bradley

**ELIZABETH SEYMOUR BRADLEY**- Daughter of Joseph Warren Bradley, was born in February 1874 and died February 1906. She married **Walter T. Clontz** in 1894. He was born February 1874, and died December 1995.

Children of Elizabeth and Walter Clontz are:

1. **Arthur Clontz**
2. **Viola Clontz**
3. **Ora L. Clontz**
4. **Elizabeth Clontz**

Walter T. Clontz was one the sons of Marion and Nancy Clountz/Clontz/Klountz at Locust. Viola Clontz was a longtime teacher at Oak Grove School and at other schools. I believe they lived close to where Hwy 121 is now located, close to Bradley Rd.

Walter T Clontz & Elizabeth Seymour Bradley Clontz, Children Arthur, Ora & Viola (Elizabeth who died shortly after the birth of their last child Elizabeth who also died). She is buried in Georgetown Cemetery.

**Denison Daily Herald March 6, 1906**

W. T. Clontz received a telegram from Cash, I. T., Wednesday, stating that Mrs. Elizabeth Clontz died there Tuesday, and would be brought here for burial Friday.

The remains of Mrs. Elizabeth Clontz arrived here Friday from Cash, I. T., and were interred in the Georgetown cemetery Friday evening. Mrs. Clontz was born Feb. 21, 1874, about six miles north of Sherman, was married to W. T. Clontz Sept. 25, 1894, and died Feb. 28, 1906. She was a daughter of Mr. and Mrs. Joe Bradley, who are pioneer settlers of Grayson county. She had lived in the neighborhood of her old home all her life until last fall, when her family moved to Oklahoma, where she died.

Elizabeth Seymour Bradley Clontz's Mother Mary Elizabeth (Bostic) Bradley, was the daughter of Solomon Bostic, also an early area resident. He was born in Tennessee in 1814 and came to the area as a member of the Peter's Colony around 1848 and his family acquired land grants, some in the Georgetown area. Solomon Bostic below:

Solomon became a Grayson County Clerk in the early 1850s and prior to 1860, he was District Clerk. As a county official, his name is mentioned very favorably as being a compassionate man to people of color in the Reconstruction days after the Civil War, in the book: Murder and Mayhem: The War of Reconstruction in Texas By James Smallwood, Barry A. Crouch, Larry Peacock – one reason for this may have been that it is said that the Bostics had some Indian heritage. The book says "several blacks were murdered by men in disguise, probably by Klansmen or by the Lee Raiders. On Feb. 16, three former slaves who lived in Grayson County's part of the Corners were sitting at home around their fire when brigand broke into the cabin and killed them. Six days later, another area freedman was found dead in the northern part of the county. The bureau man added that he was virtually a prisoner, for he could not leave Sherman without military protection. The professional men of the brush were numerous here and the slaughtering of freedmen was still going on…the section of the region bordering the Red River was in deplorable condition according to the bureau man, Evans. Dave Johnson (maybe "Dick" Johnson of the Lee gang) murdered several blacks in northern Grayson. Even if Dave was not a Lee man, he was doing terrorist work for Lee's guerrillas and the area's Klan groups. As late as August of 1867, Bureau Agent Anthony Bryant, who had replaced Evans, lamented that of all the civil officers in Grayson County, only one, **Solomon Bostick,** would give Freedpeople justice. Quite an accolade.

**Seymour B Bradley's son Thomas Norman Bradley**

His daughter was Sarah E. Bradley and she married a member of another Georgetown family – the Ridenhours – Martin & Sarah E. (Bradley) Ridenhour below left; Thomas Norman and Margaret Bradley

The house below was built by Seymour Bradley's son Thomas about 1842. He came to this area with his parents in 1838. Bradley married twice and reared 14 children in this one-room cabin.

Above left: George W Blankenship Jr. stands in front of the Bradley-Bodkin cabin which was donated by Coy and Hallie Wooten to the Grayson County Frontier Village.

Below: W. S. Bradley, picture from Jim Allen

# RUSSIAN RESIDENTS OF GEORGETOWN

Seaborn A. Perdue had land just east of Fink and just north of present day Spur 406. Perdue descendant Fred Perdue Jr. said that when Seaborn was elderly, he went blind. The family put wires on all the fence posts around the house and Seaborn would hook the handle of his cane on the wire to guide him as he walked around the yard.

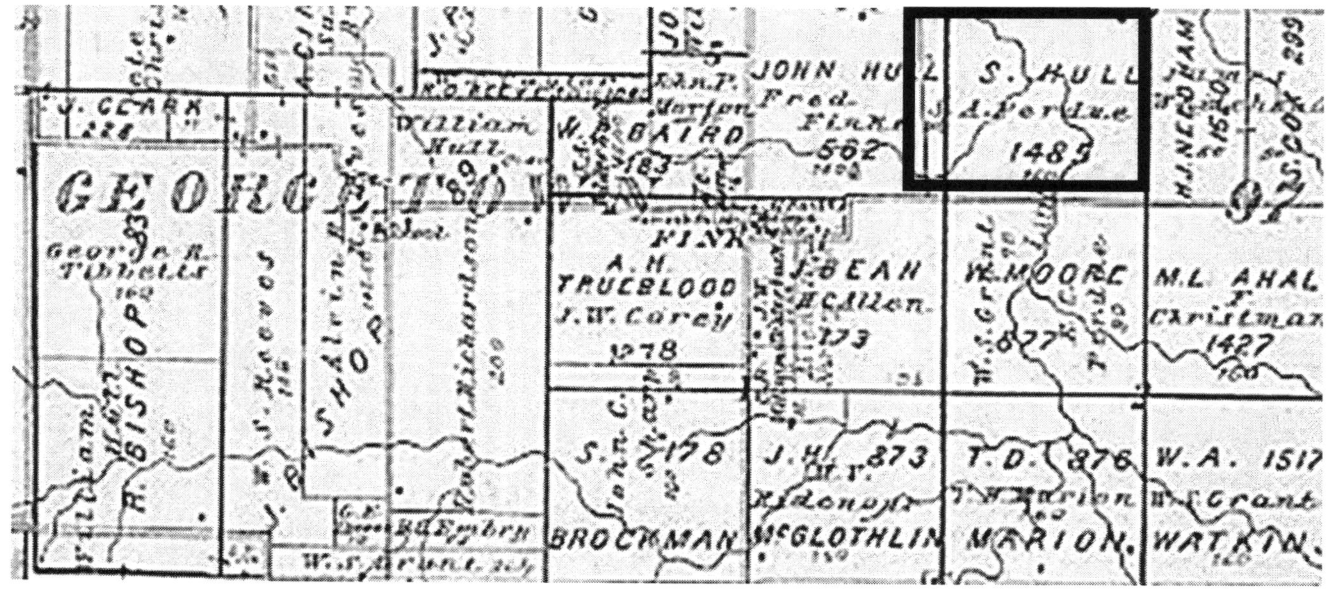


Sunday Gazetteer. (Denison, Tex.), October 9, 1887

Seaborn A. Perdue was listed in the Progress district as a delegate in the gathering of the Farmer's Alliance regular fall meeting in Gallagher's hall. March 24, 1889 "Messrs. Reeves & Perkins are receiving large invoices of dry goods from the east. The Spring fights have opened up. On last Thursday evening John Perdue, a very estimable young farmer, living about three miles north of here, became involved in a quarrel with one of his renters, named Cheatwood, over the use of a team Perdue was furnishing him, with which to make a crop, when Cheatwood attacked him with a knife, cutting him severely in the side, neck and shoulder. Perdue finally obtained a wrench, when Cheatwood's business "lay rolling," and is still rolling, as our Constable, William Creed Porter, has been searching for him in vain. Perdue, although, very weak from loss of blood, made his way to the house, and Dr. Carey, assisted by Dr. Geo. Noble, dressed his wounds. His chances for recovery are good."

# Seaborn Augustus Perdue

**BIRTH** 12 DEC 1834 • Greene, Georgia, United States
**DEATH** 3 JUL 1913 • Grayson County, Texas, USA

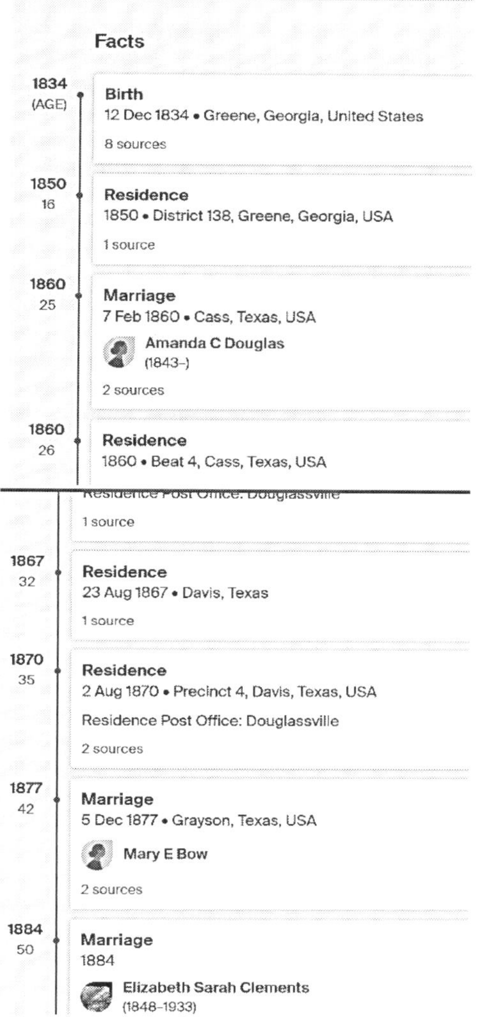

## Facts

1834 (AGE)
**Birth**
12 Dec 1834 • Greene, Georgia, United States
8 sources

1850 16
**Residence**
1850 • District 138, Greene, Georgia, USA
1 source

1860 25
**Marriage**
7 Feb 1860 • Cass, Texas, USA
Amanda C Douglas
(1843–)
2 sources

1860 26
**Residence**
1860 • Beat 4, Cass, Texas, USA
Residence Post Office: Douglassville
1 source

1867 32
**Residence**
23 Aug 1867 • Davis, Texas
1 source

1870 35
**Residence**
2 Aug 1870 • Precinct 4, Davis, Texas, USA
Residence Post Office: Douglassville
2 sources

1877 42
**Marriage**
5 Dec 1877 • Grayson, Texas, USA
Mary E Bow
2 sources

1884 50
**Marriage**
1884
Elizabeth Sarah Clements
(1848–1933)

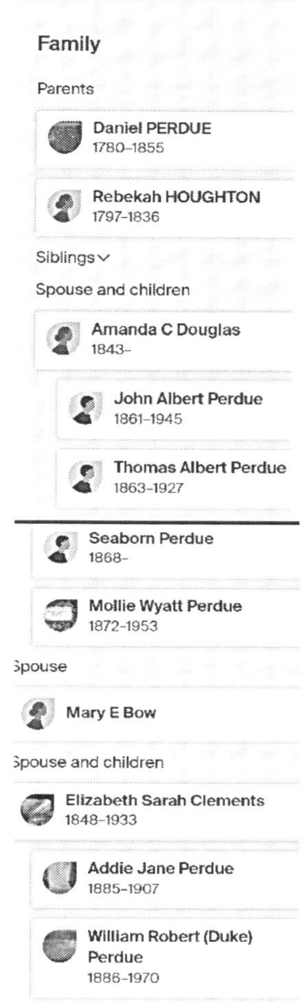

## Family

Parents

**Daniel PERDUE**
1780–1855

**Rebekah HOUGHTON**
1797–1836

Siblings

Spouse and children

**Amanda C Douglas**
1843–

**John Albert Perdue**
1861–1945

**Thomas Albert Perdue**
1863–1927

**Seaborn Perdue**
1868–

**Mollie Wyatt Perdue**
1872–1953

Spouse

**Mary E Bow**

Spouse and children

**Elizabeth Sarah Clements**
1848–1933

**Addie Jane Perdue**
1885–1907

**William Robert (Duke) Perdue**
1886–1970

Seaborn A. Perdue

# The Georgetown Signature Quilt

Signature quilts in the old days were typically made by a family group or community of people as a gift of remembrance for a loved one on the occasion of a wedding, anniversary, or for someone moving away from the group. Georgetown was just such a close-knit community and in 1932 over sixty of the area residents each produced their own signature quilt piece for inclusion to a quilt presented to Lou Christman Perdue. She lived to about age 97 and died in 1984, having been born in 1887 in Russia. This quilt still exists today and is in possession of her great granddaughter Jeannie Perdue Kartchner, the pictures are courtesy of Jeannie. Below: Quilt and Lou Christman Perdue

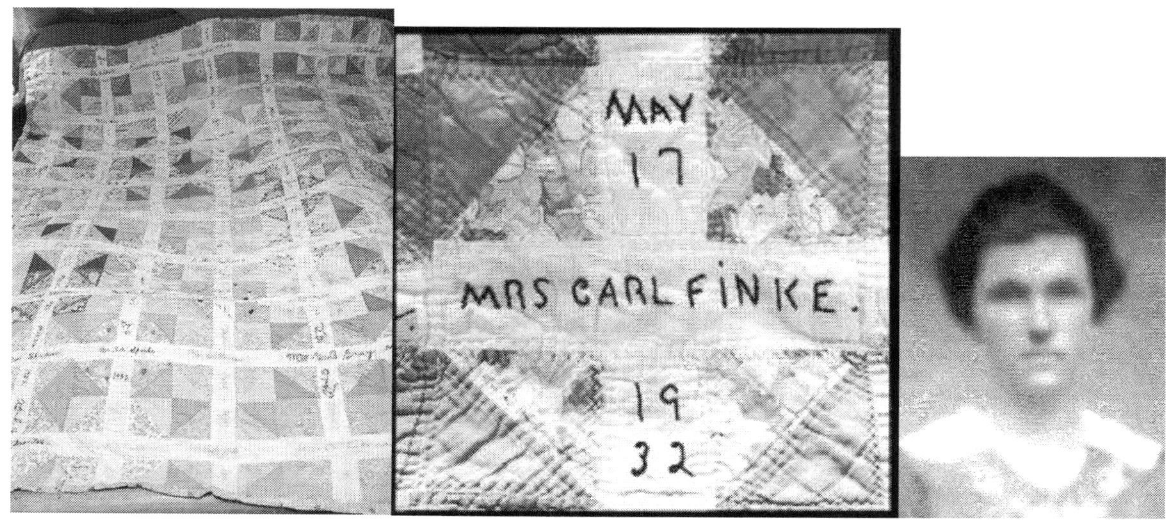


There was not enough room in the book for pictures of all the quilt pieces, but all the names and dates will be listed here below. It seems from the dates that the friends wrote the date they worked on the quilt, the Perdue family squares recorded the person's birth date. Mrs. Carl Finke May 17, 1932; Mrs. B. H. Holder May 193?; Mrs. Edmond Jones July 11, 1932; Della Owen April 15, 1932; Minnie Allen April 26, 1932; Alex. Christman March 25, 1932; Mrs. William Vest March 15, 1932; Mrs. E. Christman Feb. 20, 1932; Mrs. R. J. Payne May 13, 1932; Eula Hull Feb 12, 1932; Ed Allen May 2, 1932; Mrs. Callie Lea Blythe, Pottsboro, Texas, April 28, 1932; Mrs. Dan Christman, April 4, 1932; Clarene? and Pauline Perdue April 17, 1911; Della Cantrell, Potts. Tex, Mar 8, 32; Mrs. Dick Christman Feb 13, 1932; Fay Webb April 1932; Mrs. Leonard Jones March 23, 1932; Jessie Lee Book? April 27, 1932; Fred Perdue Sept 16, 1907; Mrs. L. A. Buford Mar 2, 1903; Miss ? Geis Mar 26, 1932; Mrs. Irene Christman April 12, 1932; Nina Hull Steele Mar 30, 1932; Mrs. Willie Sharpe April 12, 1932; Lou Perdue Oct 30, 1887; Eunice Wiest Mar 9, 1932; Simmie Buckley March 25, 1932; Willie Perdue Oct 12, 1915; Della Hull May 1, 1932; Barbara Lou Kee....? (there is an outline of a child's hand embroidered over the name) June 20,

1932; Betty (with an outline of a child's hand embroidered over the name) Mar 15, 1932; Mildred Wall Mar 15, 1932; Mrs. Bill Crook Feb 23, 1932; Mr. & Mrs. Will Carpenter Foss, Okla, April 26, 1932; Thelma & Geneva ??? Foss, Okla. April 26, 1932; Mrs. J. T. Carpenter April 4, 1932; Gene, Earlene, Ted and Hazel Strealy, Foss, Okla, April 6, 1932; Mrs. E. G. Geis May 18, 1932; Mrs. Clide Wall May 3, 1932; Dad (Fred) Christman Feb 24, 1932; Myrtle Forisha March 18, 1932; Mrs. Lydia O'Dell March 25, 1932; Mrs. Vivian Perdue February 11, 1932; Mrs. Bertha Luck April 11, 1932; Mrs. Effie McKee April 14, 1932; Mr. F. A. Sparks May 20 1932; Miss Emma Christman Feb 22, 1932; Thelma Allen March 17, 1932; Mrs. G. W. Wall April 5, 1932; Mrs. R. B. Gray April 5, 1932; Bob Perdue Mar 29, 1886; Mrs. Allen Clement 1904? 1932; Bill Crook July 8, 1907; M. A. Christman Feb. 23, 1932; Mrs. A. Christman Mar 25, 1932; Mrs. J. G. Geis.

PERDUE and STRATTON families intermarried

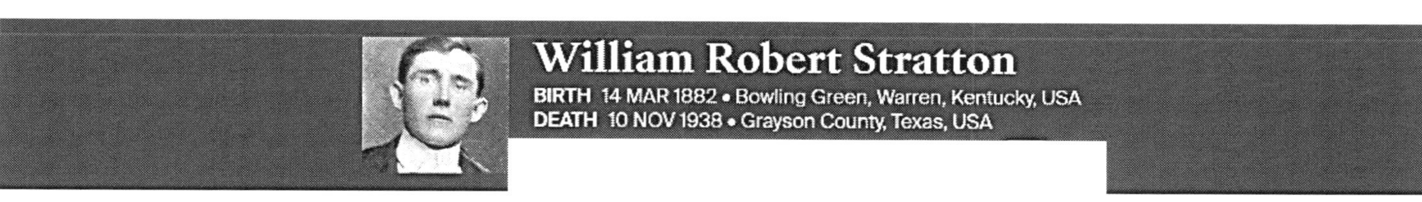


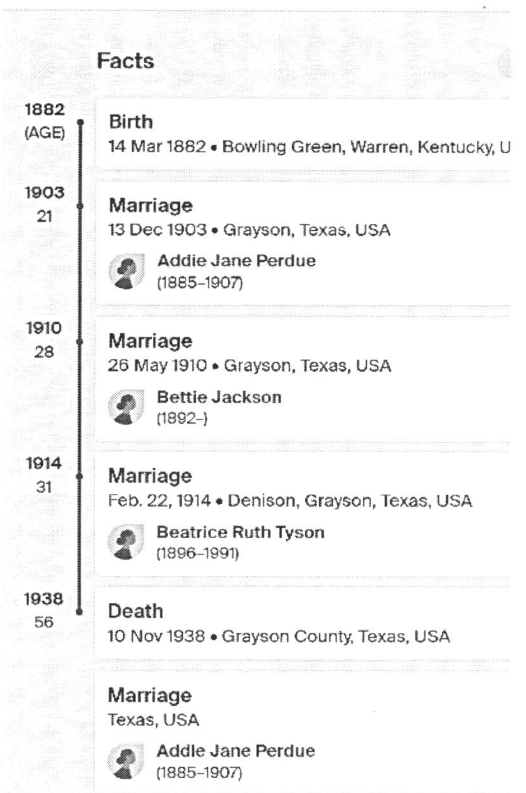


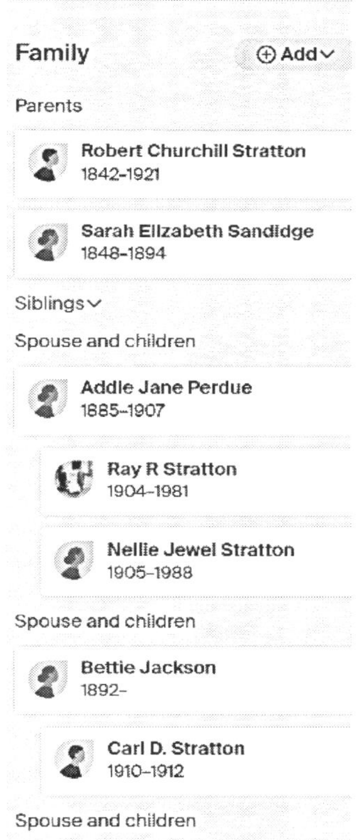

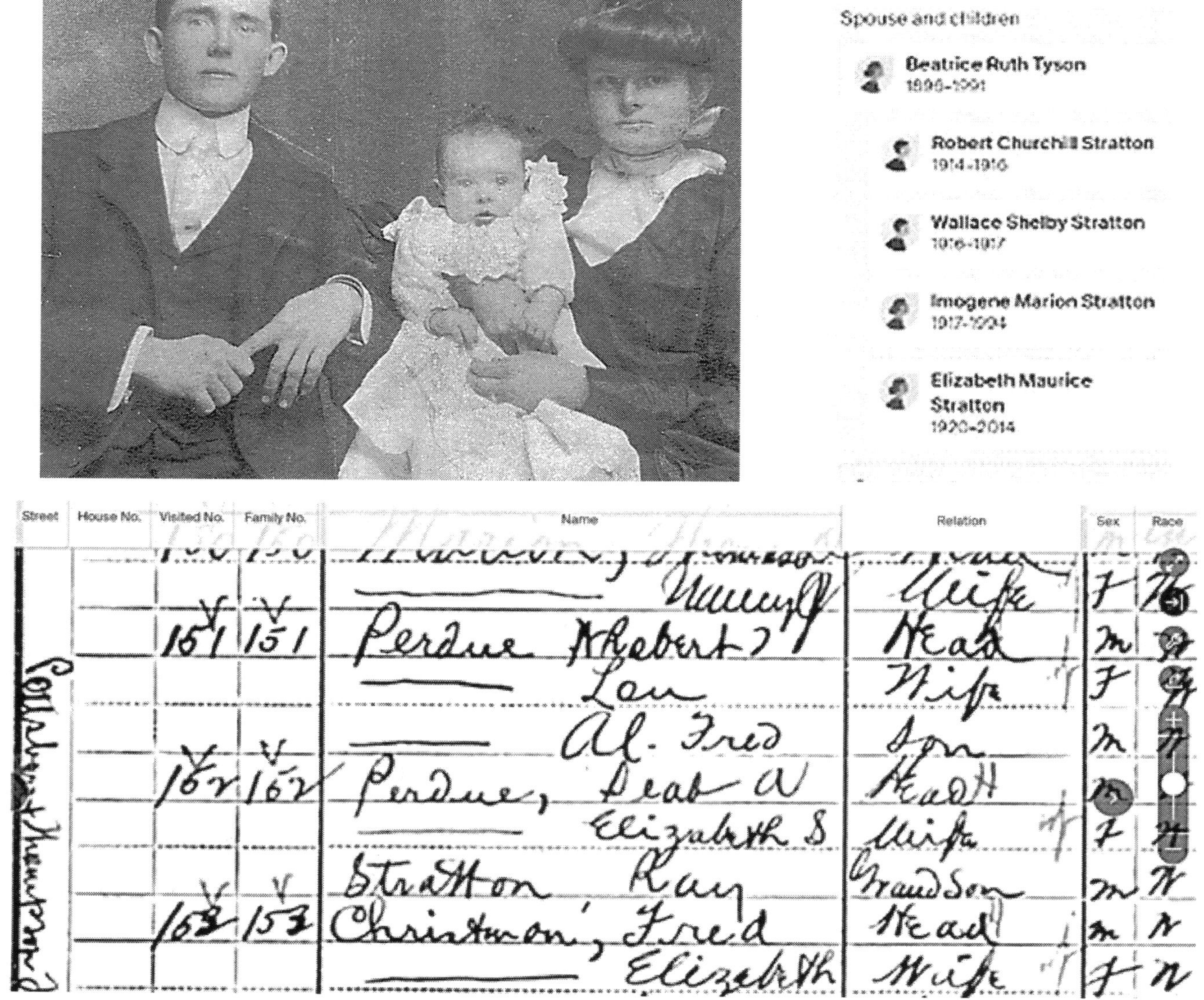


| Street | House No. | Visited No. | Family No. | Name | Relation | Sex | Race |
|---|---|---|---|---|---|---|---|
| | | | | —— Nancy J | Wife | F | |
| | | 151 | 151 | Perdue, Robert | Head | M | |
| | | | | —— Lou | Wife | F | |
| | | | | —— Al. Fred | Son | M | |
| | | 152 | 152 | Perdue, Seab A | Head | M | |
| | | | | —— Elizabeth S | Wife | F | |
| | | | | Stratton, Ray | Grandson | M | |
| | | 153 | 153 | Christmon, Fred | Head | M | |
| | | | | —— Elizabeth | Wife | F | |

1900 Census

Above: L to R – Elizabeth Clement Perdue, Nellie Stratton, Ray Stratton, Seaborn Perdue, Perdue Photos Courtesy Emma Stratton Cayton. The parents of these children were William Robert Stratton and Addie Perdue Stratton who was Seaborn and Elizabeth Perdue's daughter.

The Denison Daily Herald on May 28th, 1907 announced Mrs. Ada/Addie Stratton, wife of Robert, died after she had been ill for a month. When she died in 1907, the son Roy Ray Stratton came to live with his Grandparents and the daughter Nellie Jewell stayed with her father.

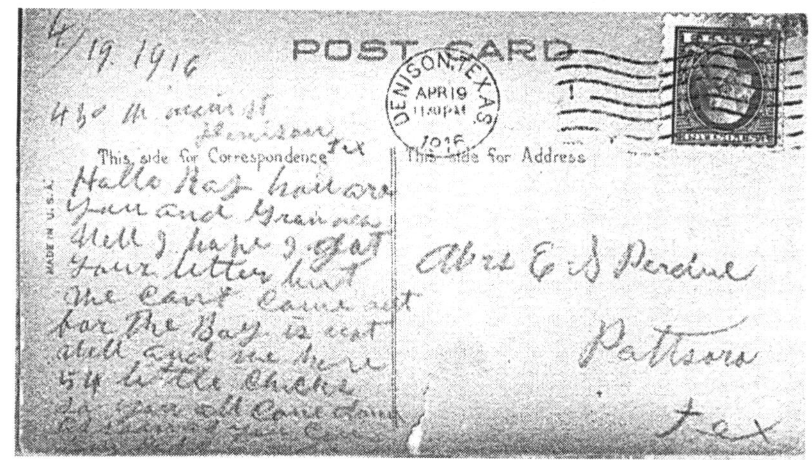


An Easter postcard sent to Mrs. E. S. Perdue (Mrs. Elizabeth S. Perdue) in Pottsboro (Georgetown) in April 19, 1916 from 430 W. Main St Denison. The card is courtesy of Emma Stratton Cayton. The card says: "Hallo Ray (Stratton?) how are you and Granma (Elizabeth Clement Perdue?). Well I have got your letter but we can't come out for the boy is not well and we have 54 little chicks. so you all come down as soon as you can...." Emma J. Stratton Cayton said she thought the postcard was sent by William Robert Stratton, her daddy's father. He was a barber in Denison, he and Beatrice, his second wife had 3 sons that died as young children. She found their gravesites at Georgetown. One of the sons, Wallace Shelby Stratton was born Feb. 1916 and died July 1917. So this could be the boy who wasn't well and prevented their visit that day. It makes it a very poignant card when you know what is about to happen. To add to the sadness, William Robert Stratton and his second wife Beatrice had just lost their one year old son Robert Churchill Stratton two months earlier on Feb. 28, 1916. He and Beatrice never had any surviving children, just those from his previous wife, Addie. Below: Roy Ray, Nellie and Robert Churchill Stratton, the baby who died.

The good old days weren't all good.

# ANTON BACHMANN/BROCKMAN

The Brockmans /Bachmanns were also Russians. As the last story stated, the Christmans and Brockmans ended up with land next to each other in Georgetown. When they got together to talk, they found out that they came from the same area in Russia as well! What a small world and what are the odds?!!

Terror on the Bachman Farm AKA The Well-Known Secret By Natalie Bauman

The moral of the following story - If you have money or valuables at your house, don't tell ANYONE, by word or deed; and also, crime doesn't pay. This story occurred in 1933 in the Great Depression after economic collapse and many bank failures. People didn't trust banks and were known to keep their money hidden at home. This caution kept some people's money safe, others were not so fortunate.... It made them targets. Local boy James Clement (who lived all his life in the Georgetown community) was about twelve years old at the time of this story, living on his father's home place near present day Simmons Shores north of Pottsboro. James said that not long before the murder, he was outside and saw two men walk up with a gun. He said they acted nervous and didn't want to look him in the eye, like they didn't want him to get a good look at them. They asked him for water. He said he heard later they had continued on to Fink to Abb Allen's grocery store there and had acted suspiciously, asking people there who in the neighborhood might have money in their house. ..... Then this headline appeared in the newspaper for the November 18th, 1933 murder: "KILLERS HUNTED AS MASS IS SAID FOR FARM WOMAN KILLED DURING ROBBERY - Surviving Sister takes Money From Hiding that Caused the Murder". As final mass was said Monday morning for Miss Antonia Bachman, 49, in St. Patrick's Church, officers of Grayson County headed by Sheriff J. Benton Davis and assisted by many citizens were combing the wooded districts of the Red River Valley in search of two men against whom Sheriff Davis has filed murder charges and offered a $50 reward. It was the most brutal murder anyone could remember in Grayson County. Antonia and Leopoldine Bachman came from Odessa, Russia with their parents 40 years earlier, settling first in Minnesota then coming to Grayson County 15 years later in about 1907. Following their father's death, the sisters farmed and prospered on their estate at Georgetown. Miss Antonia was murdered Saturday evening when a charge from a twelve gauge shotgun tore away part of her face. The home was ransacked but no money was found. Her sister was plowing I n a field when she heard the shot. Running to the home she called neighbors and officers who began the search as an ambulance from Denison hurried the wounded woman to a Sherman hospital where she died later. Money the victim and her sister had concealed in a trunk, behind a picture and in a clock was blamed for the murder. The money, undisturbed and covered with dust, was taken from its hiding place by the younger sister after officers arrived. It is not known if Miss Bachman refused to show the men where the money was hidden, or if they simply shot her, intending to search for themselves.

Later.... H. H. Buchanan, a transient formerly of Denison, worked on farms in the Georgetown neighborhood where the murder took place, leaving several weeks ago for Oklahoma, returning with John H. McCoy from Jay, OK last week. When apprehended, Buchanan's statement to district attorney Hubert Bookout was that McCoy told him "them old women probably had $30,000 or $40,000; and as I was acquainted (in this area), I could get a gun". He borrowed a shotgun and shells from a neighbor, saying they were going duck hunting. He said McCoy took the gun and walked away. A shot rang out and McCoy ran back to Buchanan asking for more shells saying "I want to kill the other one". On December 13th, Buchanan got a life sentence and McCoy received a 99 year prison sentence, though the jury voted 10 to 2 for the death penalty. But since it was not unanimous, death could not be the sentence. McCoy later got a conditional pardon. They were rushed to Dallas at once, although no mob violence was feared, nor any attempt was made. It was a well-known "secret" that the women kept money in the house as they paid cash to their workers. Buchanan had worked the farm for them during threshing time. Their parents died on the farm five years earlier, leaving the sisters a sizeable estate. Belief of the men that a lot of money was secreted in the Bachman home led directly to the robbery and murder. So if you are hiding something valuable, don't advertise the fact by word OR action to folks around the community, because word may get out to someone you don't want it to. (Oh, and crime doesn't pay, they didn't find the money, but they sure did do the time – in prison).

For more on this story, get my book "When The West Was Wild In Pottsboro Texas".

## GERMAN RESIDENTS - **Clement**

Picture above of James Issac Clement homestead at Georgetown near present day Simmons Shores on or before 1920. These Clement pictures courtesy of Dusty Williams.

Below: Fellow Georgetown resident Seaborn Perdue's second wife Elizabeth Clement with her siblings, James Issac Clement & Ambrose Clement,

round portrait – James Issac Clement

Bottom row, L to R: Nanny, Lillie, Carrie and Mary Clement. Second Row L to R: John, father James Issac Clement and wife Sarah Clement, and Minnie; Back Row L to R: Alfred, Bill, Jim and George Clement.

Below: Left -Nancy and Lillie Clement with their boyfriends; Right on horse - James Issac Clement

Funeral of James Issac Clement in August 1925 from Tracy Christman

Funeral Notice of James Issac Clement

# Pete, Fred and Alexander CHRISTMAN

Pete Christman was born in Germany on Feb. 5, 1865 and moved to Odessa, Russia where farmed land was better. Here, he married Eula Smythe. They immigrated to the US through a port in Bremen Germany on the ship Hermann in 1887 and sailed to Baltimore MD arriving the 23rd of November.

1887 Baltimore, Passenger Lists, 1820-1964 Name: Friedr Christmann 52 farmer Russia, Elizabeth 46 wife; ????? 26 farmer, Eva 25 wife; Friedr 25 farmer, Elisa A. 25 wife; Peter 22 farmer, Juliana 18 wife; Philipp 19 farmer, etc.... Christmann

Arrival Date: 23 Nov 1887 Port of Departure: Bremen, Germany Ship Name: Hermann Port of Arrival: Baltimore, Maryland

Elizabeth Christman refused to learn English because she said she didn't want to be here. According to the family, they traveled to New York and there learned about the Grayson County Texas area with its excellent farming lands and railroad jobs available. First, they lived in Coalgate, Indian Territory for a little while before moving to Georgetown. Elizabeth and Effie Christman were born there in 1890 and 1895. The other children were two sets of twins who died at or shortly after birth. Eula Christman died in 1898 and is buried at Oakwood cemetery. Around the turn of the century, the Christmans moved to Georgetown in northwestern Grayson County. They moved into an existing log cabin on a parcel of land at the corner of modern day Georgetown Road and Tanglewood Trail. On the mantle piece of this cabin, someone long ago wrote or etched "1840" into it. This old cabin was moved to nearby Texoma Estates and was, in the 70s, the property of Mrs. Clarence Jones and was called Chris Oaks, according to family accounts from Tracy Christman, and the Grayson County Frontier Village history book. Tracy believed the cabin was moved from there to Leonard, I am not sure where it is today.

If this log cabin which the Christmans moved into was built in 1840, in this place, which is directly across the road from the old Fort Johnston, then this was either built by some of the soldiers building the Fort for shelter that winter or perhaps some early pioneer in that area, like George Ivey, who had land in that immediate area at the time. In 1900, Pete married Callie Stromire and their children were Katherine , Emma and Fritz. Pete was a farmer and dairyman. Multiple sources (Tracy Christman and Grayson County Frontier Village history book) said that Mr. Christman stood up on the hill where the cabin was shortly after they moved to Georgetown and there were no trees. He could see another man standing acres away. They walked to meet each other. It was Anton Bachmann/ Brockman and they found out they were from the same town in Russia or Germany, not sure which. Tracy Christman: "Alexander Christman bought the cabin from his uncle Pete. The beds were made of feathers, Alex and his wife Roxie Farrell Christman were good people. Always had quilts to sit on and Roxie's cookies tasted like soap!" He also had a wine cellar which he dug next to his house.

1900 census - Name: Fred Christman Age: 36 Birth Date: abt 1864

Birthplace: Russia Immigration Year: 1887 Relation to Head of House: Head

Spouse's Name: Lizzie Christman Household Members: Fred Christman 36 Lizzie Christman 35 Lula Christman 13 Alexander Christman 11 Edward Christman 6 Emma Christman 4 Daniel Christman 3 Lizzie Christman 6/12

1910 census – The Christmans came from Russia, and in Georgetown, became neighbors of fellow Russians, Anton Brockman and Seaborn Perdue.

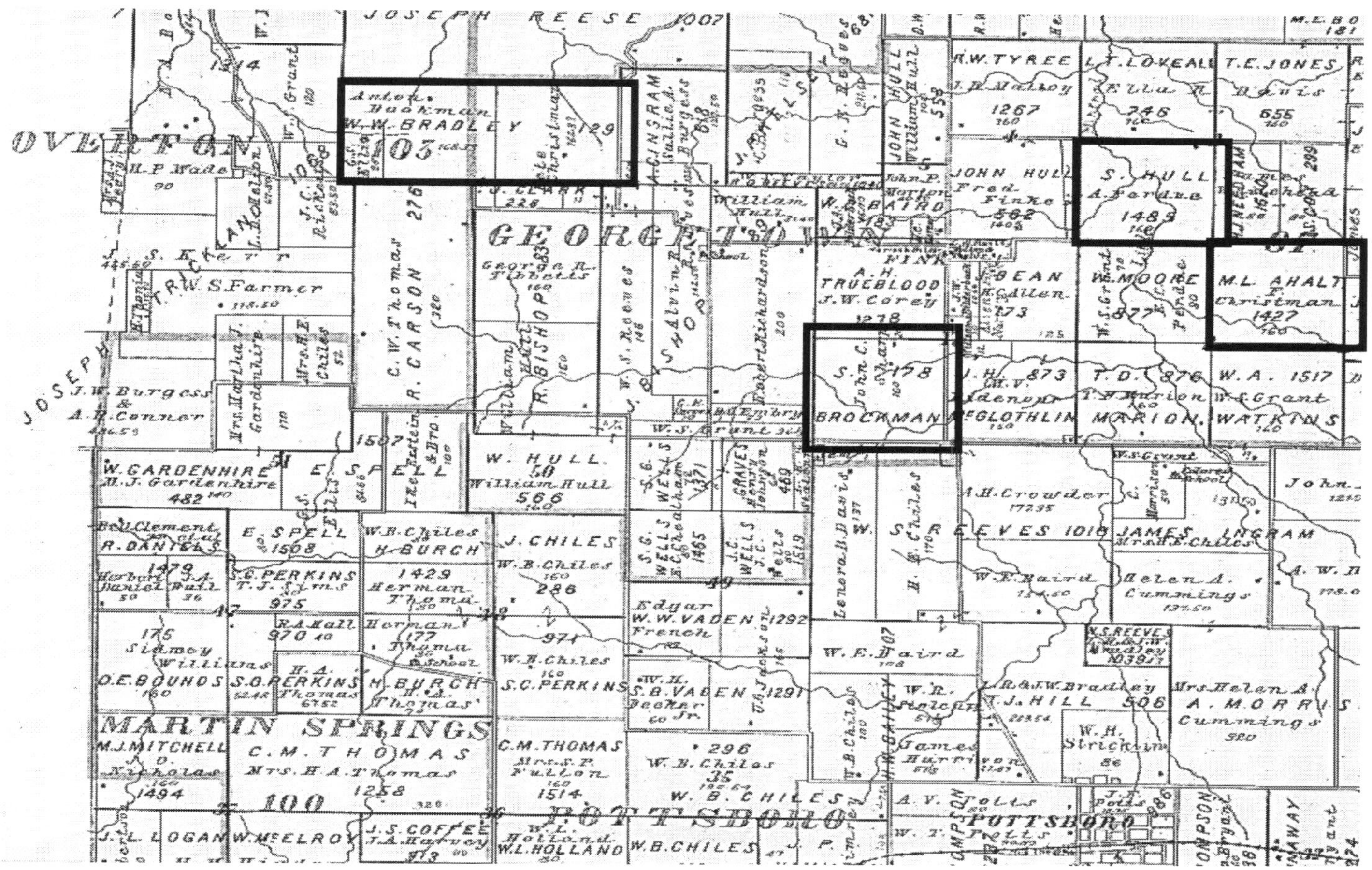


Above: 1908 plat map of Georgetown showing Brockman, Christman & Perdue land

| | | | | | | | | | | | |
|---|---|---|---|---|---|---|---|---|---|---|---|
| 154 | 154 | Dunning, Lillian A | Daughter | F | W | 10 | S | | | | Texas |
| 160 | 160 | Christman, John | Head | M | W | 44 | M1 | 28 | | | (Russ) German |
| | | Effie | Wife | F | W | 48 | M1 | 28 | 11 | 6 | (Russ) German |
| | | Pete | Son | M | W | 24 | M1 | 1 | | | (Russ) German |
| | | Mary | Daughter | F | W | 20 | S | | | | Texas |
| | | Carthe | Daughter | F | W | 18 | S | | | | Texas |
| | | Liddie | Daughter | F | W | 15 | S | | | | Texas |
| | | Bennie | Son | M | W | 10 | S | | | | Texas |
| | | Carlie | Daughter-in-law | F | W | 22 | M1 | | 1 | 1 | (Russ) German |
| 161 | 161 | [illegible], Sam H | Head | M | W | 39 | M1 | 11 | | | Arkansas |
| | | Alice | Wife | F | W | 3[illegible] | M1 | 11 | 6 | 6 | Arkansas |
| | | Ruth | Daughter | F | W | 9 | S | | | | Arkansas |
| | | Carrol D | Son | M | W | 8 | S | | | | Arkansas |
| | | Iola | Daughter | F | W | 6 | S | | | | Texas |
| | | Lice | Daughter | F | W | 4 | S | | | | Texas |
| | | Elsie | Daughter | F | W | 2 | S | | | | Texas |

| Dwelling | Family | Name | Relation | Sex | Race | Age | Marital | Yrs. married | Children born | Living | Birthplace | Father's birthplace | Mother's birthplace |
|---|---|---|---|---|---|---|---|---|---|---|---|---|---|
| 136 | 136 | Davis, Bille | Head | F | W | 50 | Wd | | 5 | 4 | Texas | Tennessee | Oklahoma |
| | | —— Elsie | Daughter | F | W | 28 | D | | | | Texas | North Carolina | Texas |
| | | —— Mary | Daughter | F | W | 21 | S | | | | Texas | North Carolina | Texas |
| | | —— Arbutal | Daughter | F | W | 17 | S | | | | Texas | North Carolina | Texas |
| | | —— Ivy | Daughter | F | W | 16 | S | | | | Texas | North Carolina | Texas |
| 137 | 137 | Dophied, J. Henry | Head | M | W | 52 | Wd | | | | Iowa | (Ger.) German | (Ger.) German |
| | | —— William | Son | M | W | 23 | S | | | | Iowa | Iowa | Iowa |
| | | —— John | Son | M | W | 21 | S | | | | Iowa | Iowa | Iowa |
| | | —— Linnie | Daughter | F | W | 18 | S | | | | Iowa | Iowa | Iowa |
| | | —— Joe | Son | M | W | 11 | S | | | | Texas | Iowa | Iowa |
| | | —— Angnes | Daughter | F | W | 8 | S | | | | Oklahoma | Iowa | Iowa |
| | | —— Henry | Son | M | W | 5 | S | | | | Oklahoma | Iowa | Iowa |
| 138 | 138 | Christman, Pete | Head | M | W | 45 | M2 | 9 | | | (Russ.) German | (Russia) German | (Russia) German |
| | | —— Carlie | Wife | F | W | 43 | M2 | 9 | 10 | 6 | (Russia) German | (Russia) German | (Russia) German |
| | | Neu —— Jacob | Step son | M | W | 20 | S | | | | (Russ.) German | (Russia) German | (Russia) German |
| | | Christman, Lizzie | Daughter | F | W | 17 | S | | | | Texas | (Russ.) German | (Russ.) German |
| | | —— Effie | Daughter | F | W | 14 | S | | | | Texas | (Russ.) German | (Russ.) German |
| | | Neu —— Charlie | Step son | M | W | 10 | S | | | | Texas | (Russ.) German | (Russ.) German |
| | | Christman, Katie | Daughter | F | W | 7 | S | | | | Texas | (Russ.) German | (Russ.) German |
| | | —— Emma | Daughter | F | W | 6 | S | | | | Texas | (Russ.) German | (Russ.) German |
| | | —— Fred | Son | M | W | 3 | S | | | | Texas | (Russ.) German | (Russ.) German |
| 139 | 139 | Moser, Alvis L. | Head | M | W | 38 | M1 | 9 | | | Tennessee | Tennessee | Tennessee |
| | | Moser, Alex. Lonnie | Wife | F | W | 24 | M1 | 9 | 5 | 3 | Texas | Ohio | Virginia |
| | | —— Annie M. | Daughter | F | W | 7 | S | | | | Texas | Tennessee | Texas |
| | | —— Ethel | Daughter | F | W | 5 | S | | | | Texas | Tennessee | Texas |
| | | —— Ada L. | Daughter | F | W | 2 | S | | | | Texas | Tennessee | Texas |
| 140 | 140 | Herndon, Fred A. | Head | M | W | 35 | M1 | 12 | | | Georgia | Alabama | Georgia |
| | | —— Sadie A. | Wife | F | W | 25 | M1 | 12 | 5 | 4 | Texas | Alabama | Tennessee |
| | | —— Violet | Daughter | F | W | 4 | S | | | | Texas | Georgia | Texas |
| | | —— Rubie | Daughter | F | W | 7 | S | | | | Texas | Georgia | Texas |
| | | —— Frank | Son | M | W | 5 | S | | | | Texas | Georgia | Texas |
| | | —— Roy | Son | M | W | 4 | S | | | | Texas | Georgia | Texas |
| 141 | 141 | Bailey, George W. | Head | M | W | 70 | M2 | 25 | | | Kentucky | Indiana | Indiana |
| | | —— Martha | Wife | F | W | 64 | M2 | 25 | 4 | 6 | Louisiana | Pennsylvania | Mississippi |

STATE Texas
COUNTY Grayson
TOWNSHIP OR OTHER DIVISION OF COUNTY Part of Precinct No. 8 (14)
NAME OF INSTITUTION X

DEPARTMENT OF COMMERCE AND LABOR—BUREAU OF THE CENSUS

# THIRTEENTH CENSUS OF THE UNITED STATES: 1910—POPULAT

NAME OF INCORPORATED PLACE X

ENUMERATED BY ME ON THE 22 DAY OF

| Dwelling | Family | Name | Relation | Sex | Race | Age | Marital | Yrs. married | Children born | Living | Birthplace | Father's birthplace | Mother's birthplace | Language | Occupation |
|---|---|---|---|---|---|---|---|---|---|---|---|---|---|---|---|
| 132 | 132 | Kilderback, Joseph W. | Head | M | W | 35 | M1 | 12 | | | Tennessee | Tennessee | Tennessee | English | Farmer |
| | | —— Nannie | Wife | F | W | 35 | M1 | 12 | 3 | 3 | Texas | Georgia | Georgia | English | none |
| | | —— Otis | Son | M | W | 4 | S | | | | Texas | Tennessee | Texas | | none |
| | | —— Loice | Daughter | F | W | 5 | S | | | | Texas | Tennessee | Texas | | none |
| 133 | 133 | Richardson, Robert | Head | M | W | 54 | M1 | 30 | | | Texas | Tennessee | Tennessee | English | Farmer |
| | | —— Sallie | Wife | F | W | 44 | M1 | 30 | 5 | 5 | Mississippi | Mississippi | Mississippi | English | none |
| | | —— Robert Jr. | Son | M | W | 11 | S | | | | Texas | Texas | Mississippi | English | Farm |
| | | —— Lou | Daughter | F | W | 14 | S | | | | Texas | Texas | Mississippi | English | None |
| 134 | 134 | Clontz, Theapolis | Head | M | W | 29 | M1 | 4 | | | Texas | Ohio | W. Virginia | English | Farmer |
| | | —— Linnie | Wife | F | W | 24 | M1 | 4 | 2 | 1 | Texas | Missouri | Texas | English | none |
| | | —— Hattie P. | Daughter | F | W | 2 | S | | | | Texas | Texas | Texas | | |
| 135 | 135 | Burgess, Conner | Head | M | W | 53 | M1 | 20 | | | Texas | Missouri | Missouri | English | Farmer |
| | | —— Sallie | Wife | F | W | 52 | M1 | 34 | 7 | 5 | Texas | Tennessee | Oklahoma | English | none |
| | | —— Wallace | Son | M | W | 17 | S | | | | Texas | Texas | Texas | English | Farm |
| | | —— Carl | Son | M | W | 14 | S | | | | Texas | Texas | Texas | English | Farm |
| | | —— Vere | Son | M | W | 14 | S | | | | Texas | Texas | Texas | English | Farm |
| 136 | 136 | Davis, Bille | Head | F | W | 50 | Wd | | 5 | 4 | Texas | Tennessee | Oklahoma | English | Farmer |
| | | —— Elsie | Daughter | F | W | 28 | D | | | | Texas | North Carolina | Texas | English | none |
| | | —— Mary | Daughter | F | W | 21 | S | | | | Texas | North Carolina | Texas | English | none |
| | | —— Arbutal | Daughter | F | W | 17 | S | | | | Texas | North Carolina | Texas | English | none |
| | | —— Ivy | Daughter | F | W | 16 | S | | | | Texas | North Carolina | Texas | English | none |
| 137 | 137 | Dophied, J. Henry | Head | M | W | 52 | Wd | | | | Iowa | (Ger.) German | (Ger.) German | English | Farmer |

SHARPE FAMILY - Georgetown Youth, Earl Laverne Sharpe, Killed Flying in Britain in WWII August 14, 22 & 25, 1942 Dallas Morning News

## Grayson Officer Missing in Ireland, Parents Notified

DENISON, Texas, Aug. 13.—Lieut. Earl Laverne Sharpe, son of Mr. and Mrs. Arthur H. Sharpe of Georgetown, twelve miles west of Denison, is missing in action in Ireland, according to a War Department message received by his parents Thursday.

Lieutenant Sharpe left the United States six weeks ago for Ireland after receiving his wings at Foster Field, Victoria, in February. He received his basic training at Randolph Field.

Lieutenant Sharpe attended Grayson County schools and Southwestern State College a Durant Okla., before enlisting in the Air Corps.

## Pottsboro Youth Killed Flying in Britain

POTTSBORO, Texas, Aug. 24.—According to information received from the War Department, Lieut. Earl L. Sharpe, an Army pursuit pilot and son of Mr. and Mrs. Arthur H. Sharpe of the Georgetown community, was killed Aug. 11 in the British Isles.

The Sharpes were informed that the youth's death occurred during a training period and not during actual combat duty. Lieutenant Sharpe left the United States six weeks ago.

A graduate of Denison High School, Lieutenant Sharpe was a student at Durant Teachers College before enlisting in the Army Air Forces.

Surviving are his parents, a brother, Aviation Cadet Richard Sharpe, Lowry Field, Colo., and a sister, Mrs. James C. Gallatin, Odessa.

## Pottsboro Officer Killed in England, Parents Notified

DENISON, Texas, Aug. 21.—Mr. and Mrs. Arthur H. Sharpe of Pottsboro have been officially notified by the War Department that their son, Lieut. Earl L. Sharpe, was killed Aug. 11 in England. No details of the accident were divulged.

Lieutenant Sharpe was reported missing a week ago. He received his wings and commission in the Army Air Corps Feb. 20, 1942, at Victoria. He received his basic training at Randolph Field. Lieutenant Sharpe went to England six weeks ago and was an Army pursuit pilot. He was a student at Southeastern State College before he entered the Air Corps.

Besides his parents, he is survived by a brother, Aviation Cadet Richard Sharpe, Lowry Field, Colo., and a sister, Mrs. James C. Gallatin of Odessa.

## KLONTZ/ CLOUNTZ / Moser/ Moon Families

The Marion Klontz family from Ohio moved to Grayson County in 1877. They were farmers, but Marion and his wife Nancy had to service as hired hands and domestic servants respectively for others to save money for their journey. There may have been some dispute in the family causing the migration, because at this time, Marion changed his name from Klontz to Clontz or Clountz by which his descendants were forever known. The Clountz family married into many other families in the Georgetown, Locust, and Oak Grove area. Some of these were the Moon, Moser, Moran Ridenhour, Myers and Cook families.

Below is a family history compiled by the Moser/Allen family where they exclusively use the Klontz family name as do many of the family relatives who have remained in Ohio.

# KLONTZ FAMILY HISTORY

Jacob J. Klontz born 1824; died 1905
Married Catherine O. ? born 18 ; died 1916
Children: Elizabeth
Jacob

Isaac Klontz born May 2, 1844; died 1908
Married Margaret S. ? ; born 1854; died 1933

William Klontz, Sr.
Born July 26, 1820; died March 17, 1898
Married Anne Blair Dec. 4, 1843;
She was born Feb. 26, 1822 in Virginia, then moved to Greene County, Ohio. Died July 27, 1903

Children:

1. Marion Klontz
   Born 1845; died June 3, 1918
   Married Nancy Hoover 1872
   She was born 1852; died 1923

2. Frank H. Klontz
   Born Jan. 19, 1846/ died Jan. 10, 1919
   Married Mary Bland Sept. 5, 1872.
   She was born July 16, 1847, daughter of Miles Bland and ? Rousch. Was said to have sneaked with her parents from Virginia to Ohio, during the Civil War; travelled only at night, so as not to be seen. Died Oct. 26, 1926.

3. Caroline Klontz
   Born May 21, 1849; died Nov. 24, 1924
   Married Alvin Lukes Saunders Jan. 25, 1866

4. Mary Klontz
   Born Nov. 29, 1850; died March 2, 1923
   Married William Hart July 5, 1888

5. Eveline Klontz
   Born Oct. 6, 1853; died Sept. 27, 1924
   Married William Klontz July 4, 1889
   He died 1909

6. Margaret Klontz
   Born Nov. 10, 1858; died Oct. 23, 1924
   Married Thomas Miller Dec. 11, 1879

7. William Klontz, Jr.
   Born Nov. 24, 1860; died March 24, 1943
   Married Emma Daugherty July 20, 1879

8. John Klontz
   Born July 2, 1862; died Oct. 14, 1941
   Married Myra Sowers Oct. 9, 1884

9. Elizabeth Klontz
   Born Sept. 11, 1866; died April 1, 1947
   Married James J. Taylor July 29, 1889

Marion Klontz
Born 1845 Died June 3,1918
Married Nancy Hoover 1872 Born 1852 Died 1923
Children;

1.Anna Klontz Born 1872 Died 1929
Married Jesse Moran
Children.
1.Delia Moran
2.Wes Moran
3.Jack Moran
4.Vera Moran
5.Minnie Lee Moran
6.Charlie Moran(Died)
7.Nannie Moran
2 8.Ethel Moran

2.Walter T.Klontz
Born Feb.26,1874 Died 1955
Married Elizabeth Bradley Sep.5,1894 Died 1906
Children;
1.William Arthur Klontz Born 1895 Died 1965
2.Ora Lee Klontz Born 1898
3.Viola Klontz Born 1902(married Brice ) Died 1970
4.Elizabeth Klontz Born 1906 Died 1906

3.Adeline Klontz B 2-28-1880 D 7-25-1947 Jess
Born 1880 Died 1947 B 6-1-1872
Married Jesse Moon ~~1901~~ 6-27-1901 D 4-5-1961
Children;
1.Stella Moon Died 1974
2.Walter Moon died 8-21-82 - he was 77 or 78
3.Dempsey Moon
4.Wayne Moon
5.Leroy Moon
6.Maggie Moon Born Jan.9,1915 - DIED FEB.1,1997
Married Lewis Carroll He died May 1976
Children;
1.Jane Carroll Sep.26,1938
2.Betty Carroll Oct.9, 1943
7.Juanita Moon
8.Weanette Moon Born 1920

4.Theopolis Klontz
Born 1879 Died 1950
Married Johnnie Ridenour
Children
1.Hattie Klontz
2.Loraine Klontz Died

5.Henry C.Klontz
Born 1882 Died 1934
Married Minnie Myers Died Oct. 1975
Children;
1.William Klontz Died May 22, 1984
2.Henry Herman Klontz Died 1969
3.Vessie Klontz
4.Bertie Klontz )boy and Died May 10, 1984
5.Gertie Klontz )girl twins
6.Infant died

Note: the number 2 son of Henry C. Clountz is Henry Sherman Clountz not Herman.

6. Dollie Maria Klontz
Born Feb.3,1884 Died 1976
Married Alexander Moser
Children;

1. Anna Mae Moser Born 1902 Married Water Moon
2. Letha Moser Died
3. Ethel Moser Born 1906 - Died 1982 Married Goug Jones
4. Ada Lee Moser - died -1-1997 Married Wilson F. Jones - died [illegible]
5. Willie Moser
6. Lena Moser Married William Feltcher
7. Esther Moser Died 1965
8. Infant Moser Died
9. Alexander Moser - DIED 1976
10. Bill Moser) - DIED 1973
11. Jack Moser
12. Dorothy Moser Married Jack Berry
13. Fatsy Ruth Moser Married Willard Allbright

# Jesse James Moon

BIRTH 1 JUN 1872 • Texas, United States
DEATH 5 APR 1961 • Grayson, Texas, United States
husband of great-aunt

### Facts

**Birth**
1 Jun 1872 • Texas, United States

**Marriage**
1902 • Texas, United States
Addie Evelyn Clountz (1880–1947)

**Residence**
1920 • Justice Precinct 7, Grayson, Texas, USA
Age: 49; Marital Status: Married; Relation to Head of House: Head

**Residence**
1930 • Precinct 7, Grayson, Texas
Age: 58; Marital Status: Married; Relation to Head of House: Head

**Residence**
1935 • Grayson, Texas

**Residence**
1 Apr 1940 • Grayson, Texas, United States
Age: 67; Marital Status: Married; Relation to Head of House: Head

**Death**
5 Apr 1961 • Grayson, Texas, United States
Age: 88

**Burial**
Pottsboro, Grayson County, Texas, USA

### Sources

Ancestry Sources

- 1920 United States Federal Census
- 1930 United States Federal Census
- 1940 United States Federal Census
- Ancestry Family Trees
- Web: Texas, Find A Grave Index, 1761-2012

### Family

Parents

- John Henry Moon 1833–1900
- Margaret Ann Shaw 1843–1924

Spouse & Children

- Addie Evelyn Clountz 1880–1947
- Stella Moon 1903–
- Walter Lee Moon 1905–1982
- Dempsey Marion Moon 1907–1981
- Wayne H Moon 1909–1996
- Leroy Moon 1913–1981
- Maggie Moon 1915–1997
- Nannie Juanita Moon 1917–1976
- Wanette Francis Moon 1921–2001

Left (as you look at the picture), to right: Wannett Moon, Dimp Moon, William Clountz, Bertie Clountz, Gertie Clountz Smith, Grandma Russell?, Juanita Russell (Sanford), Bub Moon, Bill Moser or Henry Sherman Clountz, Grandpa Jessie James Moon, Juanita Moon, Minnie Myers Clountz, Addie Clountz Moon, A. L. Moser?, Florence Clountz? In back; Doll Clountz Moser on right.

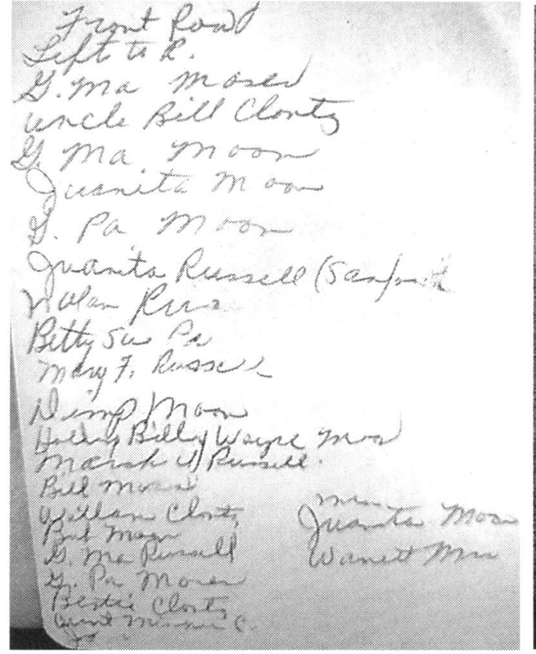

Front Row
Left to R.
G. ma Moser
uncle Bill Clontz
G. Ma Moon
Juanita Moon
G. Pa Moon
Juanita Russell (Sanford
Nolan Russ
Betty Sue Pa
Mary F. Russell
Dimp Moon
Holding Billy Wayne Moon
Mariah W Russell
Bill Moser
William Clontz
Bub Moon
G. Ma Russell
G. Pa Moon
Bertie Clontz
Aunt Minnie C.

Juanita Moon
Wanett Moon

Above: Nannie Clontz (later Moran) and Maggie Moon

Below: Jess and Addie (Clountz) Moon family;

Front Door

Old Moon residence above at the corner of Georgetown Road and Squirrel Lane, it is still there but is so overgrown it cannot hardly be seen. Picture from Jim Allen

Below: Left: Pic from Jim Allen, possibly a wedding picture of Alexander Lafayette Moser and Doll Clountz. Right: Alexander L. Moser I, Doll Clountz Moser and baby Anna Mae Moser.

Previous pictures; left from Lynn Cherry, He said: "This is Walter "Son" Moon, husband of Annie Mae Moser, plowing his famous vegetable garden about 1964 that fed so many people in the Georgetown area for years. This was located where the Black mansion now sits on Georgetown Road (just west of the Tanglewood entrance). Walter was a great man. He was the funniest man to be around that I have ever known. He enjoyed life and worked hard. He was my uncle, my mother's brother." From Myrna Roy Collins: He was my great uncle, married to my great aunt Annie Mae Moser. I spent many years in his gardens picking vegetables and fruits along with the other cousins. And when he put out the tomato and pepper plants, we either covered them with coffee cans or milk cartons so the wind wouldn't blow them away before they took root. From Scott Galyon - I believe this is down by the gate and the background is to the east. Those pecan trees are huge now. Left: 4 generations of the Georgetown Moon family - Anna Mae, Frankie, Walter & Newton Jasper. Right: Anna Mae Moser Moon

Below: Two of Alexander Moser and Doll Clountz Moser's daughters were nurses in WWI. They are pictured here on the first ever Veteran's Day, November 11, 1919, at Georgetown

and during a Veteran's Day parade in Denison, Texas. You may recognize a building. From Jim Allen.

**C. A. White's Blacksmith Shop and the Largest Tree in Grayson County** – The Moser family were said to have rented a house and farmland at one time on the "S" curve on Georgetown Road just east of Fort Johnston across from the old Atnip/ White place where an historic old hardwood tree and bartlett pear tree still stands.

Below: from Jim Allen, pictures of the old Moser home in 1920, side and front; could this be the home across the road from the C.A. White Blacksmith shop?

Above; Starnes Moser and children at old Moser place at White's blacksmith shop 1920

Below is a picture of the old barn in 2017 where Carla A., whose grandfather C. A. White had a blacksmith's shop right here under a towering old oak tree in the 1920s. There is still a large hardwood tree next to this barn, I am sure they are the same tree surviving today, and in comparing pictures, the present one is in the same place as the picture of the large tree taken in the 70s in a newspaper article with the same old barn in the background. Hardwoods in this area, including oaks, hickorys, and ash are very long lived trees. The present tree has a large solid base with a separated double trunk halfway up as if it was traumatized or cut off as a young sapling and regrew with two trunks.

Below: Lawrence "Jake" Brown holding lumber tongs, used to move lumber in the early 1940s. Right: Later Ivey residents in the area: Joe and Stella Ivey

Above: Annis Brown in 1946. Photo was taken about a mile west of Georgetown Church, just past the "s" curve in Georgetown Road. “The old house is demolished now but you always knew when you went to see Grandma that you were going to leave with eggs” from Joe Brown who was born under the old hardwood tree at the old blacksmith shop near Fort Johnston in **Old Georgetown** – most probably the location of the old town of **Reevesville.**

**The Great White / Atnip Oak Tree** – The newspaper article back then called it Grayson County's largest tree, and I wouldn't argue with that! The pictures are looking at the tree from different directions, one from the west, the other from the south. No doubt in my mind, Indians have taken their rest under the shade of this tree before the arrival of white settlers here. Oaks are very long lived here. At the time of one of the pictures below in the 1970s, the property belonged to B. V. Atnip. But C. A. White set up his forge and anvil under this same tree in 1929 and began his blacksmith shop. Pat (Moser) Albright, at that time the Mayor of Fink, recalled the shop being a gathering spot for local children including herself. Her family, Alex and Doll Moser, lived just on the other side of the creek from where this tree is and she said you could hear his hammer echoing as he worked. A shovel made by White once was on display at the Fink Museum. Edgel Clement who also lived here in those days remembered when White moved from another location to the site with this tree. He stayed there from 1929 to about 1940 when Mr. Atnip bought the place. Edgel Clement wasn't sure, but he thought the tree is a pin oak since it has small acorns. Bill Clement brought a tape measure in the 70s to see how big the tree was. He found its circumference was 13 feet 2 inches, and was about 50 feet tall.

**Old Oak Tree in 2018**

Left: tree from the west 2018; Right: tree from the south mid 1970s with old barn in the background which is still standing.

## "Don't Take Rides From Strangers!"

James R. "Jim" Allen recounted the following story told to him by his mother Dorothy Marie Moser Allen Berry. We have probably all had our parents admonish us as children to beware people we did not know and to never accept rides from strangers. Young Dorothy Moser, daughter of Alexander L. and Myra Dolly Clountz Moser, ignored this sage advice one rainy day and wished she hadn't. They lived on the old Atnip / Smith place on what is known as "the S curve" just past the intersection of Georgetown Road and Squirrel Lane. In those days in the 1930s, area schools sent buses throughout the area to collect this area's students to bring them to school. However, the bus would not take all the students to their houses, they would be dropped off in groups within walking distance. Dorothy had just exited the bus one soggy day at the corner of Preston Rd and Georgetown Rd at the town of Fink. She still had to walk about a mile and a half or so to get home. The first obstacle was Clay Hill, which was a steep red clay hill that on that rainy day was very slick and hard to climb. There is still remnants of that hill in front of the Georgetown Baptist Church, except it is paved today, Georgetown Road was all unpaved then. She grew tired quickly and as the other children arrived at their homes, she was walking alone. Her brother was already at work at the local milk barn near Spout Springs and could not walk with her that day. A car came up the road and stopped, there was a man and woman in it and they offered her a ride. She had been told by her Dad never to take rides, but she was tired of the deep mud and slippery clay! She gratefully got in the front door of the Model A Ford to stand in front of the lady in the passenger seat and held on to the "man rope" above the door. She told them to let her out before she got in front of her house because she didn't want her Daddy catching her riding with a stranger in their car. As she turned around to step out of the car, she saw what was lying in the back seat – various guns including automatic machine guns they were trying to cover with blankets. The next day, the whole neighborhood was talking about how others had encountered Bonnie and Clyde in the area of Fink and Locust, north of Pottsboro (including my own Aunt Lottie Cook Mosier). In fact Bonnie and Clyde had just left Ab Allen's store at Fink where they bought some things before they drove up Georgetown road. It was then she realized who the nice couple of strangers were who had kindly offered a tired little girl a ride home from school on a wet, muddy day.

**Dorothy Marie Moser Allen Berry Obituary** - Birth: Sep. 16, 1925, Death Mar. 5, 2011, Texas. Dorothy Moser Allen Berry was called home to be with her Lord and Savior on March 5, 2011, surrounded by her most cherished possessions, her family.

She was born Sept. 16, 1925, to Alexander L. and Myra Dolly Clountz Moser of Fink. She attended Georgetown School in Fink, Denison High School and subsequently graduated from La Jolla High School in La Jolla, Calif. in 1943. She attended Texas State Women's College studying home economics and was captain of the college golf team. As a rest of her winning the team championship, she was selected to caddy for Byron Nelson in the 1946 Pro-Am. Dorothy returned to Pottsboro and married her lifetime friend, James Farrell Allen on January 19, 1947. Dorothy was an avid golfer, hunter and fisherwoman. She was a lifetime member of Woodlawn Country Club and spent many hours on the courses in this area. She was a member of the Texas Woman's Golf Association. Some of her accolades include: multiple Ladies Club Championships at Woodlawn, Katy Golf Course, Denison Rod & Gun Club and Tanglewood Golf Course. She also was runner-up in the 1967 Trans-Mississippi Golf Championship.

Dorothy was recently honored as a Golden Circle recipient of Beta Sigma Phi Sorority, representing 50 years of service in that organization. She was an area businesswoman, owning and operating the Georgetown Store and Service Station in Fink.

Dorothy is survived by her children: James R. Allen and wife Janie; Joel D. Allen and Cindy, all of Pottsboro; Judi Howard and husband, Billy of Colbert, Okla. Dorothy resided with her granddaughter, Dori Smith and husband, Bart, as well as her great-grandson, Jacob Allen Eggenberg, all of Denison. She had six grandchildren and 18 great-grandchildren. Dorothy was widowed upon the death of James Allen in 1965. She subsequently married Texas Jack Berry of Denison on Feb. 10, 1972. T. Jack passed away in 1987. She was also preceded in death by her parents, three brothers, nine sisters and one grandson, Samuel E. Yates Jr. Funeral services were scheduled for 10 a.m. Wednesday, March 9, 2011 at Georgetown Baptist Church, 207 Georgetown Road, Pottsboro, Texas. Graveside services at Georgetown Cemetery.

Jack Moser Above

More about the Moser Family, below Ben Moser Family, pictures from Jim Allen

Willis Godwin reunion - Above pictures from Jim Allen

1973 Georgetown Map and Residents

From Grayson County Rural Directory, Excellent!

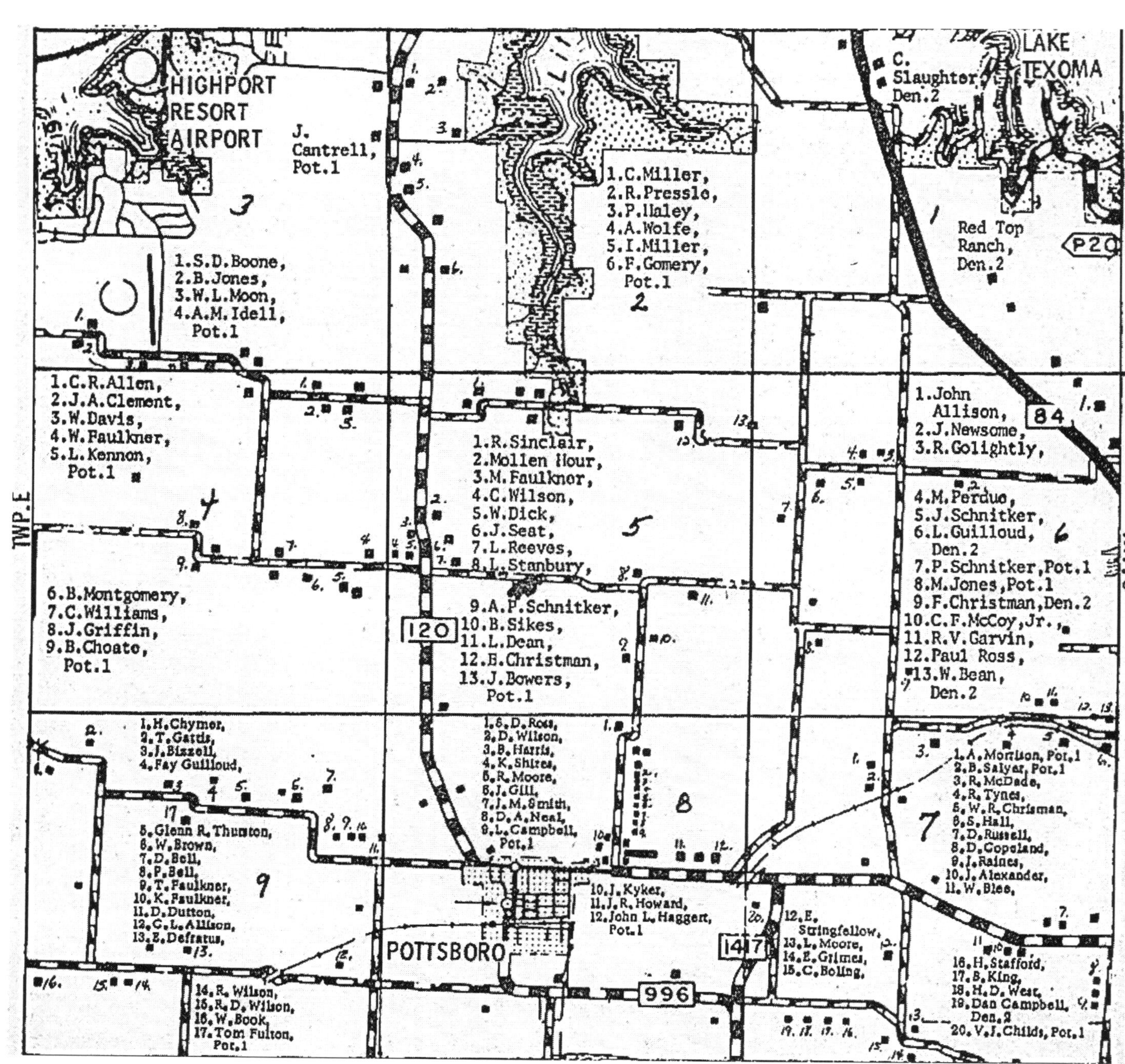

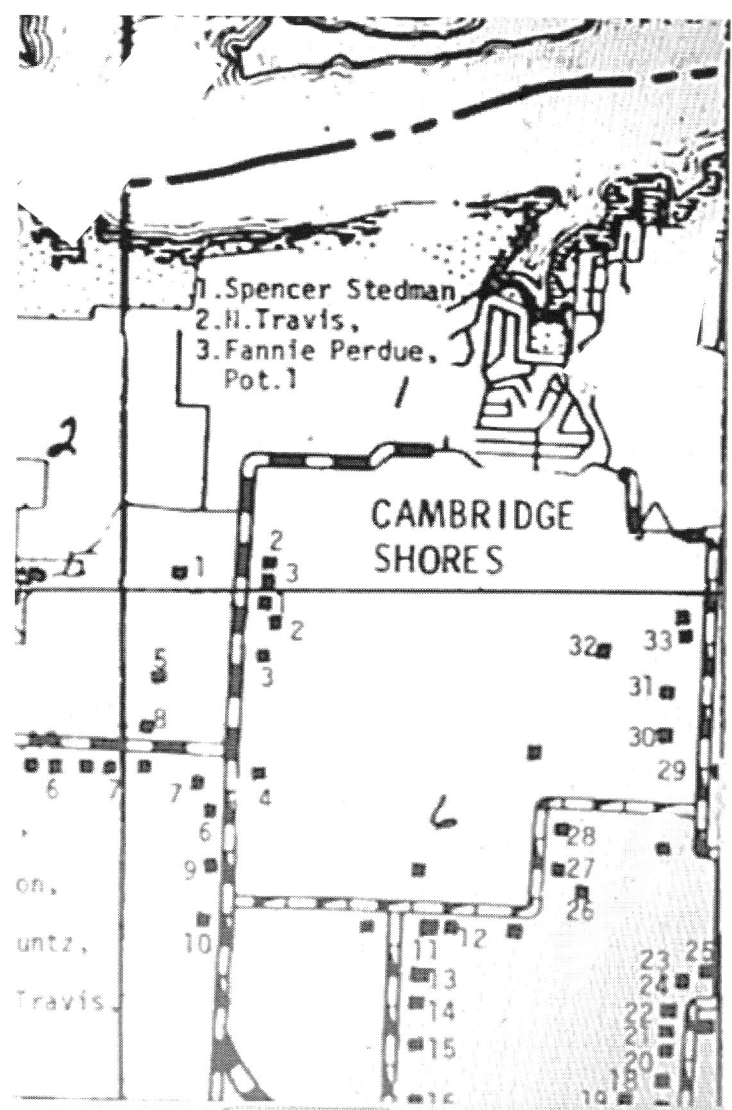


**Note- Number 1 is Dade or Dadie Cook and Lottie Cook Mosier – Sisters. 12 – Cleo Daugherty**

**SECTION 6**

1. Dave & Lottie Cook
2. Patricia Malone
3. Gurdy Smith
4. Joe L.Wastoskie
5. Rev.Roy Duff
6. J.Cartini
7. William B.Squires
8. David Wagner
9. Ed Dutton
10. Mrs.Bertha Pearson
11. J.R.Pearson
12. Cleo Dorty
13. Roy M.Smith
14. Harvey Anderson
15. Joe Baze
16. Carlos Waggoner
17. Wayne Moon
18. David D.Roy
19. Sam Roy
20. Alex Moser
21. Earnest Thomas
22. Jack Moser
23. Claude Roy
24. Herbie Roy
25. Larry D.Shaffer
26. Joseph H.Baker
27. Mrs.Henry Clountz

# More of 1973 Georgetown Map and Residents

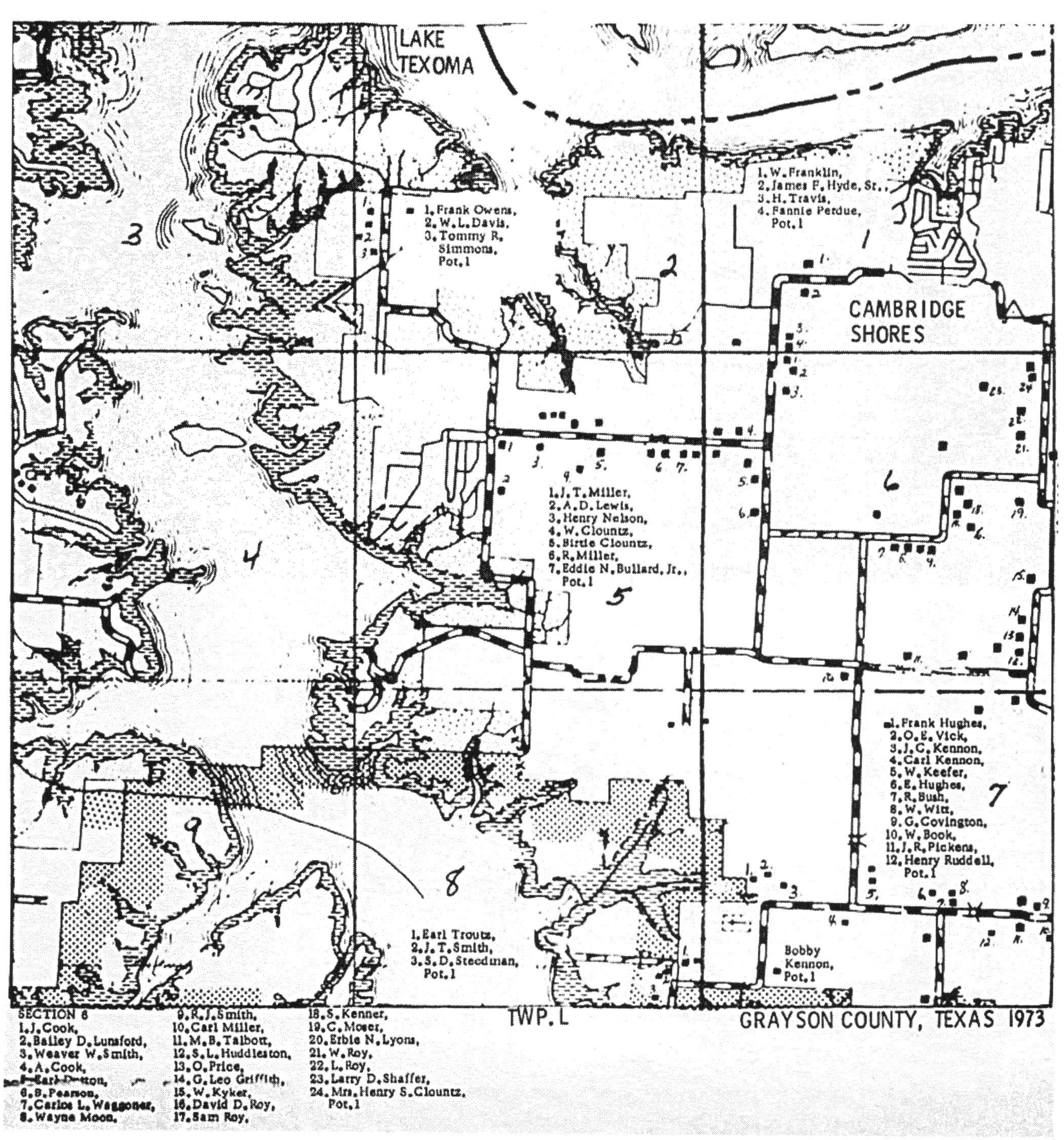

# GEORGETOWN IN THE NEWS

## Horse Thieves Always a Problem – Until They Aren't

Dallas Herald, Dec 14, 1872 - Several horses were stolen in Sherman last week. Incidentally, the Sherman Patriot said a horse thief was killed on 29th in the vicinity of Georgetown, Grayson County.

Denison Daily News, August 6, 1876 - Mr. Randell, who came in From Georgetown Saturday, says at every farmhouse on that road within five miles of Denison they have a shingle sticking out announcing watermelons for sale. I guess everyone in Georgetown planted them, they had a bumper crop, and there were more than everyone could eat.

## No Bundle of Joy Today

The Denison Daily News reported on Oct 20, 1877 that a woman living near Georgetown gave birth on October 15 to a remarkable baby (or part of a baby) with malformations after a fifteen hour labor. The lower portion of the trunk was lacking and there was not the slightest membrane supporting the bowels which were hanging loose. The head, neck, shoulders, arms and upper portion of the body were perfect. The legs however, protruded at or near the nipples on the chest. The right leg was perfect, except the foot. Just below the left nipple the left leg protruded and was perfect to the foot. There was a deficiency of lung tissue, the liver seemed normal in size, but no diaphragm was visible and no covering or support for the abdominal viscera. It was such a remarkable case it was deemed of sufficient importance to place it on record at the request of Dr. Williams, of Georgetown, who was present at the birth. The baby lived only two or three minutes after birth. C. Williams, M. D. Grayson County.

The Denison Sunday Gazetteer. Oct. 21, 1876 & Denison Daily News Apr 22, 1877

.........The wife of T. J. Cashion, who lived three miles west of Denison, died suddenly of a congestive chill at Burlington Sunday. She was visiting her daughter and Mr. Cashion started after her Friday to accompany her home, expecting to find her in her usual health, but she died about an hour before he arrived. She was buried at Georgetown.........Denison was the best buffalo hide market in Texas, and the

The News of the same date mentioned a fishing party leaving for Georgetown in carriages. The names of the following young folk who composed the party will sound familiar to old-timers: Misses Hughes, Simpson, Lottie and Evie Picton, Sandford, Mr. and Mrs. Joe Perry and the Messrs Carbry, Brutsche, Owens, Hughes and Rockwall.............The same paper

## Georgetown is a Gathering Place for Picnics, Revivals and Marriage

Georgetown is Popular Elopement Spot Aug 31, 1876 and Denison Daily News. January 6, 1880 and Married at Georgetown Picnic Denison Daily News Aug 5, 1879

**August 31, 1876**

For some time it has generally been believed that J. E. Dickson was paying marked attention to Miss Katie Bassett, of this city and that his attentions were favorably received. Still as Miss Kittie had numerous admirers nothing serious was anticipated and it was left for the public to be pleasantly surprised at the sudden announcement, yesterday that the above parties had quietly driven out to Georgetown early in the morning and there they were united in the holy bonds of matrimony by Parson Gentry, in the presence of a few friends and acquaintances. After hearty congratulations of all present the happy couple returned to this city in time for breakfast and were joyously received by their host of friends. It appears that some opposition to the marriage by the family where Miss Bassett was stopping was anticipated and rendered the elopement expedient.

up a good wagon road west; J. E. Dickson and Katie Bassett elope to Georgetown on the 29th, are married, and return to Denison in time for breakfast; W. A. Arey's wife

A young man and woman from Denison, who attended camp meeting at Georgetown on Sunday, were married at the conclusion of the servies. It was not exactly an elopement, but the father of the girl is said to be looking for his son-in-law with a stout hickory stick.

Mr. F. A. Utiger called at the NEWS office Monday to have the statement that his horse lost a race Saturday corrected. Mr. Utiger says he never owned a race horse, and never expects to own one. The horse alluded to belonged to W. A. Jones.

## Thompson-Beard Wedding at Georgetown

The Sunday Gazetteer. (Denison, Tex.), June 3, 1888

Miss Ella Overton, daughter of Ex-Gov. Overton, of the Chickasaw Nation, was in the city Thursday, and attended the Episcopal Social at the residence of Mr W. A. Hallenbeck Thursday night.

A pic nic party, composed of the lady teachers of the public schools and others, spent Thursday at Dripping Springs, and enjoyed a most pleasant time.

Mr. Frank Thompson, of Preston Bend, and Miss Sallie Beard, of Georgetown, were married Wednesday evening at the residence of the bride's mother at Georgetown. A grand reception was held Thursday night at the residence of Mrs. Judge Porter, at Preston Bend, and that full justice might be done to the happy event the popular bride and groom were tenndered a grand ball and fete Friday night at the residence of Mr. Joe Meadows, also of Preston Bend. The honeymoon of Mr. and Mrs. Thompson promises to not become monotonous for want of social divertisement.

THE GEORGETOWN GRANGE MEETING AT JUDGE AND SOPHIA PORTER'S PLANTATION The Sunday Gazetteer. (Denison, Tex.), July 12, 1875

lic a location......The Georgetown Grange held a meeting at Judge Porter's plantation at Preston Bend Saturday, and there were a number of parties present from Denison. The old grangers brought their wives with them and a jolly time was had. Judge Preston and his estimable wife had a good old-fashioned dinner prepared. There was barbecued beef, pork and mutton, all the vegetables of the season, cakes, pies and jellies, and the "bestest" coffee you ever drank. Tom Crooks said if that was the fourth degree in the Grange, he was a granger thenceforth. The judge and his wife passed over the divide several years ago, but those who partook of their hospitality will never forget the happy hours spent at their pleasant home at the Bend......Mr. L. H.

Aug 28, 1878 & Denison Sunday Gazetteer Jan 14, 1875

Camp Meeting at Georgetown

the Hughes family......The News noted that Col. Chiles, Col. Reeves, and Judge Porter of Preston Bend were engineering a big campmeeting at Georgetown......Hiddleston and Ingersoll put in a sixty-saw cotton gin and press on Crawford street......Sherman quarantined against yellow fever in the summer of 1878, but Denison didn't......

Masonic Lodge in Georgetown

THURSDAY, JANUARY 14, 1875.

D. J. Eddleman, now residing at Denton, and still an active Mason, spent the second week in January, 1875, in Denison on business connected with masonry. At that time he was deputy Grand Master and on leaving Denison went to Georgetown on similar business......Mr.

Camp Meeting at Georgetown Denison Daily News July 31, 1879

The following ladies and gentlemen leave this evening to attend camp meeting near Georgetown: Misses Lillie Andrews, Louisa Sibley, Emma and Jeanette Rue, Sady Greenwood, Nellie Graham and Mrs. M. F. Dearing; Dr. Nagle, A. K. Waddell, John Simpson. Tom Yates, Fox Platter, Asa Runyon. G. G. Randell and M. F. Dearing. After camp meeting a moonlight pic-nic will be indulged in.

Donaldson & Campbell are selling a box-toed calf shoe for $3, which is worth $4. Call and examine them. 7 26 tf

### The Blackmailing Case.

T. J. Head, the laundry man, who attempted to levy blackmail on L. S. Bearce in this city a short time ago,

at Guiteau & Waldron's. 7 25 tf

### Dead in the Woods.

On Tuesday an Indian visited Denison, imbibing copious draughts of fire water. In the evening he started for home on horseback. Since then all tidings or traces of him were lost until yesterday, when the body was discovered in the woods near a stream known as Little Mineral.

Mr. White, of the Flag Store, our informant, states that the Indian apparently died from the effects of heat, as there was no signs of violence on the body. The Indian was probably very drunk and laid down in the sun with fatal results as above stated.

Masonic and Temperance Picnic at Georgetown    Denison Daily News June 25, 1880

## THE PIC-NIC.

### Masonic and Temperance People's Jolification.

A Masonic and temperance pic-nic took place at Georgetown, nine miles west of Denison, yesterday. Nearly one thousand persons were on the grounds, many from Sherman, Denison, and adjacent towns.

A procession was formed, composed of Masons and temperance sosocieties, headed by a band, which marched to the pic-nic grounds, where the installation of officers of the Masonic lodge took place. After the installation services everybody sat down to a grand banquet.

Several candidates being present, they were called on for speeches, when Captain Turner, candidate for county attorney, mounted the rostrum and delivered an off-hand address, which was received with great favor by the audience. Dr. Feild followed Captain Turner, and was enthusiastically received. The Doctor gave the people a short talk, defining his position on the educational question and other state issues.

R. C. Crenshaw was introduced, and spoke at length on the temperance question, which he discussed in a very able and effective manner.

Rev. McFarlan also spoke in favor of temperance. He lead off in a strong appeal, contrasting the condition of the temperance man with the one addicted to strong drink. He spoke of the good work they had wrought in Georgetown and vicinity. When the Reverend gentleman sat down the band played an air.

Rev. Ranon next spoke on the subject of temperance, and Mrs. Cocks and Mrs. Vaughan, assisted by Messrs. Conner and Cox, sang an appropriate air. Dr. Scott made the closing talk on the subject of temperance.

Everything passed off in the most delightful manner.

Mr. Gordon, candidate for sheriff, County Attorney Turner, the editor of the Chronicle, J. W. Stewart, Mesdames Peters, Jouvenarl and Green, of Sherman, and Mr. and Mrs. Fred Dunn, Mr. Massey, J. W. Burson, Dick Cummins, Dr. Feild, Thos. Robinson and others from Denison attended.

Colonel Reeves was publicly installed as W. M. of Reeves Lodge, named in his honor.

It was one of the most memorable and pleasant social gatherings ever held in Grayson county.

Denison Daily News August 14, 1880 & June 11, 1889

### Sunday School Pic-Nic.

There will be a Sunday school convention and pic-nic two miles west of Denison at the junction of the Rock Bluff and wire roads on Saturday 14th, given for the purpose of collecting together the children and workers in Sunday schools from Denison, Pottsboro, Georgetown, Preston Bend and all other schools within a radius of ten miles of Denison.

Our brass band has been engaged and the Denison schools will assemble at the Methodist church at 8 o'clock where ample conveyances will be in attendance to transfer everyone who chooses to go. Arrangements have also been made for a large supply of vocal music, speeches, etc.

Political speeches will not be in order, but candidates will have ample opportunity to make good impressions.

Saturday evening, on Red river, near Baer's ferry, six miles north of Denison, Charley Colbert attempted to swim his horse across the river, but the current was too strong. His horse was carried under and drowned, and had it not been for the timely assistance of the ferryman, who went to his rescue in a boat, Mr. Colbert would also have drowned.

Charles Colbert of the Chicasaw nation and Joel Nail of Caddo, I. T., were in Denison to-day. Mr. Colbert brought down a bunch of extra fine beef cattle, which were disposed of in the local market.

At the annual meeting of the Gov. R. Reeves lodge No. 386, A. F. and A. M., held at Pottsboro June 8, the following officers were elected for the ensuing year: Worshipful master, F. A. Utiger; senior warden, J. H. Hubbard; junior warden, W. E. Baird; secretary, J. W. Carey; treasurer, T. J. Perkins; senior deacon, A. W. Hulett; junior deacon, John Hull; tiler, G. Davain. The officers will be installed at the next regular meeting.

B. W. Merrill will leave to-morrow for the national park and the mountains of the west, where he expects to remain until next fall.

Georgetown Described – Methodist Camp Meeting in Progress

The Sunday Gazetteer. (Denison, Tex.), July 27, 1884

## THE CAMP MEETING.

Tuesday morning a GAZETTEER reporter, accompanied by I. M. Standifer, Esq., set out for the scene of the Methodist camp meeting now in progress at Georgetown, this county. Seated in a light buggy and drawn by a span of Gilroy's spirted ponies, we skimmed along with remarkable rapidity and soon reached the place of worship. The country along the road from here to Georgetown is just lovely, being almost a continual farm of corn and cotton, and dotted with orchards, vineyards and gardens—all promising the husbandmen rich rewards for their labor. At interval of every few minutes farmers were met coming to market with wagon loads of hay, wheat, oats and other pro-

++++++++++++++++++++++++++++++++++++++++++++++++++++++++++++++++++++++++++++++++

ducts. Occasionally we got off the road, and once we were likely to go entirely astray, but fortunately we met Mr. Gilchohecuphurybury, who kindly showed us aright.

We found the meeting not very well attended, but the gospel seed seemed to be falling in good ground, to use a preacher's term.

At dinner-time we were invited to the table of Mrs. Judge Porter where our keen city appetite was soon appeased by the good things this estimable lady had in waiting, and we especially compliment her elegant coffee and Methodist chicken. Mr. Standifer took dinner with Mrs. James Thompson, and we presume that no candidate for legislative honors ever fared more sumptuously, as he continued at the ta-

---

ble until time for evening service.

At 3:30 we left the sacred encampment and run down to Pottsboro for an hour's stay. Here we captured some subscribers for the OFFICIAL paper of Denison, while our friend received many assurances of support from the citizens of the thriving little village and surrounding country. The candidacy of Mr. Standifer is certainly growing very popular, and we predict for the young gentleman a successful race.

As we came up from Pottsboro we stopped at the residence of Mr. D. East and drank dry a pitcher of good fresh buttermilk given us by Mrs. East.

For a young man, Standifer loves children better than any gentleman we ever knew; in fact he has a passion for them that almost equals a mother's love; at almost every house he drew rein to kiss the dear little urchins and ask after mamma's and papa's health. Oh, to be a candidate is to make one a true lover of the beautiful!

Grayson County Protective Society Picnic at Georgetown Grove – Pursuit of Horse Thieves Re-enacted

The Sunday Gazetteer. (Denison, Tex.), June 27, 1886

The Grayson County Protective Society will give a picnic at Georgetown Grove, three miles west of Pottsboro, next Saturday, to which they invite all Denison and surrounding country. The following is the programme for the occasion:

The members of the society and others will meet at the grounds at 10 o'clock a. m.; mounted field drill by the society; address by a prominent speaker; dinner; there will be a sham battle between the G. C. P. and imaginary horse thieves, which will open by the thieves stealing some horses from camp and being followed by part of the society, who will be driven back and fail to capture the thieves, but will rally their whole command and continue the pursuit until all are captured and returned to camp. A grand ball and ice cream supper will be given in the Hall at Pottsboro at night.

Mr. James Crutchfield, merchant of Pottsboro, was in the city Thursday and called at the Gazetteer office to make arrangements with Murray's Steam Printing House to print the programmes for the Grayson County Protective Society picnic at Georgetown Grove, next Saturday, July 3, 1886. Mr. Crutchfield has just recently returned from a visit to friends in Platte county, Missouri, where he says the Gazetteer goes regular and is highly appreciated by the subscribers.

**What the Newspapers Throughout Texas Are Talking About.**

The Denison Morning News advertises this singular gathering under the misleading title Horse-thief Picnic:

The Grayson County Protective society will give a grand picnic at Georgetown grove, three miles north of Pottsboro, on July 3. The order of the day will be:

1. Mounted field drill by society. 2. Address by a prominent speaker. 3. Dinner. 4. There will be a sham battle between the Grayson County Protective society and imaginary horse-thieves, which will open by the thieves stealing some horses from the camp and being followed by part of the society, who will be driven back and fail to capture the thieves, but will rally their whole command and continue the pursuit until all are captured and return to camp.

Nothing is said of hanging the thieves.

## Religious Georgetown Camp Meeting, Large Group of Sinners Gathered In

The Sunday Gazetteer. (Denison, Tex.), August 2, 1885

Mr. and Mrs. Long, who have been attending the camp meeting at Georgetown, near Pottsboro, reports great religious excitement prevailing. The attendance is very large and sinners are being gathered in A party of young men and women, who went from Denison in carriages, were among those who professed religion last Sabbath.

Denison Gazetteer August 22, 1888 Another rousing camp meeting is in progress at Georgetown. Sixteen conversions are reported for Wednesday night, and twenty-six for Thursday night, with a prospect of doubling the amount the preceding evenings. The weather has been exceedingly favorable the past week, for teaching the wayward sinner of the "warmer" climate.

August 16, 1888 Dallas Morning News & Denison Daily News January 24, 1880

A very successful Methodist campmeeting is in progress at Georgetown, four miles northwest of here. About sixty conversions was the result of the past three evening services.

A freight wreck on the Missouri Pacific railway at Buzzard's curve, near Gainesville last Saturday, delayed all trains for about six hours. No lives were lost, but a great number of freight cars were demolished.

G. E. Reeves, A. R. Harris, Robert Potts and Zack Smith, merchants of this place, went to Galveston Saturday to recuperate for a week.

It has been just eight weeks since any rain has fallen in this vicinity and the consequence is that corn, cotton and late vegetables are suffering and in some cases are entirely burned up.

Hardy Thomas constable of Georgetown, is in the city.

Below: 1930s era Mass Baptism at Georgetown Area Gospel Meeting for the Church of Christ; I think Florence Clountz is 5th from the left and Henry and Birtie Clountz are the men on the right.

## THE PRETTIEST GIRLS IN TEXAS ARE IN GEORGETOWN

The Sunday Gazetteer. (Denison, Tex.), Sunday, August 14, 1887

We do not wish to disparage the good looks of Denison girls, but in justice to the country and our own conscience we must say that six of the handsomest young ladies that have ever graced our streets, were in the city Friday, from Georgetown. They went into the Star Store to make a few purchases and caused a war among the clerks who should have the privilege of waiting on them. Young mar, if you want to see the prettiest girl in Texas, pay a visit to Georgetown, Grayson county.

# Prohibitionists and Anti Advocates Have Picnic at Georgetown

The Sunday Gazetteer. (Denison, Tex.), July 31, 1887

## BASKET PICNIC AT GEORGETOWN.

The prohibitionists and antis had arranged to have a grand picnic at Georgetown, three miles north of Pottsboro, on the 23d of July, and have this all important question thoroughly discussed by the best speakers on each side, and it was to be the crowning effort of the season for the people of that neighborhood, consequently Hon. J. W. Bailey was engaged early in the action to represent the pros and efforts were made to secure Capt. Tom Brown to speak for the antis, but it was doubtful whether he could come or not, as he had an appointment for that day at VanAlstyne, and it was whispered among the pros that Brown would not be there, as he was afraid to meet Bailey in joint discussion, but Brown was there early in the action, "and don't you forget it."

Mr. Bailey spoke in Whitesboro the night before and was telegraphed to be sure and come to Pottsboro on the night train, but he did not come, but waited for the 11.45, a. m., train, which would make him late if the train had been on time, as he was to speak first. For several days the train has been 2 hours late on account of a burned bridge near Denton, and it was highly probably that it would be late that day, and such proved to be a fact, but when it did come to Whitesboro it jumped the track in tha town, and therefore Mr. Bailey never came at all. When it was known that Mr. Bailey could not possibly get there until 2 or 3 o'clock it was arranged for Capt. Brown to speak immediately after dinner, which he did in fine style, and drew the records of other States on them in such a manner that no one could deny. It is unnessary to comment on his speech, as all who ever heard him know what he can do. Mr. Bailey's scheme was to arrive at the grounds about 2 or 3 o'clock and as he was to speak first he would hold the audience spellbound for 2 hours, and then they would begin to disperse, and Capt. Brown would have no chance to reply, but the pro's failed at every point, and the picnic was a victory for the antis.

The worst feature of the occasion was that some of the pro's went there loaded with applause for Bailey and they had no opportunity to unload, and it is about to sour in them unless they soon get some one to shoot off at.

There were about 1000 people on the ground, plenty of free ice water, lemonade ice cream, confectioneries, cigars, shooting gallery, throwing rings for knives, and an abundance to eat, and would have been a success if the Hon. J. W. Bailey had showed up.

Dr. Morrison and wife, from Denison, who are visiting Mr. James

Cummins and W. B. Chiles, were present, and enjoyed the occasion. Mrs. Harper, of Gainesville, who is visiting Miss Maude Cummins, attended to see a mixed picnic, but it turned out differently. The whole affair wound up pleasantly with a ball at night in Pottsboro.

The Sunday Gazetteer, September 4, 1898

GEORGETOWN.—A holiness camp meeting is being conducted here by Rev. L. L. Pickett of Fort Worth, who has a reputation as a forceful exhorter.

Georgetown Plagued by Grasshoppers, Denison Daily Cresset April 10, 1877, Mr. Newcomb from Kentuckytown reported the grasshoppers have not as yet done any damage to that section yet. However, at Georgetown, Denton and other points west, the farmers are greatly alarmed at the presence of the grasshoppers. Note from the author: I have seen the damage a "plague of grasshoppers" can cause. This happened again here in Georgetown for three straight years in the 1990s when we were in throws of a horrible drought and string of record high temperatures for year after year. I saw the grasshoppers some in such numbers, they ate cactus plants, poison castor bean plants, entire heads of dense cabbage in one day and stripped all the bark off all the trees, killing them. The roads were paved with dead grasshoppers and still they came. There was nothing green left, much less anything blooming or bearing fruit. Hummingbirds were so desperate for sustenance, I saw one fly up to the red stripe on a US flag hanging by my porch and try to get nectar from it, hoping it was a flower. Sounds like a joke but it's a true story. It was truly a plague and I hope I never see the like of it again. No wonder the farmers were alarmed. **Denison Daily News reported on Oct. 28, 1877 that grasshoppers were still in great numbers in Georgetown. That's seven months later. I'm not surprised. I bet they were back the next spring too.**

**Runaway Team - Wagon Wreck**! Denison Daily News, December 8, 1877 - A wagon belonging to A. B. Tillman, who resides near Georgetown, was standing in front of Sharp's grocery store. A dog jumping at one of the horses startled the team, and they dashed up Main Street. Near Burnett Avenue, they ran into a wagon loaded with groceries for Burneyville, Indian Nation. The tongue and other parts of the wagon were destroyed. The two horses however, by making a jump to each side, broke their harness and fell to the ground, thereby escaping injury. The wagon which was run into was also somewhat injured, and some barrels of sugar were broken open. The driver of the wagon was just in the act of climbing to his seat when the horses started, and was thrown to the ground with great violence. His arm was somewhat hurt, but he suffered no other injuries.

Sunday Gazetteer. (Denison, Tex.), August 18, 1895 & August 25, 1895

## McClain Family Strikes Again - This Time Killing Tom Walker

(For more about the many feuds and misadventures of the McClain / McLean family from Ireland, refer to my books "When the West Was Wild". It is a very long and interesting story involving the maiming of neighbors over fence disputes (the Connors), burning other neighbors barns (the Mills), getting in gunfights with the constable, etc. Here is a new one.)

### Killing at Pottsboro.

The little city of Pottsboro was the scene of much excitement Thursday when it became known that Ed McClain had killed Tom Walker in the country about seven miles distant. The deed was committed with the handle of a pitchfork, Walker receiving a terrible blow on the head, breaking his skull. He lived only a few minutes, and when the officers arrived McClain had disappeared, but was captured at Sherman late in the evening. The parties are well known around Pottsboro, and the killing was the result, it is said, of damaging reports circulated by Walker concerning McClain.

Ed McLean, who is charged with killing Tom Walker near Pottsboro, last week, waived examination before a justice of the peace in Sherman Friday, and was granted bail in the sum of $1000.

The Sunday Gazetteer. (Denison, Tex.) July 4, 1886

The Fourth of July was duly celebrated Saturday at Savanna, I. T., at Gainesville and at Georgetown Grove, near Pottsboro, Texas.

Ft. Worth Daily Gazette, February 1, 1887 - **A Tramp Horribly Mangled at Pottsboro**

Pottsboro, Tex., Jan. 31 - Last evening about 6 p.m. as the second section of freight 155 was passing through this place a tramp attempted to board the train, but by some means he fell under the wheels and was horribly mangled, and killed instantly. He was found a few minutes after the body was taken in charge by D.W. Odell, Justice of the Peace, who had the remains taken to his office, and summoned a jury of inquest, who rendered the following verdict: "That the unknown deceased came to his death by being run over by section 155 freight, south bound on the Missouri Pacific Railroad."

The body was cut nearly in two, the entrails torn out and the liver was found some distance from the body. One arm was nearly torn off at the shoulder, one leg and foot nearly cut off, and a large hole cut in the head. He had been in the town all day, begging for something to eat. He had on jeans pants and jacket, blue overalls, black sack coat, black hat, had red hair and appeared about 20 years of age. There was nothing found on the body to identify him, except a railroad map, and written on that was "Wyandotte Red, the Bum from Kansas," also part of a letter that he had received from someone signed "Dick." The letter stated, among other things, that Chas. Wait had gone back to the army, as he was too lazy to work, and that Beva Kay and Lou Acres had joined the Salvation Army, want of business the cause. A switch-key of some railroad was found on him. The body was interred in the **Georgetown cemetery**, at the expense of the county.

**Political Opinions in Georgetown** - Southern Mercury. (Dallas, Tex.), February 21, 1901

The present weather couldn't be prettier if it had been ordered.

A large barn, the property of Mr. M. C. Looney, near Pottsboro, was recently burned. Estimated loss on grain, etc., was $4,000 with no insurance.

The country, especially the woods, are getting very inviting just now. The frost has not yet touched the trees, but they are putting on their autumn tinges. Out of the dirt and rattle and confusion of the city comes the country that is clean, sweet, odorous; sunny with welcome; silent with peace.

**Georgetown and Pottsboro a pretty place to visit** - October 23, 1904

W. J. Bilderbuck of Fink, Texas, writes: "I favor a straight Populist ticket, and oppose fusion in any form. It is useless to organize a new party. The Omaha platform has in it every essential principle for good and economical government. I will never vote a Democratic tcket. The best plan to adopt just now is to distribute reform literature and encourage investigatons by the honest but uninformed. I endorse Direct Legislation and believe it an important measure."

Denison Daily Herald. March 1, 1906

GEORGETOWN.

Georgetown, Tex., Feb. 28.—The hail storm Friday evening was the heaviest in years.

Oat sowing is about over and farmers are preparing for corn and potato planting.

Mr. and Mrs. Frank Coonrod of Denison spent several days last week visiting relatives here.

Rufus Sharpe come out from Denison Friday and remained until Monday visiting his parents.

A. H. Burgess of Sadler was here Tuesday to attend the funeral of his great grandmother, Mrs. Zibble Connor, late, of Pottsboro.

Keel Williams of New Mexico was the guest of his father Monday and Tuesday.

Mr. and Mrs. W. S. Reeves of Sherman were the guests of the latter's parents Saturday and Sunday.

A number of our citizens attended court at Pottsboro Saturday.

John Clements is on the sick list.

Mr. Porter is building a new blacksmith shop, which will be a great benefit to the people.

Mrs. W. J. Bilderback spent Saturday and Sunday with her son, Sam Bilderback, at Preston.

Miss Minnie Lostic has accepted a position with Sidney R. Elkin of Denison.

Mr. and Mrs. Mack Jones went to Denison Saturday.

Ab Allen has resumed his duties as agent for the Texas Nursery Company.

The Denison Daily Herald Friday, March 2, 1906

GEORGETOWN.

Georgetown, Tex., July 16.—The recent rains will insure a good corn crop in this neighborhood. June corn is doing nicely.

Theshing has commenced in this community and the grain crop will be fair.

J. A. Porter has been repairing his store building the past week.

Capt. J. C. Sharpe, who has been very low, is some better at this writing.

Captain W. S. Grant and Homer Taylor returned last week from a two months' visit in the Northwest.

Vance Sharp of Wynnewood, I. T., who has been at the bedside of his father, has returned home.

Ernest and Ab Allen will leave this week for a six weeks' trip through Oklahoma, New Mexico and Western Texas.

Mesdames G. M. Elkins of Lawton and B. F. Bynum of Arapaho, Okla., are visiting their parents, Mr. and Mrs. J. E. Sharpe.

Mr. and Mrs. Albert Burgess of Sadler were here Sunday.

Dan Utiger was a Sherman visitor Sunday.

Misses Dena and Dollie Abbie of Denison spent Sunday here.

The year-old child of Mr. and Mrs. Mose Smith is very sick.

Misses Ara and Myrtle Holley returned home Tuesday from a visit with relatives at Durant.

Mrs. W. S. Reeves and children returned to Sherman Sunday after a visit with relatives here.

Miss Mary Davis is on the sick list.

C. H. Marion and father left Sunday for a trip to Greer county, Okla.

W.S. Grant and Homer Taylor went to the Northwest because that is where Mr. Grant's son had settled.

Pottsboro, Tex., March 1.—J. V. Greenup stopped off here and spent a day or so with relatives, while on his way to Corsicana, where he goes to assume his duties as assistant postmaster.

Rev. E. R. Edwards went to Whitesboro Friday.

Prof. J. B. Jared went to Wolfe City Saturday.

Pottsboro and vicinity were visited Friday by one of the heaviest hailstorms that has fallen here in years. It was specially severe about Georgetown and Fink.

F. M. Anderson left Saturday for the Territory on business.

Mr. and Mrs. W. S. Reeves of Sherman were here Saturday and Sunday, visiting Mrs. Reeves' parents, Mr. and Mrs. Wm. Hull.

John Grayham and Hall Buckley went to Sulphur Sunday.

Mrs. J. S. Gibson has gone to Blossom to visit relatives.

J. D. Rowland and family and Jim Rangely and family left Monday for Gunter, where they will make their home.

Z. G. Scott of Dallas was here this week to attend the funeral of his grandmother, Mrs. Conner.

C. R. Conner, Capt. J. H. Lee and M. A. Lee of Archer county were here this week on account of the death of Mrs. Conner.

G. A. Jones went to Sadler Monday

som to visit relatives.

J. D. Rowland and family and Jim Rangely and family left Monday for Gunter, where they will make their home.

Z. G. Scott of Dallas was here this week to attend the funeral of his grandmother, Mrs. Conner.

C. R. Conner, Capt. J. H. Lee and M. A. Lee of Archer county were here this week on account of the death of Mrs. Conner.

G. A. Jones went to Sadler Monday evening, returning Tuesday.

Keel Williams was here this week to see his father. He was on his way to New Mexico, leaving for there Wednesday.

W. T. Clontz received a telegram from Cash, I. T., Wednesday, stating that Mrs. Elizabeth Clontz died there Tuesday, and would be brought here for burial Friday.

Frank Boggs of Sherman was here Wednesday.

J. C. Leatherwood has torn down the old building formerly occupied by Buckley and Boggs Barber shop, and is preparing to move the big iron ware house that stands at the rear of his business house now, to that site. This will be quiet an improvement to this side of the street.

Workmen are rapidly completing Dr. Hogan's new building on the east

## GEORGETOWN NEWS Denison Daily Herald March 6, 1906

The remains of Mrs. Elizabeth Clontz arrived here Friday from Cash, I. T., and were interred in the Georgetown cemetery Friday evening. Mrs. Clontz was born Feb. 21, 1874, about six miles north of Sherman, was married to W. T. Clontz Sept. 25, 1894, and died Feb. 28, 1906. She was a daughter of Mr. and Mrs. Joe Bradley, who are pioneer settlers of Grayson county. She had lived in the neighborhood of her old home all her life until last fall, when her family moved to Oklahoma, where she died.

West Texas to visit relatives. Mrs. Alexander expects to spend a month on the plains for her health.

Miss Ella Bowen of Van Alstyne, was here last week the guest of Miss Clara Thoma.

L. L. Davis' team ran away with him last Thursday. He was thrown from the wagon, and received some very painful and dangerous wounds.

The remains of Mrs. Elizabeth Clontz arrived here Friday from Cash, I. T., and were interred in the Georgetown cemetery Friday evening. Mrs

---

Will Dickerson and Will Crane of Cedar Mills, were here Saturday.

Ed Judd and Miss Edna Looney, students of Grayson College, with Miss Margurite Looney and Miss Odessa White, friends of Miss Edna Looney, came up from Whitewright Saturday, and spent Saturday and Sunday here.

Rev. F. McFarland, of Sherman passed through town Saturday on his way to Georgetown, to fill his regular appointment there Sunday.

Mrs. Rachel Sledge of Ada, is here to see her mother, Mrs. Sallie Burgess, who is very sick.

R. B. Leatherwood of Hillsboro, is here this week visiting home folks.

Mr. and Mrs. A. M. Owens of Hartford, Ind., are here visiting Mr. Jackson and Mr. and Mrs. W. P. Hardwick.

The Pottsboro W. O. W. Camp held its regular meeting Saturday, at which two candidates were initiated into the mysteries of the lodge.

The Denison Daily Herald. Monday, March 12, 1906

### Georgetown News.

Georgetown, Tex., March 7.—All farm work is stopped again in consequence of the rain.

There are a few who are not through sowing oats yet. All are behind with all other farm work, many not having an acre prepared for corn.

There will be a pretty fair crop of potatoes planted, perhaps quite as many as were planted last year.

Wheat is looking promising, though but a small acreage was sown.

Ab Allen was a visitor at Honey Grove Sunday.

Mr. and Mrs. Tom Coonrod of Denison spent last Wednesday with relatives here.

Miss Zula Slayden spent Saturday and Sunday with home folks in Sherman.

Miss India Allen spent few days in Sherman last week.

There was a surprise party at the home of Mr. Holley Friday night.

Albert Burgess of Sadler was here Sunday.

Rufus Elliott, who was quite sick last week, is reported better.

.....................................

Mrs. Hull spent a few days in Denison last week with her daughters, Misses Beulah and Edith Hull.

Rev. McFarland of Woodlake filled his regular appointment Sunday.

Miss Eula Allen of Sherman spent Sunday with her parents, Mr. and Mrs. H. C. Allen.

Misses Nora Jones and May Farrell spent Sunday at Cashion.

Jim Cheatham visited his brother in Sherman Saturday and Sunday.

Capt. W. S. Grant and Homer Taylor went to Denison Monday.

J. L. Baird was elected superintendent of the Sunday school Sunday.

Will Mitchell of Basin Springs was here Sunday.

The Denison Daily Herald March 30, 1906 & April 4, 1906

Albert Burgess made his regular business trip to Georgetown last Saturday.

Prof. R. H. Smellege of Willow Springs was here on business last Saturday.

Mr. and Mrs. Spivey of Pottsboro were visiting friends here Sunday.

J. W. Hayse, the cashier of our bank, visited his parents at Collinsville Sunday.

Messrs. Ernest and Ab Allen of Georgetown were visiting Albert Burgess of this place yesterday.

### William Low.

William Low, aged 19 years, an employe of the cotton mill, died last night at his home near the cotton mill after a week's illness from a complication of diseases. The remains were taken to Pottsboro this afternoon and interred in the Georgetown cemetery near that place.

The Denison Daily Herald March 19, 1906

## DEATH OF MRS. FRENCH.

### An Old Settler of Grayson County Passes Away.

Pottsboro, Tex.. March 19.—Mrs. Susan A. French, wife of W. H. French, died at her residencey in the east part of town at 6:30 o'clock this morning.

Mrs. French was born Oct. 2, 1832, in Perryville, Boyle County, Ky. Her maiden name was Susan A. Penney. She was married in October, 1867, to W. H. French. The family moved from Kentucky to Missouri in 1868, where they lived until 1875, when they came to Texas and located just east of Sherman, where they lived until 1879, when they removed to Pottsboro, where they have lived continuously ever since with the exception of two years spent in Denison. She leaves besides her husband two stepsons, E. L. French of Pottsboro and Tom French of Paul's Valley, I. T., whom she raised from childhood, and three step grandchildren.

Mrs. French joined the Baptist Church when a girl and has been a faithful and consistent member of same for over fifty years. Besides her relatives she leaves a host of friends having been an active and useful member of Pottsboro society for over twenty-five years.

The funeral services will be conducted from the Baptist Church at 2 o'clock Tuesday, March 20th. Interment in the Georgetown cemetery at 3 o'clock.

The Denison Daily Herald, March 22, 1906

Georgetown, Tex., March 21.—Misses Edith and Beulah Hull of Denison spent from Friday until Monday with their parents.

Mrs. J. D. Holley left yesterday for a visit with relatives at Durant.

Rufus Sharpe of Denison spent the latter part of last week with his parents.

The Woodmen celebrate the fourth anniversary of the camp tonight with a supper for themselves and families.

Mrs. Ira Crause of Sherman is visiting her parents, Mr. and Mrs. R. R. Richardson.

Miss Dollie Abby of Denison visited at the home of Mr. Sharpe last week.

Mrs. Will Johnson of Pottsboro was the guest of her parents, Mr. and Mrs. Hull, a few days this week.

Miss Myrtle Brannon of Cashion was the guest of Miss Nora Jones Saturday and Sunday.

Miss Mary Gardenhire returned to her home in Rockwall, yesterday, after a visit with her brother, George Gardenhire, and wife.

Miss Aline Scott returned yesterday from a visit to Miss Beulah Speakes in Greenville. Miss Speaks accompanied her for a visit here.

## GEORGETOWN The Denison Daily Herald May 4, 1906

### GEORGETOWN.

Georgetown, Tex., May 4.—W. S. Reeves and family of Sherman are visiting relatives here this week.

Miss India Allen returned home Sunday from a week's visit with relatives in Sherman.

Capt. W. S. Grant and Homer Taylor left Monday for an extended visit in Washington and Montana.

Miss Elsie Davis returned Thursday from a visit with relatives in Sherman.

E. C. Cheatham and family spent Saturday and Sunday in Sherman.

Rev. S. E. Burroughs of Denison will preach at Georgetown the third Sunday in May.

Mrs. Belle Davis is quite sick.

Ephriam Williams is visiting his father, Dr. Williams.

W. J. Bilderback has purchased Homer Taylor's stock of groceries.

Miss Esla Allen of Sherman is spending the week with home folks.

Misses Edith and Beulah Hull, who are attending school in Denison, were at home from Friday till Monday.

J. W. Marion was on the sick list last week.

A new telephone line is being erected from Georgetown into Potts-

The Denison Daily Herald April 19, 1906

### GEORGETOWN.

Georgetown, Tex., April 18.—Mrs. S. E. Mitchell has returned from a visit with relatives at Whitesboro.

Mrs. Wm. Hull returned home Friday from Sherman, where she had been attending the bedside of her daughter, Mrs. W. S. Reeves.

Frank Williams of Clinton, Okla. is visiting his father, Dr. C. Williams.

Homer Taylor is on the sick list this week.

Miss Minnie Sharpensteen of Cashion spent Saturday night and Sunday with Miss Nora Jones.

Misses Myrtle and Robbie Brannon of Cashion visited friends here last week.

Miss Elsie Davis is visiting relatives in Sherman.

Mr. and Mrs. Hake gave a concert last night and organized a class in crayon portrait drawing.

We would like to see the road overseer on the road from the gin past the school house use the split log or some other device on it, as there are several places that are almost impassable.

Fred Finke was re-elected school trustee in last Saturday's election.

H. C. Allen is putting in a telephone.

Crops are looking promising now most all the corn is planted, and some few have plowed it.

Cotton planting is on; the crop will be increased a little over last year's acreage.

Denison Daily Herald May 8, 1906

### GEORGETOWN.

Georgetown, Tex., May 4.—W. S. Reeves and family of Sherman are visiting relatives here this week.

Miss India Allen returned home Sunday from a week's visit with relatives in Sherman.

Capt. W. S. Grant and Homer Taylor left Monday for an extended visit in Washington and Montana.

Miss Elsie Davis returned Thursday from a visit with relatives in Sherman.

E. C. Cheatham and family spent Saturday and Sunday in Sherman.

Rev. S. E. Burroughs of Denison will preach at Georgetown the third Sunday in May.

Mrs. Belle Davis is quite sick.

Ephriam Williams is visiting his father, Dr. Williams.

W. J. Bilderback has purchased Homer Taylor's stock of groceries.

Miss Esla Allen of Sherman is spending the week with home folks.

Misses Edith and Beulah Hull, who are attending school in Denison, were at home from Friday till Monday.

J. W. Marion was on the sick list last week.

A new telephone line is being erected from Georgetown into Pottsboro.

The heaviest rain in years fell Tuesday evening.

Mail carrier of route 3 out of Pottsboro failed to make his trip yesterday.

Crop conditions are very unfavorable owing to the recent rains.

Denison Daily Herald May 8, 1906

Pottsboro, Tex., May 7.—The weather is getting to be a serious question with our farmers. Everybody is behind with work, of all kinds. There is not more than half of the cotton planted yet, and what is planted is not doing well on account of the excessive rain. The rain has damaged the fruit and grain crops considerably.

J. L. Davis had a fine mare killed last week by the lightning.

Robt. Potts, Mrs. J. A. Potts and Mrs. W. C. Bennett returned Friday from a two weeks' visit in New Orleans. Mr. Potts says all the South part of the state is suffering from the want of rain. It was so dry down there that the crops could not come up.

F. M. Anderson left Saturday for Sulphur Springs, I. T.

Mrs. J. P. Steel came near being drowned last Thursday, while attempting to cross a swollen stream. Her son, Walter Steel, was with her and her son-in-law, Alvin Henderson, was just ahead of them when the accident happened. The buggy was washed down the creek and the men did not catch Mrs. Steel until she had floated some distance down the stream. She lost her purse, which contained $15. She escaped without any serious injuries.

Capt. W. S. Grant, and Homer Taylor, left last week, for an extended trip, in California, Oregon, and Washington. They went by way of San Francisco. They intend to spent the summer in Washington and Oregon.

Mr. McAden of Gainesville is here visiting his son, W. H. McAden.

Mr. and Mrs. H. L. Kimmery left Friday for Howe, to visit friends and relatives.

Dr. A. Q. Gentry is in Decatur this week on business and visiting friends.

Will T. Watts of Madill was here last week the guest of Dr. N. C. Parrish.

Miss Minter of Greenville is here visiting her uncle, Mr. R. H. Minter.

Mrs. Burleson of Sherman is here visiting her son, George Burleson.

Mr. and Mrs. M. C. Bacon went to

Denison Friday.

While working on a bridge on the road last Friday Boyd Holland dropped a heavy plank, that had a nail in it and the nail was driven through his foot, making a very severe wound.

Mr. and Mrs. W. S. Buster of Whitesboro were here Friday the guests of Mr. and Mrs. W. S. Cummins.

H. C. Bennett went to Denison Friday.

Ed Judd, who is attending school in Denison, was home Friday and Saturday.

G. E. Reeves and son, Master Pernie, and Mrs. Nelson went to Shawnee Saturday.

Prof. Jesse Ruyle of Gordonville was here Saturday.

Miss Estella and Fay Greenup went to Denison Saturday.

Mr. and Mrs. G. A. Jones went to Denison Monday to take in the carnival.

The protracted meeting that was to have begun at the Methodist Church Sunday has been postponed on account of the illness of the pastor, Rev. F. R. Edwards.

The Denison Daily Herald. May 24, 1906; June 21, 1906 & July 10, 1906

GEORGETOWN.

Georgetown, Tex., May 23.—Crops all growing nicely now and farmers are rushing their work, battling with the grass and weeds.

Misses Della Hull, India and Thelma Allen and Raymond Hull returned home Saturday from Sherman, where they were the guests of relatives during the carnival.

Rev. S. E. Burrows of Denison filled his appointment here Sunday and will preach again the third Sunday.

Misses Beulah and Edith Hull, who have been attending school in Denison, have returned home, the school having closed.

The trustees of the school have employed J. R. Malloy as teacher for the next term.

Mrs. Belle Davis, who has been sick for several weeks, is able to be up.

Joe Bilderback is on the sick list.

ENTERPRISE.

Enterprise, Tex., May 22.—Quite a crowd gathered Sunday afternoon at Sunday school, but were scared away on account of the heavy clouds.

PROGRESS.

Progress, Texas., June 17.—Mrs. M. E. Steel and little niece, Miss Lillian Sharpe, went to Wynnewood, I. T., last week to spend the summer with Mrs. Steel's daughter, Mrs. Sharpe.

Harvesting is in full swing in this neighborhod now. There is very little wheat here and it is sorry. The oats crop is good although damaged some by rust. The last ten days of fair weather has been just what the farmers needed.

It is impossible to get hands. Wages are very high and some are offering $1.50 a day and still can not get hands.

Alvin Henderson went to Pottsboro last Saturday.

M. A. Steel and wife spent Sunday at the home of John Mitchell of Georgetown.

J. I. Clements went to Denison Friday.

M. A. Steel went to Pottsboro Friday.

Wm. Crissman and family visited in the Georgetown neighborhood Sunday.

The cotton crop in this part is beginning to grow. The early planting is beginning to bloom, but there is a large per cent of the crop that is very late.

Below: Harvesting Wheat in May

GEORGETOWN NEWS The Denison Daily Herald, June 1, 1906

About fifteen members of the L. O. T. M. were in Denison last week to attend a social function given by the Denison Hive.

G. E. Reeves and E. T. Judd went to the Territory last Friday.

W. C. Hatfield went to Denison Saturday.

A. S. Noble of Preston was in town Saturday.

F. P. Thompson went to Sherman Saturday .

Dr. and Mrs. Gipson of Preston were here Saturday.

W. C. Nevitt of Appleton went to Sherman Saturday.

Albert Burgess of Sadler was here Saturday and Sunday.

Mr. and Mrs. B. M. Flanery of Denison were here Saturday and Sunday visiting relatives.

Reverend Ball of Sherman preached at the Methodist Church Sunday morning and night.

Porter Jackson and Miss Edith Loveall of Preston were married here Sunday evening, Rev. T. A. Davis, the pastor of the Presbyterian Church, performing the ceremony.

The Pottsboro W. O. W. Camp will unveil the monument of J. W. Holland at the Georgetown cemetery Sunday evening, June 3. Everybody invited to be present.

Mrs. G. N. Greenup is visiting her sister, Mrs. W. A. Winham, at Southmayd this week.

Henry Reeves, who has been attending Grayson College the past session, returned home Tuesday.

The farmers are all complaining of the ground getting very hard and dry and say that they need a good shower. Small grain needs rain as well as the other crops. The rains were so heavy that the ground was packed very hard and has dried out so quickly that it left the ground hard and tough.

Capt. A. W. Hulett returned from South McAlester Monday where he visited his daughter, Mrs. Reeves, who had been in the sanitarium in St. Louis so long, but is now rapidly recovering. Captain Hulett went fishing while he was in the Territory and brought four or five big fine bass back with him that he said weighed five pounds apiece. He requested that the Herald reporter give special notice of the fact, that he had them and that he caught them with a hook and line with his own hand, for the special benefit of Col. Nathaniel Hawthorn Longfellow Decker of Denison, as the latter is somewhat of a doubting Thomas in regard to the Captain's piscatorial ability.

The Citizen's Bank has moved into new quarters on the west side of Main street.

The Georgetown Cemetery Association will hold a meeting at the cemetery Sunday evening, June 3. Every one interested in the cemetery is requested to be present.

Denison Daily Herald June 12, 1906

**Georgetown Cemetery Association Holds Business Session.**

Pottsboro, Tex., June 11.—Misses Estella Greenup and Edna Looney went to Denison shopping Saturday.

G. E. Reeves went to Denison Saturday.

The Georgetown Cemetery Association held a business session at the cemetery Sunday evening at which there was a report from the financial committee and an election of the officers of the association. The following officers were elected for the ensuing year: W. S. Grant, president; D. R. Harris, vice president; G. E. Reeves, secretary and treasurer; J. D. Holley, superintendent, and Captain Hulett, assistant superintendent. The executive committee was called to meet at D. R. Harris' business house in Pottsboro Saturday, June 16.

B. N. Greenup returned from the West Saturday evening.

Miss Mary Scott returned Thursday from a three weeks' visit with her brother, Lave Scott at Jacksboro.

W. T. Potts, an old Pottsboro boy who is located now at Denton, was here Friday and Saturday visiting relatives and old friends. He returned home Saturday evening.

Rev. E. L. Silliman, who has been sent here by the authorities of the Methodist Church to fill out the unexpired time of Rev. E. R. Edwards, arrived with his family Saturday evening and preached Sunday at the morning and evening services.

Mr. Scott of Hereford was here this week looking at some property with a view to locating.

Dr. J. H. Stiver and family moved to Denison Saturday. Doctor Stiver has been here fifteen or sixteen years, has been one of our best physicians, and he and his esteemed family have a host of warm friends here who will sincerely regret their departure.

Mrs. J. F. Bennett went to Sherman Saturday.

Mrs. R. P. Elrod returned from Steadman Saturday. She had been visiting friends there the past week.

Mr. and Mrs. William Watts of Madill are here visiting Dr. and Mrs. N. C. Parish.

The Pottsboro W. O. W. Camp No. 426 unveiled the monument of J. W. Holland at the Georgetown Cemetery Sunday evening.

Mrs. Loughmiller and children went to Sherman Monday.

Mr. and Mrs. J. V. Greenup left for Sulphur Springs, I. T., Monday.

The new crop of potatoes are coming on the market.

Oat and wheat harvest are being pushed to the utmost this week while the sun is shining. The oat crop promises a good yield but the wheat is very light.

## GEORGETOWN NEWS

The Denison Daily Herald June 14, 1906

### GEORGETOWN.

Georgetown, Tex., June 13.—Mr. and Mrs. W. S. Reeves of Sherman spent Saturday and Sunday with relatives here.

Ernest Allen, who has been sick for several weeks, is no better.

A large crowd was present at the cemetery Sunday, to witness the unveiling of Walter Holland's monument by the W. O. W.

Miss Eula Allen of Sherman spent Sunday here with her parents.

A. H. Burgess of Sadler was a visitor here Sunday.

D. R. Utiger was a visitor in Sherman Sunday.

Mr. and Mrs. Frank Coonrod and Miss Minnie Bostic of Denison spent Saturday and Sunday with relatives.

J. A. Bilderback, who has been sick for several weeks, is able to be up.

Miss India Allen spent Monday in Sherman.

Mrs. M. E. Steele and granddaughter left last week for Wynnewood, I. T., for a visit with her daughter, Mrs. Vance Sharpe.

Misses Elsie Davis and Etta Sharpe are on the sick list this week.

Harvesting is on for sure. Quite a number of binders have been purchased this year in this neighborhood and all are running early and late. The oats crop has been pretty badly damaged by the rust.

Those who have potatoes are digging and marketing them. Only a few, however, are fortunate enough to have any to sell no matter what the price is. It is doubtful whether the potato crop is a profitable one, as it is at the same time of gathering as the small grain crop, both of which cause the corn and cotton to be neglected to such an extent as to cause a loss greater than the gain on the potato crop.

Corn is in silk and tassel and is being laid by.

The Denison Daily Herald June 27, 1906

Miss Viola Hudgins visited Miss Nora Jones of Georgetown Sunday.

The health of the community generally is good.

GEORGETOWN NEWS The Denison Daily Herald June 22, 1906

## GEORGETOWN.

Georgetown, Tex., June 20.—Mr. and Mrs. Crouse of Sherman came out Saturday. The former returned Sunday. Mrs. Crouse will remain several weeks with her parents, Mr. and Mrs. R. R. Richardson.

Miss India Allen and sister, Thelma, went to Sherman Friday, returning Sunday.

Miss Dollie Abbey of Denison spent Sunday at the home of Mr. Sharpe.

Miss Eula Allen of Sherman is at home for a two weeks' visit with her parents.

Mr. and Mrs. Tom Coonrod of Denison spent yesterday with relatives here.

Rev. S. E. Burrows of Denison filled his appointment here Sunday.

Jim Cheatham went to Sherman Saturday.

Mesdames Connor Burgess and H. C. Allen spent Saturday in Denison.

Mr. and Mrs. J. C. Sharpe and daughter, Lottie, were shopping in Denison Friday.

John Hoyle left for Beaver County, Okla., Saturday.

Connor Burgess had the misfortune to cut his hand pretty badly on the binder sickle Monday.

W. S. Reeves of Sherman was here Sunday.

Harvesting and potato digging are about over. The yield of both crops will be tolerably fair.

Corn is now in full silk and tassel and is needing rain.

The cotton crop is flourishing. The first planting is fruiting fast and will have blooms in a week or ten days.

The farmers are all about up with their work.

The Denison Daily Herald June 28, 1906

## GEORGETOWN.

Georgetown, Tex., June 27.—The rain Sunday night will prove beneficial to all growing crops.

Miss Ella Covey and brother, Enoch, of Sherman spent Sunday with the Misses Bostic.

Misses Annie and Bessie Stewart of Sherman spent from Saturday until Monday with their aunt, Mrs. Allen.

Married, at the residence of the bride's parents, Mr. and Mrs. H. C. Allen, Sunday afternoon at 6 o'clock, Miss India Allen and Albert H. Burgess of Sadler, Tex. After an elegant supper the bride and groom accompanied by friends drove to Pottsboro, and took the 8 o'clock train for a week's visit at Ada, Okla., after which they will be at home to their friends at Sadler, Tex.

Miss Minnie Bostic of Denison spent Sunday with home folks.

Mrs. T. J. Coonrod is visiting relatives in Denison.

Mr. and Mrs. W. S. Reeves and children of Sherman spent Sunday with relatives here.

Mr. nad Mrs. Sam Bilderback of Preston were here Sunday.

Mr. and Mrs. Smith from the Territory visited Mr. and Mrs. Latham Friday and Saturday.

Miss Ella May Perry of Fort Worth is the guest of her aunt, Miss Jennie Coonrod.

Dan Utiger was a Sherman visitor Sunday.

Miss Viola Hudgins of Cashion was the guest of Miss Nora Jones a few days last week.

Miss Vera Jones is visiting in the Territory this week.

Misses Della and Edith Hill were shopping in Denison Thursday.

Denison Daily News Friday, July 20, 1906

## GEORGETOWN.

Georgetown, Tex., July 16.—The recent rains will insure a good corn crop in this neighborhood. June corn is doing nicely.

Theshing has commenced in this community and the grain crop will be fair.

J. A. Porter has been repairing his store building the past week.

Capt. J. C. Sharpe, who has been very low, is some better at this writing.

Captain W. S. Grant and Homer Taylor returned last week from a two months' visit in the Northwest.

Vance Sharp of Wynnewood, I. T., who has been at the bedside of his father, has returned home.

Ernest and Ab Allen will leave this week for a six weeks' trip through Oklahoma, New Mexico and Western Texas.

Mesdames G. M. Elkins of Lawton and B. F. Bynum of Arapaho, Okla., are visiting their parents, Mr. and Mrs. J. E. Sharpe.

Mr. and Mrs. Albert Burgess of Sadler were here Sunday.

Dan Utiger was a Sherman visitor Sunday.

Misses Dena and Dollie Abbie of Denison spent Sunday here.

The year-old child of Mr. and Mrs. Mose Smith is very sick.

Misses Ara and Myrtle Holley returned home Tuesday from a visit with relatives at Durant.

Mrs. W. S. Reeves and children returned to Sherman Sunday after a visit with relatives here.

Miss Mary Davis is on the sick list.

C. H. Marion and father left Sunday for a trip to Greer county, Okla.

The Denison Daily Herald August 3, 1906

### Election Results at Pottsboro.

Pottsboro, Tex., Aug. 2.—Frank Thompson was elected county commissioner; W. H. McAden, justice of the peace; W. C. Porter, constable, and W. C. Hatfield, public weigher for this precinct at the primaries last Saturday.

G. E. Reeves went to Dallas Saturday.

Mrs. Henderson has returned from Greer County, where she had been visiting the past month or so.

W. S. Moore of Van Alstyne was here Saturday.

The following are the delegates to the county convention from this box: A. W. Hulett, Dan Utiger, J. D. Holley and G. H. Harding.

W. T. Potts and family of Denton were here and spent the first of the week with home folks. Mr. Potts is preparing to take a trip through the Western country soon.

Mr. and Mrs. J. F. Bennett spent Sunday at Tioga Wells.

The Denison Daily Herald August 3, 1906

Miss Clara Thoma left for Ambrose Wednesday for a week's visit with her sister, Mrs. Rosco Grissom.

W. E. Waddle, formerly a citizen of this place but who has been located at Fort Gibson for the past three years, is here with his family this week visiting relatives and friends.

Miss Lela Liles went to Sherman Wednesday.

The Citizens Bank has completed its fine fire proof vault.

The officers of the Georgetown Cemetery Association are still urging the members who have not paid their dues to pay up as soon as possible, as Superintendent Holley said Wednesday evening that if he did not succeed in letting the contract for cleaning the grounds to some one this week he would employ a force of men and go and clean the grounds himself.

Mr. and Mrs. G. A. Jones and son, R. W. Jones, left on the early train Wednesday morning for Epworth on the gulf near Corpus Christi to attend the annual meeting of the State Epworth League. They expect to be gone about three weeks.

Frank Thompson, G. E. Reeves and several others went to Sherman Thursday to attend the old settlers' picnic.

The prospects for cotton in this community are very flattering, considering the fact that the crop must be at least three weeks late. If the hot winds and boll worms will let the plant alone we will have a fine crop.

Georgetown News The Denison Daily Herald August 10, 1906

Georgetown, Tex., Aug. 8.—Still it rains. These continued rains are very detrimental to the crops, especially the cotton crop.

The threshing has stopped until the rains cease; there is a great deal of grain yet to be threshed.

Among those attending the picnic at Sherman were, Mrs. H. C. Allen and daughter, Thelma, Mr. and Mrs. John Mitchell and children, J. D. Holley and family, R. R. Richardson and son, Bob, and daughter, Miss Lillie.

Misses Hull and brother, Raymond, were the guest of their sister, Mrs. W. S. Reeves during the picnic.

Miss Lillie Richardson and Jim Cheatham were married in Sherman Thursday.

B. F. Bynum of Arapaho, Okla., is the guest of relatives here.

Mrs. Nannie Baird of Canyon City, Tex., is visiting relatives here.

W. E. Waddle of Fort Gibson is the guest of his brother-in-law, F. Farrell.

Capt. J. C. Sharpe is still improving.

The year-old child of Mr. and Mrs. Mose Smith died Friday night and

Georgetown News cont'd The Denison Daily Herald August 10, 1906

was laid to rest Saturday afternoon in the Steel cemetery.

The Misses Bostic spent last week in Sherman.

Mrs. Ben Bynum is quite sick at the home of her parents, Mr. and Mrs. J. C. Sharpe.

Mr. and Mrs. Jim Marion spent Sunday at Preston.

Mrs. G. W. Matthews is on the sick list.

Mr. and Miss Smellage of Kentuckytown were in the community Saturday.

J. A. Porter made a business trip to Sherman yesterday.

M. W. Jones and family spent Saturday and Sunday with relatives near Isom Spring, I. T.

Mrs. Johnnie Clontz who has been sick is better.

Miss Ollie Utiger is visiting friends at Caddo, I. T.

---

Eva Stanley, the 9-year-old daughter of Mr. Stanley, living seven miles west of the city, died yesterday from an attack of typhoid fever. The remains were buried at the Georgetown cemetery this afternoon. The child's mother has been dead for some time.

Mr. Holley has let the contract to clean up and repair the Georgetown cemetery to Warren Morrison.

Aug 14, 1906

Charley Burgess of Georgetown's Crops Sunday Gazetteer (Denison, Tex.) Aug 19, 1906

There was another rain fall last Saturday morning which extended to the Indian Territory. The Boggy at Atoka overflowed and was miles wide. The Katy was water bound between Atoka and Coalgate. Crops in the Territory have been seriously damaged and also throughout this section cotton has received a very black eye. Charley Burgess of the Georgetown community, was in Denison Wednesday. He says the late rains have damaged crops considerably, having caused him to lose at least 50 bushels of tomatoes in the last few days. He brought in a lot of tomatoes to the Denison Brokerage company, this making the second he brought in. While here he engaged a car load of oats to the Knaur Lindsey company, to be shipped from Pottsboro.

Denison Daily Herald August 23, 1906

## GEORGETOWN.

Georgetown, Tex., Aug. 22.—The boll worm is ravaging the cotton crop; the wet weather is also hurting the crop considerably.

Holley and Taylor are overhauling and repairing their gin.

There is considerable interest manifested in the protracted meeting at Progress.

Miss Eula Allen of Sherman spent Sunday at home with her parents.

Mrs. Belle Davis and family spent several days last week with relatives at Gordonville.

Mr. and Mrs. Jim Cheatham of Sherman spent Saturday and Sunday with E. C. Cheatham.

Mr. and Mrs. Albert Burgess of Sadler were guests of relatives here Sunday.

Miss Maude Bostic is visiting in Bonham.

S. J. Hull and father, Wm. Hull left Saturday for a western trip.

M. W. Jones has returned from Caddo, I. T. While there Mr. Jones purchased a farm and will move to it the first of next year.

Lloyd Pery and sister, Miss Barnanah, of Preston were the guests of friends here Monday afternoon.

Miss Minnie Bostic of Denison spent Sunday with her parents.

Joe Knighten and family of Roberta, I. T., are visiting J. D. Holley and family.

The Denison Daily Herald August 31, 1906

## GEORGETOWN.

Georgetown, Tex., Aug. 29.—The meeting at Progress closed Sunday afternoon. There wer twenty-one additions to the church.

Miss Maude Bostic has returned from Bonham.

Mrs. Mercer and daughter, Miss Eula, of Denison, spent Sunday with Mrs. Hull and family.

Mrs. S. E. Mitchell left Tuesday for Jacksboro, Tex., where she will make her home.

Miss Jennie Coonrod is visiting friends at Gordonville this week.

Mrs. J. P. Wheat and children returned to Sherman Monday after a visit with her sister, Mrs. H. C. Allen.

Miss Della Hull accompanied by Miss Eula Allen of Sherman left Monday for Canyon City, Tex., to attend the reunion. Miss Hull will remain several months the guest of relatives.

Miss Ella May Perry, who has been spending the summer with her grandmother, Mrs. T. J. Coonrod, left Sunday for her home in Fort Worth.

Mrs. W. S. Reeves and children returned to Sherman Sunday after a visit with her mother, Mrs. Hull.

Capt. J. C. Sharpe is still in a critical condition.

Mr. and Mrs. B. F. Bynum and little daughter, Winifred, have returned to their home in Arapaho, Okla.

The Farmers' Union of this place will give an ice cream supper Thursday night for its members and their families.

The Denison Daily Herald September 25, 1906 & October 25, 1906

## I. N. Hall Dies Near Pottsboro.

Pottsboro, Tex., Sept. 25.—I. N. Hall died at his residence three miles south of Pottsboro yesterday afternoon at 1:25 o'clock and will be buried this afternoon at 4 o'clock in the Georgetown Cemetery.

Mr. Hall was born in Virginia in 1845, served in the Federal Army. He moved to Texas in 1880, locating in Fannin County, where he lived for seven years. From there he removed to the Territory, where he lived for fourteen years and then returned to Texas about four years ago and bought the farm south of town, where he has lived ever since.

Deceased leaves a wife and seven children to mourn the loss of a kind, loving husband and father.

## LETTER IN A COTTON BALE.

### Mr. Allen of Georgetown Has Received Over Thirty Answers.

Georgetown, Tex., Oct. 23.—Last January, A. S. Allen placed a letter in a bale of cotton, asking the one who opened it to write and tell him when and where the bale was opened and to recommend a good looking girl for social correspondence. Oct. 15th he received an answer stating that the bale was opened Sept. 30 at Manchester, England. Also a newspaper clipping headed "A Texas Boy Wants a Wife." To date Mr. Allen has received thirty letters from various places in England, Ireland and Scotland.

The Denison Daily Herald Nov 1, 1906, Nov 9, 1906 & Nov 22, 1906

## GEORGETOWN.

Georgetown, Tex., Oct. 31.—An oil, gas, coal and asphalt mining company is securing leases on a great deal of land in this community, and will commence operations soon.

W. J. Bilderback went to Nocona Friday, returning home Sunday.

Wm. Hull is on the sick list.

The young folks had a surprise party at the home of Mrs. Utiger Friday night.

Eb Hull and Will Mitchell spent Sunday at Sandusky.

The home of J. D. Holley was entered Monday night and over $100 stolen from Chai'lle Hash and Bob Trammell, boys who are working for Mr. Holley. A party was arrested on suspicion, but was turned loose because of lack of evidence.

Mr. and Mrs. J. W. Marion visited in Sherman Friday and Saturday.

Mr. and Mrs. Porter Mosley of Midland, Tex., who are visiting Mrs. Mosely's parents, Mr. and Mrs. W. E. Baird, in Sherman, visited relatives here last week.

## GEORGETOWN.

Georgetown, Tex., Nov. 21.—The first real blizzard of the season has been with us since Sunday. Every thing is covered with ice and snow.

There is still some cotton in the field, though the majority are through picking.

The young folks enjoyed their annual pecan hunt Saturday. They spent the day in the river bottoms, returning late in the afternoon with few pecans, but well pleased with their trip. A surprise party at the home of Mr. Richardson that night wound up the festivities.

J. W. Bilderback returned home Wednesday from Nacona, where he sold a span of mules for $300.

School opened last Monday with a good attendance, under the management of J. R. Malloy.

J. W. Marion returned Sunday from a prospecting trip to New Mexico.

John Hosford has returned from Nacona. While there he sold a span of young mules for $300.

Drilling an experimental oil well northwest of Pottsboro in 1906 in Georgetown

Denison Daily Herald, May 28th, 1907

Pottsboro, Tex., May 27.—W. C. Bennett is making some improvements on his property on North Franklin avenue.

B. M. Flanner of Stringtown, I. T., was here last week, gathering teams to haul lumber from the Lingo-Leeper mills east of Stringtown, in the Territory, to the railroad. He secured a couple of good teams of mules and left Wednesday with them for the mills.

The seventeen months old baby boy of Mr. and Mrs. J. L. Klinglesmith drank some carbolic acid last Thursday evening about five o'clock and died from the effects of the poison in about two hours. The funeral services were delayed until Saturday, waiting for some of the relatives of the family to reach here from San Saba, Texas. The funeral services were held Saturday evening at the residence, conducted by Rev. E. J. Silliman. Interment was in the Georgetown cemetery.

The Denison Daily Herald December 6, 1906 & January 4, 1907

## GEORGETOWN.

Georgetown, Tex., Dec. 5.—The ginning season is about over, the gin only running twice a week after this week.

There will be a box supper at the school house Friday night, Dec. 14, to raise money to have the house repainted. Everyone is cordially invited to come.

Miss Orado Bostic returned Sunday from a week's visit with her sister, Mrs. Frank Coonrod, in Denison.

Mr. and Mrs. A. H. Burgess of Sadler came up Sunday for a short visit with relatives.

M. J. Lathan and W. H. Sharpe are in Lawton, Okla., to file on land in the "big pasture."

Miss Laura Wilson of Pottsboro spent from Friday until Monday with Miss Ava Holley.

Misses Beulah and Edith Hull entertained a number of their friends Monday evening in celebration of their birthday.

## GEORGETOWN.

Georgetown, Tex., Jan. 2.—Three telephone lines are being built into Pottsboro from this community and will enter the Southwestern telephone office.

Mrs. Mercer and daughter, Miss Eula, and Mrs. Jackson of Denison spent Sunday with Mrs. Hull and daughters.

Mr. and Mrs. W. S. Reeves and children have returned to Sherman.

Miss Mary Davis is visiting relatives in Sherman.

Mr. Embry, who has purchased Jim Marion's place, moved to it Jan. 1.

Mr. and Mrs. Frank Coonrod and

HERALD, FRIDAY, JANUARY 4.

Miss Minnie Bostic have returned to Denison, after spending Christmas with their parents.

Charlie Beckham of Basin Springs is visiting friends here.

Jim Marion is down with the rheumatism.

# Old Pioneer Ebenezer Loss Buried at Georgetown

The Denison Daily Herald, January 7, 1907 EBENEZER LOSS

Sherman, Texas, January 7 - Ebenezer Loss, aged 79 years, died Saturday night at the residence of his son-in-law, L. Holmes, on South Walnut street. Decedent was one of the oldest residents of Grayson County, having lived here for 50 years. He was a veteran of 2 wars, having fought in the Mexican War and the Civil War under the Confederate flag.

The remains were interred this afternoon beside his wife in the Georgetown Cemetery near Pottsboro.

# E. T. and M. E. Judd

E. T. Judd and Wife, on Wedding Day.

E. T. Judd, Banker and Ginner.

The Judd Gin at Pottsboro.

Residence of E. T. Judd, Pottsboro.

E. T. Judd owned the cotton gin in Pottsboro and was the President of Pottsboro's Citizen's Bank and one of the nicest houses in town. However, E. T. and his wife M. E. Judd knew tragedy, they lost at least three of their children and had to make that dreaded final trip to Georgetown Cemetery. The children were as follows:

The Sunday Gazetteer, October 17, 1897 - Friday, October 15 - At Pottsboro Wednesday a fatal accident happened. Luther Judd, the 7-year-old son of E.T. Judd, the ginner, stepped into the seed augur at the gin and was buried into the saws and literally ground to pieces from which he died half an hour later. Luther R. Judd, 28 November 1889 - 12 October 1897.

The Denison Daily Herald - October 26, 1906 - Leroy Judd, infant son of Mr. and Mrs. E.T. Judd, died at Tioga Sunday night and was buried in the Georgetown cemetery Tuesday evening. The child had been sick for some time and Mrs. Judd had taken the little fellow to Tioga, hoping that the change would benefit him.

Buddie Judd Born 1903 died 1906. Georgetown Cemetery is full of stories like this.

## GEORGETOWN NEWS The Denison Daily Herald March 5, 1907

Miss Orado Bostic of Georgetown is the guest of her sister, Miss Minnie Bostic, this week.

The Denison Daily Herald, March 28, 1907

### GEORGETOWN.

Georgetown, Tex., March 27.—Farm work is progressing nicely. Since the green bugs have left oat sowing has commenced anew. Early corn is up to a nice stand. Irish potatoes are up and ready for the plow. Cotton is being planted earlier this year than ever before, all working to head off the boll weevil.

Mr. and Mrs. Ira Crause of Sherman spent the latter part of the week here.

Mrs. Essie Hosford and children of Denison spent last week with her parents, Mr. and Mrs. Hull.

Mr. and Mrs. Jim Cheatham have removed from Denison to this place. They are with the former's parents at present.

Miss Dennie Bragdon has returned home after a visit with relatives here.

Miss Louise Utiger spent last week in Pottsboro with her sister, Mrs. Jim Bryant.

There was a surprise party at the home of Mr. Bostic Saturday. All report a most enjoyable time.

(Above: That was Brogdon rather than Bragdon)

The W. O. W. supper Thursday night was a decided success, there being about 150 present, including a number of visitors from the Pottsboro Camp.

The Denison Daily Herald February 29, 1908

## GEORGETOWN.

Georgetown, Tex., Feb. 27.—Everything is moving along nicely since the rain. Farmers are all busy, some planting potatoes and onions, while others are still sowing oats.

There is a great deal of sickness in the community at present, mostly measles, la grippe and bad colds.

Misses Minnie Bostic and Jennie Coonrod of Denison spent several days with friends and relatives here the latter part of last week.

Mrs. M. E. Steel returned home Monday from a several months' visit with her daughter at Wynnewood, Okla.

Mrs. Vance Sharpe of Wynnewood, Okla., is visiting relatives here.

Mrs. Myrtle Connor has returned to her home at Claude, Texas. Mrs. Connor was called here on account of the illness and death of her mother, Mrs. John Steel, of Preston.

Miss Eula Mercer of Denison visited friends here Saturday and Sunday.

Mr. and Mrs. Kapye and Misses Eula Allen and Annie Stewart of Sherman spent Sunday here.

The Denison Daily Herald February 7, 1908

## GEORGETOWN.

Georgetown, Tex., Feb. 6.—A few of the farmers are sowing oats, while others are preparing their land for potatoes and corn.

Mrs. Steel of Preston is very sick at the home of Mr. and Mrs. Claude Campbell, where she is visiting.

Mrs. Hull returned home Sunday from Denison where she had been visiting her daughter.

Born, to Mr. and Mrs. J. D. Holley, a boy.

A league entitled the Georgetown Schoolground Improvement League, was recently organized for the purpose of fencing and beautifying the school grounds. This is to be a permanent league to keep the grounds in good order.

Mrs. Dennie Cox is visiting her uncle, Connor Burgess.

Miss Mary Davis has returned from a visit in McAlester, Okla.

Ab Allen was a Denison visitor Sunday.

W. A. Mitchell was a Denison visitor Sunday.

The young people had a leap year party Friday night at the home of Mr. and Mrs. J. R. Molloy. All expressed themselves as having had a delightful time.

The Farmers' Progressive League recently organized in the Georgetown community, northwest of Pottsboro, for the purpose of co-operating with the Denison Board of Trade in its work for progress along agricultural lines, will meet at the Georgetown schoolhouse tonight. Secretary Larkin will attend and will be accompanied by C. O. Moser, expert in charge of the Denison Demonstration Dairy Farm, who will deliver an address on dairy farming; H. P. Pratt and Harry Sampson, representing the recently established Royal Creamery; A. L. Jones, John R. Haven and James Kono.

Denison Daily Herald, March 16, 1908

The Denison Daily Herald April 6, 1908

## PROGRESS.

Progress, Tex., April 6.—A party of fox hunters caught a grown red fox and seven small ones near here a few days ago

Mrs. M. E. Steel is visiting her daughter in Denison.

Alvin Henderson has been on the sick list the last two weeks, but is up and around now.

Mr. and Mrs. John Sharpe spent last Sunday with Mr. J. C. Sharpe of Georgetown.

The Denison Daily Herald April 29, 1908

## GEORGETOWN.

Georgetown, Tex., April 23.—The Georgetown School Ground Improvement League has been doing some fine work on the school ground. They have recently set out a hundred roses and have sown many flower seeds, besides doing other much needed work.

The school, which was to have closed April 24, will not close until the 29, the teacher, Mr. J. R. Malloy, having been sick for several days and unable to attend to his duties. The closing exercises will be held the night of the 29th.

Mrs. John Hosford has returned to her home in Denison, after spending a month with her parents here.

Jim Marion who has been sick for six weeks is very low.

Misses Maud and Orado Bostic are visiting relatives and friends in Denison this week.

Mrs. E. M. Utiger of Eureka Springs, Ark., is visiting relatives here.

E. J. Covey and brother, Otis, of Southmayd are in the community.

A. S. Allen was in Denison a few days this week.

## Georgetown News -

Denison Daily Herald May 8, 1908 & May 15, 1908

E. C. Allen of Georgetown was in the city yesterday and reports the farmers very busy in his community. He says there is a great interest in dairying in his community and many farmers are adding to their dairy herds.

H. A. Martin of Georgetown is spending the day in the city on business.

The Denison Daily Herald May 11, 1908

Georgetown, Texas, May 7.—The frost last week, while very heavy, didn't do much damage. This cool weather is harmful to the crops, especially cotton.

The closing exercises of the school were held last night. There was a large crowd present, the house being packed, and all were well pleased with the entertainment.

Mrs. A. H. Burgess of Ada, Okla., who has been visiting relatives here, is visiting in Sherman, where she was taken suddenly ill, and is unable to return home.

Mrs. Ira Crause and little son of Sherman are visiting her parents, Mr. and Mrs. R. Richardson.

Misses Eula Allen of Sherman and Eula Mercer of Denison spent Sunday at the home of Mr. and Mrs. Allen.

Miss Etta Sharpe returned home Sunday after a short visit in Sherman and Denison.

Miss Minnie Bostic of Denison spent Sunday here.

Miss Eula Harmon and Zella Richardson of Dripping Springs are visiting Misses Eva and Zula Covey and Ada Mercer.

Miss Orado Bostic returned Sunday from a visit with relatives in Denison.

Jim Marion is still very ill.

The Denison Daily Herald May 22, 1908

Miss Eula Mercer has for her guests Misses Edith and Beulah Hull of Georgetown, at her home, No. 825 West Hull Street.

The Denison Daily Herald May 23, 1908

A bolt of lightning struck a horse of G. W. Thompson residing near Georgetown in this county Thursday and instantly killed it. The same flash felled a sixty-foot tree some 100 yards from the scene and stripped it of every vestige of foliage.

The Misses Etta and Lottie Sharp of Georgetown are guests of Miss Eula Mercer at her home, No. 825 West Hull Street.

The Denison Daily Herald March 28, 1908

**GEORGETOWN.**

Georgetown, Tex., March 26.—The W. O. W. supper Saturday night was well attended by the Woodmen, their wives, children, sisters and sweethearts, there being more than a hundred present.

Oats are looking nicely since the rain. Corn planting is about over in this community. Potatoes are coming up, while the onions are up to an average stand.

J. T. Marion is reported as being quite sick.

Mr. and Mrs. Ora Crause have returned to their home in Sherman after spending a week with Mrs. Crause's parents, Mr. and Mrs. R. Richardson.

Mrs. Essie Hosford and children of Denison are visiting relatives here. Mrs. Hosford's youngest child has been very sick for the past two months, and was brought here for a change.

Mrs. Dennie Cox, who has been visiting her uncle, C. Burgess, has returned home.

The Grayson County Singing Convention was held at Georgetown last Sunday with a fine attendance.

There was a Bailey Club of forty or fifty members organized here this week. Capt. W. S. Grant is the president and E. A. Wright secretary. Quite a number of delegates were appointed to go to Fort Worth Saturday to attend the "rally."

J. D. Holley, Superintendent of the Georgetown Cemetery Association, requests the members to begin to send in their dues, as he desires to get up the money to take care of the grounds before any work has to be done. The grounds are in fine condition now but the way vegetation is growing it will not be long until they will have to be gone over.

Capt. A. W. Hulett of Denison was in town Wednesday, shaking hands with old friends.

Mr. Bush of Gainesville was here Wednesday in the interest of the Gainesville Creamery.

Johnny Grayham went to Denison Tuesday evening on business.

B. M. Flannery of Denison was here Tuesday.

Mrs. Nannie Johnson, daughter of Mrs. Gardenhire, who lives a few miles west of town, died at her mother's residence Wednesday evening, and was buried in the Georgetown Cemetery Thursday evening. Mrs. Johnson had been suffering for several years with tuberculosis and her death was not unexpected.

This community has not had a better crop prospect for the past five or six years than it has now. The oat crop is looking very fine and no prospects of the "green bug" are visible.

The Denison Daily Herald May 19, 1908

## THE DEATH ROLL.

### Mrs. A. R. Reeves.

A telegram received in the city announced the death this morning at her home in McAlester, Okla., of Mrs. A. R. Reeves. Her father, Capt. A. W. Hulett, left on the noon Flyer for that place. A sister, Mrs. W. R. Hopson, who has been visiting at Tecumseh, Okla., also went to McAlester this afternoon. Other members of the family will go later. The body will possibly be brought to Georgetown, near Pottsboro, for burial.

Mrs. Reeves, formerly Miss Sophie Hulett, eldest daughter of Capt. Hulett, was about thirty-one years old. She had been ill several years, and several operations and the care of the best physicians failed to give permanent relief. Her last serious illness dated from three weeks ago. She had lived in this county till after her marriage several years ago, and has a host of friends over North Texas who will be grieved at news of her death. Besides her father, she is survived by three brothers, Harry and Robert Hulett, of Altus, Okla.; Amos Hulett of this city; and two sisters, Mrs. W. R. Hopson of Denison, and Mrs. Jesse Foster of Port, Okla.

The Denison Daily Herald May 20, 1908

The body of Mrs. A. R. Reeves, who died yesterday morning at her home in McAlester, Okla., arrived in the city this afternoon on Katy train No. 1, and was taken to the home of her father, Capt. A. W. Hulett, No. 420 West Sears Street. Services will be held tomorrow morning and the body will be taken to the Georgetown Cemetery, near Pottsboro, for interment.

The Denison Daily Herald May 30, 1908 & June 11, 1908

### GEORGETOWN.

Georgetown, Tex., May 28.—Considering the rain we have had, the crops are doing very well. Potatoes will soon be ready for market. Oats are looking fine and are beginning to ripen.

Claude Bostic and sister, Miss Maude, went to Denison Wednesday.

Misses Beulah and Edith Hull and Etta and Lottie Sharp returned home Monday from Denison, where they visited friends and attended the carnival.

W. E. and A. S. Allen, W. E. and Herbert Hull were carnival visitors in Denison.

Jim Marion, who has been sick for two months, is still quite sick.

Mrs. W. S. Reeves and children of Sherman are visiting her parents here.

Miss Della Hull has returned from Sherman.

Misses Beulah and Della Hull of Georgetown community, who have been visiting Miss Eula Mercer at her home, No. 825 West Hull Street, during the past few weeks, have returned home.

### Mrs. Minnie Christman.

Mrs. Minnie Christman, 36 years old, wife of Frederick Christman of Pottsboro, who died yesterday morning at the City Hospital after a short illness, was the mother of seven children the elder of whom is 14. The younger are twins, baby girls, 10 months old. Mrs. Christman was apparently in good health until shortly before her death, it was reported.

She was born in Russia, the daughter of Frederick Woulghmoot and Rosa Smith Woulghmoot. She came to this country with her parents at an early age. She and Mr. Christman, son of Mr. and Mrs. W. M. Christman of Georgetown, were married about fifteen years ago and made their home in Pottsboro.

The funeral is to be held at 4 o'clock this afternoon at the home of Mr. and Mrs. Christman in Georgetown, interment following in Georgetown cemetery. The Swank Undertaking Company will have charge of the funeral.

Sunday Gazetteer. Denison, Tex November 27, 1904 & November 26, 1905

Several persons have been arrested in Georgetown, a prohibition town, for soliciting C. O. D. orders for whisky. The cases have been set for trial in the county court in December and will be hotly contested.

been confirmed..........Col. Chiles, of Georgetown, was in Denison Wednesday and returned home that evening with $186 50 in his pocket. That night some one entered his house and abstracted the money from his pants' pocket. He did not discover his loss until he got up in the morning..........The city council

The Denison Herald November 11, 1921

## John G. Geis

Funeral services for John G Geis, Pottsboro farmer who died a the city hospital Tuesday, were conducted from the home of his sister at 314 West Morton street Wednesday afternoon, with Rev. Father J. J. McGran, pastor of St. Joseph's Catholic church, officiated, interment being in Calvary cemetery.

Mr. Geis had been ill for several weeks but the immediate cause of his death was pneumonia which developed a short time before he passed away. He was born in Bastrop, Texas, December 9, 1876, and was the son of Christian and Barbara Schaffer Geis. He was a former resident of Denison but moved to Pottsboro five years ago where he has been engaged in farming.

Surviving are his wife and five children: Lester Lee, Viola Elizabeth, J. G., Milton and Wilbur, also his mother, Mrs. Barbara Geis, and sisters, Mrs. Margaret Hoppe of Bastrop, Mrs. Bertha Dougherty, Tom Bean, Mrs. H. A. Schuelke and brother, C. W. Geis of this city.

Mr. Geis was a prominent citzen of his community and his death is mourned by a large circle of friends.

**Card of Thanks**

We take this means of thanking our many friends in our affliction in the loss of our dear husband and father, for the floral offerings, and also the Ladies Aid of Georgetown.

MRS. J. G. GEIS
AND CHILDREN.

The Sherman Courier August 18, 1917

## ALLEGED BOOTLEGGER KILLED BY OFFICER

Ty Tippett, an alleged bootlegger, was killed after midnight Thursday night at the Henderson ferry, north of Pottsboro. He was crossing the river into Oklahoma when fired on by officers. A man said to be named Watkins escaped. In the automobile in which Tippett was riding was found a quantity of liquor. He was well konwn to peace officers on both sides of Red River. It is said that he was married and lived at Madill, where the body was taken by the officers.

# OFFICERS HELD UP AND PISTOLS TAKEN FROM THEM

## WERE MADE TO "PUT 'EM UP" INSTANTER

## WAS IN PRESTON BEND

## But Guardians of the Law Stage Come Back and Get Their Men.

Deputy Sheriffs Bart Shipp and George Brinkley and Deputy Constables Sam Franks and Tim McCormick Friday night raided the farm of Jess McClure, west of Preston, and destroyed a fifty gallon whiskey still and arrested McClure and one other man, after they had been disarmed by McClure and held at bay with a double barrel shotgun while McClure and others destroyed and hid the finished whiskey on hand.

Another chapter in the story of law enforcement in Grayson County was written Saturday when the remaining members of McClure's alleged band were safely confined in the county jail, and to the level headed actions of the officers participating in the raid, and more particularly the persuasive powers of Deputy Sheriff George Brinkley must go the credit for the final outcome of Friday night's experience, which, for a while at least, was potent with tragedy for the officers attempting to enforce the law. For, according to the humor which McClure showed while holding the officers at bay: after having one of his associates take their guns from them, it is remarkable that no bloodshed marked the efforts of the officers upon the occasion

### How It Happened.

Deputy Sheriff George Brinkley told the story in the Sheriff's office Saturday afternoon. The four officers had reached McClure's place, which is situated off the Georgetown road, leading west from Preston, Bend, about one mile into the timbered hills skirting Red River. Three of the officers were proceeding through the timber, Deputy Sheriff Bart Shipp having remained at the car to repair a puncture in a tire. Out of the darkness of the wood, the men suddenly heard the command to throw up their hands, and found themselves looking into the twin barrels of a shotgun, held in the hands of a determined appearing individual, who was recognized at once as McClure.

### Brinkley Has Silver Tongue.

The officers readily complied. McClure's next action was to have a confederate, who appeared out of the darkness from behind him, take the guns from each of the officers. And while the officers were thus held, according to their story, McClure's helpers began systematic work nearby, which they later learned was directed to doing away with the stock of whiskey which the gang had distilled in a plant located but a short distance away.

At least one of the three men was not idle, however, and while McClure's band was engaged in "destroying the evidence," Deputy Sheriff George Brinkley started talking with McClure, pointing out the risk he was running and the consequences which would certainly follow if he put into execution his threat to put all of the officers out of his way for good.

### Invited to Inspect Plant.

McClure then asked the officers if they would return to Sherman and say they had found nothing, Mr. Brinkley said. Upon their refusal to promise this and upon the gang's completion of their jobs of concealing or destroying the whiskey, McClure lowered his gun, and invited the officers to come over and inspect his plant. Still disarmed, the officers complied and found a mammoth outfit set up in the open, but complete in every detail.

Deputy Sheriff Brinkley having succeeded in convincing McClure of the folly of his actions, and McClure's band having succeeded in disposing of the stock on hand, McClure asked the officers if they could identify their guns. When they said they could, he permitted the officers to secure their guns.

### McClure Thought He Was Safe.

According to Mr. Brinkley, McClure evidently believed himself safe from any actions of the officers, after the manufactured whiskey was done away with, and the still stopped running. He made some resistance to arrest, and it is stated that one of the officers struck him with a gun when a member of the band attempted to come to his rescue. This member promptly dropped a club he held, however, after Brinkley got the drop of his gun on him.

Mr. Brinkley and his party started a systematic cleaning up and breaking up of the plant before starting back to Sherman, using an axe on the still. The plant was put totally out of commission. McClure was placed in the car and brought back to Sherman. Saturday officers again visited the place and arrested Sam Blythe, McClure's son-in-law, and Luther Lamb of Oklahoma, McClure's nephew. Two of McClure's sons are also implicated in the illicit business, the officers state, but had not been arrested Saturday afternoon.

McClure was arrested about a year

ago at his farm by county officers, and a smaller still destroyed. He told the officers that distilling was a matter of "meat and bread" with him, but according to the officers, his home was well provisioned with hog meat and other food.

McClure's efforts to conceal the finished whiskey included the burning of a small shed containing part of the plant, the officers state. He showed them this while attempting to persuade them to return to Sherman and report they had found nothing.

The destruction of this plant destroys one of the largest moonshine distilleries in the county, the officers believe, and will do away with one of the chief sources of illicit whiskey in the county.

State of TX Versus Jess McClure Sherman Daily Democrat March 29, 1922

**Week of April 10th**

State of Texas vs. Jess McClure, 3 cases; State of Texas vs. Scotty Mangrum.

The State Vs. Jess McClure Sherman Daily Democrat April 23, 1922 – Criminal cases set for the 59th Judicial District court, April Term, week of May 1st: 16299 and 16297 – State vs. Jess McClure

The Denison Press, August 12, 1949

## G. H. (BUD) JONES

G. H. (Bud) Jones, 92 years old, and a retired farmer of the Georgetown community, died at the home of a daughter, Mrs. E. W. Miller, in Abilene, Texas, Sunday, after a six months illness. He was brought to Denison where funeral services were held Monday at Bratcher-Moore chapel with Church of Christ ministers, Foy Wallace and Littlejohn officiating. Burial was in the Georgetown cemetery.

Mr. Jones was born in Green County, Ark., on Nov. 15, 1856, and came to Texas with his parents in 1863. He was educated in the Georgetown schools, and married in 1881 to Miss Elizabeth Straud, who died in 1901. He was a member of the Church of Christ.

Survivors include four sons, L. F. Jones of Pottsboro; W. H. Jones of Los Angeles, and Leonard and L. F. Jones of Denison; three daughters, Mrs. Miller and Mrs. J. I. Ammons of Abilene, and Mrs. J. W. Bacon of Colbert, Okla.; three great-great grandchildren and 33 great-grandchildren.

Oct 1935 & Dec 18, 1935 Denison Herald

## GEORGETOWN

Mrs. Pauline Walker of Austin has returned home after few days' visit with her aunt, Mrs. Fred Riddle.

Ray Stratton and family have moved to Preston Bend.

John Perdue of DeQueen, Okla., was a recent business visitor here.

Raymond and Bob Hale left Sunday for the western part of the state where they have employment.

Jack Allen has gone to Fort Worth to reside.

Mr. and Mrs. Edmond Jones spent Sunday at Howe, the guests of relatives.

Paul Owen and Louie Forisha have gone to Dalhart, Texas, to assist in the harvesting of feed crops on the Gullloud farm.

Mr. and Mrs. Ernest Eldridge of Denison were recent visitors of their parents, Mr. and Mrs. T. L. Clontz.

Mrs. Grace Bowden, who has resided with Miss Minnie Bostic the past several months, was called to Amarillo Thursday due to the accidental death of her brother.

## GEORGETOWN

Mr. and Mrs. M. R. Peeples and Billie Martain of Wichita Falls were recent visitors of Mr. and Mrs. H. C. Hale.

Ben Baker of Arkansas is a guest of the Clements family here.

Mrs. A. H. Finke is in Dallas at the bedside of her father L. Davis, who is seriously sick.

Several club ladies from here attended council meeting at Sherman Saturday.

Walter Clontz and family of Oak Grove were Sunday visitors in the A. L. Moser home.

Mr. and Mrs. H. C. Hale, Mrs. Eula Hull and Mrs. A. H. Sharpe were visitors in Sherman Monday.

Walter Moon of Gordonville was a recent guest of relatives here.

Mrs. Fred Finke has returned to her home here after an extended stay with her son, Fritz Finke of Pottsboro.

Mrs. John Clements and son were recent visitors with the Lee family at Oak Grove.

Miss Margaret Ansley spent the week-end in Sherman.

The Denison Press August 16, 1938

# Alcoholism Claims Man In City Jail

## Police Bring Former Banker In Then Call Physician To Attend Him Here Monday

Sam Bennett, 61, former bank employee at Denison, Durant and Pottsboro, the Denison tie plant and once well-to-do, died early Monday night in the city jail from what physicians reported was "acute alcoholism."

Fellow employees at the tie plant Monday afternoon late, noticed Bennett was acting peculiarly and called the Katy hospital which refused him admittance. Police were called at 6:45 p. m. and Bennett was taken to jail where officers noticed this peculiar actions and condition.

Police placed Bennett on a mattress in the cell block and immediately called a physician, who pro-

++++++++++++++++++++++++++++++++++++++++++++++++++++++++++++++++++

nounced Bennett dead at 8 p. m.

Mr. Bennett was born in Alabama, July 23. 1876, the son of Mr. and Mrs. W. C. Bennett, but moved to Gainesville, Texas as a youth where he lived a number of years before residing in Pottsboro. He was married in Kendrick, Okla., to Miss Nellie Horton.

He had been a resident of Denison the past 14 years. living at 205½ West Main street. He had been connected with several business concerns in Texas and Oklahoma before moving to Denison.

Surviving are his widow. a son, Sam, Jr., of Baton Rouge, La., two daughter, Miss Daisy Bennett and Miss Nelda Bennett of Baton Rouge; two brothers, Frank of Whitesboro and Harper of Denison; three sisters. Mrs. Jessie Hogan of Whitesboro, Mrs. J. B. Jared of Riverside, Calif. and Mrs. J. E. Dishman of Denison.

Funeral services will likely be held Thursday afternoon. Burial will be at the Georgetown cemetery.

Grayson Native Steele Found Slain - Dallas Morning News, Mar 05, 1938

**Grayson Native Found Slain.**
**Special to The News.**

DENISON, Texas, March 4.—Mase Avaunt Steel, 70, his entire life a resident of the Pottsboro and Georgetown communities west of Denison, was found dead Friday near a smokehouse of his farm, six miles north of Pottsboro. A shotgun was near by and a wound was in his left side. He was born near where he died, was educated in the schools of Pottsboro. Surviving are his wife, five sons, two daughters and four sisters.

The Denison Press August 10, 1937 & August 25, 1937

# Local Talent Entertains At Georgetown

Denison entertainers presented a lengthy program at Georgetown Monday night, as a part of an entertainment to raise school funds.

With A. C. Wimpee as master of ceremonies and Mrs. Bebe Bodamer accompanist, the local program included: Blue family orchestra; song, Doris Gene Douglas; Crabtree string trio; vocal, Florine Hodges; song, Sammy Carrao; xylophone solo, Desmond Brewer.

Mr. Wimpee is chairman of the summer progam committee. J. F. Landers, another member of the committee, was present for the program.

## MISSES SUMMERVILLE RECEIVE DEGREES FROM DENTON COLLEGE FRIDAY

Misses Maggie and Rommie Summerville, daughters of Mrs. Mary Summerville have taught in the Pottsboro public school for the past eight years and last Friday they received bachelor degrees at the Denton teachers college together. The Misses Summerville are well known in Denison.

This year they will separate, however, with Miss Maggie going to teach English next year in the Rochester, Haskell county, school while Miss Rommie continues in Pottsboro. Their degrees were different, with Miss Maggie recipient of bachelor of arts and Miss Rommie, bachelor of science. The former taught at Riverside and Georgetown before joining the Pottsboro faculty. She is a member of the national council of English teacher.

The Denison Press December 15, 1938

# Former Local Man Dies Wed.

Injuries received in an automobile accident near Waco about 4 o'clock Wednesday afternoon proved fatal to Marvin Griffith, 34, a former Denisonian and farmer living at Valley Mills, Tex. He died at a Waco hospital Wednesday night at 10 o'clock.

Short-Murray, funeral directors will return the remains overland to Denison today. Funeral services will be held at the home of his parents in the Cotton Mill community Friday at 2 p. m. followed by interment at Georgetown.

Griffith was born October 2, 1900, the son of Mr. and Mrs. James Griffith in Coryell county, Texas. He married Miss Mattie Sandoff at that point, later moving to Denison.

Surviving are his wife, parents, two sons, Wayne and Travis, both of Coryell county, two brothers, Luther and Gerald Griffith of Denison.

The Denison Press September 10, 1937

# Katy Man Dies On Job Driving Terminal Bus

## J. W. Loughmiller Succumbs To Heart Trouble After Making Round Trip today

J. W. (Jake) Loughmiller, about 42, resident of Denison and Katy employee for a number of years, was found dead early this morning in a bus he operated from Ray terminal to the city. Judge E. A. Wright, in an inquest said he had died from heart failure.

Mr. Loughmiller, from a well-known Pottsboro family, resided at 2312 West Walker street and is survived by his widow and a small son, J. W. Jr., both of Denison.

The Katy man had driven the bus to Denison and returned to Ray terminal, parked the bus and had evidently went to the back end to rest. A negro employe, entering the machine to give it a routine cleaning, found Loughmiller doubled up in the back.

Judge Wright said Mr. Loughmiller had been treated for heart trouble by physicians several months and had been recently told to take a rest from his duties.

Deceased was born June 18, 1896, the son of Mr. and Mrs. J. W. Loughmiller, at Pottsboro, where he was reared and educated. He was married at Sherman June 3, 1920 to Miss Gladys Opwalt. He was a member of the Methodist church.

Coming to Denison he served with the Katy, then enlisted in the army for eight months. Returning to Grayson county, he farmed near Pottsboro for serveal years before entering the Katy service again in 1927 which position he held until his death.

Funeral services will be held Sunday at 2:30 p. m. with interment at Georgetown, Short-Murray directing.

The Denison Press December 15, 1938

## POTTSBORO RESIDENT ALL OF HER LIFE, DIES

**Mrs. Belle Clement, 72, a resident of Pottsboro practically all her life, died Wednesday afternoon at 2:25 at her home following a year's illness.**

**Funeral services are to be held Friday at 3 p. m from the home with Rev. Kirk Beard officiating. Interment will be conducted at the Georgetown cemetery, Shot-Murray in charge.**

**Mrs. Clement was born as Miss Belle Daniel, daughter of Mr. and Mrs. Robert Daniel in Grayson county July 25, 1866 and was reared and educated in Pottsboro.She married Issac Clement, a general merchandise store operator Nov. 8, 1883.**

**Mr. Clement died Nov. 20 this year.**

**She is survived by two sons, R. F. and Owen of Pottsboro; two daughters, Mrs. Reed Jones of Denison, and Mrs. Houston Loughnie of Parsons, three brothers and one sister, eighteen grandchildren and two great grandchildren.**

The Denison Press August 25, 1938 & September 3, 1938

## Denison Woman's Brother Injured

Dick Allen, son of Mrs. Edythe Allen of Georgetown, is a patient in the St. Vincent's hospital in Sherman, suffering from a serious internal injury sustained Wednesday. Young Allen fell forty feet from a tree in his yard, where he was playing. He was removed immediately to the hospital where an operation for the removal of a ruptured kidney was performed.

The boy is a brother to Mrs. Harry Painter of Denison. Mrs. Painter said this morning that his condition was as good as could be expected.

Dick Allen, twelve year old son of Mrs. Edythe Allen of Georgetown has been removed to his home from St. Vincent's hospital in Sherman where he underwent a major operation following a fall at his home recently. He is a relative of Mrs. Harry Painter of Denison.

Dick Allen did not die from his injuries, but recovered to lead a full life until he passed away at the age of 86 and was buried at Georgetown Cemetery.

Charles Richard "Dick" Allen, 86, passed away on Friday, July 13 at The Heart Hospital Baylor, Plano. Richard was born on October 1, 1925, in the Georgetown community near the town of Pottsboro, to Edyth Hull and William Ernest Allen. He attended school at Georgetown and graduated from Denison High School in 1942.

He was raised Baptist and read the Bible daily. He was an endowed member of the Lone Star Masonic Lodge 403. He married Verna Mae Schnitker June 22, 1946, who has preceded him in death. After graduating from high school, Richard worked at Perrin Air Force Base as a flight line mechanic during World War II. He left there and became employed in February 1947 with Ballard & Ballard to open the refrigerated dough plant at 314 S. Chandler in Denison. The company was purchased in 1951 by the Pillsbury Company and in 1962 the refrigerated foods plant moved to FM Hwy 84 where Richard was Distribution Manager until he retired in 1989, giving 42 years of faithful employment to the Pillsbury Company.

He was elected to the Georgetown school board and became president. As president he assisted with the development and creation of bond elections to build Pottsboro High School, which had its first graduating class in 1967. He served as a school board member for many years after the creation of PHS. Richard was a life long avid hunter and fisherman.

He took trips to Alaska, Mexico, Montana, Colorado and various other parts of the U.S. hunting and fishing. He found especially great joy in quail hunting and training bird dogs. For over a decade, he maintained a quail lease in the Texas Rolling Plains and happily spent days at a time following bird dogs in the hills and canyons in pursuit of bobwhite and blue quail. He had a reputation as an exceptional shotgun marksman. He was a Life Member of the National Rifle Association.

His other life passion was as an amateur archaeologist, and was very knowledgeable about the early America's indigenous people and their stone tools with emphasis on early Texas history of the Comanche and Apache Indians.

Following in the footsteps of his nurseryman father, Richard enjoyed gardening and created a producing peach orchard, as well as plum and cherry trees; and he grafted varieties of pecan trees. He enjoyed working with his cattle herd and raised calves for market for over 40 years.

Richard is survived by son, Charles Edwin Allen and wife, Jody of Denison, daughter, Carol Brownlee of Denison; four grandchildren, Michelle Gomez, Stephanie Rice, Brandy Humphrey, and Colby Choate; nine great-grandchildren, Chelsea Gomez, Grant Gomez, Stephanie Allen, Devyn Rice, Dylan Rice, Brandon Humphrey, Blake Humphrey, Zoe Carlile and Zaiden Choate; son-in-law, Donny Conary as well as numerous nieces and nephews. He was preceded in death by parents, Edyth and William Ernest Allen, daughter, Mary Kathryn "Kathy" Conary, sisters, Margaret Jane (Allen) Parham, Lorene Beulah (Allen) Gillean, and Ruth Christine (Allen) Dunn, brothers, Hull Forrest Allen, and William Ernest Allen Jr. Funeral services held at 11 a.m. Thursday, July 19, 2012 at Georgetown Baptist Church with Pastor Bobby Hancock officiating. Interment in Georgetown Cemetery. Pallbearers: Brunson Choate, Chris Humphrey, Donnie Rice, Lonnie Brownlee, Jim Nelson, and Curtis Clement.

The Denison Press March 8, 1941 & DMN December 8, 1927

MRS. G. N. WORTHLY

Mrs. G. N. Worthley, 62, a resident of Pottsboro 30 years, died suddenly Friday night at 7:30 at her home.

Funeral services will be held at 3 p. m. Sunday from the Pottsboro Methodist church, Rev. William Greenhaw officiating. Interterment will be at Georgetown cemetery, Short-Murray directing. Pallbearers will be Otto Wilson, O. P. Clontz, E. P. Crowder. Jess Cooke, Bill Atwell and W. H. Young

Mrs. Worthley was born Feb. 18, 1879 in Fannin county, daughter of Mr. and Mrs. G. S. Lamb, where she was reared and educated She was married to Mr. Worthley in that community. He died Oct. 6, 1933. She was a member of the Methodist church.

Surviving are a son, Dawrence Worthley off Wichita Falls; two daughters, Miss Jean Worthley of allas and Mrs. W. E. Favors of Aylesworth, three brothers and two grandchildren.

# Will Drill Oil Tests In Pottsboro Vicinity

Special to The News.

SHERMAN, Texas, Dec. 7.—For the oil test to be drilled by J. N. Burnham on the 447-acre tract of the Texas Nursery Company of Sherman, about four miles west of Pottsboro, a ninety-six-foot derrick has been erected and all equipment has been received for beginning of operations. The well will be drilled to 900 feet and will be carried deeper if conditions warrant.

A depth of 180 feet has been reached in the well being put down by J. T. Miller and associates on the Mouldin farm, one and three-fourths miles north and west of the gasser.

The Herbert and Big Indian Oil Companies are planning to erect a derrick on the 1,285-acre Ike Exstein tract within the next ten days. This test is contracted to be put down 2,500 feet.

June 11, & Oct 9, 1948 Grayson County Road Plan Via Georgetown

## Advisory Groups Locating Precinct Roads Get Active

With the approach of road building time for lateral roads in Grayson county for farmers to reach markets and to better serve rural schools, representatives of various communities are meeting to lend assistance and advice to engineers and county commissioners in locating such roads to be improved.

This week a meeting was called for the Pottsboro area with representatives from that area present. Interested points around Pottsboro are Willow Springs, Preston, Georgetown, Hagerman, and Pottsboro.

The Pottsboro Chamber of Commerce is taking active part in the movement, Fred Lannon, president, states.

SHERMAN, Texas, Oct. 9.—The Grayson County commissioners court has approved a project in the lateral road program of the county which covers a 5-mile stretch of road north from Pottsboro via Georgetown, in the Lake Texoma area. The road is one of the county projects being financed by the $750,000 bond issue voted this year. The commissioners authorized advertisement for bids for labor and equipment to apply 45,000 square yards of double asphalt surface on the project.

The Denison Press August 5, 1941 & Sept 7, 1951

Mrs. Dadie Griffith and Clarence Kyker

**MRS. D. GRIFFITH**

Mrs. D. Griffith, 67, living near Collinsville, died at 11 a. m. Monday, after an illness that lasted two years. Funrela services will be conducted Tuesday at 3 p. m. with interment at Georgetown cemetery.

Mrs. Griffith was born at Range Creek, Tex., Oct. 22, 1873, her parents being Mr. and Mrs. Harry Cook. She was married in 1895 to Martin Lee Griffith She was a member of the Methodist church.

Surviving are the husband and three sons, Wm. A. of Springdale, Colo., Joe C. of Collinsville and Robert L. of Pearl Harbor, Hawaii Daughters are Mrs. O. L. Allison, Orange and Mrs. W. D. Webb, Sherman

Brothers surviving are Jim Cook, Joe Cook, Jess Cook and Luther Cook, of Pottsboro. Sisters are Mrs. Mollie Taul and Mrs. Cora Griffin, of Denison.

**CLARENCE MITCHELL KYKER**

Funeral services were held at Bratcher-Moore chapel Monday, September 3, at 3 p. m. for Clarence Mitchell Kyker, 45, of Pottsboro, who died in a local hospital, Sunday morning at 2:25 o'clock. He had been ill for three weeks. Otto Johnson, Church of Christ minister, officiated and interment was in Georgetown cemetery with Bratcher-Moore directing.

Mr. Kyker was born in Celina, Texas, Nov. 26, 1905, the son of Mr. and Mrs. E. W. Kyker. He was a dairy farmer.

Survivors include three brothers, Arlie Kyker, Dallas, Joe Kyker, Pottsboro, and Clayton Kyker, Los Angeles; six sisters, Mrs. Edna Taylor, Mrs. Mattie Atwell and Mrs. Dell Snyder, all of Denison, and Mrs. Dollie Brogden, Chicago; Mrs. Hattie Finke, Pottsboro and Mrs. Florence Barrier, Amarillo.

Dallas Morn News 1 4 1964

# Third, Last Son Of Couple Meets Violent Death

DENISON, Texas (Sp.)—Violent death has taken the third and last son from Mr. and Mrs. M. V. Jones of Pottsboro.

The couple's oldest son was killed during World War II in action. Their second son drowned in Lake Texoma when he and his father operated Little Mineral Dock on the Preston Peninsula.

Thursday, violent death struck again. Jack Alexander Jones, 27, the youngest and last son, was killed when he slipped and fell into a rock crusher at Crushers, Inc. The rock quarry on Preston Peninsula is just two miles from where his brother met his death in Lake Texoma.

Justice Homer Gaddy ruled death due to suffocation from rock dust.

Funeral will be held Saturday at 2:30 p.m. in the Georgetown Baptist Church with burial in Georgetown Cemetery.

Survivors include his parents; his wife, two sons and one daughter.

Thank you for reading my book, I hope it has been a blessing to you. I also hope it has been interesting and informative for you. I have many other books about the history of the people and the area I love in North Texas. They include:

The History of Building the Denison Dam

When the West Was Wild in Sadler and Basin Springs Vol 7

When the West Was Wild in Gordonville and Cedar Mills (Wild West Vol 6)

When the West Was Wild in Delaware Bend -Wild West Vol 5

When the West Was Wild in Pottsboro Texas -Wild West Vol 4

Gone With the Water The Saga of Preston Bend & Glen Eden

Crime & Calamity in Preston Bend When the West Was Wild Vol 3

When the West Was Wild in Denison Texas Wild West Vol 2

When the West Was Wild in Pottsboro Texas Vol 1

Quantrill's Raiders In North Texas & Jesse James Gang in Grayson County Texas

The Many Faces of Texoma's Red River

Pottsboro Texas and Lake Texoma, Then and Now Volume One and Two

School Days Around the Pottsboro Area & NW Grayson County

Ghost Towns of Texoma, Vol 1 – Preston Bend

Ghost Towns of Texoma, Vol 2 – Hagerman

Ghost Towns of Texoma, Vol 3 – Martin Springs

Ghost Towns of Texoma, Vol 4 – Georgetown, Fink Ghost Towns of Texoma, Vol 5 - Locust, Willow Springs

Reflections on the Beauty of Lake Texoma

Texoma Tales Volume 1 – NW Grayson County's People & their Stories

The Old Country Store

True Ghost Stories of Grayson County Texas...and Other Strange and Scary Tales Vol 1, 2, 3, 4 & 5

THE LAST DAYS AND THE BOOK OF REVELATION UNVEILED - THE REAL BIG BANG! A Book of Comfort and Encouragement VOLUMES ONE and TWO

I am, God willing, intending to write many more history-related books, since we have such a rich heritage here, and I am sure I will only scratch the surface. People ask me why I don't think I will run out of material. I respond, there have been a LOT of people in this area and they ALL have a story.

I have given several local history related speeches and costumed living history presentations.

All my books are available on:

Amazon.com, my author name is Natalie Clountz Bauman,

On etsy.com from the store PottsboroTexasBooks

You can order books directly from the author

and you can get the books in Denison on Main Street at The Book Rack and The Main Street Antique Mall;

They can also be found at the Frontier Village Museum at Loy Park in Denison and at my personal event appearances.

I also have a tour company called Red River Tours. We give Ghost Tours and Wild West Tours. To get tickets, go to our Facebook page Red River Tours. Thank you for considering my books. I hope you find them interesting and informative. God bless you!

About Natalie Clountz Bauman: Just a few years ago, Natalie was laid off from a job of 11 years due to failing health. She was a middle-aged lady with multiple autoimmune diseases that are chronically painful, don't have cures, progressively get worse, and are disabling. Some might just quit. The doctor "prescribed" she needed a mental hobby to keep from becoming depressed and deteriorating physically because of inactivity. She got busy doing something she loves - writing about local history and especially about God and His Word. HER story is, never give up, don't get discouraged, whatever your challenges. If you trust God, He will help you. If you keep swinging, you at least have a chance to hit the ball out of the park!

Natalie is a graduate of the Brown Trail Church of Christ preacher's wives School of Preaching in 1992 and has an accounting degree from Grayson College. She has taught Bible classes to children and adult women all her adult life, from her local congregation to area-wide seminars.

She has so far written a couple of dozen Grayson County history books and Bible lesson books including "The Many Faces of Texoma's Red River"; "Quantrill's Raiders in North Texas Including the James Gang" and "The Last Day and the Revelation Unveiled".

Her books are available at Amazon, at local venues locally and on the author's Facebook page "Natalie Clountz Bauman - Author" and "Pottsboro Texas History". Natalie does historical speeches for groups, living history demonstrations and has been a historical columnist for the Pottsboro Sun newspaper.

Made in the USA
Columbia, SC
11 July 2024

38433395R00163